Y0-BCG-497

# *BEGINNINGS:*

# THE SOCIAL AND AFFECTIVE DEVELOPMENT OF BLACK CHILDREN

# CHILD PSYCHOLOGY

A series of books edited by **David S. Palermo**

# *BEGINNINGS:*

# THE SOCIAL AND AFFECTIVE DEVELOPMENT OF BLACK CHILDREN

*Edited by*

Margaret Beale Spencer
*Emory University*

Geraldine Kearse Brookins
*Jackson State University*

Walter Recharde Allen
*The University of Michigan*

**LEA** LAWRENCE ERLBAUM ASSOCIATES, PUBLISHERS
1985   Hillsdale, New Jersey                              London

LIBRARY
COLBY-SAWYER COLLEGE
NEW LONDON, NH 03257

E
185.86
.B377
1985

# 11399607

Copyright © 1985 by Lawrence Erlbaum Associates, Inc.
All rights reserved. No part of this book may be reproduced in
any form, by photostat, microform, retrieval system, or any other
means, without the prior written permission of the publisher.

Lawrence Erlbaum Associates, Inc., Publishers
365 Broadway
Hillsdale, New Jersey 07642

**Library of Congress Cataloging in Publication Data**
Main entry under title:

Beginnings : the social and affective development of black
children.

Bibliography: p.
Includes indexes.
1. Afro-American children—Psychology—Addresses,
essays, lectures.   2. Afro-American families—Addresses,
essays, lectures.   3. Afro-Americans—Race identity—
Addresses, essays, lectures.   I. Spencer, Margaret B.
II. Brookins, Geraldine K.   III. Allen, Walter R.
E185.86.B377   1985        155.4'5796073        84-24742
ISBN 0-89859-520-7
ISBN 0-8058-0228-2 (pbk)

Printed in the United States of America
10  9  8  7  6  5  4

Dedicated to the Memory

of

Jean V. Carew
1936–1981

Committed scholar, faithful colleague,
and friend of black children.

# Contents

**PART III: Theories, Policy Implications and
        Recommendations**

# List of Contributors

**Yvonne R. Abatso,** *Fisk University*
**Walter R. Allen,** *The University of Michigan*
**Urie Bronfenbrenner,** *Cornell University*
**Geraldine K. Brookins,** *Jackson State University*
**Louis A. Castenell, Jr.,** *Xavier University of Louisiana*
**William E. Cross, Jr.,** *Cornell University*
**John Dill,** *Memphis State University*
**Aimee Dorr,** *University of California-Los Angeles*
**Glen H. Elder, Jr.,** *University of North Carolina*
**V. P. Franklin,** *Yale University*
**Bruce R. Hare,** *State University of New York*
**Beverly F. Harris,** *Prince George's School System*
**Bertha G. Holliday,** *George Peabody College of Vanderbilt University*
**Velma LaPoint,** *Howard University*
**Vonnie C. McLoyd,** *The University of Michigan*
**Gerald A. McWorter,** *University of Illinois*
**Elsie G. J. Moore,** *Arizona State University*
**John U. Ogbu,** *University of California-Berkeley*
**Marilyn O. Pickett,** *National Institute of Mental Health*
**Chester M. Pierce,** *Harvard University*
**Morris Rosenberg,** *University of Maryland*
**Leachim T. Semaj,** *University of the West Indies*
**Diana T. Slaughter,** *Northwestern University*
**Margaret B. Spencer,** *Emory University*
**Ewart A. C. Thomas,** *Stanford University*
**Marguerite N. Alejandro-Wright,** *Yale University Medical School*

# Foreword

Much of what has been written about black children and families has been based on the assumption that attitudes and patterns of behavior observed among Euro-Americans are normal whereas those observed among other racial/ethnic populations are deviant. Sociological and psychological research and theory have not adequately appreciated the importance of different environmental circumstances in which family life styles and child-rearing practices have developed. Because racial/ethnic groups inhabit different cultural niches, they face different subsistence demands, provide different role models, and have different conceptions of adult success. These different experiences result in a variety of socialization settings that are associated with numerous socialization goals and outcomes. The notion of a universal pattern of human development does not pass the test of human experience, even within the boundaries of a single diverse nation such as the United States. Unfortunately, modern social science has been slow to take into account this diversity in its conceptualizations of human development and family life styles.

This timely book provides a welcome change from the normative stance of most previous research on minorities. It presents a rigorous examination of black children and youth from a pluralist perspective while maintaining a developmental focus. Black child development is viewed from the perspective of the social ecology of black life experiences. The questions asked and the issues addressed focus on the central theme of adaptive life styles. How do families who face certain kinds of subsistence (survival) demands prepare their children for adult roles? The contributors to this volume address a broad range of issues with considerable insight and make a substantial contribution to our understanding of socialization and child development among black Americans.

I find this volume especially appealing because many of the topics discussed in the essays have engaged my research interests for the past 20 years. It is gratifying to see some of my work extended in the research of younger scholars. I think it is also worth noting that eight of the authors and coauthors, including two of the editors, are products of University of Chicago graduate programs in sociology, education, and human development. Six of the authors were students during the 1970s when Diana Slaughter was my colleague on the University of Chicago faculty. In their writing, I can see the maturation of many of the ideas discussed in seminars and during the development of their own research projects. Several of these former students have told me repeatedly how the presence of black faculty members in the social sciences enabled them to maintain or develop alternative ways of viewing black family life, socialization and child development. The very presence of black faculty members on dissertation committees provided the students with a sense of conceptual freedom that might otherwise have been missing.

James E. Blackwell, professor of sociology at the University of Massachusetts in Boston, has recently completed *Networking and Mentoring: A Study of Cross-Generational Experiences of Blacks in Graduate and Professional Schools.*[1] This research demonstrated the utility of networks for creating positive experiences for blacks during their graduate and professional school years. I would extend that notion to career experiences as well. There is rarely a sufficient number of black scholars with common intellectual interests at a given university to provide a critical mass of collegiality and creative stimulation. Thus, it is important that networks of scholars with complementary interests be developed and nurtured so that they can provide encouragement for each other and share the results of their research and thinking—as well as their experiences in coping with the academic establishment. Society for Research on Child Development Study Groups, such as this one, are examples of small networks that can provide the type of stimulation and interaction that results in productive collaboration.

This collection of essays will become, in my opinion, an important addition to our knowledge of how racial experiences (experiences that are shaped by the societal patterns of subordination and superordination that influence life chances and everyday encounters) affect child-rearing patterns and family and individual coping styles. *Beginnings* is a good title because it reflects an emphasis on early childhood development that appears in some of the papers; as well, it reflects the authors' perceptions that important work from a specifically black perspective is in its beginning phases.

While the research in this volume focuses on black children and families, the basic theme of the work is applicable to other populations. The authors are

---

[1]James E. Blackwell, *Mentoring and Networking: A Study of Cross-Generational Experiences of Blacks in Graduate and Professional Schools* (Atlanta, Georgia: Southern Education Foundation, 1983).

saying that each group must be understood from the context of its historical experiences and current circumstances. The influences of race, ethnicity, and class on socialization patterns and family styles must be viewed from a variety of perspectives, free of the implicit ethnocentrism that idealizes the middle-class Anglo-European life style.

The papers in this volume make stimulating reading. They should be widely read by students of family sociology, child development, education, and race relations. Certainly more questions are raised than answered, but they provide a challenge for other researchers to expand the search for new understandings about the processes involved in child development among an oppressed minority.

Some of the topics covered in this collection have been the focus of research by earlier generations of black scholars. Most readers are familiar with the work of E. Franklin Frazier (the black family), Charles S. Johnson (black youth), Allison Davis (child-rearing practices, ability testing), and Kenneth and Mamie Clark (racial self-image). The early scholars (including W. E. B. DuBois and John Hope Franklin among historians, economist Vivian Henderson, and educator Horace Mann Bond) served as role models for my generation. They left a legacy of serious scholarship, focused on issues of vital concern to black Americans. My predecessors were the products of their era, an era when racial integration and assimilation were viewed as desirable goals by the majority of black intellectuals. Thus, it is not surprising that their research emphasized values and behaviors that were deemed likely to promote social equality.

The researchers whose work comprises the meat of this volume are no less products of their era. They matured during the 60s and 70s of the 20th century, an exciting period of rapid change in black Americans' political goals and racial self-images. It is to be expected that their research will reflect a more pluralist, or even separatist, stance than that of earlier scholars. The fact that scholarly work reflects the social and political climate of its era should not detract from its usefulness or its validity. Its significance lies in its ability to help us understand the important research questions of the era. After all, each generation learns from the errors, as well as the successes, of its predecessors.

Edgar G. Epps, Ph.D.
Marshall Field IV Professor
of Urban Education
University of Chicago

# Preface

*A great many people think they are thinking when they are merely rearranging their prejudices.*

—William James

William James' insightful observation underscores the oft political nature of research. Although the point might be contested vigorously by some, research is by nature political. The work of Clark and Clark (1939, 1940, 1947) played an important role in the Supreme Court's *Brown vs. the Topeka Board of Education* decision in 1954, outlawing segregated public schools. More recently, Moynihan's assessment of black family life as essentially pathological, produced a deluge of political discussions and related social policy decisions. Likewise, Jensen's 1969 *Harvard Educational Review* article, suggesting that intelligence is biologically inherited, caused politicians and academicians to seriously question the feasibility of government funded "enrichment" programs for the "disadvantaged." Although rhetoric advocates—or more correctly, exalts—the separation of political issues from scientific questions, publications by Clark, Moynihan, and Jensen selectively illustrate the political power of social research. Equally powerful, however, are the assumptions upon which much of the research is based and the exclusion of alternative research interpretations from "mainstream" publication outlets.

Previous researchers have drawn many conclusions concerning the psychological functioning of black children. Yet, most research on black children and their families reflects minimal understanding of psychological processes as these relate to the unique ecological experiences of minorities in a majority white society. Process refers, in this connection, to necessary questions surrounding the "how." The literature abounds with assumptions concerning the "why." Too frequently these assumptions offer only descriptive models of causality (e.g., theories of oppression) and reflect minimal empirical verification. Too often missing is a broader theoretical understanding of minority child development under adverse conditions. This society publicly lauds the ideal of cultural pluralism, while often behaving in ways totally antithetical to this creed. Discriminatory attitudes and practices adversely affect the life-chances of black and minority children through all developmental stages. They and their families are "at risk." In sum, the literature conveys a general misunderstanding of, and gap in, theoretical and methodological approaches necessary for sensitive interpretation of black children's development. In this volume, we attempt to fill that conceptual and empirical void.

"*Beginnings: The Social and Affective Development of Black Children,*" is a collection of papers about African-American children's development. The book offers theories, paradigms, empirical studies, and commentaries by psychologists, sociologists, anthropologists, historians, and psychiatrists. Their perspectives acknowledge the history of black children in America as one characterized by hardship, deprivation, coping, and optimism in a seemingly hopeless world. These investigators enlarge our understanding of black children's social and emotional development by providing empirical assessments of the ecological contexts, interpersonal relationships, and psychological states which influence their growth and development.

Although focusing specifically on black child development, the volume serves as a useful model for studying developmental processes among minority group children generally. Each section of the volume addresses an important issue: socio-historical and conceptual perspectives for the study of black children and their families, the development of competence, identity formation and family relationships. Each paper addresses a specific set of concerns in the literature on black child development.

The opening section initiates the "how" versus "why" perspective or a process versus outcome delineation. Its several papers offer alternative conceptual perspectives, important for informed study of black children. Next, empirical research and theoretical papers in the area of social competence, identity formation, and the family are introduced to illustrate key considerations in the study of black child development. A synthesis of the research and theory presented, stated as a research agenda for the future, concludes the volume.

This book offers a substantial body of research and theory which suggests alternative approaches to the study of black children and the interpretation of behavioral outcomes. The volume serves several purposes: (1) as a reference guide for education and public policy makers; (2) as a teaching text for graduate students and upper-level undergraduates; (3) as a guide for scholars and researchers.

## Background and History

This volume is the product of a series of study group meetings held at Emory University in Atlanta, GA. The meetings were intended to explore the complex process of black child development in the area of social-affective functioning as a consequence of maturation and social experiences in a variety of settings. The idea for a study group on the "Social and Affective Development of Minority Status Children" originated during the 1975 Society for Research in Child Development (SRCD) meetings in Denver, CO. At that time, members of the SRCD Black Caucus expressed the need for more systematic, sensitive, and representative studies of black and minority child developmental experiences, processes, and outcomes. One approach to addressing the problem was to establish a study group which would focus on such concerns.

In the spring of 1979, following the San Francisco SRCD meeting, Margaret Spencer and Geraldine Brookins met at Jackson State University (Jackson, MS) to make plans for the creation of a study group. Later that same year, Walter Allen consented to join the effort. An initial planning meeting was held in December, 1979, in Atlanta at Emory University and was attended by the editors along with Glen Elder and Diana Slaughter. At this meeting, the goals, participants, and schedules of meetings were finalized. Given the importance and complexity of the issues to be addressed, it was decided that the study group should meet over a two-year period.

## Acknowledgments

Because the work represented in this volume has been ongoing for almost four years, there are many people and organizations who must be thanked for their contributions and support. First among these are the contributors whose papers appear in this volume. During the initial stages of this project, Donna Banks was immensely helpful in executing tasks ranging from typing proposals to arranging meetings. Brenda Summers, Rhonda Butler, Webster Smith, Marina Shoemaker and Deborah Jones contributed by performing necessary clerical and organizational tasks. During the "middle passage," Aisha Ray, Anne-Marie Debritto, Blondell Strong and Angelle Cooper, all graduate students at The University of Michigan, provided incisive and thorough critiques of drafts. Successive drafts of this volume were typed by Ed Sammons' will, skill and patience, despite never ending changes. Nesha Haniff's rigorous, creative, sensitive editing of drafts was essential.

Of course this volume would not have been possible without the financial support of the Society for Research in Child Development, the Foundation for Child Development and the Carnegie Corporation of New York. Our respective universities contributed necessary in-kind resources. We are indebted to each. Much of our work as editors was done in conjunction with our individual research efforts, and we must therefore recognize the National Institute of Mental Health, the Spencer Foundation, the Charles Stewart Mott Foundation, the Ford Foundation, and the Rockefeller Foundation.

Encouragement, patience, support and love were provided in abundance by our spouses, Charles, Phillip, and Wilma. Thank you for being there when we most needed you. Thanks also for the love, inspiration and living examples provided by our children Tirzah, Natasha, Chaz, David, Rena, Binti, and Bryan. Special thanks to our extended families and friends who contributed so much to our own "Beginning" and "Becoming." Words fail, but you know who you are, what you have done, and how much it has meant. Finally, the three of us found in each other a wellspring of faith and strength, which always emerged at the appropriate time. Through the process we have moved from being just colleagues to loving, abiding, close friends.

Margaret B. Spencer<br>
Geraldine K. Brookins<br>
Walter R. Allen

# ORIENTING ISSUES FOR THE STUDY OF BLACK CHILDREN

# Introduction

The four papers in this section outline a holistic, conceptual perspective useful for studying black children and their families. These approaches provide important extensions of the developmental perspective. Social researchers need to consider black child development as it is influenced by socio-historical, cultural, life course and ecological imperatives. How these imperatives affect black children's personalities differs, depending on individual life stage. Together, the papers in this section provide a comprehensive orientation to guide empirical research on child development generally, and black child development in particular.

While varying in tone, direction of emphasis and orientation, Slaughter and McWorter, Franklin, and Elder each rely on a historical context for their discussion of present thrusts in studying black children and their families. As such, these papers enhance our understanding of the current knowledge base, or lack thereof, of blacks in this country.

Slaughter and McWorter in "Social Origins and Early Features of the Scientific Study of Black American Children and Families," demonstrate the theoretical and practical consequences of social research views of black life. In the process, they examine a half-century of research on black children and their families. By assessing the "Chicago School," they demonstrate how this paradigm and its adherents, have shaped the contours for intellectual inquiry regarding black life especially, but for others as well. One major lesson to be learned from research on black families and children prior to the 1970s is that, "Black families cannot be accurately described without simultaneous and systematic consideration of their cultural context, history, familial course of development, and economic and political realities."

Franklin in "From Integration to Black Self-Determinism: Changing Social Science Perspectives on Afro-American Life and Culture," also notes the significant role of some of the "Chicago School" scholars—most notably E. F. Frazier—on perceptions of the black experience. Using the 1980 uprising in Miami as a springboard, Franklin examines the historical relevance of civil rights programs in juxtaposition to scholarly treatises on black life. In the course of this analysis, the role of social science in determining how blacks are perceived and responded to in this country is discussed. Franklin's paper "From Integration to Black Self-Determinism," demonstrates the importance of understanding the historical underpinnings of current black experiences.

Elder's paper, "Household, Kinship and the Life Course: Perspectives of Black Families and Children," examines important, recent shifts in how black families are conceptualized and studied. The new emphasis is on family resilience and resourcefulness; black families are studied as examples of effective coping. Elder relates changing perspectives on black family life to changes in the field of family studies generally. Researchers rediscovered the analytical themes of time, process and context, proposed earlier in the work of W. I. Thomas and E. Franklin Frazier, thus moving them closer to a life course perspective on families and individuals.

Ogbu's paper, "A Cultural Ecology of Competence Among Inner-City Blacks," demonstrates the importance of studying the ecological contexts and cultural settings where black children grow and experience life. By addressing one specific context—the inner city environment—he demonstrates through his cultural-ecological model, the contextual origins of interpersonal competence and school achievement among young blacks. These, and other developmental outcomes are related to the socio-cultural imperatives of their community environments. Finally, Bronfenbrenner concludes this section by summarizing the major issues running through the four papers. He uses Ogbu's paper as a focal point for his discussion.

# 1 Social Origins and Early Features of the Scientific Study of Black American Families and Children

Diana T. Slaughter
*Northwestern University*

Gerald A. McWorter
*University of Illinois—Urbana*

## INTRODUCTION

The 1980s will be a period for new possibilities—a fitting optimism in an introduction to scholarly studies of black families and children undertaken by black scholars educated in the 1970s. This introductory paper focuses on a tradition that these studies have reexamined and replaced where necessary. Here the concern is with two issues: a description of social science as practiced by the early Chicago School of the University of Chicago, and a critique of how this perspective was applied to the black American experience in general.

Our paper describes pre-1970 approaches to the scientific study of black families and children. The perspective of socialization and individual development is emphasized. We think certain societal factors affecting black people as a group precipitated the growth of this field. First, some of these precipitating factors are enumerated, then key dimensions of the Chicago School are reviewed. Research on blacks from this perspective is presented, followed by a critique of the ''School.''

### The Impact of Social Change on the Scientific Study of Black American Families and Children

Black migration to northern urban settings occured in three different waves. The first wave occurred around 1896 when the boll weevil destroyed the cotton crop in the southern Black Belt, about 20 years after former President Hayes' withdrawal of the Union troops from the South. The effects of the withdrawal were keenly felt. Because of the action of Hayes and subsequent presidents (Logan, 1969), blacks lost the political power initially gained during Reconstruction. Mob violence, lynching, and terrorism reigned supreme. Ginzberg (1962), using Tuskegee Institute data, observes that nearly 5000 persons were lynched between 1885–1924, with the peak period occurring from 1890–94. Further, the 1896 *Plessy vs. Ferguson* Supreme Court decision, supporting the "Separate But Equal" doctrine, legitimized black codes, buttressed Jim Crow laws and racial segregation (Guillory, 1974), thereby providing black Americans with strong impetus to migrate.

The larger second and third migratory waves were directly linked to World Wars I and II. These wars increased factory production and thus employment opportunities for blacks in the North (Baron, 1971). Spear (1967) notes migrants initially sent encouraging reports back to relatives and friends in the South. Black-owned news media, such as the *Chicago Defender,* painted the North as the "promised land." Certainly, the isolation and terrorism, as well as the "Black Codes" and legally imposed constraints on voter eligibility—so pervasive in the rural South—were not characteristic of the more subtle discriminatory practices in the North. Blacks came north, for example, to learn the concept of "de facto" segregation.

The Society for Research in Child Development was founded in 1933. Thus, from about 1933 to the early 60s white American children were the objects of scientific study and research by developmentalists (Sears, 1975; Senn, 1975). However, black American children were usually not included in these studies, nor were they studied in their own right (Guthrie, 1976). This is not surprising; these early studies were largely psychological studies of presumed "universal" truths about individual growth and development. Only recently have many social and behavioral scientists discovered how relative our scientific truths can be. However, given the earlier perspective, there was no initial need to study black families and children. The study of black families and children began when scientists and others perceived them to pose a significant social problem.

By 1950, the majority of black people resided in the urban areas (Farley, 1968). Four historical developments paralleled the black mass migrations to the North between the late 1800s and 1950: (a) the institution of the White House Conferences on the nation's children and youth, which were held approximately every 10 years, beginning around 1909 (U.S. Children's Bureau, 1967); (b) the rise and consolidation of the American public educational system (Bremner, 1974; Woodring, 1975); (c) a trend toward antiauthoritarianism or pro-democracy as a political ideology, as a result of Fascism and Nazism in World War II (Arendt, 1951; Erickson, 1942); (d) creation of the University of Chicago in 1892 (Goodspeed, 1972), and the subsequent emergence of the "Chicago School" of Sociology (Diner, 1975; Faris, 1967; Hunter, 1980; Matthews, 1977).

Each of these early developments had consequences for the relationship between black people and the social sciences. This paper has given special attention to the influence of the Chicago School of Sociology and its associates on early interpretations of black behavior and development. The pioneering studies of black families and children were primarily conducted by associates of the Chicago School.

## The Chicago School: Focus on the Black Experience

The Chicago School has greatly influenced the social sciences and how they developed; nowhere is this more clear than with sociology (Hunter, 1980). For the first few decades, American sociology was dominated by the Chicago School. A Chicago-based journal (*American Journal of Sociology*) was the profession's single official publication until 1932. Over half of the first 12 presidents of the American Sociological Association held degrees from Chicago.

Associates of the Chicago School also influenced other related social science disciplines (e.g., education, human development, psychology). Greene's (1946) book, *Holders of Doctorates Among American Negroes,* reports Chicago among the top 10 schools, accounting for 234 of 381 doctorates awarded to blacks between 1876–1943. Chicago was the leading school in the number of doctorates awarded in the social sciences. Twenty-nine years later, Conyers and Epps (1974) surveyed black sociologists. Their list of the 10 black sociologists believed to have made the most important contributions to sociology included seven who had received doctorates, graduate training or postgraduate work from the University of Chicago: E. Franklin Frazier, Charles Johnson, Oliver Cox, Hylan Lewis, St. Clair Drake, Mozelle Hill, and Allison Davis. Three of the 10, Frazier, Johnson, and Davis, have written extensively in the areas of family socialization and development. The historical link is further demonstrated by the extent to which the historically black colleges were influenced by Chicago: Johnson at Fisk, Frazier at Howard, and Cox at Lincoln.

Contributors to this book have been influenced by this tradition as well. We are both products of graduate training in the 60s at Chicago in Human Development (Slaughter) and Sociology (McWorter). Further, many of the contributing authors are graduates of Chicago. For these reasons, it is important to first depict, and then critique, ideas inherent in the Chicago School perspectives, especially as applied to black families and children.

## The Chicago School: Ground Work—The Contributions of Park and Others

The titles of Robert E. Park's early publications (1914–18) indicate a great deal about his perspective and the evolution of the Chicago School of Sociology: "Racial Assimilation in Secondary Groups with Particular Reference to the Negro," "The City Environment," "Methods of Forming Public Opinion Applicable to Social Welfare Publicity," and "Education in its Relation to the Conflict and Fusion of Cultures: With Special Reference to the Problems of the

Immigrant, the Negro, and Missions.'' Park arrived at Chicago after having worked as a special assistant to Booker T. Washington at Tuskegee Institute from 1905–1914 (Matthews, 1977). Park's experiences, as well as the competencies he developed while at Tuskegee, were well-received by Chicago faculty and students:

> Initially, Park's formal teaching duties were confined to a single quarter—the fall term in 1913, the summer term in later years. Thomas had arranged that he give a single course, 'The Negro in America', to a small group of graduate students for a stipend of $500. Park reported to Washington that he was assigning a heavy load of Tuskegee books—*Up from Slavery, My Larger Education,* and *The Story of the Negro*—and that his lectures should "do a lot of good". The course was evidently a success, since when Park resumed teaching in June, 1914, the number of students had doubled (Matthews, 1977) [p. 85].

From his initial essay in 1914, Park maintained a consistent interest in the sociological study of the black experience. Subsequent generations of scholars and graduate students have continued this traditional focus. It is a tradition of research and educational activities presently summed up as the Chicago School.

Park made a profound contribution to the development of the basic elements of sociological research at the Chicago School (White & Smith, 1929; Wirth, 1940). There were five elements or components: (a) empirical, (b) ecological, (c) multi-disciplinary, (d) historical, and (e) policy components.

*Empirical.*    The main approach to research was always rooted in direct observation, the Aristotelian method of induction. Much of the previous work had been non-empirical, Platonic, philosophical reflections on social reality. Park insisted that social research should focus on both the objective external environment that influences human interaction and development, and the subjective level of attitude and values. His main emphasis was to learn from concrete social investigation. He also refused to use science as an intellectual rationalization for a particular political or social viewpoint. However, Park was a liberal and a social reformer. According to one author, "Empathy combined with objectivity was the standard he held up to his students." (Matthews, 1977, p. 114) This provided the basis for 20th century liberal scholarship.

*Ecological.*    The Chicago School was based on the theoretical position that social forces made up the community. These forces were independent of policy decisions and constituted an objective environment impacting social development. The School focused on this structure of social forces, and the development of urban social sciences, with an emphasis on "human ecology." Park's notion was that in each city there were "natural areas" where people and institutions were concentrated, and where there was a common cultural linkage and related economic activity. Burgess advanced a "zonal hypothesis," which consisted of a taxonomy of natural areas. Although this schema offered classification rather than explanation, graduate research vigorously described a wide variety of ecological patterns. Noteworthy here, for example, is Frazier's work (1932, 1957a) on the black populations of Chicago and Harlem.

*Multi-disciplinary.* Chicago-based research was not limited to a specific discipline, but was usually undertaken by researchers from several disciplines focusing on a common problem. This was clearly stated in every volume in the University of Chicago Social Science Studies Series edited by the Social Science Research Committee (Hunter, 1980). As early as the 1929 conference, Chairman Wesley C. Mitchell confronted this issue:

> We recognize the artificiality of considering the behavior of an economic man, a political man, a social man. We admit that few social problems can be treated adequately on the basis of knowledge possessed by an economist alone, a political scientist alone, a sociologist alone, or a lawyer alone (Wirth, 1940, pp. 113–114).

The early founders of the Committee on Child Development came from eight different disciplines. W. Lloyd Warner and Robert Havighurst, two of the original members, were concerned with bringing a developmental perspective, notably the perspective of the child and its family, to educational problems.

*Historical.* One of the major mandates of this School was to consider all phenomena within its natural history, based on first hand ethnographic techniques of description. It was more oriented to social process than structure. The search was for general laws of social development characteristic of all groups. Park developed a four staged theory (contact, competition, accommodation, and assimilation) which was known as the race relations cycle. This taxonomy of social process became a type of liberal view for the ameliorization of race relations conflict.

*Policy.* The purpose of research, in the School's view, was ultimately to find solutions to social problems. While the Chicago School held that disinterested observers should conduct value free research, it also held that the role of social science was to solve problems associated with man's relationship to man. In short, the world should, as a result of this impersonal, detached research, become more humane.

The scholar-activist role was thus an integral part of the tradition of the Chicago School, if activist is construed as the full range of possible sociopolitical premises. Park, for example, was the first president of the Chicago Urban League, and remained connected to social causes throughout his life.

## Perspectives on the Black Family: E. Franklin Frazier, 1932–1967

The 1932–1967 period of research on the black family at the Chicago School better was dominated by E. Franklin Frazier who published the *Negro Family in the United States* in 1939. Nowhere are the basic elements of the Chicago School better illustrated than in his work, *The Negro Family in Chicago*. This doctoral work was the foundation of his more widely known later study. The Frazier model has been described as historical-evolutionary (Staples, 1974; Hare, 1976).

In the 1932 study, he mapped ecologically-based zones on Chicago's black southside. He then researched these zones using social survey and participant observer methods. These data, along with census data and related records, were drawn on to document that as one traveled south from zone one, to the last zone, ending at 67th street, the incidence of reported unemployment, crime, and vice decreased. Indices of social-community disorganization also decreased, as did examples of family instability. Less juvenile delinquiency and fewer one-parent families were observed. Social disorganization decreased as adaptation to urban life and industrial society increased; each zone represented a different level of acculturation.

In interpreting these findings, Frazier argued that notions of genetic transmission, or African heritage, were not useful. Rather, he believed black families were severed from their African culture heritage during the middle passage and the American slave trade. He also thought black families were structurally weakened as a consequence of slavery and reconstruction. He argued that with adaptation to an urban ecological setting, blacks would freely choose to assimilate white middle class American behavioral patterns in regard to both family structure and life style. Further, Frazier (1964) theorized that the bases for a new family foundation emerged in the Americas. The origins of social stratification within the black community were to be found in the invidious distinction made between the more privileged house slaves and the less privileged field slaves.

Normative standards for lower or working class black families were to be set by middle and upper class black families. Families in the latter groups were perceived to be morally and socially superior to other black families. More conventionally moral conduct was to accompany even the smallest increments in education or economic advantage. Lewis (1936) conducted an earlier study in which he argued that socioeconomic indices became the bases for social differentiation among black Americans relatively late, 1910–1930, by comparison to white Americans. Thus, he sided with Frazier in viewing this emergent stratification as a tangible sign of "Negro progesss".

Moynihan (1965) reasserted that portion of Frazier's thesis dealing with black family instability during a peak period in the civil rights movement (Rainwater and Yancy, 1967). Moynihan argued that the lower socioeconomic status of most black families, reinforced by the earlier negative legacies, combined to render black families especially weak and vulnerable. According to Lewis (1966), this resulted in a "vicious cycle" where these families perpetuated their own poverty generation after generation.

## Perspectives on Black Childhood Socialization and Development: 1934–1970

So far as we can determine, the first ethnographic account of black child behavior was presented by Johnson (1934) in a chapter in *Shadow of the Plantation*, a study of black rural family life. Johnson stressed the adaptive folk culture of his study participants. Later, in a special focus on the victims of prejudice and discrimination, the Clarks published in 1939–1940 their early research of black preschoolers, using the now famous projective doll technique. The results of their studies seemed to document the budding self-hatred of black children and youth. Black children were more often prone to be favorably evaluated, and chose as a preferred playmate, an other-race doll.

Around the time the Clarks published their work, four major books sponsored by the American Council on Education were also published (1940–41). They were: *Children of Bondage* by Allison Davis and John Dollard, a study of the personality development of black youth in the urban South; *Negro Youth at the Crossways* by E. Franklin Frazier, a study of black youth in the middle or border states; *Growing up in the Black Belt* by Charles Johnson, a study of black youth in the rural South; and *Color and Human Nature* by W. Lloyd Warner, et al., a study of black youth in a northern city (Chicago).

According to Reid (1940), the ACE studies began with the question, How does the fact of being born a Negro affect the developing personality of a boy or girl? These studies looked at the socialization experiences and environmental contexts which influenced the youths' personality development. They stressed self-hatred, relative to being a black person—especially one of lower socioeconomic status. The concepts of class and color/race were essential to interpretations of the data. Reid's policy recommendations, to offset the potentially negative influences of inferior social status, included such items as adequate housing, employment, education, and a political voice (Reid, 1940).

Under the influence of Davis and Havighurst (e.g., Davis & Havighurst, 1946) who examined social class and color differences in childrearing practices, the emphasis on color/race as an explanation of black behavior was diminished. The authors concluded that the class-linked were better explanations of group differences in achievement behaviors than color/race-linked explanations. They also found it expedient to adopt Warner's concept of social class in their research. This definition of social class stresses consensual community agreement about existing patterns of intimate adult social participation. In 1948, Warner argued that such behavioral patterns would best be indexed by ratings of individual (a) occupational prestige, (b) educational level, (c) income, and (d) place of household residence, prioritized in descending order.

This openly assimilationist model was used throughout *Children of Bondage* by Davis and Dollard in the study of black personality development. The psychological parallel to occupation of a particular class or caste position is the individual emotional reaction to perceived immediate social status. Black youth at the extremes of the upper and lower classes were least likely to emotionally link personal life experiences and changes with either skin color/race or the friendships and social networks of the immediate family members. The youth most sensitive to barriers stemming from color/race or class contacts, according to the assimilationist model, are those who are either upwardly or downwardly mobile in the American social strata. However, the model has been most consistently applied to analysis of the behavior of black youth who strive for higher social status.

In summary, from the perspective of early research, being of lighter or darker skin color determined the class-linked privileges a black was likely to enjoy among his or her fellow blacks. Further, openly expressed antagonisms toward white Americans were assumed to be projections in the service of status strivings within the black community, rather than honest beliefs and attitudes. Other than this, however, it was assumed that existing psychological theories (e.g., Freudian, social learning perspectives) and methods (clinical interviews, later supplemented with projective personality tests) could be used to study black behavior. In 1951, Kardiner and Ovesey extended the concept of black self-hatred to include all blacks.

It was also assumed that an optimally functioning black family would function precisely like the white middle class family. If it did not, it was (a) deviant, even pathological, in orientation and (b) likely to produce children with defective personalities, whether or not a high degree of class or race consciousness was part of the individual's personal expression of attitudes and feelings. The Moynihan report (1965), which stressed the maladaptive functioning of black lower socioeconomic status families, continued a thesis first elaborated by Frazier. However, in 1970 two important critiques of deficit-oriented psychological theories were published (Baratz & Baratz, 1970; Sroufe, 1970). These critiques, and others that followed (e.g., Tulkin, 1972) challenged the preeminence of the Chicago School's interpretations of lower class, as well as black, behavior.

## Critique: Black Children and Families, the Assimilationist Paradigm, and the Chicago School

The two preceding sections in this paper discussed the (pre–1970) assimilationist perspective of the Chicago School. The assumptions, methods, and procedures of the specific research generated have been the major targets for critiques of the Chicago School perspective. Usually the content of these appraisals could be classified under one or more of the broad dimensions characterizing The School: (a) empirical, (b) ecological, (c) multidisciplinary, (d) historical, and (e) policy-referenced. Few have evaluated the strengths and weaknesses of the perspective as applied to the study of black children and families. This is the thrust of our critique, organized by these characteristics of the School.

*Empirical.*    A definite strength of the early Chicago School was its conviction that actual systematic data collection should accompany armchair theorizing and speculation. Perhaps the major problem was that these activities often were neither balanced nor comprehensive. Three examples illustrate this point. First, the authors of the American Council on Education studies assumed self-concept and attitudes toward oneself as a black person, to be identical. Two recent reviews (Cross, 1980; Porter & Washington, 1979) of research in this area indicate that levels of personal esteem and pro-black identification are quite independent dimensions of personality. Had this knowledge been available, a more balanced and comprehensive appraisal of the self-concepts of blacks would likely have emerged from the American Council on Education studies.

A second point, and the one most critical of research such as that by Hess and Shipman (1965), questioned the assumed equivalence of meaning for the three socioeconomic groups of mother–child pairs studied in the experiment arranged at the University of Chicago laboratory setting (Baratz & Baratz, 1970; Sroufe, 1970; Tulkin, 1972). If the primary issue was how mothers of different social statuses actually taught their children, then it was important that the experiment be equally familiar and meaningful to all concerned. Conversely, if the issue is merely to document that in certain contexts mothers of different statuses will, on average, behave differently with their children, then of course, the 1965 study did that very well. The black mothers who could be presumed to be most assimilated, were the most effective teachers of their children according to the middle class criteria generated.

Finally, we are reminded of the "strength of black families" arguments which undoubtedly developed in opposition to the Frazier-Moynihan thesis of widespread black family instability in the lower classes. Early on, these important counterassertions were made by black social scientists such as Billingsley (1968), Ladner (1971), and Hill (1972) who stressed the strengths and resiliencies of black families generally, and lower income black families in particular. For example, Ladner's research significantly opposed the prevailing view of single parent households need be headed by women who lacked resoursefulness, social competence, and parenting skills. Children born out of wedlock were not considered illegitimate nor were younger mothers pressured to marry the fathers of these children in order to become more respectable. Billingsley (1968) documented the diversity of black family organizational patterns; Hill (1972) observed that the consistent and persistent work ethic of black families was one of their major assets.

An eclectic, empirical approach assumes investigators to have the background and resources necessary for informed judgments about what data to collect and how. The Chicago School too often unfavorably portrayed blacks, especially blacks of lower socioeconomic backgrounds. The environmentalist approach, initially stimulated by W. I. Thomas (1912), was a definite advance over approaches which espoused openly racist and genetic hypotheses about black behavior. Still it appeared to reject that which was positive and progressive about black people generally, and poor black people in particular. Because of this, the research reports were frequently neither balanced nor comprehensive. More information about black children and families is necessary to achieve a more balanced assessment of the black experience in this nation. At the same time, we must reexamine many of our theoretical assumptions in order to offer viable alternatives to the assimilationist paradigm.

*Ecological.*    Park, as the early exponent of the Chicago School most clearly linked to black people, believed in the vibrancy and resiliency of group processes and social forces within the city. He also believed in the merits of their further study. However, his ideas about "human ecology" were neither (a) linked to a concrete analysis of black social history nor (b) sufficiently appreciative of the essentially social and political character of knowledge, both in terms of historical content and social result. Park fed the ambiguity associated, for example, with how race relations conflicts were to be ameliorated because he never presented a systematic theory to account for historical changes in the black experience. He himself may have chosen to utilize available scholarly research in his own area selectively, and so perhaps critical studies were ignored.

In his essays on the historical development of research on the urban experience, Park (1952) censures W. E. B. DuBois by not acknowledging the critical importance of his community study, *The Philadelphia Negro* (originally published in 1899). DuBois lived with his wife in the black community in Philadelphia for about one and one-half years while conducting this seminal study of black community and family life. DuBois' early study findings, based in part on interviews with more than 250 people, reflected a more balanced portrayal of black life than that of subsequent studies generated by advocates and devotees of the Chicago School (DuBois, 1903).

DuBois, as a Harvard educated black intellectual, could scarcely have been unknown to Park, since for years Park was secretary/special assistant to Booker T. Washington. He must have been aware of the ongoing debates between DuBois and Washington over the nature of the black experience. Yet he chose not to reference or discuss DuBois' perspective in his courses and writings. On the other hand, Park chose to link up with relevant social agencies and put a concern for social problems at the heart of his overall program. This stance stimulated and legitimized the action oriented research of many of the black researchers trained at Chicago. At a theoretical level, we reject the liberal paternalism of the early Chicago School approach and affirm social science research which supports black self-determination and empowerment. The case of Park and DuBois easily explicates the importance of this point via negativa.

When we studied at the University of Chicago, and even today, the separateness of the University community and the neighboring black community (often even the city) was stressed to students. Students of all backgrounds were taught fear and parochialism, within the confines of this otherwise highly cosmopolitan setting. This approach to inducting students into the University had the net effect of discouraging independent community contacts. This separation of students from community reinforced the Chicago School based interpretations of the urban black experience. While we salute the early community/family studies' focus on the concepts of class and race/color in analyses of the black experience, it is now clear that we need to introduce the concept of black culture. An alternative model inclusive of the entirety of the black experience must be devised.

*Multi-disciplinary.*    The multi-disciplinary approach was derived from the early Chicago School's emphasis on the solution of social problems. It is certainly true that the black experience has always been best studied and illuminated in this type of interdisciplinary approach. Thus, most of the major early black researchers spanned several disciplines: W. E. B. DuBois, Charles Johnson, Carter G. Woodson, E. Franklin Frazier, Allison Davis, Alain Locke, Horace Mann Bond, and J. A. Rogers, to name but a few. These authors, using various means and approaches, set out to understand black people, not to generate or validate specific, theoretically based laws of economics, psychology, or sociology, for example.

Not surprisingly, however, the Chicago School never encouraged development of a visible vehicle for interdisciplinary work on the black experience. In effect, social and cultural pluralism was uniformly practiced and acknowledged as a format of student body composition much earlier in Chicago's history. The outcome of this on-campus heterogeneity of social background was to be a kind of democratization of the elite. That is, one came to know, appreciate, and enjoy, upper-middle class white American culture regardless of one's social origins. However, origins, if other than upper middle class white American, were not considered to be a part of the ensuing intellectual debate.

It is not surprising that, despite its early contact with blacks and its emphasis on a multidisciplinary perspective in the solution to social problems, the Chicago School did not promote a tradition of serious study and analysis of the rural or urban black experience. Rather, blacks have been studied in relation to the problems they posed for groups who wished to contain and control them rather than to service and liberate them. The researchers in this volume are to be commended for attempting to establish such a tradition in the study of black children and family life.

*Historical.*    An accurate, balanced rendering of black history is essential to any theory of social change and the black experience. Until recently, however, the black family suffered from an essentially negative rendering of its history during and immediately following slavery. The altered appraisals emanated from new data sources. Gutman's (1976) close examination of southern plantation birth records and related documents over several generations, as well as Blassingame's (1972) examination of slave narratives from the perspective of (a) implicit family functioning and (b) related individual psychology, have produced a more balanced perspective. There is, for example, documented evidence of a distinctively black domestic and kinship style which emerged during slavery. Patterns of mating, marital choice, and child naming practices were especially unique. Further, slave narratives implied that the black family was, at least partly, a source of resistance to the oppressive conditions of slavery. American slavery was not, as Elkins (1959) had earlier argued, so comprehensive that virtually all of the slaves' attachments and identifications were linked directly to their slavemasters and mistresses. The legacy of slavery, relative to black family structure and functioning, includes ample evidence of black self-determination.

Despite these revisionist perspectives, as recently as 1978 a publication by the University of Chicago Press continues to promote the "negative legacy of slavery" approach. In an otherwise informative volume, Martin and Martin's (1978) study of extended black families continues to espouse the idea that blacks lost their African heritage during slavery. The black extended family was viewed, not as a construction within the context of the African-American experience, but as a self-help or survival unit generated by an ahistoric group of people living in a rural or agricultural setting.

The distinction we make is important. If the black extended family is an American adaptation of a longstanding African tradition, then clear cultural links to the diaspora are implied and can be expected to continue. This would occur because of a people's thrust for cultural continuity, even in a changed geographical setting (i.e., urban by comparison to rural). If it is merely a self-help or survival unit, then the black extended family will wane in scope and influence in accordance with any societal change which heralds significant social and economic improvements for black people. Further, if its functioning is impaired under crises, its scope and influence will wane, bringing many attendant policy implications. For example, Martin and Martin (1978, p. 1) define the black extended family as: a multigenerational, interdependent kinship system which is welded together by a sense of obligation to relatives; is organized around a family base household; is generally guided by a dominant family figure. They then make the following conservative statement about the black extended family's prospects in urban environments, where the majority of blacks now reside:

> Extended family members in our study were in general agreement that urban life is less conducive to the maintenance of the extended family structure than is rural or small-town life. . . . Welfare grants are given to various needy units within an extended family, not to the extended family itself, and usually such grants are in amounts insufficient either to allow family aid or to break their chain of dependency on government assistance [pp. 85–87].

This position essentially portrays the black extended family as merely an economic self-help unit, and not also as a proactive, positive, political, and cultural force. In assuming this position, the Martin and Martin view is certainly consistent with the earlier view of the Chicago School.

We can safely assume that most recent studies of black families were conducted in the context of the controversial Moynihan report. As increasing numbers of politically and socially aware black Americans entered higher education during the late 60s and early 70s, studies of the black family as well as of the black child were conducted. Prior to 1975, *Dissertation Abstracts* lists about 50 theses whose content pertains to the black family; this same guide lists about 40 between the years 1975–80 alone. Many of these more recent studies are not reiterating the Frazier–Moynihan line about family instability but rather, are attempting to say something qualitatively different about black families. This is certainly true of the studies in the present volume. However, from our perspective, these early outpourings reveal one important lesson: Black families cannot be accurately described without simultaneous and systematic consideration of their cultural histories and context, familial course of development, and economic and political realities.

*Policy.* Many policy-oriented criticisms of the Chicago School have already been made. The assimilationist model, as developed and elaborated by the Chicago School, dominated perspectives on the black family and on the relationship between black parenting styles and black child development during the years 1932–1970. We have described and critiqued this perspective because others have not had as powerful an impact on public policy decisions affecting black children and families. Alternative models, stressing not only class and race/color, but cultural and social history as well, should inform public policy. Regrettably, previous culturally based perspectives (e.g., King, 1976; Nobles, 1976) have often ignored the class and race/color questions, thereby limiting both their comprehensiveness and effectiveness for policy purposes. Too often the Chicago School promoted conservative, reformist policies for black people and, more importantly, neither nurtured, developed, nor promoted ideas which portrayed blacks as an historically independent social force in American society. There is a clear need for pluralism to be practiced at the level of social knowledge and exchange of ideas about black people.

## SUMMARY AND CONCLUSION

In summary, we have argued that the Chicago School was the principal intellectual and scholarly force influencing academic and policy-referenced perspectives on black people between roughly 1932–1970. We have also argued that this School arose from a concrete need to understand processes of urbanization and immigration. Its application to black people was timed with the urban migrations which began in response to increased political and economic oppression of blacks in the south after 1876. The theoretical orientation of the school emphasized social and cultural assimilation. As a result, a balanced appraisal of black family life in relation to family, black children, or the larger black community, was not possible.

We have outlined the dimensions of the School and identified its weaknesses in application to the study of the black experience. These weaknesses adversely affected policy decisions. The use of inappropriate concepts, methods, and procedures for data gathering caused the data presented for these decisions to be less than accurate or comprehensive. Further, the invalid, distorted interpretations of the black experience have caused black people to view research and evaluation as another instrument of social control serving only the controllers.

Finally, throughout this paper we have indicated our warm support and encouragement for the efforts of current scientists to establish a new tradition in this field—one which emphasizes the social and cultural integrity of black people generally, and black children and families in particular.

# From Integration to Black Self-Determination: Changing Social Science Perspectives on Afro-American Life and Culture

2

V. P. Franklin
*Yale University*

In an editorial that appeared in the May 24, 1980 *Amsterdam News* following the racial explosion in Miami, black columnist Louis Clayton Jones, in trying to account for the situation in the devastated black neighborhoods, provided this unencouraging declaration:

> To the civil rights types who are frantically rushing to Miami to quell the rebellion, this writer would remind you that you have never had a program for the disaffected masses and you have none now. Go home before you get shot and, for once, stop acting like house colored helping "Massa" put down a slave revolt.

As a student of the comings and goings of Afro-Americans, including on occasion "the masses," I would have to disagree with the idea that the civil rights leaders "never had a program" for the black masses. Moreover, the response of some black rioters and journalists to the civil rights leaders who tried to soothe racial tensions and relieve black frustrations must also be questioned and analyzed by black social scientists. To what extent have the theories and research of blacks in the social sciences sanctioned and supported the program espoused by the civil rights leadership? What over the last half century has been the program of the civil rights leadership? Was it effective? What was the relationship of social science action research and theories to the development of this program? What has been the role of black social scientists in trying to improve the conditions of the black masses? Have the black leaders and the social scientists been acting like "house colored," aiding the further exploitation of the black masses? Do black leaders and social scientists have a responsibility to try to mitigate the short term effects of unorganized violent eruptions? Or should they ignore the immediate results of these outbursts and begin to focus on the most appropriate long term objectives that could bring about significant improvements for the masses? Although it would be difficult to address all these questions in detail in one essay, it is important to begin to try to find some answers.

Examining the overall thrust of social scientific research on blacks in the United States, there are significant differences in the emphases of studies conducted by black as compared to those produced by white researchers. During the first half of the century, both white and black sociologists, political scientists, and anthropologists were describing and analyzing the impact of social class oppression, political subordination, and caste discrimination upon blacks in the United States; however, studies by black scholars always tended to be more positive and optimistic about the possibilities for improvement and advancement. Black and white psychologists assessed the impact of the depressed social environment upon the academic achievement of black children, but black psychologists carried out experiments that demonstrated the improvements in the performance on mental tests by blacks who were familiar with the test materials and procedures (Franklin, 1980). Even those black anthropologists who believed that America was (or is) a caste society, also suggested that conditions would change once blacks were no longer legally defined as a degraded, inferior group (Davis et al., 1937). When we examine the program advocated by black social scientists in the 20th century, it too often accepted the debased condition of blacks as an initial premise. It rarely entertained the idea, that regardless of what white Americans were doing, Afro-Americans should be moving toward greater control over the resources and decisions that affect their lives and their children's lives.

It should also be noted that from the end of the 19th century some black intellectuals posited black self-determination as the primary objective of organized social activities among Afro-Americans. W. E. B. DuBois, for example, recognized very early that black self-determination must be an important objective of the "spiritual strivings of black folk."

> We cannot reverse history; we are subject to the same natural laws as other races, and if the Negro is ever to be a factor in the world's history—if among the gaily colored banners that deck the broad ramparts of civilization is to hang one uncompromisingly black, then it must be placed there by black hands, fashioned by black heads and hallowed by the travail of 200,000,000 black hearts beating in one glad song of jubilee (DuBois, 1897, p. 181).

In order to accomplish these objectives, Afro-Americans will need "race organizations: Negro colleges, Negro newspapers, Negro business organizations, a Negro school of literature and art, and an intellectual clearing house for all these products of the Negro mind." Moreover, in his later years DuBois, over and over again, expressed his faith in the ability of the Negro masses eventually to bring about their own social and cultural advancement. At the same time he called for training at the highest levels for the "talented tenth" of the race to serve as leaders, "who through their knowledge of modern culture could guide the American Negro to a higher civilization." DuBois knew that "without this the Negro would have to accept white leadership, and that such leadership could not always be trusted to guide this group into self-realization and to its highest cultural possibilities" (Du Bois, 1971). As long as the possibility for training black leadership existed, Du Bois was optimistic about the future advancement of Afro-Americans in the United States as a distinct social and cultural group.

Carter G. Woodson, the Father of Negro History, founded the Association for the Study of Negro Life and History in 1915 for "the collection of sociological and historical data on the Negro, the study of peoples of African blood, the publishing of books in this field, and the promotion of harmony between the races by acquainting one with the other." Like Du Bois, Woodson believed that "Negroes had their own ideas about the nature of the universe, time and space, about appearance and reality, and about freedom and necessity." Woodson was also acutely aware of the need to train competent black leaders, but he often expressed his fear that "the educated class of Negroes" might not be up to the task. "The only question which concerns us here," Woodson asked rhetorically in *The Mis-education of the Negro* (1933), "is whether these 'educated' persons are actually equipped to face the ordeal before them or unconsciously contribute to their own undoing by perpetuating the regime of the oppressor" (Woodson, 1933, p. XI–XII). However, because of his faith in the liberating aspects of education, Woodson was basically optimistic in his conclusions about the ability of educators and other community leaders to assist in the development of Afro-American life and culture.

> Can you expect teachers to revolutionize the social order for the good of the community? Indeed we must expect this very thing. The educational system of a country is worthless unless it accomplishes this task. Men of scholarship, and consequently of prophetic insight, must show just the right way and lead us into the light which shines brighter and brighter (Woodson, 1933) [p. 135].

There was also a great deal of optimism about the future prospects for Afro-Americans expressed in the writings of black social scientists of the 1930s, 40s, and 50s. It usually did not stem from the same source as that of Du Bois and Woodson—a growing faith in the black masses for self-determination and advancement. These black researchers often subscribed to a theory of race relations that posited assimilation as the end result of interracial contacts in the United States, and as each barrier to the integration of blacks and whites was pushed aside, their optimism appeared more justified. Led by the students of sociologist Robert Park at the University of Chicago, including Charles Johnson, E. Franklin Frazier, Bertram Doyle, Allison Davis, Horace Mann Bond, and St. Clair Drake, these black social scientists published richly documented studies of the impact of class and caste upon the black personality, family, community, and culture. For most of these researchers, assimilation or integration of blacks and whites was inevitable, despite the objections of most whites and some blacks. Therefore progress in breaking down barriers to black advancement through greater desegregation was a constant source of optimism (Smith & Killian, 1974).

Charles Johnson, noted black sociologist, fully subscribed to his mentor, Robert A. Parks' theory of the "race relations cycle," which predicted that when different racial groups come together they move from contact to conflict to accommodation to assimilation. Johnson viewed the conflict that existed between the reaces as dangerous and deadly, and even where blacks and whites had erected a system of "racial etiquette," blacks were still the victims of unequal and discriminatory treatment. Moreover, despite this tradition of accommodation and economic exploitation, Johnson believed that changes were occurring in race relations. According to Johnson (1934), the isolation of the black masses caused a cultural lag. In pointing out areas where changes were occurring, Johnson believed he was undercutting the belief in "the ineptness of the members of this group in taking on the white man's civilization." [p. 8]

Whereas Du Bois and Woodson demonstrated a healthy respect for black culture and achievements, Johnson and many of the other black social scientists influenced by Parkian theories, generally had few positive statements about Afro-American culture. At their best, they subscribed to a vague sort of cultural materialism, suggesting that what passed for culture among blacks was really the result of the plantation social structure and black folk traditions. At their worst, these social scientists, some trained in anthropology, suggested that just because some black individuals have rhythm, does not mean blacks possess a culture.

In the book, *Race Relations* (1934), coauthored with Willis Weatherford, Charles Johnson directly addressed the question, "Can there be a separate Negro culture?" After concluding that "the original African culture of the American Negro is very largely lost," Johnson noted three important efforts on the part of blacks "in the direction of separate culture development." The first was the abortive Garvey movement of the 1920s, which tried to "salvage Negro self-respect through all-black activities." By 1934, however, the movement was in complete disarray. The second effort involved activities to try to inculcate "race pride and respect by substituting Negro characters of history for white characters, or of supplementing history with the addition of these neglected names." Johnson believed this strategy did little to raise the opinion of whites about the character of the average Negro [p. 550].

The third effort occurred during the 1920s, when the "younger generation of Negroes . . . turned back frankly to discover the beauty and charm of the life of the folk Negro." The works of Claude McKay, Jean Toomer, Countee Cullen, and Langston Hughes, according to Johnson, tended to "enrich the general culture rather than to develop a distinctly Negro expression." According to Johnson and Weatherford (1934):

> When it is asserted that Negroes have a peculiar aptitude for music, the statement can mean nothing more than that there are among the Negroes more talented individuals per million of the population than among the whites. No one would assert that all Negroes have a talent for music nor deny that some white men are especially gifted in that respect. Musical composition is the work of individuals and not of groups. Quite irrespective of race, individuals will be attracted to and succeed in vocations along the line of their special abilities. It might conceivably be that Negro individuals in the future will write ten or a hundred musical compositions for one of equal rank produced by white men. But this would not make a Negro music: it would simply mean that Negro individuals contribute more than do white artists to the development of an art. The art itself is not racial [p. 549–554].

In quoting these remarks, Johnson indicated that he subscribed to the viewpoint expressed. But even Johnson should have questioned the idea that "cultural contributions are individual rather than group contributions." How could the development of the black spirituals, religious practices, jazz, blues, or language be considered individual as opposed to group contributions? Johnson espoused these negative views on black culture because he believed that certain cultural traits and practices were a hinderance to the further integration of the Negro into American, i.e. Euro-American, culture.

In his examination of the *Negro Family in Chicago* (1934), noted sociologist E. Franklin Frazier discussed the earlier studies, mainly by white researchers, that described the black family as demoralized, dissolute, and disorganized and went on to draw distinctions among the various types of black families emerging from the antebellum black experience. Indeed, Frazier's (1934) optimism with regard to the contemporary situation, despite the negative impact of the city upon migrant families, stemmed from the existence of a "leavening element" in the form of free Negro families that took the lead in the "progressive stabilization" of the black family in the 20th century.

> From emancipation to the opening of the twentieth century there has been a progressive stabilization of Negro family life. With the collapse of the social organization of the ante-bellum South, nearly all that the Negro had achieved in the way of stable and organized family life went to pieces. Remnants of the past were salvaged here and there and became the basis of orderly sex relations under freedom. Among the already free Negroes there was a leavening element with solid family traditions that formed the nucleus for future progress. Since the opening of the twentieth century the steady urbanization of the Negro has set adrift large sections of the population. Customary forms of control have been broken down, and new conceptions of life have been acquired. In the city, especially the northern city, the process of emancipation from the old ways of life has gone farthest. Even the casual student of Negro life has been aware of these changes since emancipation [p. 49].

Once these blacks arrived in the city, Frazier believed that "family disorganization measured by dependency, desertion, illegitimacy, and juvenile delinquency varied according to the economic organization and social structure of the Negro community." The lower elements, especially the southern migrants, did not fare as well as the higher classes in the better areas of the city. In contrast to the crippling disorganization of the masses of black migrants, Frazier felt that,

> In other cases family traditions had been established by ancestors who had succeeded in accumulating property, or education, or had acquired some distinction that had given them status in their community. Accessions to this small group of families had constantly come through the more intelligent and energetic members of the Negro group who had succeeded in acquiring a higher status in the Negro population. While the city tended to dissolve established forms of social life and brought about disorganization, it had created an opportunity for more to escape from the condition of the masses [pp. 250–252].

Frazier was much more optimistic about the status of the black family than earlier researchers because of the existence of a significant and growing upper status group that could compete and survive in the urban social environment.

As was the case with Charles Johnson, Frazier believed that the African cultural heritage and southern black folk traditions were more a detriment to the advancement of the "civilizational process" and the integration of whites and blacks in the United States. "Although the Negro is distinguished from other minorities by his physical characteristics", wrote Frazier in *The Negro in the United States* (1957), "unlike other racial or cultural minorities the Negro is not distinguished by culture from the dominant group." Frazier was optimistic about the ultimate integration and assimilation of the black minority because of the strong desire of Negroes for assimilation.

> The Negro minority is striving for assimilation into American life. The Negro has striven as far as possible to efface or tone down the physical differences between himself and the white majority. He does not take seriously the notion of a separate Negro economy. In his individual behavior as well as in his organized forms of social life he attempts to approximate as closely as possible the dominant American pattern [pp. 680–681].

The interpretations of black life by other black social scientists trained in the Parkian theories of race relations echoed many of the themes found in the work of Johnson and Frazier. For example, even the black anthropologists trained in the Chicago School designed their research in order to demonstrate the significance of "caste discrimination" upon the social and cultural development of Black Americans. The caste and class discrimination studies of Allison Davis, Horace Cayton and St. Clair Drake tried to demonstrate that the relations between blacks and whites in the South and the urban North were determined by caste and class norms, not by race, which is a biological rather than a social category. In *Deep South,* Allison Davis, Burleigh Gardner, and Mary Gardner, used the term caste to describe the principle used in the United States for allocating political and economic power and social prestige. Blacks were labeled an inferior, degraded group from whom social prestige was systematically withheld, and for whom a specific inferior economic and social position was legally established.

It should be noted that Charles Johnson criticized the use of the term caste in describing the black-white situation in the United States. There has been "constant change" in the attitudes of whites toward blacks, but Johnson believed that in a caste system "changes are socially impossible". There were, of course, no examples of societies with high and low castes where change was "socially impossible", but they were nonetheless considered "caste" societies, such as Hindu society in India. In fact, Allison Davis, John Dollard, and St. Clair Drake use caste and class as organizing principles for their examination of blacks in the United States in pretty much the same way that Johnson and Frazier had used the term race (Myrdal, 1944).

More importantly, the theoretical underpinnings of the research of all of these black and white social scientists came under attack when Gunnar Myrdal severely criticized the race relations theories of Robert Park. In his investigation of the Negro problem in the United States, Myrdal agreed with the empirical information that had been previously produced by black and white social scientists as well as that produced specifically for his study: The Negro suffers from class, racial, and caste discrimination; the Negro family is disorganized; and the Negro culture and community are pathological versions of white American culture and community. "In practically all its divergences, American Negro culture is not something independent of general American culture. It is a distorted development or a pathological condition, of the general American culture . . ." (Myrdal, 1944, pp. 928–930). Unlike the studies of the black social scientists, however, Myrdal was much less optimistic about the future of the American Negro or the realization of the American Creed—the traditional American belief in freedom and equality. Myrdal was pessimistic because of what he considered the acceptance by Americans (black and white) of Robert Park's fatalistic, naturalistic theories of race relations. Rather than serving as the theoretical justification for movement toward change and improvement in the social conditions of blacks, and thus facilitating eventual integration and assimilation, these race relations theories provided rationalizations for "race prejudice", racial discrimination, and the existing accommodation between blacks and whites in American society. The race relations cycle was evidently stuck between conflict and accommodation, and assimilation was still a long way off because it was valued primarily by blacks and they were in the distinct minority.

Myrdal believed that a more dynamic view of society was needed, informed by practical research, in which value judgments were related to factual situations and trends in social change. Therefore, if a certain end result is sought, such as the realization of the American Creed, then practical research should be carried out with this particular objective in mind (Myrdal, 1944). One of the immediate results of Myrdal's critique was a shift in the focus of the research of many black social scientists to the practical ways of bringing about the immediate desegregation of public life among black and white citizens (Frazier, 1968).

It must also be pointed out that throughout the first half and well into the second half of the 20th century, the social scientific approaches and theories that black scholars used in their research on contemporary conditions facing the black individual, family, and community, were generally inappropriate. They did not lend support to the optimistic tone of their assessments of the possibility for improved race relations and black social advancement in the United States. Moreover, because of their failure to appreciate the role and function of cultural development in the Afro-American experience, these black and white social scientists ignored empirical evidence that noted the strength and significance of Afro-American culture in black life and American society at large (Hershkovits, 1936; 1941).

Nonetheless, this social science research served as the empirical and theoretical underpinning for the attacks on Jim Crow segregation and second-class citizenship during the Civil Rights movement. But ultimately the theoretical weaknesses and gaps in empirical information in the social science research supporting Martin Luther King's non-violent protest movement became apparent. The civil rights campaigns became engulfed in the flames of the big-city riots of the 1960s and the demands from within for Black Power in controlling the movement. For example, when King visited Watts after the riot in August, 1965, he encountered a group of young people who shouted triumphantly: "We won." King was quoted as having then asked: "How can you say you won when 34 Negroes are dead, your community is destroyed, and whites are using the riot as an excuse for inaction?" The reply was: "We won because we made them pay attention to us." Subsequently, when King tried to address a group at a community center, he was booed and shouted down: "Get out of here, Dr. King" (Brisbane, 1974, p. 159). In Miami following the riot in May, 1980, Andrew Young, Jesse Jackson, and other civil rights leaders were booed and told to get out. It is no coincidence that the program for black advancement espoused by Young and Jackson is really the very eloquently stated one of King in the 1960s. Just as the program of non-violent protest and integration or desegregation was unsatisfactory to the black masses in the 1960s, it remains unsatisfactory to those Afro-Americans who are still the victims of racism, unemployment, police brutality, and social oppression in the 1980s.

During the 1960s and early 1970s, many black intellectuals began to challenge the organizing principles guiding social scientific research on black life in the United States. They suggested that the social sciences had been used as "instruments of racist ideology" and that there was a need to examine social phenomena from a "Black perspective." These black researchers discussed

Black Psychology, the Sociology of Black Liberation, and the Ideology of Black Social Science, and unfortunately heralded the *Death of White Sociology* (Ladner, 1973) before a full fledged Black Sociology had appeared on the scene. For example, in much of this writing the possession of a finely tuned sense of black consciousness is the crucial ingredient in interpreting empirical evidence on the black condition. Therefore, having lived the black experience is a necessary, though not sufficient, factor in making a contribution to black social scientific knowledge. The narrowness of this perspective became patently clear during the 1970s when the great diversity in the experiences of blacks was finally recognized and assessed (Wilson, 1978). Developing an incisive and sophisticated black consciousness is a very important objective for black social scientists working in the United States. However, practical and theoretical social scientific research geared toward black social advancement and increased self-determination can be conducted by black or white, native or foreign born, brilliant and not so brilliant scholars.

At the same time, integration–desegregation began to play out as a theoretical objective for Afro-Americans in the United States as early as the 1940s. Then the failure of blacks to gain social, economic, and political equality was beginning to be attributed to the minority status of black Americans. Therefore, the reason why blacks were not allowed to vote, to gain employment or reap the benefits of higher education and skilled training, was because they were a minority. The dominant white majority objected to black advancement in these areas. But one must ask: Why should the dominant white majority be expected to allow changes that increase social competition for the limited resources in the society—resources that the whites already control? An emphasis on the minority status of blacks served as another excuse for lack of black social advancement in many areas (Frazier, 1957a).

For the black masses the integration–desegregation objective began to be repudiated when it became clear that only a certain number of blacks in certain areas of American social life were to be integrated. Many blacks also began to realize that desegregation served as a threat to many of the public institutions already under the control of competent black professionals. Desegregation in effect closed off for lower income blacks many traditional avenues of advancement that were previously open, and at the same time, did not open up enough new areas for black penetration. Contrary to the suggestion of journalist Louis Clayton Jones, the black leaders and social scientists had a program, it was just inadequate and ineffective for the advancement of the masses of blacks in this country. The fact that it was effective for some blacks, most notably educated blacks who were able to take advantage of the limited opportunities that were made available, also helps to explain the disaffection between the black masses and the civil rights leadership (Wilson, 1978; Washington, 1979).

Increasing the degree of control exercised by blacks over those things that affect their lives and the lives of their children is a viable alternative to integration–desegregation as the major objective of social science research on Afro-

Americans in the United States. Recent research by anthropologists and historians on the distinctness of the Afro-American experience and culture in this society provides much support for the black self-determinist approach in other areas. Sociological research suggesting the similarity of the experience of blacks, European, and Asian immigrants to the United States often fails to take into account that the treatment of voluntary immigrants to a country is often very different from that of a group brought into a society enslaved, and treated as inferior (Glazer, 1971; Franklin, 1980). Historians have begun to examine the African input in the response of enslaved blacks to their oppression, and have documented many of the cultural themes of the Afro-American experience. Even sociologists must come to recognize that Afro-American cultural values and perspectives are significant in explaining the resistance of the Afro-American masses to demands for further assimilation into Euro-American culture (Gutman, 1976; Lovell, 1972; Levine, 1977; Webber, 1978).

It is possible that a shift to an emphasis on black self-determination in social science research on blacks in the United States may alienate some white researchers in this area. But at the same time, many black and other Third World peoples are also engaged in research, and struggle to bring about real power and control over institutions, resources, and social processes that affect their lives and nations. Therefore, Afro-American and Third World social scientists who embrace black self-determination as a primary objective of their theoretical and practical research can support each other through scholarly contacts and intellectual solidarity.

# 3 Household, Kinship, and the Life Course: Perspectives on Black Families and Children

Glen H. Elder, Jr.
*University of North Carolina—Chapel Hill*

Studies of black families and children have undergone major changes since the 1920s. The central question up to mid-century concerned the etiology of family disorganization, a theme now challenged by growing interest in the resilience and adaptiveness of families under stress (McCubbin et al., 1980). This change increased awareness of three family dimensions; time, process, and context. Increasingly, black families are now studied across historical time, life course, and successive generations. They are more frequently depicted as actors who shape their own lives within the constraints of structured environments.

Explanations for the shift in problem orientation inevitably lead to ideology. "The more at odds a black family is with the white, middle-class family model, the more pathological in orientation that family is considered to be" (Allen, 1978) [p. 170]. The new emphasis on family resilience is consistent with Allen's "cultural variant" perspective, in which black families are represented as a social form distinct from that of the white family. Black families differ from white families for reasons of culture and socioeconomic environment (Billingsley, 1968; Stack, 1974).

I propose another view of such change, an interpretation which defines it as part of a general conceptual transformation of family studies since the early days of the 20th century. The observed changes in the research question, from pathology to resilience, can be seen within the broad field of family research, and reflect the changing times and conditions of the post 60s (Elder, 1984). This chapter presents three views of the analytic change, beginning with research themes of family disorganization and reorganization that represent a link between Thomas and Znaniecki's *The Polish Peasant in Europe and America* (1918–20) and E. Franklin Frazier's *The Negro Family in the United States* (1939). The

29

second theme concerns the shift from insular to embedded household. Burgess's work is one source of an insular view of the household. He treats the domestic unit as divorced from the kin system of generational members and collaterals. In contrast, an embedded concept of the family and household draws upon a multi-generational approach to the life course. The third theme outlines temporal views of the family and individual from an age-based perspective. Family reorganization and coping, the embedded household of a kin network, and a temporal account of family and individual histories then depict an emerging approach to black families and children.

## The Research Problem: Disorganization Versus Reorganization

My point of departure on research is with W. I. Thomas and Florian Znaniecki's landmark study, *The Polish Peasant in Europe and America* (1918–20) (1974), completed more than 60 years ago. *The Polish Peasant* revealed an historical process of profound importance for family change and social character: migration to urban-industrial areas of Poland, Germany, and the United States. There was a breakdown of traditional life patterns as recent immigrants accommodated themselves to the new world. Thomas and Znaniecki's analysis revolved around two often simultaneous processes, social disorganization and reorganization. Family stability represented "a dynamic equilibrium of processes of disorganization and reorganization" (1974, p. 1130). Reorganization extended beyond the reinforcement of a decaying family pattern to the "production of new schemes of behavior and new institutions better adapted to the changed demands of the group."

The analytic structure and disorganization theme of E. Franklin Frazier's (1939) major work on black families up to the 1950s owes much to *The Polish Peasant*. This same theme reappears 25 years later in the conclusion to Moynihan's controversial essay, *The Negro Family*. Moynihan wrote, "At the heart of the deterioration of the fabric of Negro society is the deterioration of the Negro family" (1965, p. 51). The reorganization theme also described in *The Polish Peasant* has resurfaced after decades of neglect through contemporary studies of black family resilience in the face of adversity (Gutman, 1976; Aschenbrenner, 1978). More than before, research is attending to the dual processes of disorganization and reorganization.

*The Polish Peasant* and *The Negro Family* have much in common beyond emphases on disorganization. Both works concern social migration and are genuinely historical in design. The two volumes were also widely regarded as the most important studies of the family by American sociologists up to World War II (Elder, 1984). Though Frazier's work generally reflected the ideas of his mentor Robert Park, as well as the urban ecology of Ernest Burgess, he turned to W. I. Thomas and Florian Znaniecki for the analytic framework used to study black families following their great northward migration. This framework is most clearly seen in *The Polish Peasant* and represents one of the study's most enduring contributions.

Stable family life implies effective social control in *The Polish Peasant*. A well-organized family is one in which existing social rules of behavior are effective in regulating the behavior of members. Disorganization thus represents a loss of social control; "a decrease in the influence of existing social rules of behavior upon individual members of the group" (Thomas & Znaniecki, 1974, p. 128). The social customs of rural Poland ensured effective control, whereas migration to Northern Europe and urban America undermined this traditional basis of family organization.

Stability also occurs when families have the resources to achieve their aspirations. In Thomas's work, control of desired outcomes is a function of the changing relation between aspirations and resources. Loss of control results from disparities that reflect sharply diminished resources, as in the economic collapse of the 1930s. Soaring aspirations that outstrip available resources establish another form of reduced control. A third example involves the disparity between new aspirations in the urban environment and resources better suited to the old agrarian world.

Thomas and Znaniecki described social disorganization as a paramount issue in American life during the first quarter of this century. Well before the appearance of *The Polish Peasant,* Walter Lippmann (1914) offered some cogent observations on the unsettled condition.

> There isn't a human relation, whether of parent or child, husband or wife, worker and employer, that doesn't move in a strange situation. We are not used to a complicated civilization. We don't know how to behave when personal conduct and eternal authority have disappeared. There are no precedents to guide us, no wisdom that wasn't made for a simpler age. We have changed our environment more quickly than we know how to change ourselves. (pp. 152–153)

The problematic disjuncture between custom and personal choice in family life became a dominant research orientation among family sociologists in the Chicago School up to 1940. W. I. Thomas, E. Franklin Frazier, and Ernest Burgess were especially prominent in this line of study.

The process of family disorganization through emigration in *The Polish Peasant* begins with changes that breakdown the isolation of the peasant community. Though emigration is linked with disorganization (and its symptoms—sexual promiscuity, vagabondage, juvenile delinquency), situational change is not a sufficient cause of family breakdown. The change itself must interact with certain pre-existing attitudes, such as hedonic interests and individualistic preferences created in pre-migrant populations by the diminished isolation of rural communities. This perspective is important because it points to circumstances in which family disruption is not a result of emigration.

An effective counterbalance to family disorganization (Thomas & Znaniecki, (1918–1920) is unlikely if the local

> . . . community has lost its coherence, if the individual is isolated from it, or if his touch with the outside world made him more or less independent of the opinions of his immediate milieu . . . In combination, these factors provide tools for exploring the process by which family disorganization is quickly replaced by reorganization. (p. 1168)

However, reorganization or the process by which families cope effectively with new circumstances, was not a major consideration in the study. By contrast, more recent studies have shown (Elder, 1974) that family outcomes in a change process depend on how families respond to the new situation. This response, in turn, varies according to the new situation, the change event itself, and what families and people bring to the event.

Frazier's (1964) final chapter of *The Negro Family in the United States* concludes that the

> . . . Black family which evolved within the isolated world of the Negro folk will become increasingly disorganized. Modern means of communication will break down the isolation of the world of Black folk and, as long as the bankrupt system of southern agriculture exists, Negro families will continue to seek a living in the towns and cities of the country. They will crowd the slum areas of southern cities or make their way to northern cities where their family life will become disrupted and their poverty will force them to depend upon charity. (pp. 367–368)

There is an inescapable bias to Frazier's account, one of pervasive family disorganization through black migration from the rural South to Northern communities, a process of assimilation and acculturation. In a major section of the book, "In the City of Destruction," Frazier moves from one symptom of family breakdown to another; "roving men and homeless women," father desertion and divorce, unwed motherhood, prostitution and crime. Just as Thomas and Znaniecki stressed the disruptive intervention of state power in Polish immigrant families (the police, courts), Frazier documented the deprivational aspects of social welfare for newly arrived black families. Instead of helping to stem the rising tide of family disruption, social and welfare agencies were more often part of the problem.

Both *The Polish Peasant* and *The Negro Family* expressed a Victorian mentality toward normative variations and alternative family forms. Preoccupation with "sexual promiscuity" among migrants is characteristic of both studies, an outlook consistent with emphasis on the disorganization side of family life. However, Frazier as well as Thomas and Znaniecki explored the reorganization process as well. Indeed the last section of *The Negro Family* centers on the revitalizing process in urban black life, especially within the family unit. At the macroscopic level, important developments include the reduction of racial barriers in all aspects of community life, improved employment and housing opportunities. Within these constraints, Frazier very briefly identifies family strategies or adaptations that could enhance family well-being and the nurturance of children. Effective parental control is one example and residential change is another. Multiple earners represent a third.

One of the clearest examples of family reorganization in Frazier's study involves single parenthood. The powerlessness of a young mother in this situation is captured well by the words of a widow concerning her wayward daughter: "I talk and talk and teach, and, when I have done all I know how to do, I can do no more. Children in these days are a heartbreak" (1966, p. 265). Some single mothers moved in with their own mothers, and others shared a dwelling with an adult sister or more distant relative. This network of kin ties is not prominent in Frazier's study, especially those of lineages that extend across three, four, and more generations. Unlike the new research on migration (Shimkin et al., 1978; Hareven, 1981), *The Negro Family* does not present and expand upon migration as a system of social exchange between origin and destination units. An account of migration within kinship networks is missing.

A useful example of such networks comes from the Holmes County (Mississippi) study (Shimkin et al., 1978, p. 76). Since World War I, nearly 70% of the black residents of the county emigrated, with two fifths ending up in the city of Chicago. The study documents the process by which migration has "resulted in the formation of extensive networks of relationships, maintained by much communication and return visiting, that serve today to direct individual movements and the formation of new colonies toward favorable opportunities." This study challenges Frazier's arguments that discontinuity exists between the rural South and the urban North. "Chain migration" forms a social bridge involving relatives and former townspeople in a network of support and exchange crossing geographic boundaries. By neglecting the broader kin relations of black households, Frazier created a portrait of family disorganization. The strengths and weaknesses of a family unit cannot be accurately judged without considering the larger kinship system. The strengths of two generations may offset the vulnerabilities of a third or fourth generation.

An exclusive emphasis on family disorganization has left a misleading imprint on black family studies, especially in the kinds of questions posed. Instead of making sense out of family survival and effectiveness under difficult circumstances, studies of the black family have given too much attention to family breakdown—as if this represents the only phase of family adaptation and change. As Prude (1976, p. 424) correctly notes from studies of families in the working class, this work has generally failed to comprehend that a "family could be both affected by and effective in its milieu, that it could be simultaneously unsuccessful in resisting changes in its own traditions and successful in aiding its members to cope with the world in which they found themselves." The same

LIBRARY
COLBY-SAWYER COLLEGE
NEW LONDON, NH 03257

family may be victor and victim in different domains, just as the same event has positive and negative consequences.

The most effective critics of the "either victory or defeat"orientation in black family studies are the Martins (1978, p. 113). They argue that both Gutman (1976) and Stack (1974) glossed over the price and limitations of black extended networks. "Black people, at least the ones we know, have always known, even if social scientists have not, that there were strong black families and terribly disorganized ones, too, but never a consistent pattern of either-or." In reference to Robert Hill's (1972) case for the adaptive strengths of black families, Martin and Martin (1978) conclude that he was no "more successful in placing the Black family in a straightjacket of strengths than St. Clair Drake and Horace Cayton (1945) were years ago in attempting to lump black experience into 'staying alive,' 'praising God,' 'getting ahead,' 'advancing the race,' and 'having a good time.'"

Emphasis on the insular household and family contributes to an image of family breakdown, disadvantage, and fragility. We see this preoccupation in the work of Ernest Burgess, as well as in the tradition of family studies that bears his continuing influence.

## From Insular to Embedded Households

During World War II, the marital unit acquired unusual significance in family studies. Social custom was fast losing power in the regulation of family behavior, and couples seemed to be largely on their own, bound mainly by love and companionship. At the end of the war, Burgess et al (1971) summed up the change in a thesis which states that

> the family has been in transition from a traditional family system, based on family members playing traditional roles, to a companionship family system, based on mutual affection, intimate communication, and mutual acceptance of division of labor and procedures of decision making. The companionship form of the family is not conceived as procedures of decision making. The companionship form of the family is not conceived as having been realized but as emerging. (p. 7)

The individualization of family life and an increasing dependence of marital permanence on happiness or satisfaction drew Burgess's attention to the basic elements of dyadic interaction. The "family interior" became even more narrowly circumscribed by marital relations and adjustment. Though keenly aware of family ecologies, Burgess showed less inclination than Thomas to relate history, social structure, and ecological factors to family interaction. This was especially true for the marital dyad where "affection, temperamental compatibility, and social adaptability" had become the key ingredients of marital success. By the end of the 1930s, Burgess and Cottrell (1939) had coauthored the first quantitative investigation of the determinants of marital adjustment.

Studies of marital adjustment and relations, often blind to the external realities of family life (Bowerman, 1964), gained momentum over the subsequent decades (Gray-Little, 1982), and by the late 1970s, the Burgess domain of family interaction was still largely divorced from the external world in empirical research. Aldous (1977) observed that "there continues to be a general lack of interest in the way influences from the outside milieu become translated into family interaction patterns" (p. 129).

Burgess's concern with marital permanence and quality did not extend to the implications of marital discord and dissolution for children and their developmental course, a research focus in studies of black families. If Burgess had explored the connection between marital instability and child development, would it have been within the broader network of kinship? Probably not if we are to judge from his previous research. Burgess's treatment of kin generally appears sequentially within a life span; the child and his or her parents, the child as adult and his or her child, and the adult in later life with mature offspring and grandchildren. The parent of childhood is not in the picture of adulthood. More often than not we are apt to see an interior view of marital discord and parent-child interaction or of the single parent apart from relatives. Such interior views invite misinterpretations of family structure and functioning. As Martin and Martin (1978) observe, a household

> with father absent appears to be a broken home, but it may really be a vital part of a strong and flexible extended family. A family with a female as the head appears to be female-dominated or matriarchal houshold, when in fact several male relatives may be influential in such a household setting. (p. 9)

Marriage and family in Burgess's perspective represent dynamic and emergent phenomena with related sources of change. Families are changed because of the changes in members, and members are changed through changes in family relationships. This link between individual and family development is characteristic of Burgess's well-known definition of the family, as a unity of interacting personalities. The formative stage of family life exemplifies the connection. The task is to account for the process by which two persons with a history at marriage form a relationship that develops a history. How does the family emerge as a social unit of interacting persons? Burgess saw marriage and parent education as institutional replacements for the family collective and social custom in building marital and family solidarity.

Despite Burgess's interest regarding individual lives and marital relations, he never developed a satisfactory concept of development change. How are family and individual histories structured? What is the process linking individual and family careers? Are there social stages of family life, from marriage formation to old age? Burgess did not explore such questions in theory or research, though colleagues such as Willard Waller (1938) were doing so in creative ways. From one vantage point, Burgess's neglect of temporal concepts and models is not surprising. His concept of the family as a unity of interacting personalities depicts a crosssection of family life. As concepts in Burgess's research, marital adjustment and personality describe functioning at a point in time.

Some implications of Burgess's approach for studies of black families and children are documented by Scanzoni's (1971) *The Black Family in Modern Society*. Unlike the insular, marital focus of the Burgess tradition, Scanzoni followed Frazier's lead and proposed a study of the relationship between economic resources, on the one hand, and family structure, on the other. This ambition was compromised in part by the metropolitan sample of intact marriages; a restriction which ruled out one major form of covariation, low resources and marital instability.

Beyond this socioeconomic link, *The Black Family* has very little to offer concerning relations between the interior and exterior of black families, particularly on the extended family context. The central picture involves black couples, their childhoods and adult roles—marriage, parenthood, and work. The study moves from past experience, using retrospective accounts, to the current situation and then to the children, the next generation. Scanzoni refers to this design as quasi-three generational. The parents' parents or grandparents are not part of the generational account.

The implicit theory behind this design is that parents only make a difference in the developmental course of lives during the preadult years. In a statement reminiscent of Burgess, Scanzoni (1971) argues that "full understanding of what goes on between husbands and wives requires knowledge of what occurred to them prior to marriage" (p. 197). The new relationship is shaped by the joining of two life histories, in which parents played a major role, but as modeled, the relationship itself is not open to the influence of parents in the present.

One underlying rationale for this truncated view of the generations comes from the assumption that inter-generational ties are dysfunctional or irrelevant in modern society. The older generation lacks control over economic rewards and restricts both geographic and social mobility (McAdoo, 1978). The pooling and exchange of resources among kin units may enable survival, but kin are unable to ensure more than survival. Scanzoni's treatment of the decline of kin control in the last chapter represents one explanation for the asserted prominence of the conjugal family in urban-industrial society.

The design of Scanzoni's *The Black Family* reflects a desire to avoid Anglo ideologies and stereotypes that were so prevalent in the empirical literature. The image of the single black mother and her brood of young children is a case in point. Since a majority of black households in 1968 were headed by a man with his wife present, Scanzoni (1971) restricted the sample to intact black couples and their households. The defect in this view is that it does not tell us about the prospects of couples and children over time. Cohort projections (Hofferth, 1985) based on children born from 1975–79 indicate that approximately 4 out of 5 black children will not be living in a first marriage household of their parents by the time they reach the age of 17. Seven out of 10 of these children will have lived in a one-parent household for a period of time. Among white children, 40% will not be living in a first marriage household by age 17. By excluding households lacking a husband-wife structure, Scanzoni produced a study that actually bears little relation to the contemporary realities of family life and children's experience. Dissolved parental marriages are a critical part of that experience.

In *The Black Family,* the functional conjugal unit in modern society, and the dysfunctionality of the extended network of family ties, favor a two generation model of parent and child. The most common version of this model is known as the family cycle, or life cycle, in which one generation is replaced by another (Hill, 1964). This version of the family cycle refers to the reproductive process (parent-child) from the standpoint of a couple's life trajectory. The sequence of stages describes this trajectory without reference to transitions and events in the lives of offspring, parents, and grandparents. Some couples enter the "establishment" phase with living parents and grandparents, while others may have only one set of living parents and no surviving grandparents. As seen within the context of family and kinship, the two types of couples occupy very different positions relative to self-definition and support. The distinction can be drawn between entry into parenthood with or without surviving parents. At the other end of the cycle, the postparental stage or experience will vary greatly according to the presence and life stage of children and parents.

The family or intergenerational cycle takes us beyond some discontinuous features of *The Black Family* by linking the life course of parent and child. The full scope of the cyclical model requires a multi-dimensional concept of the life course for adult offspring; a moving set of interlocking career lines, such as work, marriage, parenting, etc. Misfortune and opportunity across these pathways may become intergenerational, so too many life problems. Failed marriages and careers frequently lead adult sons and daughters back to the parental household, and have profound implications for the parents' life plans. Early misfortune, such as pregnancy in adolescence, may postpone home leaving (Furstenberg, 1976). Similarly, economic setbacks and divorce among the parents of adolescents may impede their transition to adulthood by postponing home leaving, higher education or employment, and marriage. Each generation is bound to fateful decisions and events in the other's life course.

This interdependence remains a primary theme as we extend our vision of the black family across three or more generations. The vulnerabilities and strengths of these generations are interdependent, but even more important is the prospect that one generation may offset the vulnerabilities of another, whether younger or older. Shimkin and his colleagues (1978, pp. 73–74) claim that the typical extended family in rural Holmes County, MS (and linking Chicago) includes four to five generational stations: elderly persons who were objects of common respect and orientation, the founders; a set of middle-aged siblings, their spouses, and cousins, the nucleus group; the married children and grandchildren of the nucleus group. This multi-generation view of black families (and of white families, for that matter) broadens the range of adaptational options under study. Contrary to the image of disorganization or pathology, single parents can be embedded in kin relations that sustain in the most difficult of circumstances.

Our discussion of insular and embedded households highlights the ecology of black families and children, and the strategic value of locating black families within a multi-generational setting. The process of kin help in this setting of black families has been documented by an increasing number of studies of all socioeconomic levels, including ". . . before, during, and after upward mobility, even into the third generations of middle-class status" (McAdoo, 1980, p. 127). The extended family also brings a temporal dimension to family studies. The statuses of grandparent, parent, and child refer to different positions along the time line of families. Growing up and old entails movement from one position to another, and often a transition from one kinship setting to another. The child in a five generation system may become a member of the first generation in young adulthood through the death of parents and grandparents. For individuals, change in the generational structure of families has implications for change of status and role, self-identity, and behavior (Hagestad, 1981). Greater distance seems to occur between parents and offspring when the former move to the last position of the generational line.

The full implications of a particular generational status vary according to age and time distinctions; life time, social or family time, and historical time. To complete this perspective on studying black families, I conclude with these meanings of age in structuring the life course of families and children.

## Age and the Life Course

Individuals are the elementary units of an age-based perspective on the life course. The lifetime meaning of age refers to the status of individuals in the maturation and aging process. Social time refers to the timing of events and roles in lives, and historical time locates people in historical settings through membership in specific birth cohorts. All three temporal dimensions locate family units through age data on their members. The distinctive theme is the timing of this placement in lives, families, and history.

An individual's life course is multi-dimensional because adult life in complex societies spans different lines of activity (e.g., education to marriage, parenthood, work, and leisure). The general picture is one of interdependent career lines that vary in timetables, synchronization, and resource management. In applying the life course perspective to marriage and the family unit, we begin with the interlocking career lines of individuals. Analysis of the young couple centers on the social patterns formed by the joining of life courses through mate selection and their implications for marital relations, child rearing, and kin ties.

Within the context of social patterns at marriage (age, class origin, education, etc.), the trajectory of family life is shaped by subsequent developments in the career lines of each spouse.

Family or life transitions are particularly well-suited to the dynamic, temporal emphases of life course research: (1) the single transition and its consequences, such as divorce or remarriage; (2) concurrent and sequential transitions, such as the transition to adult roles, especially work and marriage; and (3) the interdependence of widely separated transitions—the effect of early family events on the planning of retirement and old age. Some transitions are normatively prescribed with regard to timing, including marriage, conception, and births, while other events are idiosyncratic (accidents, acute illness, etc.) or historical (job loss in an economic recession). Studies of family development have generally stressed the normative timing and sequence of family events, especially in relation to childrearing. Life course theory highlights the implications of departures from this format: very early and late marriage, childbirth before marriage, young widowhood or a prolonged dependency on parents. Atypical events of this sort have become a major object of study for their psychological effects and disruptive social consequences.

Problems in the life course approach arise from the interlocking career lines of family members and their pattern of reciprocity and synchrony on needs, options, and resources. Differentiated careers in the life course imply some differentiation in social worlds whose demands compete for the scarce or limited resources of a family—the time, energy, affections, material resource of each member. This model of interlocking careers implies a dynamic interactional concept of the family economy which has long been a conceptual mainstay of life course studies (Oppenheimer, 1981), though some analysts regard it as a novel perspective of the 1980s. Thus Levinson (1980, p. 271) concludes that "sociologists have generally not investigated the individual life course in its complex patterning." He attributes this failure to the specialization of fields. "The expert in occupational careers usually has little interest in the family, religion, or other systems." Refuting this view, Wilensky (1981) observed that trajectories of work, family, consumption, and community participation have implications that stem from their interlocking temporal pattern. Consistent with recent national surveys on life quality, Wilensky found that job satisfaction, participation in community life, financial and psychological well-being tended to hit bottom among married men during the early childbearing and childrearing stages.

Strong pressures arise from the asynchrony of family income and consumption curves, especially during the childbearing years. Life course planning may reduce income and consumption pressures by developing more strategies: (1) reducing expenditures; (2) reallocating resources such as replacing service expenditures with family labor, as in child care; or (3) increasing the match between income and outgo through savings, loans, and additional earners. Examples include particular responses, such as maternal employment and doubling up, which reduce the disparity between family income and claims and restore control relative to preferred family outcomes. Such responses alter the family's course in ways that may have consequences that differ for the family and children. The shortrun benefits of family survival may entail severe costs for children in the long run, as in the tensions of multi-generation households.

The life course approach captures well the building up and breaking down of family patterns. Individuals form relationships and groups, and they also dissolve them. Consequently, the individual represents the essential unit of study over time. The need to study individuals over time, as contrasted to households, was recognized at an early stage by the staff of the well-known Panel Study of Income Dynamics at the University of Michigan. Ever since the late 1960s, a team of social scientists has been following a large, nationwide sample of American families, both white and black. From the very beginning, the problem of tracking everchanging domestic units made individuals the most feasible unit of study and data collection.

This panel study was launched in the late 1960s to generate knowledge regarding the poverty class and its members' lives. Is the poverty stratum a stable group in society? Are poverty and welfare passed on from one generation to another? One of the motivating ideas behind the project assumed that poverty was self-perpetuating. People entered through misfortune, the inheritance of dependency from parents, or other circumstances; and they seldom managed to become self-supporting again. Acquired values and beliefs from adaptations to poverty presumably increased the chances of continued deprivation. The panel design offered a way to determine whether such views corresponded with reality.

The results of empirical work to date show that only a very small fraction of sample members who actually experienced poverty did so for a year or more (Coe, Duncan, & Hill, 1982). Transient members of the poverty category turned out to be indistinguishable from members of the general sample, while chronic cases were typically in one or more of the following categories—black, elderly, female. Household composition, employment status, and earnings were the main determinants of entering, staying in, and leaving poverty. One third of the persistently poor are over the age of 65, and two thirds of the remainder live in households headed by women. A large majority of these women are black. On matters of public assistance, Coe, Duncan, and Hill (1982, p. 52) conclude from the Michigan Panel that most "welfare recipients remain on the welfare rolls for relatively short periods of time, most are never dependent on welfare income in a given year, and even if they are, this dependency is short-lived."

Out of such research on families and children has come a perspective on the life course dynamics of interaction between economic change and family adaptations (Moen, Kain, & Elder, 1983). Economic adversity prompts adaptations outside the household through multiple earners and other means, and within the household through alterations in family composition as people leave or enter. These adaptive responses, in turn, serve to modify the family's resources and economic situation which, once again, influence family decisions. Change in household composition thus represents both a determinant and an outcome of change in economic status. Divorce usually results in a diminished economic position for children in an evolving one-parent household, and the economic pressures of this new situation may require doubling up with relatives in a strategy of "pooling resources."

An age perspective on the life course gives particular emphasis to the role of timing and timetables in families and lives. Likewise, the death or imprisonment of a head of household entails deprivations for a young mother that are generally more severe than for an older woman. The timing of motherhood provides a third example. The birth of children to adolescent mothers entails a substantial risk for the well-being of mother and child, especially when it leads to the absence of one or more other adults in addition to the mother. Relevant data come from the Woodlawn longitudinal project (see Kellam et al., 1977; Brown et al., 1981; Kellam et al., 1982), a study of black mothers and children from Chicago.

Ten specific types of family structure were identified in the Woodlawn sample: mother alone, mother/father, mother/grandmother, mother/aunt, mother/stepfather, etc. The mothers who gave birth to a child in adolescence were most likely to be living alone in 1966–67 and this residential arrangement was also most common 10 years later among the mothers with teenage births. Mother alone households ranked at the bottom on receiving help in rearing children (60% vs. 7% or less for other households in 1975–76). The deprivations of mother alone families are not merely a reflection of maternal age or income variations.

The increasing risk of social isolation among teenage black mothers has been found in a Baltimore study by Furstenberg and Crawford (1978) and appears to be a major factor in the developmental disadvantage of children from mother alone households. Kellam and his associates (1977, 1982) found that these children were at greatest risk of social maladaptation to first grade, and that the developmental handicap increased with age. Children in mother/father households represented the other end of the social adaptation continuum, a position they shared with the children of mother/grandmother families. The absence of a second care taking adult, whether father or grandmother, emerges as the critical finding.

The Woodlawn study points to both social and psychological factors that threaten the development of black children in mother only households. These mothers lack social support in the mothering role, experience extreme economic pressure, and are susceptible to a high level of psychological distress. The more children they have, the greater the distress. In rare detail, the Woodlawn project documents the intimate relation between individual and family development, an analytic feature of life course studies.

As expressed in these studies, age brings a concept of age-graded trajectories and differential timing to studies of the individual and to the emergence of family relations. An age-based approach is especially conducive to developmental or psychological considerations because it involves properties of individuals. Age in the life course suggests at least two models of the relation between individual and family development. Families or relationships may be changed by changing the personality or behavior of individuals; and individuals may be influenced through changes in their family environments.

Kinship distinctions (the family cycle, a generational hierarchy) broaden the life course perspective beyond a single life span, following the assumption of intergenerational dependence. Though most life event inventories still imply independence between members of adjacent generations, studies are beginning to document the extent to which events in one generation directly impinge on the well-being of another generation. The divorce of a middle-aged son or daughter may directly alter the lives of parents, whether through sharing a household once again or in losing contact with grandchildren. Kinship extends the conceptual framework of life course analysis through the family cycle (the process by which an older parent generation is replaced by the younger generation) and across the sequence of generational stations (child, parent, grandparent) that people traverse in their lifetimes.

What does all of this have to do with an understanding of children's lives and developmental courses? Most importantly this is an approach to the environment of children which is compatible with their increasingly more diverse lives and developmental courses, an approach that views children in social contexts, across evolving interactions with others, and in historical time. Children change as their environments change, but prevailing models of environments are typically static. As an exception, the life course provides one way to relate various ecologies to the course of human development (Bronfenbrenner, 1979b; Elder & Rockwell, 1979). The ecology is not merely one situation after another, or one setting inside of, or linked to, another. On the contrary, the ecology of human development is patterned over time by age and kinship. Careers are age-graded. With its focus on the individual, the life course provides a way of relating social worlds in the lives of children, family, neighborhood, and school. Children often live in many households during their maturing years, a diversity which has implications for their upbringing. This point is especially relevant to black children, who due to norms of extended kinship systems, poverty, etc., are more likely to reside in many different households (Martin & Martin, 1978; Edelman, 1980). Life course analysis follows such paths across time and place. The objective is to understand how children live and the developmental consequences of their life ways. Why do some children thrive, even in very difficult circumstances, while others fail to do so? The family, with its network of kin and friends, represents an appropriate point of departure for answers to such questions.

## CONCLUSION

The past decade has witnessed a remarkable change in studies of the family and children generally, whatever the nationality, social class or race. The change is marked by greater attention to three analytic themes: context, process, and time.

All three are elements of the newly emerging life course perspective on families and individuals. Equally noteworthy is a dramatic shift in type of research question. For many years, the central question had to do with the conditions that enhance the breakdown or disorganization of family life. This research orientation has now been turned on its head. The more common question today concerns the process by which families and individuals manage to function effectively under difficult or demanding circumstances. How do families avoid disorganization?

During the first six decades of this century, studies of both white and black families were strongly influenced by a disorganization perspective, as most fully detailed in Thomas and Znaniecki's *The Polish Peasant in Europe and America.* E. Franklin Frazier borrowed heavily from this analytic theme in his series of studies of black families in the United States. The same theme appears in Daniel Moynihan's mid-1960s report on the state of the Negro family. The irony of this intellectual development is that Thomas and Znaniecki outlined a broader, more differentiated model of family adaptation and change in their classic study, although they did not devote as much space to this model. Nevertheless, the reorganization theme appears with some prominence in a recent archival study of 1930s families (Elder, 1974), a study which actually drew upon the adaptational perspective of *The Polish Peasant.*

Another source of a disorganization view of black families is lodged in what I have called the Burgess tradition of family research, one largely focused on the interior of households, and especially on the marital relationship. Neglect of the extended family is one consequence of such priorities, as illustrated by Scanzoni's *The Black Family.* Single parent households cannot be fully understood apart from the extended family options. Households clearly vary in their degree of embeddedness within a system of kin and friends, and thus in adaptational options. This social anchorage of families represents one example of the new contextual emphasis in family research.

A second example of the contextual theme comes from age-based models of the life course. The link between age and time identifies two contexts of families; the historical setting as indexed by the birth year of members, and the age-graded life stage of family members. By locating families according to historical time, we also place them in relation to social, legal, and economic changes. Age distinctions, such as birth year, draw attention to the process by which social change influences the family and its members. This process operates through individual lives and family relationships. Individuals are changed through change in families, and the latter are changed through change in people. Concepts of age and kinship in the life course are bringing context, process, and time to the study of family change, individual development, and their relationship.

# 4 A Cultural Ecology of Competence Among Inner-City Blacks[1]

John U. Ogbu
*University of California—Berkeley*

The first part of this paper reviews two current approaches to the study of competence development among inner-city black Americans: a universal model and a difference model. In the second part, I propose another approach—a cultural-ecological approach—particularly for cross-cultural research on competence. This cultural-ecological model is used in the third part to reinterpret existing data on development of competence among inner-city blacks. The conclusion reexamines the relationship between black instrumental competencies and schooling.

## TWO CURRENT RESEARCH MODELS OF BLACK CHILD DEVELOPMENT

### Universal Model

Mainstream developmentalists did not seriously study black children until the 1960s. Moreover, when they began to study black children, they did not study them in their own right, but because black children were perceived as a social problem and because mainstream developmentalists were searching for universal truths about child development. The field of formal education has provided the ground for both rationales, leading to the enormous growth in mainstream developmentalist research about black children since the 1960s.

---

[1]Except where otherwise specified all references in this chapter are to inner-city Black Americans.

Mainstream developmentalists and educational psychologists have long believed that the disproportionate school failure of black children is due to a lack of cognitive and other competencies required to do well in school. One group (the hereditary proponents) has held that this lack of abilities is due to genetic definiencies, whereas the environmentalists held that it is due to environmental deficiencies (Ogbu, 1978). Mainstream developmentalist studies of black children have grown because the reformist orientation of the Kennedy-Johnson administrations encouraged the environmentalists by giving them opportunities to prove their point.

The environmentalists believe that white middle-class children do well in school because they possess the right kind of competencies—cognitive, linguistic, motivational, and social—as a result of white middle-class parents' childrearing practices. Black children, on the other hand, are thought to do poorly in school because they lack such competencies. It is further believed that black children lack the competencies because black parents do not use the same childrearing practices as white middle-class parents. The way out of this black developmental and educational dilemma, the environmentalists say, is to enable black preschool children to acquire white middle-class children's early childhood experiences and the instrumental competencies they generate through specially designed programs. The other strategy is to teach black parents how to use white middle-class parents' childrearing practices in bringing up their children (see Bloom, Davis, & Hess, 1965; Connolly and Bruner, 1974; Hunt, 1969; S. White, 1973).

These conclusions were reached, however, before a sufficient number of studies had been done to warrant the assumption that black children were failing in school because their parents did not transmit, or were not capable of transmitting to them, white middle-class competencies. Thus as early as 1963, a conference on Compensatory Education for the Culturally Deprived at the University of Chicago, attended by influential researchers in education and child development, concluded that 75 percent of all black children were culturally deprived. Black parents were deemed incapable of training their children to succeed in school; and as a result there was a need for early intervention programs (Bloom, Davis, & Hess, 1965). An earlier conference at Columbia University in New York City had reached the same conclusion (Passow, 1963).

However, both conferences called for more research on childrearing practices and child development among blacks. Because of the underlying assumption of cultural deprivation, subsequent studies have proceeded from the position that, at least in the United States, white middle-class childrearing practices and development are the normal patterns. Thus in comparative studies of blacks and other minorities, differences in childrearing practices, motivational-social competencies and self-concept have usually been designated as deficient.

This research perspective portraying white middle-class patterns as the standard by which others are judged must be rejected for the following reasons. First, populations in different societies, or within the same society, may differ in cognitive, linguistic, motivational and social competencies, not merely because they use different methods of childrearing, but because they live under different cultural imperatives requiring different instrumental competencies. The cultural imperatives of a given population (Cohen, 1971)—the political, social and economic realities of the population—dictate the cultural tasks (e.g., subsistence tasks or economic activities) of its members and it is these activities that determine the adaptive or functional personal attributes prevalent in the population. Such competencies usually become the qualities which parents and other childbearing agents perceive as desirable to foster in children (LeVine, 1967). Current studies of black childrearing and development either do not take into account the requirements of black cultural imperatives, or they erroneously assume that blacks and whites share the same cultural imperatives. In any case, by narrowly focusing on intrafamilial relationships (Inkeles, 1968a) these studies decontextualize competence from realities of life. In so doing they confuse the process by which adaptive and culturally valued instrumental competencies are transmitted with the reason for their very presence or absence in a given population.

Second, there may be no universally correct method of childrearing for developing instrumental competencies (Baumrind, 1967). Therefore the white middle-class pattern cannot be used to judge others. Cross-cultural studies suggest that child-rearing techniques depend, at least in part, on the nature of the instrumental competencies which adults in a given population seek consciously and unconsciously to inculcate in the young and which children consciously and unconsciously seek to acquire as they grow older (Aberle, 1962; Inkeles, 1968; LeVine, 1967; Mead, 1939; Ogbu, 1981a). This paper argues that there are genuine differences in both instrumental competencies and child-rearing techniques among geographically distant populations, particularly among populations occupying different resource environments in a modern industrial society like the United States.

Third, a general theory of relationship between childrearing and development of instrumental competencies should not be based on data derived from studying one population. Rather, such a theory should emerge from knowledge of childrearing and development in different populations. A first step toward developing such a general theory is to study the phenomenon in different populations contextually. For example, black childrearing and development should first be studied qua black childrearing and development. Chicano childrearing and development should be studied qua Chicano childrearing and development. White middle-class childrearing and development should also be studied qua White middle-class childrearing and development. Mapping out patterns of childrearing and development in these and other populations should provide the only valid data base for generating a theory of human socialization and development. The objection is to the mere search for a pattern of childrearing and development derived from studying one population in other groups.

At the level of social policy, the theory of social change implicit in the universal model is unsupported by historical and cross-cultural evidence. The case for early intervention is based on the belief in the determinism of early childhood events—"that much that shapes the final human product takes place during the first years of life" (B. White, 1979, p. 192). "The cognitive set of the culturally disadvantaged child, the pattern of perception which handicaps him in learning tasks demanded by the school, is *irrevocably cast in preschool years*" (Kerber & Bommarito, 1965, p. 345; emphasis added). It is also based on the belief that an effective strategy to improve the social and economic status of black Americans lies in changing their childrearing practices so that they would be more successful in school (Hunt, 1969).

The latter argument is weak for two reasons. First, there is no historical or cross-cultural evidence that any population has ever achieved a significant social and economic change by first changing its method of childrearing. It is usually the case that social and economic changes precede changes in childrearing practices (Aberle, 1968; Kaplan and Manners, 1970). The latter situation is precisely what is happening today in most developing nations of the world. Furthermore, children from different cultural backgrounds (and therefore with different childhood experiences) do learn successfully in the same school and under the same teacher in the United States as illustrated by a comparison of the school success of White middle-class and immigrant minorities like the Chinese, Japanese and others (DeVos, 1973; Ogbu, 1978). Also, in Third World countries there are some populations which do well in Western-type schools even though they do not follow white middle-class childrearing practices (Van den Berghe, 1980).

The universal model has dominated research in childrearing and development but has produced doubtful conclusions because of inadequate conceptualization of context, or environment; because it ignores the possible influence of instrumental competencies on childrearing techniques; and because it is based on an ethnocentric conception of development. Moreover, it embodies a theory of social change not supported by historical or cross-cultural data. Programs based on the theory have not been particularly successful in inculcating permanently the missing competencies in black children (Goldberg, 1971; Ogbu, 1978).[2]

## Difference Model

From the late 1960s some minority researchers have proposed an alternative model which may be designated as a *difference model*. They argue that minority groups have their own cultures; that their cultures embody different child-rearing

---

[2]Our criticism here refers only to the primary focus of the early childhood intervention programs, which is cognition. Recent studies show that although these programs may fail in their primary goal of raising children's IQ permanently, they do have other beneficial effects, such as teaching children how to go to school: children who participate in the programs are more likely to stay in school longer, have less school absences, less likely to be assigned to special education classes and more likely to be promoted to the next grade (Lazar and Darlington, 1979, cited in Tomlinson, 1980).

practices which inculcate different instrumental competencies; and that minority children probably fail in school because schools do not recognize and utilize their unique competencies for teaching, learning, and testing (Boykin, 1978, 1980; Gibson, 1976; Ramirez & Castenada, 1974).

Proponents of the difference model have not generally spelled out the specific instrumental competencies of black culture except in expressive life styles (e.g., adaptability, interactional skills), styles in dress, walking, etc.; language and communication (see Abrahams, 1976; Keil, 1966; Kochman, 1972; Labov, 1972(a); Mitchell-Kernan, 1972).

The psychologist, Wade Boykin (1980) has probably been the most explicit in specifying distinctive black attributes bearing on school problems. He postulates five distinctive black stylistic cultural manifestations; (a) an affective-feeling propensity manifested as a person to person emphasis, with a personal orientation toward objects, rather than a person to object emphasis and an impersonal orientation toward people; (b) a psychological verve or enhanced responsiveness to variability and intensity of stimulation; (c) a movement orientation which emphasizes intensity of music as opposed to movement comprehension; (d) an improvisation quality which emphasizes expressive individualism as opposed to possessive individualism; and (e) an event orientation toward time, such that time is what is done, as opposed to a clock orientation. Boykin argues that black children want to learn when they begin school but are turned off by the educational process which confronts them with "artificial, contrived, and arbitrary competence modalities, such as reading and writing, that are presented in ways that undermine the children's cultural frame of reference" (p. 11).

There are some problems with present formulations of the difference model. One is the tendency on the part of some to overemphasize the African origins of black culture and competencies without a comparative perspective based on knowledge of cultural changes in Africa and, without sufficiently accounting for the persistence of the African elements among black Americans. Second, again from a comparative perspective, the cultural difference model does not explain why children from other minority groups, who also have distinctive cultural frames of reference, are not turned off by the same educational process. In the next section we suggest an approach—that of cultural ecology—which enables us to discover distinctive black competencies, and the relationship of these instrumental competencies to black child-rearing practices as well as to black school experiences.

## CULTURAL ECOLOGY OF COMPETENCE

### Childrearing As Culturally Organized Formulae

One fundamental assumption underlying the cultural-ecological approach is that childrearing is a culturally organized formulae to ensure that newborns survive to become competent adults who will contribute to the survival and welfare of their

social group (Fishbein, 1976; LeVine, 1977). The formulae, under normal circumstances, make it possible for most children in a given population to grow up
able to perform cultural tasks competently as defined within their population.

The formulae consist of teaching children the skills or instrumental competencies which already exist when they are born. Parents do not invent the knowledge, beliefs, and skills they teach their children. Except in a period of rapid
social change, the competencies parents teach their children are more or less
preordained. For example, the competencies contemporary white, middle-class
Americans teach their children, such as self-direction, initiative, independence,
competitiveness, certain cognitive and communicative skills, are not the in-
ventions of individual parents, but those proven functional to the higher level,
high paying white middle-class occupations and social positions (Connolly &
Bruner, 1974; Kohn, 1969; Vernon, 1969). In a hunting and gathering population, these would probably not be the adaptive competencies parents would try to
inculcate in their children.

The formulae also work because parents in a given population use more or
less the same culturally standardized techniques of childrearing. It can be argued,
for example, that contemporary white middle-class Americans share the same
standardized knowledge, skills, and practices of childrearing which are suited for
producing the kinds of instrumental competencies adaptive to their type of occupations and other cultural tasks. In contrast to white middle-class parents of
earlier periods, they have increasingly employed culturally standardized techniques invented by experts in child development. These experts, in a special
cultural role, study, devise, and pass on to the general population, appropriate
techniques for inculating new competencies required by changing technoeconomic tasks. (Consider the number of books appearing in recent decades on how
to raise children; e.g., Dr. Spock). We should add, however, that the experts are
keen observers of changing cultural tasks, particularly technoeconomic tasks and
their required competencies, although they do not usually acknowledge the influence of such historical and structural forces on their work.

In no human population, under normal circumstances, are child-rearing practices an irrational or random set of activities; rather, they form a part of a
culturally organized system which evolved to meet people's needs within their
effective environment (LeVine, 1974). Most children in a given population grow
into competent adults because there are societal rewards for employing the formulae, and penalties for not doing so.

The incentives for using culturally prescribed child-rearing practices to teach
adaptive competencies can best be understood through the concept of status
mobility system (LeVine, 1967) or the native theory of success. Members of a
given population usually share some ideas of how one gets ahead or succeeds in
cultural tasks and reward system. How one makes it is defined differently in
different populations, but it is always a shared cultural knowledge. The native
theory of making it generally includes knowledge of the range of cultural tasks

and status positions available; their relative importance, the competencies essential for attaining and performing the cultural tasks; the strategies for obtaining higher status positions; and the expected societal rewards and penalties for success or failure. Parents employ the formulae because they want their children to become competent and successful adults. Cultural images of successful members of the population, living or dead, guide child-rearing agents in their child-rearing tasks and the growing child's responses to these efforts respectively.

## Environmental Context Of Transmission Of Competence

The second assumption underlying the cultural-ecological approach is that the environment which influences childrearing and development is much broader than is usually defined in current developmental studies. These settings are merely the micro environments within which instrumental competencies are transmitted and acquired. The concept of environment must be expanded to include the nature of the cultural tasks faced by the population, and the way in which these tasks determine the competencies that are transmitted and acquired. This is particularly necessary in comparative or cross-cultural studies, including the studies of stratified populations in modern industrial societies like the United States.

Cultural ecology provides a useful framework for broadening the concept of environmental influences on transmission and development of instrumental competencies. Cultural ecology is the study of how a population uses its natural environment influences, and is influenced by, its social organization and cultural values. It also explores how the relationship between the personal attributes (i.e., instrumental competencies) and behaviors of its members and the environment is influenced by the strategies or tasks they have devised for coping with environmental demands (Bennett, 1969; Goldschmidt, 1971; Netting, 1968). Within this relationship between the population and its environment, the adaptive competencies and behaviors are the properties of the entire population, and may be found to characterize most common types of persons in the population.

One aspect of this broad or macro environment, which exercises an enormous influence on human competence, is the subsistence or economic system. Strategies with which people respond to subsistence needs vary, however, from population to population, because the latter do not occupy the same physical environment. Different populations, therefore, have evolved different strategies appropriate to their respective environments and these strategies determine to a large degree the repertoire of instrumental competencies—practical skills, cognitive skills, communicative skills, social-emotional skills, etc.—characteristic of members of each population.

Other cultural tasks play important roles in determining instrumental competencies, but in modern industrial societies, economic or subsistence tasks (i.e., the job and related factors) are the most influential. This is widely recognized by mainstream researchers in child development and education (Baumrind, 1976; Bloom, Davis and Hess, 1965; S. White, 1973). Moreover, debate on black children's competence generally centers around the acquisition of a particular type of competence, purported to cause school and job market success.

The challenge for research is, therefore, to map out (a) the nature of the macro environment and cultural tasks, especially the subsistence tasks of the population under study; (b) the nature of the instrumental competencies required by these cultural tasks; and (c) the formulae evolved to inculcate the adaptive instrumental competencies. From the perspective of the proposed model, this goal can best be achieved through a methodology that allows the investigator to discover what competencies exist and why and how, rather than impose preconceived and precoded categories on the population.

## ORIGINS OF BLACK COMPETENCE; A REINTERPRETATION

The cultural-ecological approach to child development is a new formulation which has not been applied to the study of Afro-American child development. What we want to do here is to use the model to reinterpret available data on black child development and speculate about possible results of research designed to use this approach. We use the following diagram both to summarize available data and to suggest a research paradigm for future study (See Figure 4.1). Each box in the diagram represents a separate set of data and the entire sets are to be integrated and analyzed in order to interpret correctly the nature and production process of black competencies. The following description is based on this re-search paradigm.

### Effective Environment

The effective environment of a given population determines the subsistence tasks of that population, and the latter, in turn, determine much of that population's instrumental competencies. Effective environment is made up of the tech-noeconomic resources of the population as well as its members' knowledge of their past and present opportunity structure. Black Americans, particularly inner-city blacks, and white middle-class Americans have not traditionally occupied, and do not now occupy, the same effective environment, even within the same city. Rather, they live in a kind of symbiotic relationship where dominant whites exploit the more richly endowed parts of the environment, leaving blacks the portions with marginal resources (Ogbu, 1981a, 1981b).

Unlike the white middle class environment, the inner-city, mostly occupied by blacks, is characterized by scarcity of jobs, dead-end, peripheral, and unsta-

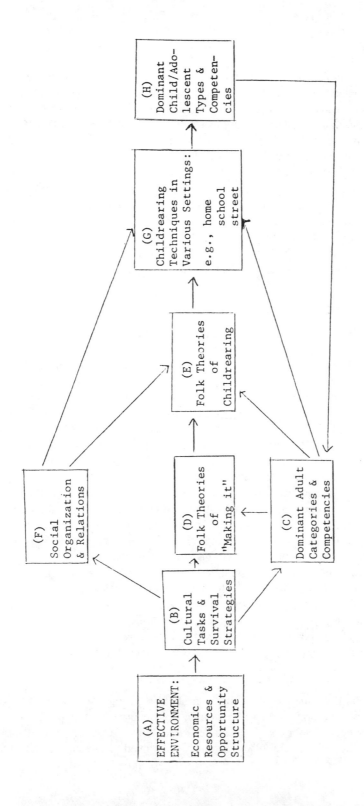

FIG. 4.1. A Cultural-Ecological Model Of Inner-City Childrearing and Development

ble jobs, and by low wages and little social credit as measured by the values of the larger society. Some blacks also occupy portions of this environment nearly devoid of any wage labor, though they contain social resources which include other residents and caretaker institutions (Harrison, 1972; Ross & Hill, 1967). Of equal importance to these conventional resources is the subeconomy, or street economy, of the inner-city (Bullock, 1973).

For generations, blacks have used the strategy of collective struggle or civil rights to increase their conventional resources or gain access to those in the white environment. They have argued their right of access to these resources as citizens and that they possess more know-how than is required for their marginal conventional resources. Although they have achieved some measure of success in these endeavors, the inner-city is still an environment of marginal conventional resources; for many, the street economy is more lucrative.

## Subsistence Tasks And Survival Strategies

Blacks have developed a number of alternative strategies called survival strategies. Besides Conventional Employment, these survival strategies include Clientship, Collective Struggle, Mutual Exchange, Hustling, Pimping, Entertainment, Sports, etc. These are normal subsistence strategies upon which blacks judge competence. There are no studies showing the kinds of instrumental competencies or skills required by the various survival strategies. But we can gain some idea of these competencies from descriptions of the attributes of adult categories employing the strategies. Membership in these categories is not mutually exclusive: One person may belong to different categories at different points in his life and/or under different situations.

A tentative list of these adult types includes the Conventional Worker (i.e., one holding a conventional job in mainstream economy), the Client, the Reformer (some would say, Militant, Revolutionary, etc.), the Hustler, the Pimp, the Sportsman/Athlete, the Entertainer, and the Street Man. Labels for the categories may differ across authors and regions. Each category tends to be associated with a given subsistence strategy, but the relationship is not exclusive. For example, a hustler may sometimes hold a conventional job and adhere to the norms of the Conventional Worker; yet s/he may occasionally find it necessary to engage in some hustling (Schulz, 1968). The point to stress here is that these are the normal competent adult types in the inner-city, given the nature of its effective environment, especially its marginal conventional resources and its alternative street economy.

*Conventional Employment.* This is probably the most common strategy. That is, most able-bodied men and women hold conventional jobs. However, there are not enough jobs for all. More desirable jobs are in even shorter supply. As a result, many inner-city blacks are underemployed or cannot earn adequate subsistence wages from conventional employment (Ferman, Kornbluh & Miller, 1968; Harrison, 1972).

The Conventional worker. According to Perkins (1975), the Conventional Worker in the inner-city shares the attributes of other American conventional workers, but is faced with special problems arising from racial barriers. Consequently, to continue his conventional strategy he tries to develop special instrumental competencies like perseverance, patience, obedience, conservatism, indifference, respect, and loyalties.

*Clientship (Uncle Tomming).*    This is a strategy whereby a black person who lacks access to jobs, good wages, advancement on the job, and other societal goods attaches himself *in his own right* to a white patron (white individual, white organization, or white-controlled caretaker institution) in return for services and/or deferential behavior.

The Client. The client is specially skilled in subservient behavior or its simulation, also a feature of Uncle Tomming. Subservient behavior is an attribute also shared by many Conventional Workers and the Welfare Clients in the respective contexts.

*Collective Struggle.*    This strategy is defined by the larger society as civil rights techniques, and has historically been used by blacks to increase their pool of conventional resources. This strategy has generally been very effective in increasing the conventional resources of the inner-city, at least temporarily (Newman et al., 1978; Ogbu, 1978; Scott, 1976).

The Reformer. The reformer is characterized by race consciousness and a degree of resentment. The nonconventional Reformer is of particular interest because of his appearance or reappearance and influence since the 1960s. His special competencies include a deep commitment to liberate black people from oppression, and greater than average knowledge of the political system and techniques of political mobilization (Perkins, 1975, p. 83; see also Blair, 1977; McCord, et al., 1969; Scott, 1976).

*Hustling.*    This subsistence strategy is employed in the street economy to obtain money, goods, and services in various ways. Some hustlers are criminally inclined and their specific subsistence techniques include peddling dope, pills, and pot; selling policy, and at times soliciting prostitutes. Others specialize in playing pool, taking bets, shooting craps, conning people, exploiting businesses, making shady deals and the ''woman game'' or extorting money from women on public assistance or who are employed (Bullock, 1973; Horton, 1970; Perkins, 1975; Rainwater, 1974).

The Hustler. The Hustler and the Pimp define society and social situations as a game where everyone is a player. The stakes are power and money. Two kinds of people are involved: those who game (i.e., Hustlers and Pimps) and those gamed on (i.e., the exploited). Using this model as a guide, the Hustler obtains his money through the ability to manipulate and exploit (i.e., exercise power over) other people; the Pimp obtains his money through exploitation of (or power over) women (Milner, 1970).

*Pimping.*    Pimping is a strategy which used "interpersonal relationships, especially relationships with women, for monetary gain" (Milner, 1970, p. 180). One type, street pimping, exploits women as a part of hustling activities. Another, professional pimping, makes the exploitation of women a full-time occupation (Hudson, 1972, pp. 419–421; Perkins, 1975, pp. 79–81).

The Pimp. The professional Pimp is generally more sophisticated than the Hustler. The ability to manipulate other people and situations is a key to his survival strategy because of the high risk of his business. The Pimp, it is said, must constantly "struggle to outwit women and to keep one step ahead of the police and enemies out to destroy him. Consequently, the Pimp must continually manipulate everyone and cannot afford to become lax, or his empire will collapse" (Perkins, 1975, p. 80; see also Milner, 1970; Hudson, 1972, pp. 419–442).

*Entertainment.*    Entertainment includes a wide range of performers, such as singers, musicians, preachers, comedians, disc jockeys, athletes, and writers (Keil, 1967). This is a traditional strategy for exploiting social and economic resources within the black community by satisfying people's needs for entertainment and for therapy in coping with problems of subordination. Some entertainers also use this strategy to exploit conventional resources.

The Entertainer. The special ability of the entertainer is to perform for a black audience in a way that arouses their auditory and tactile sensibilities. He must be able to make proper use of oral expressions, to "style out" and employ other dimensions of "black talk", as well as use appropriate bodily movements. In some respects the entertainer demonstrates the same instrumental competencies characteristic of the hustler so that some entertainers (e.g., preachers) have been called entertainer-hustlers (Keil, 1967; Holt, 1972; Williams, 1972).

*The Street Man.*    The survival strategy of the Street Man is primarily using physical strength to achieve his desired ends: money, sex, services, and goods. His most important instrumental competencies include physical strength, although styles of dress, stance, walking, and verbal communication are important and distinctive. He is said to be indifferently violent and proud of his ability to meet any challenge that involves physical contest. His communicative style is characterized by specialized vocabulary (Ellis & Newman, 1971; McCord et al., 1969; Perkins, 1975; Silverstein & Krate, 1975).

*Mutual Exchange.*    There are mutual exchange groups in the black community made up of kin-based households and friendship networks. Members of such groups are expected to help each other out. They may join one another's household temporarily, share food, clothing, childrearing, and other goods and services. Through these mutual exchanges, people find subsistence and other supports when they are unemployed or in other difficult situations (Stack, 1974; Ogbu, 1974).

These are the common and important adult categories (or, as many would prefer to label them, lifestyles) and their distinctive competencies in the inner-city. Their subsistence tasks within the conventional and street economy are the normal cultural tasks demanding competence. To be competent in these cultural tasks requires the instrumental competencies characteristic of these adult categories. From a cultural-ecological perspective, black childrearing is organized to inculcate the instrumental competencies which have proven functional in the exploitation of conventional and street economy of the inner-city and to ensure that black children grow up competent in these adult tasks. We now turn to how these competencies are instilled in inner-city children or the process of acquisition of competence among inner-city children.

## Theories of Making It In The Inner-City

The first clue about how inner-city black children acquire their instrumental competencies lies in the folk theories of success in the inner-city because they tell us the kinds of people parents want their children to be, and perhaps, the kinds of people older children themselves strive to be, when they grow up. Folk theories of making it in the inner-city, as elsewhere, are based on knowledge inherited from previous generations, on images of present and future opportunity structures. Inner-city theories of success differ from those of white middle class. The difference lies largely in the strategies for achieving these goals (Foster, 1974; Milner, 1970). For example, although inner-city blacks and middle-class whites desire formal education for jobs, wages, and social prestige, blacks do not believe as strongly as whites that school credentials are sufficient to achieve these goals. Having experienced a long history of unequal rewards for equal school efforts and credentials, blacks tend to be bitter and frustrated that a job ceiling and other racial barriers prevent them from using this conventional strategy to achieve success as defined by American society. And they have responded to the barriers by (a) developing alternative theories of making it; (b) developing alternative strategies for making it; (c) developing an admiration for those who make it outside conventional strategies of schooling and wage labor; and (d) by valuing positively the attributes of the latter individuals.

The point is that black theories of success also stress the importance of other strategies and competencies besides those of the white middle-class. Thus blacks teach their children to acquire formal education for conventional jobs, but also consciously or unconsciously teach them the instrumental competencies of clientship, hustling and other survival strategies. Nobles and Traver (1976) report how the sense of "mother-wit" is conveyed to children through proverbial sayings.

## Theories of Childrearing In The Inner-City

Childrearing among inner-city blacks, as among other populations, is, to a large degree, a future oriented activity that prepares children for competence in their adult cultural tasks. Folk theories of childrearing in the inner-city do not necessarily correspond to the scientific model of the same phenomenon. They exist nonetheless to guide inner-city parents and other adults in their relationship to children and to rationalize what happens between them and children. From a cultural-ecological perspective, an adequate study of childrearing in the inner-city must probe the people's conscious and unconscious ideas of how children should be raised and the sources of these ideas (Mayer, 1970). As researchers, we should ask inner-city blacks, "What works?," or "What makes people competent and successful in their community?" We should then examine how their knowledge of what works affects their child-rearing values and practices.

It may be asked whether inner-city blacks consciously want to raise their children to be competent hustlers, pimps, clients, and the like. We cannot answer this question on the basis of existing data, because conventional research has not been designed to probe this matter systematically. There is some evidence, however, that hustlers, pimps, and related adult categories are not rejected in the inner-city, as they may be in the wider society; in fact they seem to be admired in the inner-city. Also, pimps, hustlers, and entertainer-hustlers appear to be popular among inner-city youths who seem to emulate them more than they emulate the Conventional Worker (see Foster, 1975; Keil, 1967; Perkins, 1975, Schulz, 1968).

## Social Organization and Relations Affecting Childrearing

Organization of subsistence activities in the inner-city affects organization of childrearing in four ways. First, the marginal conventional economic roles of males undermine their power in the family and result in more single parent, female-headed households. Contemporary high unemployment among inner-city males also weakens their ability to support families, thus sustaining the high incidence of female-headed households (Gonzalez, 1961). One consequence of this household organization is that males participate less in childrearing as fathers-in-residence, and thus have less influence on their children. Second, a significant number of black families depend on public assistance. Some receive supplementary childcare under sponsorship of government or private agencies because they are on welfare. Such supplementary childcare usually involves introduction of alien (middle-class whites') ideas and techniques, which may not be strongly endorsed or willingly adopted (Billingsley, 1968).

Third, the necessity to meet subsistence and other needs under marginal resources has encouraged some inner-city households to organize into cooperating mutual-exchange groups based on kinship or friendship (Stack, 1974). This organizational form of childrearing is most noticeable in the role of extended family members, including aunts and uncles, grandparents, cousins, and others. As Ladner (1978) observes, when parents work, grandparents may serve as permanent babysitters and co-residents of the same households. Some children are also brought up almost entirely by grandparents or other relatives, especially when parents' subsistence activities severely interfere with their child-rearing tasks. Lastly, a major influence on the social organization of inner-city children is the free enterprise of the street economy. Success in this economy requires nothing less than the ultra individualism, abundant mistrust and impersonal attitude of hustlers and pimps. This limits participants' share in family activities like childrearing. It also affects the economic socialization of children, which may include formal and informal teaching of street economics.

## Childrearing Techniques in The Inner-City

Parents and other child-rearing agents in the inner-city have developed appropriate and standardized techniques of training children at home, in the street, and at school to become competent inner-city adults. We do not know much about the relationship between these settings. A more accurate assessment of the relationship among these settings and their influences must await future systematic research. Here we can only attempt to review findings of studies which have not been designed to examine children's experiences in all the settings. Ideally it would be most useful to indicate specific techniques used to inculcate particular instrumental competencies in the home, school or street, and show what changes in these techniques and competencies occur as children pass through different stages to adulthood.

*The Home.*  The few extended observational studies we have show that during infancy children receive a great deal of nurturance, warmth and affection (Rainwater, 1974; Silverstein & Krate, 1975; Young, 1970). Investigators generally agree that the infant's individuality is stressed. In post infancy, nurturing is greatly reduced if not entirely terminated, especially with the arrival of a new baby. A new element is now introduced—contest between the child and adult, particularly the mother. Young, (1974) points out that the mother structures the contest relationship more or less purposely as a means of teaching the child independence, self-reliance, and skills in manipulating persons and situations.

The techniques outlined appear to inculcate several attributes which facilitate children's development into inner-city adolescent categories:

1. The use of physical punishment discourages emotional dependency while simultaneously encouraging early independence and self-reliance bordering on "defiance" (Silverstein & Krate, 1975).

2. Purposive training in early independence and self-reliance makes black children independent and self-reliant much earlier than white middle-class children and thus shortens the duration of effective parental control of black children (Ladner, 1978; Young, 1974).

3. Emphasis on aggression in early play and parental insistence that the child fight back when attacked by peers encourage children to accept physical action as a legitimate technique for solving problems (Foster, 1974; Ladner, 1978; Silverstein & Krate, 1975).

4. Parental demand for early independence and self-reliance, coupled with inconsistent physical and verbal sanctions, encourage early affiliation with street culture (Ladner, 1978; Silverstein & Krate, 1975; Young, 1970).

5. Early withdrawal of emotional support, coupled with inconsistent restrictiveness and punitiveness, probably leads the child to develop mistrust for parents which is later generalized to other adults and authorities (Ladner, 1978; Silverstein & Krate, 1975).

6. The mother-child contest develops the child's ability to manipulate persons and situations, to become competent in certain procedures of interpersonal interaction rather than to learn conventional rules of moral conduct (Young, 1974).

7. Before the civil rights revolution of the 1960s, parental emphasis on obedience, respect for self and others, and on "knowing your place" taught the children to express deferential behavior to whites, an important element in the survival strategy of clientship (Cooke, 1974; Nobles & Traver, 1976).

Finally, parental emphasis on mother-wit teaches children that formal education is but one alternative survival strategy and inculcates in children the value of manipulative skills in dealing with people and situations (Nobles & Traver, 1976). These are some of the essential competencies the inner-city child must learn in order to grow into a competent adult.

*The School.* Aside from its preparation of children for formal credentials, the school contributes in two ways to the inculcation of the instrumental competencies of black children. First, schools provide a setting for contact with a large number of peers, and an opportunity for self-selection into peer categories. Rainwater (1974) reports that in St. Louis, some groups and cliques formed in the neighborhoods oriented themselves to school. Second, schools contribute to further differentiation and the sorting process of children into categories; a process begun earlier in the home. Sorting in the school context occurs when conflicts develop between the attitudes and capabilities of non Mainstreamers and those attitudes and capabilities valued by the schools.

As early as first or second grade, the school uses both subjective teacher judgments and formal testing testing procedures to separate children who respond well to its rules of behavior, from those who do not (Silverstein & Krate, 1975). Those in the latter category are labeled immature, incompetent, or unlikely to succeed. Children are then channeled into two tracks, one for those not expected to succeed academically, the other for those expected to succeed academically. Among those who respond well to school norms—the Mainstreamers—girls usually outnumber boys by a ratio of 2 to 1, whereas in the worst classes, two thirds are often boys (see Ogbu, 1974, 1978; Rainwater, 1974). The school sorting process appears to be completed by the third grade, so that by this time, ''the worst class in each school (has) usually become, in effect, a 'maximum security' class to 'control' the most deviant children, the troublemakers, for whom teachers and supervisors could see no good future'' (Silverstein and Krate, 1975). This sorting process reinforces children's negative experiences in school, facilitates early entry into, and encapsulation of some in, street culture.

*The Street.*    Street culture plays a powerful role in furthering the development of inner-city children into adult categories. Induction into peer group may begin as early as 3 to 4 years of age, with initial groups consisting of older siblings and neighbors (Ladner, 1978, p. 222; Young, 1974, p. 410). By the time the child enters school, the peer group expands in age, number, and territory. Moreover, by this time the child has begun to run into conflicts with his or her family and has achieved a fair amount of independence of parental control.

During the remainder of the preadolescent period, the child's self-assertiveness continues to be more pronounced as he becomes less and less dependent on the family and more and more on peers for emotional and other supports (Ladner, 1978; Rainwater, 1974). Between the ages of 8 and 12, many inner-city black children are already drawn into street culture proper, lured by excitements of street life and gangs. This is particularly true of children who do not find school interesting or meaningful (Silverstein & Krate, 1975; Perkins, 1975). There is limited information on the actual instructional techniques used in the street to mold children into adolescent categories, but it appears that street techniques include modeling, apprenticeship, peer contests (e.g., verbal contests in joking, playing ''the dozens'', etc.), peer pressures, and direct instructions (see Foster, 1974; Ladner, 1978; Perkins, 1975).

*Other Sources of Role Models.*    There are hardly any studies of the full role of the church in the transmission of competence, but it is very likely that the church does indeed play an important role. Other sources of influence are black folktale characters (e.g., the signifying monkey, shine and titanic, Brer Rabbit, etc.), the mass media characters (e.g., cowboy, gangster, sports figures, entertainers, etc.), characters in school textbooks (e.g., Frederick Douglas, Abraham Lincoln, etc.). These characters have attributes admired and emulated by inner-city youths (Hickerson, 1980).

## DOMINANT CHILD & ADOLESCENT CATEGORIES AND THEIR COMPETENCIES IN RELATION TO ADULT CATEGORIES

The following diagram shows the major child, adolescent and adult categories and possible developmental relations in the inner-city. A few points should be noted about the diagram. Except for childhood period, the categories refer to males only. Furthermore, no one has yet systematically studied the development from childhood to adulthood. Our discussion of the probable course of development is therefore speculative and suggestive of a future research agenda.

### Childhood Categories And Competencies

Silverstein and Krate (1975) identify four child categories and their distinctive attributes, emphasizing mainly social competencies in the context of school-related behavior.

*The Mainstreamer.*   The Mainstreamer behaves more or less like white middle-class children and possesses similar values. Two thirds are girls.

*The Submissive.*   Two-thirds of the Submissives are boys. They are generally quiet, inactive, nonassertive, stoic and socially isolated. They talk very little and rarely show any initiative or self-confidence.

*The Ambivalent.*   Most Ambivalents are girls. They have intensive and frequent conflicts between a desire for dependency, attention, nurturance, and belongingness on the one hand, and on the other a tendency to mistrust others, expect them to be manipulative and eventually rejecting.

*The Precocious Independent.*   These are mostly boys and are distinguished by stubbornness and rigid self-direction, early functional independence, lack of cooperativeness, "dramatic and forceful identities," and a readiness to display a lot of "guts" or courage. They are disliked and feared by their peers. Generally they channel their intellectual capacity early into survival skills and are often marked for early death.

### Adolescent Categories And Competencies

Early school experiences reinforce the categories emerging from the home. In the street, however, there is a further differentiation, reformation, and sorting into new and old categories. The process is not entirely clear, but we may speculate on the following course of events. First, children who are marginal members of the child categories may be easily recruited into other groups, depending upon their street encounters. Second, depending upon opportunity for imitation, apprenticeship, peer pressure or direct instruction, regular members of the child categories can be influenced to join any other emerging types.

The major categories are the Square, Ivy-Leaguer, Regular, Cool Cat, Jester, and Gowster. There are differences in labels used by different writers and in different regions, but authors describe more or less similar types (see Foster, 1974, Ellis & Newman, 1971; Hunter, 1980, Perkins, 1975). Although we have no studies showing how these adolescent categories developed from child categories, some trends appear recognizable or make sense. Also, while inner-city adolescents share competencies of adaptability, verbal manipulation, role-playing, and interactional skills, membership in a given category is marked by a distinctive constellation of these and other attributes (Perkins, 1975).

*The Square.*    Squares seem to have developed mostly from Mainstreamers of earlier stage, but street encounters may have molded some Ambivalents and Submissives to become Squares. The Squares are a deviant group in street culture, rejecting its norms, activities, and regular membership.

*The Ivy-Leaguer.*    Ellis and Newman (1971) describe the Ivy-Leaguer as probably a subcategory of the Square. He "emulates middle-class behavior, belongs to social clubs or fraternities in college, abides by school laws and routines, dresses well by middle-class standards" (p. 304). He also tends to be a church-goer and is well liked by his family and the authorities. At school he is generally considered a good student.

*The Regular.*    The Regular is an accepted member of the street culture, although he does not subscribe to all of its norms. The Regular may have developed from the Mainstreamer, the Submissive, and the Ambivalent. He is distinguished by the fact that he knows how to get along well with everyone, without comprising his own values.

*The Cool Cat.*    This is probably an outgrowth of the Ambivalent, though some Mainstreamers could later have developed into this type. All inner-city children learn how to keep cool under difficult conditions, but this survival skill seems perfected in the Cool Cat. He is not only "cool," but also "hip," "together," and "able to function under considerable pressure." He is characterized by a neat appearance, skill in verbal manipulation, and "an uncanny ability to stay out of serious trouble." The Cool Cat is indifferent to problems around him. In summary, he has learned "to be cool, stern, impersonal, in the face of all kinds of adversities" (Perkins, 1975). (p. 40)

*The Jester.*    This may have developed from the Submissives and from the Ambivalents. His distinguishing attribute is that he handles threats and pressures by acting foolishly to avoid facing problems head on. He gains attention and status by being funny. To maintain his role he lets others use him as a foil and for

FIG. 4.2. Relationship Between Child/Adolescent Categories To Adult Categories In The Inner City. (Categories not mutually exclusive.)

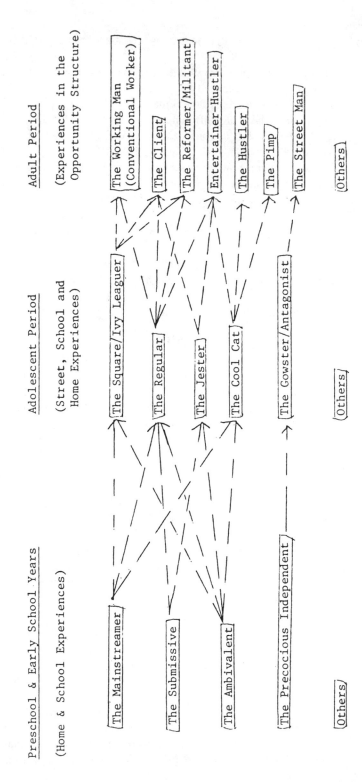

pranks and mischevious acts. Because he is easily manipulated to do such things, he is often in conflict with the law and authorities.

*The Gowster/Antagonist.*    This adolescent type must have developed from the Precocious Independent of earlier years. The Gowster seeks status through sheer "ability to outfight, bully, and harrass, and intimidate others" (Perkins, 1975, p. 42). "A Gowster tends to acquire his reputation as early as the age of 10 and often dies young from violence associated with his reputation" (Perkins, 1975, p. 40).

If we compare these adolescent types and their attributes with the adult types described earlier we find many resemblances. We may speculate that most Squares, Ivy-Leaguers and Regulars become Conventional Workers, Clients, and Reformers in adult life; Jesters mature into Conventional Workers, Clients, and Entertainer-hustlers; Cool Cats become Hustlers, Entertainer-hustlers, and Pimps; while the Gowster turns into Street Man. However, the development from child type to adolescent type to adult type does not follow a rigid course.

## CONCLUSION: BLACK INSTRUMENTAL COMPETENCIES AND SCHOOLING

From the perspective of cultural ecology, neither the universalists nor the relativists capture the reality of the situation of black school failure. I have tried to show that the problem is not merely that inner-city black children lack white middle-class competencies as a result of black parents' lack of know how in white middle-class child-rearing tasks. True, many inner-city black children do not acquire the instrumental competencies of the white middle-class. But it is because black parents teach black children those instrumental competencies required by the cultural imperatives of the inner-city black communities. These validate the survival strategies which blacks have developed for exploiting the marginal resources of their effective environment and for generally coping with life in the inner-city.

Before the 1960s, the conflict between black rules of behavior for achievement and instrumental competencies on the one hand, and those of the school on the other, was functional. The result was a disproportionate number of black children achieving only the minimum education levels; all that was necessary for the menial jobs available to blacks in the conventional economy. That is, the conflict helped prepare blacks for menial jobs below the job ceiling, which did not require white middle-class type of educational credentials (Ogbu, 1978).

Some efforts are being made to improve black education, so that many blacks appear to be receiving a more middle-class type of education than before. But the disproportionate school failure remains because of institutional, structural, and cultural factors discussed here and elsewhere (Ogbu, 1974, 1978, 1981a, 1981b). This failure persists because the social and economic changes begun in

the 1960s have not had a significant impact on the conventional economic resources of inner-city blacks (Ogbu, 1981b; Willie, 1979; Wilson, 1978). These
changes have not been large enough to diminish the importance of the street
economy and therefore make alternative survival strategies less attractive.

For the same reason, the solution proposed by the relativists is bound to have
only a limited success. The relativists are right in saying that inner-city black
children acquire different, rather than deficient, instrumental competencies, but
their analysis does not go far enough and their solution is simplistic. In their
analysis, they ignore the fact that some other minorities with distinctive cultural
frames of reference and competencies are more successful in school than blacks.
There must be an understanding for the success of these other minorities who are
not brought up like white middle-class children.

It has been suggested elsewhere (Ogbu, in press) that there are different kinds
of cultural differences with different implications for minority schooling. Some
of the rules of behavior for achievement and instrumental competencies of inner-
city blacks described in this paper fall under *secondary cultural difference*. This
means that inner-city blacks, for example, tend to define black culture, competence, and behavior in opposition to white culture, competence, and behavior.
One gains the impression from ethnographic study of inner-city blacks that many
people, especially the males, consider it inappropriate to behave like white
people in school and community, although one should know how to deal with
white people—how to manipulate whites in such a way as to retain one's safety
and identity. This type of bicultural learning probably dates back to a period in
black American history when it was not safe to behave like white people.

Increasing the proportion of black school success will, therefore, require more
than interventions which focus on family and school experience and on reducing
institutional and structural barriers. It will require programs designed to deal with
the problem of secondary cultural discontinuities. Specifically, some children,
particularly older ones, will need help in separating behaviors and skills which
facilitate school success and later socioeconomic success from behaviors and
skills that imply *assimilation* into white middle-class culture, and a threat therefore to their identity. Developing a pragmatic attitude is essential in reducing the
problem of disproportionate school failure, given the phenomenon of secondary
cultural discontinuity. Some inner-city black children need to know, for example, that one person can be a good mathematician and black; another person
could be a good mathematician and Chinese; another can be a good mathematician and Chicano; and still another can be a good mathematician and white. Yet
all four may have become good mathematicians because they learned similar
rules of behavior and skills that make people anywhere good mathematicians,
without requiring them to give up their cultural, ethnic, or racial identities.

# Summary

Urie Bronfenbrenner
*Cornell University*

The preceding offers four contrasting, but yet complementary perspectives for the scientific study of minority child development. Surely, the most important, and also the most neglected of the four theses, is John Ogbu's insistence that children and their families be seen in the context of the reality in which they live.

Ogbu contends that in every society children are brought up to deal effectively with the particular situations they face at successive points in their lives. Moreover, in his view, the great majority do in fact acquire the motivation, knowledge, and skills that they need at each step of the way so that, in the end, "most children in a given population grow up as confident adult men and women."

Difficulties arise, however, if the environments of children and adults are assessed in terms of criteria appropriate to a different milieu. Under such circumstances, minority members are apt to be misjudged as inferior, and their developmental capacities and achievements left unrecognized. This is typically what happens, says Ogbu, when minority groups are evaluated by the majority, be it in the realm of science, or in the more comprehensive and consequential sphere of everyday life. To remedy this state of affairs, Ogbu urges developmental researchers, and indeed all members of the society, to adopt what he calls the cultural-ecological perspective. For students of development, the first step in implementing this perspective requires an analysis of the reality that a given minority group faces. The second task is to identify those attitudes, knowledge, and skills necessary for coping with the situations that the group confronts. Without such information about minority groups and their experiences, Ogbu asserts it is impossible to make valid assessments of developmental status, to identify key developmental processes, or to design programs appropriate to the realities where the children and their families live.

It is useful now to consider some difficulties inherent in Ogbu's adaptive cultural model. In Elder's study of "Children of the Great Depression" (1974), he followed two groups of subjects. The first group were teenagers whose families experienced economic loss. Surprisingly, for these youngsters, economic deprivation appeared to have a positive effect on subsequent development. They did better in school, were more likely to go to college, had happier marriages, and exhibited more successful work careers. Elder concludes that financial misfortune forced the family to mobilize its own human resources, including those of its teenagers, and to take on new responsibilities to work toward the goal of getting and keeping the family on its feet. In the words of the Banished Duke, "Sweet are the uses of adversity."

But adversity was not so sweet for the second group of children who were of school age when their families were hit by the Depression. By contrast, these youngsters, in particular the boys, subsequently did less well in school, showed less stable family and work histories, and exhibited more emotional and social difficulties—some still apparent when subjects of the study were in late middle age. These effects were particularly marked among those whose families were already poor when the Depression hit.

The subjects who exhibited the previously discussed life pattern were not merely a few exceptions. They were representative of a large group of Americans who, as children, had lived in families that suffered severe loss of income during the Depression. Elder's report of the long-range effect of economic hardship in this group, especially among families that were poor to start with, is difficult to reconcile with Ogbu's assertion that, "most children in a given population grow up as confident adult men and women." It would appear that, at least in some ecologies, neither the adults nor the peer group can fully succeed in producing a next generation that effectively adapts to the realities that it confronts. In such situations, human beings, both the adults and the children, are simply doing the best they can under the circumstances.

Putting the issue in another way, the research evidence, of which Elder's study is but a single example, requires adding another, more sobering element to Ogbu's Panglossian paradigm: the possibility that the outcome may not be adaptive to the person's life situation. Thus Elder's research, conducted with a sample of white families, suggests that the consequences of environmental stress may be favorable or unfavorable for development depending on the age of the child, and the resources available to the family prior to their misfortune. Is there any reason to believe that these qualifications are any less applicable to children growing up in black culture?

As the above question indicates, the application of a life course framework to Ogbu's cultural model reveals not only important dissonances but also notable gaps in the latter—the absence of a developmental and historical perspective. In the "cultural ecology of the ghetto," age appears solely as a sociological status bereft of any distinctive psychological characteristics or environmental requirements; and culture is treated as a static given, to which the growing individual has to conform, with no allowance for possible developmental costs.

The recognition of developmental changes, for better or for worse, in the lives of individuals as a function of the successive contexts they inhabit lies at the core of research on human development based on a life span or life course perspective. It is noteworthy, however, that although this approach is American in its origins and has been on the scene for more than a decade (Baltes, 1968; Schaie, 1970; Riley, 1973), it has yet to be applied in research on American minority groups. For example, to my knowledge, among all the longitudinal studies that have been carried out in this country, none has focused specifically on black families. Thus the literature gives no indication of the specific relevance of the life course approach to research on minority groups, the kinds of investigations that might be conducted in this sphere, or the special problems and opportunities presented by a dilemma highlighted in Ogbu's analysis: the necessity of having to adapt to two cultures simultaneously.

Franklin's paper illustrates the changing social science perspectives in minority research. In effect, Franklin documents the existence and development of two different scientific cultures, each exhibiting a distinctive historical course, and viewing similar phenomena from divergent points of view. The first scientific tradition Franklin identifies is essentially based on what Ogbu calls the "universal" but is perhaps more accurately described as a "deficit model" (Bronfenbrenner, 1979a). This line of research views black children and adults as impaired by social and economic conditions, hence as inferior when judged by white middle-class criteria, and therefore in need of resocialization in accord with middle-class norms. Franklin's second scientific stream is indigenous to black culture, affirms its strength and capacity for self-determination, and seeks to demonstrate the validity of both. Franklin clearly identifies himself with the latter position, whereas Ogbu rejects it, primarily on the ground that it fails to specify the competencies that are unique to black culture or to show how these competencies relate to black child-rearing practices and black school behavior.

Ogbu sees his cultural-ecological model as a third alternative. His contemporary, ahistorical solution, however, reflects a curious blending of Franklin's two historical themes. Ogbu's list of what are presumably "competencies unique to blacks" consists of the skills he views as required for survival in a "street economy." These cover a wide range from "Uncle Tomming," "mutual exchange," "mother wit," "entertainment," and "conventional employment" (one wonders how this is unique), to "making it by not working" through "hustling and pimping." Success in the latter activities, he points out, requires a variety of attributes, among them "smartness," "perceptiveness," "indifference," and "independence mixed up with a good deal of mistrust in interpersonal relations." In order to survive in the immediate environment in which they live, black children must somehow acquire these skills, if only to protect themselves. But they must also learn to deal with the wider world of the white middle-class majority. Black culture accomplishes this double task, Ogbu argues, through distinctive patterns of socialization not only in the family but also in the peer group.

Although Ogbu offers his analysis as constituting a third and different alternative to the two prevailing models of black socialization, the terms he employs to describe the minority child-rearing practices and outcomes have a curiously familiar ring. They resemble those used by proponents of the deficit model, but are expressed more forthrightly, without the usual note of moral disapproval. In his effort to represent these patterns as adaptive features of black culture, is Ogbu making a virtue of necessity? Even so, if the necessity is real, is it not the obligation of social scientists to say so, to tell it like it is?

The necessity that Ogbu sees derives from the model he has set forth, and from the way in which this model has guided the selection and interpretation of data. As the Slaughter/McWorter and Franklin historical analyses show, the choice of models determines the nature of research questions that are asked, and hence limits the answers that can be obtained. Thus, social scientists in the first half of this century, convinced that destructive social and economic forces had impaired the development and reduced the capacity of black children and adults, sought, and believed they had found, evidence in support of their expectations. Correspondingly, (during much of the same period), black scholars, pointing to the rich Afro-American heritage and strength exhibited by successive generations of black people in withstanding the onslaughts of slavery and continuing racism, have sought to reorient research to focus on manifestations of black competence and its special cultural origins. In both perspectives, the orienting assumptions are made rather explicit, so that they can readily be taken into account in evaluating research results. The assumptions in Ogbu's model, however, are not so obvious. There are several of them.

(1) Although at the outset Ogbu promises to specify the competencies unique to black culture, and ends up speaking of "black culture and its own instrumental competencies," what he deals with are solely the strategies and states of mind presumed necessary for survival in the ghetto. To be sure, a great number of Black Americans do live in urban ghettos, but they are far from the majority, certainly under 30% (U.S. Bureau of the Census, 1982). What of the remaining 70% or more? Ogbu's exposition is unclear on this point. Does he expect non-ghetto blacks also to exhibit the ghetto pattern, but in milder form? If not, would their socialization practices and outcomes resemble those of the white majority, or do they constitute some other, culturally distinctive form? The answers to these questions are, as yet, unknown. It seems reasonable to expect, however, that, as with data on white samples (Deutsch, 1973; Hess, 1970; Martin, 1975), the picture will be a varied one. For example, it seems likely that differing patterns of child rearing and developmental outcome would be revealed by the following groups of black families:

a. the 8% of all black families who are in the top two fifths of the income distribution (annual income of $46,000 or more in 1981);

b. the 32% of all black families whose income falls in the middle 40% of the distribution ($15,000–$32,000 in 1981). Virtually none of these families fall below the poverty line (to do so they would have to contain eight or more members).

c. the 23% of all black families who are living outside metropolitan areas (over a third of whom are below the poverty threshold).

(2) Even if Ogbu's conclusions are interpreted as applying only to a ghetto population, one may question whether they can be accepted as characterizing a particular aspect of *black* culture. Rather, they may reflect what happens to socialization processes and effects in any group of human beings exposed to ghetto conditions. For example, what basis is there for expecting a difference between child rearing practices and outcomes among the 6.2 million blacks living last year in poverty areas within central cities, and the 4.5 million whites classified as residents in the same kinds of environments?

(3) An examination of Ogbu's model from a life course perspective reveals two additional, complementary assumptions. The first is his principal thesis that the ghetto socialization pattern he describes does in fact lead to adult acquisition of the array of skills defined as essential for ghetto survival. I refer to this proposition as an assumption because, insofar as I could determine from the sources cited, no empirical link has as yet been established between these socialization processes and outcomes. The linkage is merely inferred from their coexistence in the ghetto environment. To establish a functional connection, it would be necessary to show, at the very least, that those ghetto residents who were exposed to the practices described are more proficient in survival skills than those deprived of the appropriate training.

Reference to the latter group calls attention to the complementary half of Ogbu's thesis, clearly implied in the original proposition but left unexamined; namely, adherence to more traditional modes of child-rearing by ghetto parents should prove counterproductive for the development of their children, particularly in adolescence and adulthood. The children should, in line with Ogbu's analysis, later experience difficulty in coping with the life situations in which they find themselves.

Although, to my knowledge, there are no data bearing directly on this complementary thesis, there is some indirect evidence that casts doubt on its validity. For example, consider Elder's findings that in economically deprived families, encouraging the child to show initiative and independence had positive longrange effects for adolescents, but not for school age children, particularly those whose families had been poor to start with. Elder also investigated exceptions to the rule: school age children from economically deprived homes who nevertheless exhibited success in most aspects of their lives. An examination of the patterns of socialization employed in these families revealed several elements that should have proved counterproductive from Ogbu's cultural perspective. Similar findings appear in other studies of competent children and adults growing up in economically deprived circumstances (Deutsch, 1973; Hess, 1970).

(4) Although Ogbu refers to his paradigm as an "ecological model," he omits consideration of one parameter that is usually viewed as critical by proponents of an ecological approach: the dimension of historical time. In his discussion of ghetto culture, Ogbu seems to assume that most ghetto residents have spent and will spend all of their lives in the ghetto environment. Again, although I know of no direct data on the point, indirect evidence calls this assumption into question. For example, recent longitudinal studies have shown (e.g., Nelson & Skidmore, 1982) that most families do not remain in poverty for extended periods of time; rather they fall in and out as a function of fluctuating circumstances, such as unemployment or illness.

It appears likely that, for many families, living in a ghetto is a transient experience. People move in for a period of time, and then move out again. Moreover, whether and when they do so is likely to vary systematically with the person's age and the stage of the family cycle. To the extent that this is so, we are dealing with a phenomenon of ecological transition rather than with an enduring ecological state. As students of human ecology have pointed out (e.g., Bronfenbrenner, 1979b), ecological transitions can have powerful developmental effects, but these influences depend as much on the environment from which the person or family has come as on the next context that is being entered; and the impact of the latter experience depends, in turn, on the settings into which the person subsequently proceeds.

Recognition of these ecological realities raises a host of new questions for Ogbu's cultural model. For example, to what extent are the characteristics exhibited by ghetto residents a function of not having been brought up in a ghetto environment, but of socialization experiences that led ultimately to moving into a ghetto? And are there socialization strategies that enable a person eventually to leave a ghetto environment? More generally, what are the social and cultural forces that lead persons to enter, leave, or remain in the ghetto; who comes, who goes, who stays? And what are the developmental effects of such experiences at different ages or stages of the family cycle?

Finally, Ogbu's ahistorical model appears to assume a ghetto culture—a black culture—that is static rather than in the process of change. Yet, there is evidence that both the narrow and the broader cultural context is undergoing rapid transformation. For example, several recent demographic studies (*New York Times,* 1982) indicate that over the past two decades, blacks have been moving out of the cities into the suburbs in ever growing numbers (from 2.8 million in 1960 to 3.6 million in 1970 to 6.3 million in 1980). Paralleling this demographic trend is another, broader development that has received little recognition. The degree of schooling obtained by black Americans has been rising steadily. To quote the conclusion of a recent study commissioned by the National Academy of Sciences (Ellwood & Wise, 1982): "The median black is now receiving almost as much education measured by years of schooling as the median white."

The significance of these trends, however, is tempered by two other recent changes that are even more rapid, and point in the opposite direction:

1. Despite their increasing educational level, blacks continue to experience rapidly rising rates of unemployment, especially among young men and single-parent mothers (22%).

2. The proportion of blacks living in poverty has been rising at an accelerating pace since 1974. The rate is highest for the young children, particularly those under the age of three. As of March, 1981, half of all the nation's black children were living in families below the poverty line. The proportion of those between three and six was only slightly lower (48%). The data for whites showed a similar trend, but at much lower levels (17 and 18%, respectively). The total number of white children living in poverty is, of course, far greater than the number of black youngsters. For example, among children of preschool age, the figures are 2.8 million versus 926,000, respectively.

This evidence of increasing hardship in the lives of black families and their children gives special urgency to Ogbu's insistence that social scientists, and the public in general, focus attention on the realities confronting minority groups in American society. As Ogbu implies, the first priority, should not be the further documentation of conditions already known to be destructive. Instead, the priority should be to reverse the economic and social policies that are depriving millions of American families of the basic resources they need. The first order of business in this sphere is surely the provision of jobs for the men and women who are family breadwinners.

Slaughter and McWorter argue that social scientists, in their roles as researchers and teachers, have a further obligation and opportunity: to counteract the fallacy equating black family and community life with the culture of poverty. They can do so by illuminating the diversity and richness of the Afro-American experience in the context of American society. This volume represents a useful contribution to that effort by setting forth contrasting perspectives which both complement and challenge each other. It is by investigating such assumptions that we learn most about the nature, complexity, and contribution of black culture to the processes and products of making human beings human.

# RESEARCH AND THEORY ON BLACK CHILD DEVELOPMENT

# Section A: Social Competence

# Introduction

This section attempts to characterize social competence. We begin to discern the subtle and dynamic interactions between the affective and cognitive domains.

In order to provide a perspective and a sense of coherence for the papers in this section, we employ the theoretical construct of competence. White has argued (1959) that competence is the organism's capacity to interact effectively with the social environment, the object and the physical environment.

According to White (1959), the development of competence is enhanced by contributions from activities which show directions, selectivity, and persistence in interacting with the environment. Such activities are oftentimes playful and exploratory as in McLoyd's paper, "Pretend Play Among Low-Income Children as a Function of Structure in Play Materials: A Question of Mind and Matter." Of particular interest is the competence in socio-dramatic play as it relates to high- and low-structure play materials demonstrated by the young black females studied.

According to Anderson and Messick (1974) an important component of social competence is role perception and apperception. In her paper, "Towards a Model of Teacher–Child Transactional processes Affecting Black Children's Academic Achievement," Holliday cogently shows that ". . . joint perceptions of teacher and child must be understood as a unitary segment of experience, and analyzed as such" in order to arrive at a comprehensive assessment and perspective of black children's school achievement.

Various aspects of cognitive intellectual functioning are also components of competence. Moore proposes in her paper, "Ethnicity as a Variable in Child Development," that ethnicity and child-rearing environments should be employed as process variables in order to better understand black children's performance on IQ tests and achievement measures.

Competence also produces a sense of efficacy which is a critical component for achievement. In her paper, "The Coping Personality: A Study of Black Community College Students," Abatso demonstrates the role of efficacy in college achievement and success for young black adults.

Returning to White's definition of competence as the capacity to interact effectively with the environment, the following empirical studies variously demonstrate that understanding the relationship between environment and the person is critical to an understanding of social competence, its origins and transitions over time.

# 5 Are Toys (Just) Toys? Exploring Their Effects on Pretend Play of Low-Income Preschoolers

Vonnie C. McLoyd
*University of Michigan*

If any one psychological concept in the child development literature captivated the attention and challenged the acumen of researchers during the decade of the 1970s, it was the concept of play. Unprecedented streams of books (e.g., Caplan & Caplan, 1973; Ellis, 1973; Garvey, 1977; Schwartzman, 1978; Bruner, Jolly, & Sylva, 1976) and research articles too numerous to cite, emerged to suggest that the frivolity of play is only apparent.

This paper focuses primarily, though not exclusively, on a specific type of play, namely, pretend play. Pretend play is defined here as a transformational and representational activity marked by an "as if" quality in which objects, actions, and/or verbal behavior are used to symbolize imaginary persons, objects, and situations (Piaget, 1962; Sutton-Smith, 1972a). Our primary purpose is to explore what we know and do not know about the functions and determinants of pretend play among black and low-income children. Findings from a recent study of how play materials of different structure affect pretend play are also presented.

First, a brief discussion of theoretical notions and empirical research bearing on the role of pretend play in children's development should clarify the significance of pretend play. Second, a critique of research on pretend play among low-income and black children and its undergirding assumptions will be presented. In the third section, data from a study of one situational determinant of children's pretend play, the structure of playthings, will be presented.

Any major departure from the deficit model of black and low-income children's behavior must be, at once, vigilant and reflective. Just as critical analysis of this model is essential to any attempt to advance our understanding of black and low-income children and their cultural milieu, so too is the generation of new concepts, realities, and frameworks. Thus, in the last section of this paper, there is a discussion of the study data and speculation regarding unique aspects of Afro-American culture as related to various types and conceptions of play. This latter section is intended to encourage future research which is conceptually and methodologically grounded in Afro-American culture.

## The Role of Play in Abstract Thought, Problem-Solving, and Social Cognition

One could conclude from early writings that the recent interest in play as a concept deserving serious theoretical and empirical inquiry was both impossible and inevitable. In 1947, Schlosberg not only acknowledged that play was a particularly troublesome concept to define precisely, but argued that since play could not even be operationally defined, it could hardly be studied empirically. However, as early as 1933, Vygotsky (see Cole, 1978), a Soviet psychologist, had made considerable progress in defining and exploring pretend play. He proposed a close link between pretend play and the development of abstract thought, arguing that in the context of pretend play the child

> . . . learns to act in a cognitive, rather than an externally visual realm by relying on internal tendencies and motives and not on incentives supplied by external things. . . . Thought is separated from objects and action arises from ideas rather than from things. . . . Action according to rules begins to be determined by ideas and not by objects themselves (pp. 96–97).

In retrospect, it is clear that Vygotsky's ideas were a harbinger of the interest in children's play during the past decade. However, Vygotsky's ideas were not translated and published in this country until 1966.

Early researchers in the West independently made similar conclusions about the role of play in children's cognitive and social development. Isaacs (1930) suggested that play assists the child in the "emancipation of meaning from the *here* and *now* of a concrete situation, which makes possible hypotheses and the 'as if' consciousness" (p. 104). On the basis of her observations of the play of 5 years olds, Griffiths (1935) concluded that imaginative play leads to a diminution of egocentrism and an increase in problem-solving in early childhood. Sutton-Smith (1971) suggested that play increases the child's repertoire of responses and adaptability to the environment. Others have maintained that play promotes problem-solving behavior because the freedom therein supports self-motivated exploration and insight (Buhler, 1930; Stern, 1924).

Peller (1952) pointed out that play bears curious similarities to abstract thought—(a) neither has direct consequences in the outer world; (b) both allow particular elements of reality to be selected and varied; (c) both are far quicker than is direct action in reality; (d) both require imagination; and (e) both overcome, with great facility, the obstacles of time and space. The hypothesis that play enhances abstract thought, problem-solving, and nonegocentrism has not received even modest empirical support until very recently. Lieberman (1965), Johnson (1976), Sutton-Smith (1971), and Dansky & Silverman (1976) explored various aspects of these hypotheses. It has been found, for example, that allowing children to do whatever they wished with objects resulted in a significantly greater number of novel uses for the objects (Dansky & Silverman, 1976).

## Pretend Play Among Black and Low-Income Children

What, then, is the significance of these theoretical notions and empirical findings for play among low-income and black children? Some studies indicate that middle-income children in preschool and the early primary grades engage in more pretend play than low-income (often black) children (e.g., Rosen, 1974; Smilansky, 1968; White, 1978), others report no differences (Golomb, 1979), or differences in the opposite direction (Eifermann, 1971). There is considerable disagreement among studies, and, in a number of cases, validity and reliability must be questioned. These issues are discussed extensively in a critique of research on social class differences in pretend play by McLoyd (1981).

The assumption that low-income children engage in less frequent, lower quality pretend play, or play that is characteristically unimaginative and desultory, is widely accepted in the available literature (Lovinger, 1974; Murphy, 1972; Singer, 1973; Smilansky, 1968). These assumptions underlie a spate of intervention studies designed to increase the frequency and quality of pretend play among low-income, often black children (Feitelson & Ross, 1973; Rosen, 1974; Saltz et al., 1977).

All the studies which provide information on the social and cognitive skills associated with pretend play among low-income and black children have been training intervention studies. Those skills (e.g., role-taking, divergent thinking) which correlate with postintervention pretend play are assumed to be functions or correlates of nondirected, spontaneous pretend play. The possibility that pretend play subjected to, or resulting from, systematic training strategies may have correlates quite different from pretend play not subjected to such intervention, is generally ignored. The significance of the presence or absence of pretend play for the social-cognitive development of black and low-income children remains unclear. Much would be clarified if we could point to data which indicates that the more pretend play very young, low-income and black children engage in, the more advanced are certain of their social and cognitive skills.

One of the most explicit deficit hypotheses regarding play among low-income children was articulated by Sutton-Smith (1972b). He argued on the basis of Smilansky's (1968) comparative study that there are "two cultures of games": (1) Play among children in the "achievement game culture," which includes children from Western, middle-class nuclear families, is imaginative, more egalitarian, and less hierarchical; (2) Play among children in the "ascriptive game culture" is imitative, not imaginative or transformational, relies on the use of realistic toy representations rather than improvised ones or none at all, and is centered around one usually bossy, manipulative individual.

"The dozens" is the only example provided by Sutton-Smith of a game of a contemporary ascriptive culture. It is a game played primarily by Afro-American elementary and high school children in which players exchange verbal, often rhyming, disparaging remarks, typically about the family members of the opponent player. It can occur between two (usually boys) who play to the crowd, trying to make each exchange funnier than the last. The laughing crowd plays a central role in the exchange as audience, inciters, and judges, giving approval to the wittiest player.

While researchers vary in their interpretations of the cultural significance of "the dozens" (Abrahams, 1962; Dollard, 1939, Grier & Cobbs, 1971), there is agreement that "the dozens" requires and rewards high imagination, creativity, and wit (Folb, 1980; Grier & Cobbs, 1971; White, 1972). Sutton-Smith's characterization of "the dozens" as unimaginative and as an example of a game in the ascriptive culture, is highly questionable. Schwartzman (1978) argues that researchers have tended to "neglect the investigation of alternate expressions of imagination or creativity, which lower-class children may display" (p. 120). Since low-income and black children are thought to lack skills related to pretend play, researchers therefore conduct their research with this presumption.

## Playthings as Socializers and Determinants of Pretend Play

Children's playthings are sources of entertainment, but more importantly and perhaps less obviously, they are a central medium by which children are introduced to the realities of their cultural and social world (Schroeder & Cohen, 1971). Recent empirical work supports the view that different types of toys promote different types of behavior. For example, Quilitch and Risley (1973) found that social play occurred very infrequently when black elementary school children were provided with isolate playthings (e.g., crayons, tinker toys, puzzles). Social play was significantly increased when the children were provided with social playthings (e.g., pick-up s stix, checkers, a deck of playing cards). Similarly, Vandenberg (1981) reported that white, middle-class preschoolers were more likely to engage in solitary or parallel play in an environment equipped with paper, pencils, crayons, and other materials designed to develop fine motor skills. They were more likely to engage in associative play in an environment equipped with a jungle gym, slides, tumbling mats, and other materials designed to exercise large muscles.

McGhee et al. reported that black preschool males used unstructured toys in a pretense manner significantly more often, but high-structure toys elicited significantly longer pretense episodes. Elder and Pederson (1978) reported that 2½ year-olds pretended more frequently when the signifier resembled the signified, whereas 3½ year-olds were able to pretend equally often, irrespective of whether the signifier was similar or dissimilar to the signifier or absent altogether.

The research discussed here attempted to provide an environment relatively free of adult constraints, within which natural and spontaneous play would occur. This study extends previous research by examining how differences in the degree of structure of the play materials affect both boys and girls of different ages. Prior studies reported sex differences in the amount of pretend play and frequency of different types of transformational modes employed during pretend play (Matthews, 1977; McLoyd, 1980; Sanders & Harper, 1976), thus sex may affect the outcomes of different types of play materials. Finally, the study examines play among low-income, black preschool children, a population which has been the focus of considerable speculation. In this regard, the study provides a test of Sutton-Smith's (1972b) thesis predicting a decrease in the frequency of pretend play when the available playthings are not replicas.

In the present study, it was hypothesized that older children would show more triadic sociodramatic play in the low-structure than in the high-structure (miniature replicas) condition. Conversely, it was hypothesized that because of their need for greater verisimilitude between the signified and signifier, younger children would show more triadic sociodramatic play in the high-structure than in the low-structure condition. Finally, differing with Smilansky's (1968) contention that economically disadvantaged children show no progress in sociodramatic play with age, it was hypothesized that older children would show more triadic sociodramatic play in the low-structure, but not in the high-structure condition. Other types and properties of pretend play were examined in the study, but no predictions were made.

## METHOD

### Subjects

Thirty six low-income preschool children, equally divided by age and sex, served as subjects. The mean age of younger girls and boys was 41.8 months (SD = 5.2) and 42 months (SD = 7.8), respectively. The mean age of older girls and boys was 61 months (SD = 2.6) and 60.3 months (SD = 3.1) respectively. Of the thirty six children, thirty one were black and five were white. All were enrolled in a preschool center in Southeastern Michigan which required low family income for attendance. Within each age group, the children were members of the same class. With a few exceptions, such as blocks and Play-Doh, the center was equipped with primarily replica toys.

## Setting

A mobile laboratory with two rooms (playroom and videotape equipment room separated by a one-way mirror), was set up at the preschool center. The playroom measured approximately 100 square feet and was equipped with a child-size table and three chairs. Prior to the investigation, two research assistants spent approximately 4 hours per day for 2 days in the preschool center to establish rapport with the children. Children were brought to the playroom in random groups of three or four; given a tour; invited to explore briefly all of the play materials (both high- and low-structure); and told that they would have an opportunity to play there sometime soon.

Same-sex and same-age children were randomly grouped to constitute six younger triads and six older triads. Each triad was escorted to the playroom and invited to play with anything they wished. The research assistant told the children she would be working in the next room and they should knock on the door if they needed her. The research assistant then left the playroom and went into the equipment room, at which time a second assistant began videotaping the children's behavior. Each triad was covertly observed for four 30 minute sessions. Triad membership remained intact throughout the four sessions. When interruptions within a session were necessary (e.g., restroom breaks), children were brought back to the playroom for completion of the session. The 30 minute sessions were usually separated by 1 to 2 days. In two of the four sessions, high-structure toys were available and in the remaining two sessions, low-structure objects were present. The order of sessions was counterbalanced.

## Materials

The high-structure play materials (defined as those which have highly specific, readily identifiable, and conventional functions) included a tea set, puppets, stove and sink combination, refrigerator, medical kit, telephone, ironing board, dolls, trucks, tool kit, and adult "dress up" clothes. The low-structure play materials (defined as those which have less specific, more varied or ambiguous functions) included a package of pipe cleaners, cardboard boxes, round, flat pieces of hard plastic, metal cans, cylindrical pieces of cardboard, construction paper, styrofoam cups, paper bags, blocks, large, square pieces of cloth, and styrofoam cartons. In addition to varying the degree of the play materials' specificity of function, these materials were chosen so that the variety of play materials across the two experimental conditions would be constant.

## Data Preparation

In conjunction with a larger study, transcripts of the 48 sessions were prepared. Each transcript was completed by one research assistant and checked by another who reviewed the videotape and transcript concurrently. In the case of disagreement with the preliminary transcript, the assistant indicated how he or she thought it should be changed. Finally, a third research assistant reviewed 24 of the 48 final transcripts in conjunction with the respective videotapes, indicating disagreements. He or she was told to ignore deletions and verify the information contained in the transcript. The percentage of transcribed words with which the third reviewer agreed ranged from 82% to 96% with a mean of 94%. Percentage agreement for objects manipulated ranged from 82% to 96% with a mean of 96%, and for speaker identification, from 90% to 96% with a mean of 94%.

## Identification of Types of Pretend Play

For each 1 minute interval, the predominant type of pretend play which occurred, if any, was identified, including:

1. *Triadic and dyadic sociodramatic play.* Three (triadic) or two (dyadic) children collectively create and enact an imaginary or nonliteral situation, assuming different and complementary roles required for the organized execution of the drama.

2. *Triadic and dyadic associative pretend play.* Three (triadic) or two (dyadic) children play with each other in a nonliteral situation, discussing with each other what they are doing. However, there is no assignment of roles or overall organization of the imaginary situation.

3. *Triadic and dyadic parallel pretend play.* Three (triadic) or two (dyadic) children engage in similar, though independent, pretend play activity, making few, if any, attempts to interact with or influence each other. Verbal exchange is sparse if present at all and unrelated to the ongoing pretend play.

4. *Solitary pretend play.* At least one triad member engages in make-believe play alone. It is different from the make-believe play of the other triad members (if existent) and is generally unaccompanied by verbal behavior directed to other triad members.

For each 1 minute interval, all of the categories of pretend play were mutually exclusive, except solitary pretend play. It was possible for solitary pretend play to occur concurrently with dyadic sociodramatic, associative, or parallel pretend play. Reliability, expressed as the number of 1 minute intervals coded the same by both coders divided by the total number of 1 minute intervals and based on 24 randomly chosen transcripts, ranged from 84% to 97% with a mean of 94%.

## Properties of Pretend Play

In addition to identification of the different types of pretend play in which the triads engaged, some properties of pretend play were assessed from the transcript, including:

1. *Variety of themes.* Number of different themes in the children's pretend play.
2. *Types of roles enacted in pretend play.* Number of distinct roles children assumed in their pretend play including family (e.g., mother, baby), occupational (e.g., fireman, nurse), and fantastic or character (e.g., Batman, Hulk) roles.
3. *Object substitutions.* Number of different instances in which an object was given a new identity (e.g., pipe cleaner becomes a knife or bottle for baby, a doctor's kit becomes a telephone).
4. *Object onomatopoeia.* Number of vocal imitations of the sound property associated with an imaginary or existent object (e.g., "ring" for telephone, "vroom" for motor vehicle).
5. *Animate onomatopoeia.* Number of different vocal imitations of a sound property associated with an action by an animal or human being (e.g., "gulp" for drinking, eating or snoring sounds).
6. *Request for clarification of pretend versus reality.* Number of instances in which one play partner specifically requests confirmation about whether the other partner's behavior, including verbalizations and actions, are to be interpreted as pretense or reality (e.g. one child makes pretend crying sounds, and another responds by asking, "You crying for real?").

Reliabilities for these categories of behavior, based on 24 randomly chosen transcripts, ranged from 95% to 98% with a mean of 96%.

## RESULTS

### Types of Pretend Play

Table 5.1 presents the mean proportional frequencies for each type of pretend play in the high- and low-structure sessions for younger and older children respectively. As shown in Table 5.2, older children engaged in significantly more triadic sociodramatic play than younger children and girls engaged in significantly more triadic sociodramatic play than boys. These findings were tempered by a significant age X sex interaction. Neuman Keuls analyses indicated that older girls engaged in significantly more triadic sociodramatic play than younger girls, while boys did not differ by age. Neither the main effect of structure of play materials, nor the interaction of age and structure of play

TABLE 5.1
Pretend Play Among Triads in High- and Low-Structure Conditions:
Mean Proportional Frequencies

| | Types of Pretend Play | | | | | | |
| | Sociodramatic | | Associative | | Parallel | | |
| Condition | Tr | Dy | Tr | Dy | Tr | Dy | Solitary |
|---|---|---|---|---|---|---|---|
| Younger Triads | | | | | | | |
| Low-Structure | .02 | .03 | .01 | .00 | .01 | .01 | .06 |
| High-Structure | .03 | .05 | .01 | .02 | .03 | .05 | .59 |
| Older Triads | | | | | | | |
| Low-Structure | .13 | .13 | .13 | .07 | .01 | .01 | .18 |
| High-Structure | .23 | .09 | .03 | .06 | .00 | .02 | .33 |

materials, was statistically significant. However, the analysis of variance yielded a significant interaction of sex and structure of play materials.

Neuman Keuls analyses indicated that girls engaged in significantly more triadic sociodramatic play in the low-structure than in the high-structure sessions; for boys there was no significant difference. In addition, girls engaged in significantly more triadic sociodramatic play than boys in the low-structure sessions but not in the high-structure sessions. Contrary to the hypotheses set forth, correlated t-tests indicated no significant differences in the amount of triadic sociodramatic play younger or older children engaged in during the high- versus low-structure play sessions.

Analyses of the relative frequency of dyadic sociodramatic play revealed no significant main effect of age. A marginally significant effect of sex was found, which indicated that girls tended to engage in more dyadic sociodramatic play than boys. Neither the main effect of structure of play materials, nor any of the interaction effects, were statistically significant.

There were no significant main or interaction effects for the proportional frequency of triadic associative pretend play. Analysis of dyadic associative pretend play revealed no significant main effects of age, sex, or structure of play materials, but the interaction of age and sex was statistically significant. Neuman Keuls analyses indicated that younger girls engaged in significantly more dyadic associative play than younger boys, while older girls and boys did not differ significantly. Other interaction effects were nonsignificant.

Analyses of the proportional frequency of solitary pretend play revealed no significant main effects of age or sex. However, the main effect of structure of play materials was highly significant. Children engaged in significantly more solitary pretend play in the high-structure sessions. The interaction of age and structure of play materials was marginally significant and reflected a tendency for younger children to engage in more solitary pretend play in the high-structure sessions but not in the low-structure sessions.

## Properties of Pretend Play

For each property of pretend play, data for children in triads were summed and triads were treated as the unit for all analyses. A 2 (age) × 2 (sex) × 2 (high- vs. low-structure) repeated measures analysis of variance of the mean number (M) of different pretend themes generated by the triads indicated no significant main effects of age or sex. However, the main effect of structure of play materials was significant. Triads generated a significantly greater number of different pretense themes in the high-structure sessions. Boys elicited significantly more themes than girls in the high-structure condition but not in the low-structure condition.

Boys and girls enacted a total of 48 and 42 roles, respectively. Forty three (90%) of the roles enacted by boys and 36 (86%) of the roles enacted by girls could be clearly categorized as either familial, occupational, or fantastic. Within this categorical scheme, the most frequent type of role enacted by the boys was fantastic (40%), followed by occupational (32%), and familial (28%). In contrast, the most frequent type of role enacted by girls was familial (75%), followed by occupational (19%), and fantastic (6%). A Chi-Square analysis indicated that boys and girls differed significantly with respect to the types of roles enacted.

An analysis of variance of the mean number of substitutions indicated significant main effects of age, sex and structure of play materials. Older triads made significantly more substitutions than younger triads and girl triads made significantly more substitutions than boys. In addition, triads made strikingly more substitutions with the low-structure play materials than the high-structure play materials.

The analysis also yielded significant interactions of age and sex and sex and structure of play materials. Older girl triads made significantly more substitutions than younger girl triads, but older and younger boy triads did not differ significantly. Older triads made significantly more substitutions than younger triads with the low-structure play materials, but did not differ significantly for the high structure play materials. In addition, girl triads made significantly more substitutions with the low-structure than the high-structure play materials, but for boy triads, the difference was not significant. Girl triads made significantly more substitutions than boy triads with the low-structure play materials, but not with the high-structure materials.

Analysis of the mean number of object onomatopoeia made by the triads indicated no significant main effect of age or sex. However, the main effect of structure of play materials was significant. Triads made more object onomatopoeia with the high-structure play materials than the low-structure play materials. The analysis also yielded a highly significant interaction of sex and structure of play materials. Neuman Keuls analyses indicated that boy triads made significantly more object onomatopoeia than girl triads with the high-structure play materials. In contrast, girl triads made significantly more object onomatopoeia than boys with the low-structure play materials. In addition, while boys made significantly more object onomatopoeia with the high-structure play materials than the low-structure play materials, girls did not differ significantly.

TABLE 5.2
Statistical Analyses

1) *Types of Pretend Play*
   A.  Sociodramatic
         Older > Younger***
         Girls > Boys**
         Older Girls > Younger Girls**
         Low Structure > High Structure for Girls**
         Girls > Boys in Low Structure**
   B.  Dy Sociodramatic
         No significant effects
   C.  Tr Associative
         No significant effects
   D.  Dy Associative
         Younger Girls > Younger Boys*
   E.  Solitary
         High Structure > Low Structure
2) *Properties of Tr Pretend Play*
   A.  Different Themes
         High Structure > Low Structure (M) = 2.5 vs. 1.5**
         Boys > Girls in High Structure (M) = 2.5 vs. 1.75*
   B.  Role Enactment
         Sex ($X^2$ = 19, 2df)***
   C.  Substitutions
         Older > Younger (M) = 10.67 vs. 5.17***
         Girls > Boys (M) = 12 vs. 3.83***
         Low Structure > High Structure (M) = 13.33 vs. 2.5***
         Older Girls > Younger Girls (M) = 16.5 vs. 7.5**
         Older > Younger in Low Structure (M) = 18.7 vs. 8**
         Low Structure > High Structure for Girls (M) = 21 vs. 3**
         Girls > Boys with Low Structure (M) = 21 vs. 6**
   D.  Object Onomatopoeia
         High Structure > Low Structure*
         Boys > Girls in High Structure (M) = 3.8 vs. 1.4**
         Girls > Boys in Low Structure (M) = 2 vs. .25*
         High Structure > Low Structure for Boys (M) = 3.8 vs. 1.4**
   E.  Animate Onomatopoeia
         No significant effects
Triad Information: N = 3 for both Girl and Boy triads

*p < .05 (M) = Mean Number, **p < .01 Tr = Triadic, ***p < .001 Dy = Dyadic, All F Statistics df = (1,8)

Analysis of the mean number of animate onomatopoeia revealed a marginally significant main effect of age which reflected a tendency for older triads to make more animate onomatopoeia than younger triads. There were no other significant main or interaction effects. Analysis of the number of requests for clarification of pretend versus reality revealed no significant main or interaction effects. Few order of session effects within the two high-structure sessions and the two low-structure sessions were found.

## Degree of Similarity Between the Signifier (Substitute Object) and Signified (Referent) in Girls' Object Substitutions

Unlike the more task-like procedures employed in previous studies (e.g., Elder & Pederson, 1978; Fein, 1975), this study allowed examination of children's spontaneous use of objects during symbolic play in a setting substantially free of adult constraints. It was conducted in collaboration with Martha Smith, a graduate student in Developmental Psychology at the University of Michigan. Of particular interest was the extent to which children spontaneously chose substitute objects generally similar or dissimilar to the referent or signified object. The aim was to examine more closely dimensions of similarity on which substitute objects and their referents conformed. Because of the relatively low frequency of substitutions among boys, and because few substitutions were made with the high-structure playthings, only the data for girls during the two low-structure sessions will be examined.

For each substitution, the degree of similarity between the signifier and signified was evaluated by means of four categories. For each substitution, a score of one was given for each category where there was a match between the attribute of the signifier and those of the signified. The four categories were:

1. *Animation.* Both the signifier and signified are inanimate objects (e.g., block as signifier and telephone as signified) as opposed to an inanimate-animate combination (e.g., pipe cleaner as signifier and mouse as signified).
2. *Functional Equivalence.* The signifier and signified can be used in an identical manner (e.g., empty can as signifier and cup as signified).
3. *Form.* The signifier and the signified are similar in terms of physical properties, i.e., shape, length, or height (e.g., pipe cleaner as signifier and straw or cigarette as signified).
4. *Texture Equivalence.* The signifier and signified are made of the same material (e.g., cloth as signifier and bed sheet as signified).

The transformation score for each substitution was the total number of categories in which there was a match between the features of the signifier and those of the signified. The maximum score, indicating a high degree of similarity between the signifier and signified, was four, and the minimum score was zero. Mean similarity ratings for each triad were calculated. The substitutions were scored by two independent raters. Inter-rater reliability ranged from 96% to 100% with a mean of 98%.

Eliminating redundancies, older girl triads made a total of 95 object substitutions, while younger girl triads made a total of 44. Preliminary analyses of the mean proportion of substitutions involving each category of similarity revealed no significant age effects. Therefore, the data were collapsed over age. In 97% of the substitutions, there was agreement between the signifier and the signified in terms of the animation category. In 44% of the substitutions, form was a dimension of similarity. Function and texture were relevant dimensions of similarity in 33% and 23% of the substitutions, respectively.

Agreement between the signifier and signified in terms of the animation category did not appear to be a sensitive indicator of similarity since such agreement characterized 97% of the substitutions. Therefore, animation was eliminated as a dimension of similarity and the data were reexamined using a simple two-category classification system:

1. *Similar.* Substitutions in which the signifier and the signified were similar on one or more of the three remaining dimensions of similarity (e.g., functional equivalence).
2. *Dissimilar.* Substitutions in which the signifier and the signified were not matched on any of the three dimensions of similarity.

This analysis indicated that 53% of the substitutions of the older girl triads in contrast with 29% of the substitutions of the younger girl triads were categorized as dissimilar. This difference was significant ($X^2$ (1) = 5.04, $p < .05$). Older girl triads, then, made significantly more substitutions characterized by considerable incongruence between the substitute object and its referent.

## Qualitative Analyses of Some of the Properties of Sociodramatic Play Among Girl Triads.

The high frequency with which girls engaged in sociodramatic play also provided the opportunity to examine some of the qualitative aspects of social pretend play.

*Clarification of Reality versus Pretend State.*   Researchers (McLoyd, 1979; Garvey, 1974; Vygotsky, 1978) have pointed out that in order to play with each other, play partners must recognize that a state of social play obtains. That is, social play requires a firm grasp of nonplay, reality, or what play is not. Children's use of the words "pretend" and "really" is one type of evidence of their ability to make this distinction. Children in the present study, especially girls, made frequent use of these words, as when a child substituted one object for another (e.g., "Pretend this is the heater right here, ok.") or created an imaginary situation (e.g., "Pretend we're at home now"). Particularly striking are instances in which one play partner specifically requests clarification about whether the other partner's actions are to be interpreted as pretense or reality. Eighteen separate occurrences of such requests were recorded, all of which occurred among the older girl triads. These requests for clarification suggested that the ambiguity in meaning required resolution before the requestor could respond appropriately to the other play partner. An illustration of specific requests for clarification of the reality versus pretense state among older girl triads is given in Table 5.3.

*Role reversal.*    Underlying sociodramatic play is the ability to jointly construct the theme of the activity and negotiate the roles and actions necessary for execution of the theme. One play partner may undergo a role change without feedback or discussion from the other play partner, so long as the role change is consistent with the jointly constructed theme. In contrast, role reversals, by their very nature, require a minimal amount of discussion, or at least acknowledgement of the reversal, since one child is supplanting the role of another. The interdependent nature of sociodramatic play necessitates that the other child assume a different and complementary role. In the case of a complete role reversal, the role assumed by the first partner is the previous role of the second partner, and vice versa.

Though several occurrences of role change were recorded for girl triads, role reversal was rather infrequent. A total of eight separate role reversals were recorded, seven of which occurred among the older girl triads. In six of the eight instances, the child who was the initiator of the role reversal was playing a subordinate family role (e.g., baby, younger sister) and was requesting that she be allowed to assume a superordinate family role (e.g., mother, father, older sister). In one of the requests, this direction was reversed, and in another (i.e., mother to doctor), the hierarchical relationship was less distinct. An illustration of role reversal is given in Table 5.4.

## DISCUSSION

In the present study, high-structure play materials significantly increased the frequency of solitary pretend play, irrespective of age and sex, and the variety of pretend themes and object onomatopoeia among boy triads. Low-structure play materials significantly increased the frequency of triadic sociodramatic play, substitutions, and object onomatopoeia among girl, but not boy triads. Thus, sex, rather than age as predicted, was the critical determinant of how play materials of differential structure affected triadic sociodramatic play. Irrespective of structure of play materials, younger girl triads engaged in significantly more dyadic associative pretend play than younger boy triads, and girl triads tended to engage in more dyadic sociodramatic play than boy triads.

TABLE 5.3
Clarification of Reality Versus Pretend State
Among 5-Year-Old Triads

| X | Y | Z |
|---|---|---|
| (X pretends to be the mother, Y the father, and Z the baby) | | |
| What? What you want baby? What's wrong? | You crying for real? Oh, I thought you was crying for real. | (playing with pipecleaners) Mommy, guess what? (makes crying sounds) No. |
| What's wrong, baby? | | Do this Mom. Do this Mom. (hands paper and pipecleaner to X) |
| (X pretends to be older sister, Y the mother, and Z the little sister) | | |
| For real? | (taking cloth off of Z) It's time to wake up. You gotta use the bathroom? OK, go to the bathroom | I've got to pee-pee. Not for real, for play. (goes behind table and squats) Mommy, I can't flush the toilet. |
| (Same girls, same roles) | | |
| (picks up pipecleaner) I got the key. | Go outside. | Mommy, Mommy, I want to outside. Give me the key. Give me the key. |
| | (to Z) No! You don't need the key, baby. OK, go outside with sister. (examining ankle) No. I'm bleeding. | Can we go outside? |
| (runs over to Y) For real? (opens door to speak to research assistant) Do you have some bandaids? ____, the big girl, she's bleeding. | I'm bleeding. Yeah. | I'm sleepy For real? |

TABLE 5.4
Role Reversal Among a 5-Year-Old Female Triad

| X | Y | Z |
|---|---|---|
| | (Initially, Z is mother, Y the older sister, and X the baby. After the change is executed, Z is the baby, Y the mother, and X the older sister) | |
| | (as though calling to someone outside) Theresa, Theresa, come in. (hits X with paper towel roll) | |
| | | (as though speaking to imaginary person at door) Would you keep her (referring to X) over your house, 'cause I'm fixing to go to work? |
| | (to X) Go get in that bed. | Stay in that bed. |
| | (to X) Get in that bed. | (to Z) Come here, come here girl. Let me take you out of that bathtub (holding a piece of cloth as if using it for a towel to wrap around Y as she pretends to take Y from imaginary tub) Come (attempting to lift Y) |
| | Let me be the mother now. | OK, I'll be the baby. |
| | OK, come on baby. (lifts Z, carries her across room) | |
| I'm the big sister. | Mmm (yes). How old you going to be? How old you going to be? | |
| Mmm (pausing as if deliberating). The big sister. | How old? | |
| | (carrying Z, and rocking her back and forth) | |
| Thirteen. | | |

The pattern of finding suggest that Sutton-Smith's (1972b) "two cultures of games" thesis, is too undifferentiated and simplistic. Girls in the present study showed twice as much triadic sociodramatic play in the low-structure condition than in the high-structure condition, a finding at variance with Sutton-Smith's prediction. At the same time, children in the present study engaged in strikingly more solitary pretend play in the high-structure condition. Also, younger girls engaged in almost three times as much dyadic sociodramatic play in the high-structure condition, though this difference was not significant.

The latter two findings are consonant with Sutton-Smith's hypothesis. Replica and nonreplica play materials appear to affect different types of pretend play, specifically triadic sociodramatic and solitary pretend play, quite differently. The finding that triads, especially girls, made far more spontaneous substitutions with the low-structure play materials than with the high-structure play materials, challenges Sutton-Smith's contention that low-income children's play is primarily replica-bound and nontransformational. Furthermore, girls showed a clear developmental pattern toward increasing dissimilarity between substitute objects and their referents. This finding is contrary to Smilansky's (1968) conclusion that economically disadvantaged children show no progress with age in their use of objects during play.

An intriguing question is, why do older girls engage in substantially more triadic sociodramatic play in the low-structure condition than in the high-structure condition? Because of their lack of clear cut functions and atypicality, particularly in the complete absence of high-structure play materials, the low-structure play materials may have represented a challenge for the older girls to "do" something with them. Perhaps engaging in triadic sociodramatic play was the easiest way for them to respond to that challenge. On the other hand, the low-structure toy condition, was a less constraining and intrusive backdrop against which girls could express their competencies in both pretense and peer interaction. In any case, a number of the children, girls in particular, commented about the unusual nature of the low-structure play materials and asked where the high-structure play materials were, when low-structure sessions followed the high-structure sessions.

Children in the present study engaged in significantly more solitary pretend play in the high-structure condition. This is consistent with McGhee et al.'s (1981) finding that among black preschool boys, high-structure toys were played with in a solitary, pretense manner longer than low-structure toys. However, it is inconsistent with Phillips' (1945) finding that play materials of different structure have no effect on amount of solitary pretend play.

The properties of the replica play materials used in the present study were sufficiently attractive that children presumably derived meaning and pleasure from them independently of other triad members. In contrast, for older girls at least, it appeared that low-structure play materials were attractive only to the extent of a triadic shared exchange. If we assume that the low-structure play materials in the present study were less complex than the high-structure play materials, the pattern of findings for older girls appears consonant with Scholtz and Ellis' (1975) finding that peer interaction decreases as the complexity of play objects increases.

Data for the younger girls' sociodramatic play might be interpreted as indicating that the complexity of peer interaction (i.e., triadic versus dyadic) decreases as the complexity of the play objects increases. The findings further suggest that this effect is likely to be obtained only if the children in question, in this case girls, have already attained a relatively high level of competence in peer interaction. Otherwise, the complexity of the play object is likely to affect the degree of solitary pretense, but not cooperative or interactive role-playing, as was the case for boys in the present study.

## Is More Necessarily Better? Putting Play in the Context of Afro-American Culture

The significance and implications of this study of situational determinants of pretend play would be far more distinct if we more clearly understood the functions or correlates of pretend play among low-income and black children. Schwartzman (1976) has argued against just such a criterion, noting that research can and should be evaluated on the basis of what it tells us about children's play, rather than cognition, social structure, or culture contact.

In the absence of data which establishes the relationship between children's play and other valued social and cognitive skills, it is risky to suggest practical implications. A particularly instructive example of how our value of a particular behavior shifts in relation to other behaviors is the case of solitary play. As Moore, Evertson, and Brophy (1974) pointed out, solitary play has traditionally been viewed as evidence of nonsociability and immaturity, and therefore a behavior which should be discouraged, or at least not encouraged. These researchers found, however, that certain types of solitary play were positively related to goal-directed activity. This finding was interpreted as indicating that some types of solitary play are functional in school situations and indicative of maturity, rather than immaturity.

The issue of how pretend play relates to black children's social and cognitive development needs to be assessed in view of certain cultural values and life circumstances. It is conceivable, for example, that certain types of pretend play (e.g., fantastic roles) may impede the development of necessary survival and coping skills among black youngsters. The converse possibility is even more intriguing. Are children who engage in high frequencies of certain types of pretend play more likely to challenge the existing social order? In short, do they show a proclivity toward critical or dialectical thinking?

The issue of unequal distribution of resources and power raises another question, that of the utility and necessity of role-taking and its potential relationship to play. It has been suggested that role-taking competence increases as social status and power decreases (Baumrind, 1977; Thomas, Franks, & Calonico, 1970). The explanation for this relationship is that low-status people, lacking power, derive control by responding in such a way to maximize reward and minimize punishment—outcomes which are significantly enhanced by the ability to accurately anticipate, and in turn, manipulate, the responses and desires of those who have power as a result of high social status. There is some research which indicates that black boys are significantly better than white boys at both depicting emotions so that observers perceive them correctly, as well as identifying the emotions of others (Gitter, Black, & Mostofsky, 1972).

Role-taking ability may relate not only to relationships between high- and low-status persons, but also to relationships among low-status persons. Actually, the notion of soul suggests that one has both insight into, and empathy with, the often adverse circumstances of one's peers (Hannerz, 1969). Are certain types of play among black children important in the ability to negotiate hierarchical relations, perceive emotions accurately, and to empathize with others? If indeed these are important values and goals in Afro-American culture, and if they are advanced by certain types of play, such play should then be encouraged.

In short, it may be less a question of how much of certain types of pretend play low-income and black children engage in, but for what purpose? Naturalistic and longitudinal research are sorely needed to address these more focused, sophisticated, and culturally relevant questions. However, we concur with Schwartzman (1976) that studies are needed which provide information on both texts (description of the play or game event itself) and contexts (social, psychological, or environmental correlates of the event).

## Play as a Phenomenon in Afro-American Culture

Huizinga (1950) examined play as a social and cultural construction. Huizinga's macro-level analysis of play is quite distinct from the study of play as it manifests itself in the individual child. He attempts to demonstrate the myriad ways by which play permeates all archetypal activities of human society (including language, contest, law, poetry, and other cultural expressions). Huizinga's analysis appears applicable to all cultures; take, for example, Afro-American vernacular.

Folb (1980) concluded that the "front" is a recurring image expressed in the vernacular of black teenagers. The expression "front off" means to show off what you are or what you have, especially in the context of male–female interaction. The front, according to Folb, represents a strategy by which teenagers play out their attempts to exert power over another's personal and psychological space. She likens it to the persona or masks we wear for the world to see; it is the role or roles we assume for the duration of the play. Some human interaction, then, might well be characterized as playing out one's scene with companions and friends as a human backdrop. While these examples are taken from the language of black teenagers, similar expressions can likely be found in the language of black adults.

There are other aspects of Afro-American culture (e.g., movement, contests) infused with elements of play which should be explored. Also, the extent or manner in which play elements are found in social expressions should be explored. For example, do children who perceive school as boring, hostile, and alienating infuse their academic performance with play elements differently from children who perceive school in more positive terms? To what extent do persons who hold boring, tedious, and terminal jobs introduce play elements into their work to make it more tolerable? What is the cultural significance of these play elements? These and related questions suggest that the study of play has cultural and social relevance which can be delineated only if such studies expand their parameters.

## ACKNOWLEDGMENTS

Partial support for this research was provided by National Institute of Mental Health grant no. MH 36519–01, a Faculty Research Grant from the University of Michigan, and the Hampton-Michigan Project funded by the National Institute of Education. I wish to express sincere appreciation to Joyce Cowan and Dwight Walls, administrators of the preschool center, and the teachers, children, and parents for their cooperation. Special thanks to Betty Morrison and Mutombo Mpanya for their continued support and advice, and Martha Smith and Kathy Wilcox for their assistance in data collection. Several undergraduate students were helpful in data processing, especially Melinda Stewart, Roger Smith, Jane Stein, Helen Gammie, and Bernice Holman.

# 6 Ethnicity as a Variable in Child Development

Elsie G. J. Moore
*Arizona State University*

America is a culturally pluralistic society. While a substantial decline in the significance of ethnicity is expected with each succeeding generation of native born groups (Blau & Duncan, 1967), in reality, ethnicity persists as an important source of identity (Glazer & Moynihan, 1963; Greeley, 1974). As investigators have attempted to understand the factors which contribute to the persistence of ethnic identification, both sociological and psychological components have emerged.

It is the purpose of this paper to suggest how the ethnicity of the child-rearing environment influences children's test performance. The specific focus of this work is the comparison of the intelligence test performance of two groups of black children, one group adopted by middle-class white families, the second group adopted by middle-class black families. It also compares the dynamics of the different ethnic child-rearing environments which may contribute to the differential test achievement observed for the two groups of black children.

George De Vos (1975) attributes the persistence of ethnicity in America to the individual's need for a sense of continuity–belonging, which, from the perspective of psychology, is essential to the development of the sense of self. While not negating the importance of structural factors in the maintenance of ethnic identity, De Vos (1975) argues that, ultimately, ethnic identity provides meaning to the life of the individual. He states that

> Ethnicity . . . is in its narrowest sense a feeling of continuity with the past, a feeling that is maintained as an essential part of one's self-definition. Ethnicity is intimately related to the individual need for collective continuity. The individual senses to some degree a threat to his own survival if his group or lineage is

threatened with extinction. Ethnicity . . . includes a sense of personal survival in the historical continuity of the group. (p. 17)

Ultimately, ethnicity is a process variable which begins to have its effects in the earliest interactions between mother and child, and continues to have its effect as parents attempt to shape the child's emerging physical and cognitive capacities. Therefore, a lifespan perspective on human development requires analysis of how socialization in different ethnic groups affects behavioral development from childhood through later life.

Unfortunately, the significance of ethnicity has been effectively ignored in the conceptual models of human development as they are applied to minority status groups in this country. There has been a tendency among American social scientists to conceptualize the nature and consequences of minority status in terms of deviation from the normative system established for the majority culture. The deviation approach has been particularly characteristic of investigators' attempts to conceptualize the development of minority status children. This is especially relevant when the lower standardized intelligence test performances and school achievement levels of minority children—relative to white children—are considered.

Sociologists posit that the structural conditions encountered by various groups and their descendants are important factors in the continual significance of ethnicity. Yancey, Ericksen, and Juliani (1976) argue:

. . .ethnicity defined in terms of frequent patterns of association and identification with common origins . . . is generated and becomes crystallized under conditions of residential stability and segregation, common occupational positions, and dependence on local institutions and services. (p. 399)

From the perspective of these theorists, ethnicity is an emergent phenomenon because the forms of the ethnic culture change as the social positions of the groups and individuals change.

Attempts to understand the meaning and origins of between-group differences in intelligence test achievement have stimulated considerable research. The theoretical and practical significance of test score differences between groups arises from two important assumptions underlying the traditional use of intelligence tests. The first is that intelligence tests yield valid and reliable measures of the intellectual functioning of all children. Secondly, the apparent differences in functioning, indexed by test scores, are assumed to play an important causal role in differential school achievement (Eckberg, 1979). Theorists who subscribe to these assumptions view the lower average scores observed for minority status children as evidence of deficits in their intellectual competence. Therefore, proponents of the deficit perspective locate responsibility for poor children's (and children from certain ethnic groups) school achievement difficulties with the children, rather than with the school systems and their failure to provide adequate instruction (Labov, 1972b; Boykin, 1979).

Performance differences between black and white children have been a particular focus of research in this area. There has been some consensus among investigators regarding the meaning of the difference. The most prevalent view has been that black children's lower test scores are indicative of deficits in their cognitive functioning, specific skill development, and/or their socioemotional functioning.

The hereditary proponents measured intelligence as a general ability underlying all specific cognitive functions, and have attempted to document that black children's intellectual deficiencies are genetic in origin (Eysenck, 1971; Herrnstein, 1971; Jensen, 1969). Theorists who subscribe to traditional environmental arguments have attempted to identify linkages between deficits in black children's home environments and the suppression of their specific skill development. This results, according to their argument, in black children's lower average test performance (Bereiter & Engelman, 1966; Dave, 1963; Deutsch et al., 1964; Hess & Shipman, 1965; Karnes et al., 1970).

As a consequence of the different views concerning the origins of black–white differences in intelligence test performance, this between-group difference continues to be the focus of vigorous debate among investigators in the area. Environmental proponents (Deutsch, 1973; Golden et al., 1971; Lesser, Fifer, & Clark, 1965) argue that comparisons are valid only where black and white child-rearing environments are standardized with regard to variables shown to affect children's intelligence test performance. Since such controls have not been used with most of the data from which hereditary proponents work, environmentalists have rejected the hereditary position.

However, there are data which indicate that even when socioeconomic status is controlled, significant differences in the average test achievement of black and white children are still observed (Sitkei & Meyers, 1969; McQueen & Browning, 1960; Nichols & Anderson, 1973; Trotman, 1977). From the hereditary perspective, black–white differences observed under such control conditions offer strong evidence of the genetic basis of this between-group difference in intelligence test achievement. These particular findings present important challenges to the traditional environment explanations. If socioeconomic status is an efficient index of the correlates of intelligence test achievement for all ethnic groups, then the tenability of hereditary formulations is strengthened. If it is concluded that socioeconomic status is not an efficient predictor of the occurrence of specific environmental correlates of test achievement for all ethnic groups, then the environment proponents must rethink their positions on the relationship between socioeconomic status, ethnicity, and intelligence. One could conclude that the black child-rearing environment, regardless of socioeconomic status, suffers from the "cultural deprivation" syndrome. One could also conclude, as we do here, that the significance of ethnicity as a variable in the differential achievement of black and white children on standardized intellectual measures and in school performance needs to be further and more carefully explored.

## ETHNICITY AS A VARIABLE IN BLACK CHILDREN'S INTELLIGENCE TEST PERFORMANCE

The term ethnic group denotes a self-perceived social grouping, within a larger cultural or social system, which is distinguished by a variety of traits. These include religious and linguistic characteristics; distinctive skin pigmentation; geographical or national origin; aesthetic cultural patterns; and socially transmitted way of life (De Vos, 1975; Montague, 1964). The influence that ethnicity of the rearing environment exerts on children's intellectual performance has been documented by numerous investigators (Lesser, Fifer, & Clark, 1965; Stodolsky & Lesser, 1967; Werner, Simonian, & Smith, 1968). These studies show different patterns of intellectual performance among the various ethnic groups observed. The differences in the patterning of tested abilities remain, even when social class is controlled.

In view of the considerable research on black–white differences in test performance and school achievement, the characteristics of black ethnicity and their relationship to black children's intellectual performance and achievement have not been the focus of systematic inquiry. The research evidence strongly suggests that the historical circumstances of black Americans in this country has resulted in the development and persistence of a distinctive culture. Young (1970) concluded from her observations on the childrearing of rural southern black families that there are distinctive cultural patterns which exist in the black community. These mediate the personality development of black children. The work of this investigator indicates that the black community may encourage a greater people orientation among its children than object orientation, which appears more characteristic of Anglo-Americans. Further, according to Young, black families value and encourage idiosyncratic behavior on the part of their children, which sharply contrasts with the conformity values expressed by the white middle-class.

Consistent with Young's observations, Hale (1980) notes, that the strong emphasis on personal uniqueness, or what she terms "style", observed in the black community provides an alternative frame of reference by which black children may develop a positive self-concept. Hale posits, that black Americans (because of socioeconomic constraints) have had to obtain respect and admiration from their peers through personal attributes, hence the value emphasis on style observed for blacks. Cohen (1969) observes that black children are characterized by a relational cognitive style, while an analytical style is more typical of white children, particularly middle-class white children. However, the school context expects and requires intelligence in the analytical mode.

In addition to differences between black and white children in their relative person–object orientations, behavioral conformity, and cognitive styles, investigators have also observed differences between the two groups in their achievement orientations. It has been generally concluded that black children are less motivated in academic situations to be correct for the sake of correctness alone, and are willing to settle for lower levels of achievement success (Seitz et al., 1975; Zigler & Butterfield, 1968). Findings such as these have encouraged some investigators to argue that black children's achievement deficiencies stem from the failure of black families to socialize the children to persist on tasks which do not offer immediate extrinsic reward (Stodolsky and Lesser, 1967).

Banks, McQuater, and Hubbard (1979) take issue with this conceptualization and point to the methodological shortcomings of the supporting research. They do not argue that the black community devalues tasks related to academic performance. Rather, they suggest that within the interest-value hierarchy of the black subculture, such tasks may occupy a lower position than others because of limited opportunities for their early practice and performance. Indeed, these researchers provide data which show that when the interest value of the task is controlled, no significant difference in the persistence behavior of blacks and whites is observed.

Traditionally, in the measurement of intelligence, it is assumed that all children are equally motivated to do well. However, as the foregoing discussion indicates, children from different ethnic groups may enter the test situation with not only a different set of skills, but also with different attitudes, orientations, and interests than those expected by the test developers. Cole and Bruner (1971) hypothesize that discontinuities between what children from different groups bring to the test situation and the demands/expectations of the test best explain consistently observed between-group differences in children's test achievement. From their perspective, the apparent deficits in the intellectual ability of low-scoring groups are related to the testing procedure. The selection of test items generally fails to recognize the cultural diversity of American society in areas likely to influence children's test performance.

## THE STUDY

The conceptual model underlying the present investigation of the childrearing practices and attitudes of adoptive black and white mothers, and the relationship of childrearing orientations to children's intelligence test performance is the cultural difference framework outlined by Cole and Bruner (1971). Based on the work of previous investigators, it was expected that black children adopted by black families would achieve significantly lower WISC (Wechsler Intelligence Scale for Children) scores than black children adopted by white families (Trotman, 1977). This expectation was also based on previously observed differences in the two groups' PPVT (Peabody Picture Vocabulary Test) scores obtained when the children were approximately 4 years old. Because all of the families included in the sample were middle-class, the effects of income on any observed differences between the two groups would be controlled. Because all the children in the sample were socially classified black children, it was assumed that potential genetic sources of variance were also controlled. With these controls established in the research design, the influence of ethnic childrearing environment on any observed differences in the children's test achievement could be assessed.

The child-rearing attitudes and practices of interest were the adoptive mothers' attitudes toward independence training and the development of achievement orientations in their children. Previous research suggests that differences in black and white children's achievement orientations may contribute to observed differences in intelligence test achievement (Zigler & Butterfield, 1968; Zigler, Abelson & Seitz, 1973). The apparent relationship between children's achievement motivation and the independence training provided by their mothers also differed by race. (Baumrind, 1970, 1972; Rosen, 1956; Winterbottom, 1958).

While other research posits that black children's lower achievement motivations contribute to lower test performance, the present investigation explores the possibility that black and white families differ in the relative encouragement given to two types of achievement motivation. Theorists now recognize the existence of two types of achievement orientations; one responsive to external pressures, the other dependent upon internal standards, or autonomous achievement motivation. The strength of each type is related to parents' encouragement of one or the other (Smith, 1969; Veroff, 1969). Since the relative strength of children's autonomous achievement orientation may be an important factor in their willingness to perform difficult tasks in virtual social isolation, differences between the two groups of children in the apparent strength of each type of achievement motivation were explored.

## METHODS

Forty three of the 46 adoptive families who participated in this study were drawn from a larger sample of adoptive families participating in a longitudinal study conducted by one of the two agencies which made all of the placements of the children included in the sample. The total longitudinal sample includes 36 traditional adoptive families (black families who adopted black children), and 36 transracial adoptive families (white families who adopted black children). Three of the families included in the sample for the current study declined participation although they had earlier participated in the agency's longitudinal study.

The total sample was 23 traditional adoptive families, and an equal number of transracial adoptive families. Within the traditional adoptive sample there were 14 males and 9 females. The transracial sample included 10 males and 13 females. A review of the agency's files on the traditional and transracial adoptive families who did not participate in this investigation revealed no significant differences (Socioeconomic status (SES) and background) from the families who chose to participate.

At the time of data collection, the mean age of the transracially adopted children was 8.6 years, with a range of 7.2 to 10.8 years. The mean age of the traditionally adopted children was 8.6 years, with a range of 7.8 years to 10.1 years. No significant differences were observed between the two groups of adopted black children in their average age at adoptive placement, average birthweight, Apgar rating, or biological mother's health rating at the time of delivery. In contrast, the average educational attainment among biological mothers of transracially adopted children was significantly higher (12.6 years of education and 11.7 years of education). The average age of transracially adopted children's biological mothers was significantly lower (20.96 years versus 23.44 years). However, the mean age of biological mothers with traditionally adopted children was inflated somewhat by the inclusion of two older mothers, one age 40 at the time of delivery, the other age 36.

Children of racially mixed parentage and children of black parents were not normally distributed between the two types of adoptive placements. There was a disproportionate occurrence of biracial children in the white adoptive homes (N=14 as compared to N=6 in the black homes). This issue was discussed with agency personnel who confirmed that this distribution did not occur by chance. The situation did not result from selective placement aimed at matching genotype and environment, but rather resulted from the agency's attempts to satisfy adoptive parents' preferences for children whose physical characteristics resembled their own.

All adoptive families included in the sample are middle-class as defined by Warner's Index of Status Characteristics (1949). The two groups of adoptive mothers are comparable in average educational attainment (white mothers average 16.0 years, black mothers average 15.7 years). Mean educational attainment of white adoptive fathers (17.3 years) is significantly higher (17.3 versus 15.6 years). The median income of black families was also significantly higher ($37,000 versus $26,000). Income differences between black and white adoptive families were largely due to the higher proportion of working mothers in the black adoptive homes. Seventeen of the black mothers worked outside the home, compared to four of the white mothers. White families had more children in the home, an average of 3.35 children versus 1.7. The majority of the black families resided in the city (15 families), while a majority of the white families lived in the suburbs (14 families). Most of the black families also lived in predominantly black neighborhoods (14 families) while the majority of white families (16) resided in largely white neighborhoods.

All of the children in the two adoptive subsamples attended preschool, however the traditionally adopted children attended preschool significantly earlier

(3.0 versus 3.7 years). Again the factor of differing rates of maternal employment in transracial and traditional families should be considered. The two groups of children also differed in the racial composition of their friendship networks. Parents of transracially adopted children indicated that they had more white friends. Transracially adopted children were also involved in more activities outside of school, such as dance lessons, gynmastics classes, music lessons, organized sports, and social organizations (average 5.6 versus 2.7 activities). Black adoptive mothers were more likely to indicate that their children played mostly at home. Finally, the reading levels of the classmates of the two groups of adopted children were examined. The average reading level of transracially adopted children's classmates exceeds that of traditionally adopted children's classmates at all grade levels except first grade. As grade level increased, the disparity between the average reading level of transracially and traditionally adopted children's classmates widened (See Moore, 1980).

*Child Measures.*    All data collection occurred in the children's homes. The first tasks administered were those designed to assess the children's achievement orientations. The initial task was one developed by Veroff (1969) to assess children's level of social comparison achievement motivation. The child was shown three identical envelopes aligned left to right before him. He was told that there was something inside each envelope for him to do, and starting with the envelope on the child's left the tester pointed and described the first task as something that most children of his age found easy. The second task was one which some children of that age found easy and some found hard and the third was a task that most children found hard to do. The child was then asked to choose the envelope containing the task which he felt he would like to perform. The choice of the middle envelope, or the one some children the child's age found easy to do and some find hard to do, was coded as high social comparison because it was assumed that the child was using social comparison as the basis for his achievement interest.

The task used to assess the children's autonomous achievement level was also developed by Veroff (1969), and involves the child in trying to remember all the familiar objects pasted on a sheet of paper. Eight sheets of paper were used with 2, 3, 5, 7, 9, 13, 16, and 20 familiar objects pasted on them. The child was presented each sheet of paper in order and told to try to remember because he would be asked to recall what was on the page. After two failures, the child was shown the first page, the last success, the first failure, and the second failure. He was told that he would be permitted to try one more page, and was asked to choose which he would most like to try again. The choice of either of the two middle tasks was assumed to be a choice of a challenge because each of them represented one that the child had been able to succeed at or had just missed. Since the middle tasks were relative to the child's own ability, it was assumed that the choice would reflect autonomous achievement striving.

Next the child was administered the Wechsler Intelligence Scale for Children (WISC). The same tester administered the WISC to all the children. The tester was a black female, experienced in the administration of the WISC. One observer was present during each test administration to record the behavior and verbalizations of the child during testing. A taperecording of the child's verbalizations during the test administration was also made.

*Mother Measures.* While the child was in the testing session, the adoptive mother was asked to respond to a questionaire designed to assess her attitudes and practices related to independence training. The questionnaire contained items from the Winterbottom (1958) and Smith (1969) schedules. Included were questions pertaining to demands for independence and mastery, restrictions imposed on the child's independence strivings, and the age at which the mother expects the child to have learned the independence demands and restrictions. The mothers were also asked to indicate the types of rewards and punishments used to encourage independent mastery or discourage failure to comform to restrictions.

After completing the questionaire, mothers were asked to perform a sorting task developed to ascertain the extent to which the mother valued different types of achievement qualities in their children. The mother was given 21 cards on which were printed different independence values. She was asked to sort the cards into three stacks of seven cards, the first containing those qualities she considered most important in children. The second set of seven was to include the qualities considered important, but not as important as those qualities included in the first stack of seven. The third stack included those qualities she considered least important for her child to possess.

Among the qulaities typed on the cards, nine were identified as independence qualities, such as "being explorative and curious", six were social comparison qualities, such as "doing well in competitive games", and six were autonomous achievement qualities, such as "doing his/her best at tasks" (Smith, 1969). The 21 cards were presented to each of the mothers in the same order. The average ratings given by the two groups of adoptive mothers for each quality were tabulated to assess differences between them in their independence and achievement values.

## RESULTS

The transracially adopted black children achieved a mean WISC full scale score of 117.1, while the traditionally adopted black children achieved a mean of 103.6. This 13.5 point difference in the two groups' scoring is significant, and of the magnitude typically observed between black and white children. It should be noted, however, that the mean score observed for the traditionally adopted black children was substantially higher than that observed for black children in general.

Similarly, the mean score observed for the transracially adopted black children was considerably higher than that observed for white children in general. No significant sex differences in achievement were observed within-group, and the between-group differences in scoring were similar across the WISC subscales.

Due to the disproportionate occurrence of biracial children in the white adoptive homes, a comparison of the scoring of these children with children having same race parents within each adoptive subsample was made. As can be seen in Table 6.1, children with same race parents placed in white adoptive homes achieved a full scale WISC score of 118.0, while biracial children in white adoptive homes achieved a full scale score of 116.5. Scores on the WISC subscales showed similar differences in favor of children of single parentage, although these differences were not significant. A different pattern in scoring emerged between the two groups of children within the traditional adoptive placement. In this group, biracial children achieved a mean full scale score of 105.7, while children of same race parents averaged 102.9. Similar differences between these two groups within the traditional adoptive subsample were found across the WISC subscales. However, in this case, favoring the biracial children; these differences were not significant.

The only significant correlates of children's test achievement were the demographic characteristics of their adoptive families. The children's full scale scores were positively correlated with adoptive mothers' education (r=.38), and adoptive fathers' education (r=.51). Significant relationships were also observed between their full scale scores and the number of whites in their neighborhood (r=.51), and the number of white children in their friendship network (r=.51). As might be expected, their scores were significantly related to the average reading level of their classmates (r=.49).

## Adoptive Mothers' Attitudes Toward Independence Training

Parents' independence training attitudes and practices have been found to be associated with children's achievement motivation and intellectual performance. The mean age of independence training indicated by adoptive mothers was analyzed for between-group differences on this childrearing dimension. Black adoptive mothers indicated significantly later independence demands than did white adoptive mothers (mean age of 6.6 versus 5.1 years). No significant differences in the age of independence demands were observed between mothers of girls and mothers of boys, nor did educational attainment significantly influence their expressed views on this dimension.

The average number of restrictions indicated by the two groups of adopted mothers, and the average age at which they expected their children to have learned the restrictions, were tabulated. These aspects of the family's childrearing appeared to affect achievement orientation and academic performance. It

TABLE 6.1

Mean Verbal, Performance, and Full Scale WISC Scores by Adoptive Status, Racial Admixture, and Sex

| | Traditional | | | | | | Transracial | | | | | |
| | Black | | | Biracial | | | Black | | | Biracial | | |
| Scale | M | F | All | M | F | All | M | F | All | M | F | All |
|---|---|---|---|---|---|---|---|---|---|---|---|---|
| Verbal | 101.0 | 105.6 | 102.9 | 105.7 | 107.0 | 106.2 | 114.3 | 119.3 | 116.1 | 113.5 | 118.0 | 116.1 |
| | (9.4)* | (14.3) | (11.9) | (13.6) | (8.0) | (12.1) | (12.5) | (8.8) | (10.9) | (0.3) | (9.74) | (10.2) |
| Perfor-mance | 101.8 | 104.7 | 103.0 | 109.8 | 97.0 | 105.5 | 117.5 | 116.4 | 116.9 | 115.3 | 117.1 | 116.3 |
| | (13.7) | (10.5) | (12.6) | (13.9) | (6.0) | (13.4) | (12.4) | (8.0) | (10.2) | (10.4) | (5.9) | (8.2) |
| Full | 100.8 | 105.9 | 102.9 | 107.5 | 102.0 | 105.7 | 117.5 | 118.4 | 118.0 | 114.7 | 117.8 | 116.5 |
| | (11.5) | (10.0) | (11.4) | (12.6) | (1.0) | (10.7) | (13.1) | (8.1) | (11.1) | (8.7) | (7.9) | (7.9) |
| N = | 10 | 7 | 17 | 4 | 2 | 6 | 4 | 5 | 9 | 6 | 8 | 14 |

*Number in parentheses is the standard deviation.

111

TABLE 6.2
Correlations Among Mothers' Independence Training Practices,
Selected Family Demographic Characteristics,
and Children's WISC Achievement (N=46)

|  | Age of Demands | Number of Restrictions | Age of Restrictions |
|---|---|---|---|
| Number of Children in family | −.16 | −.21 | −.18 |
| Mother's Employment (1=employed; 2=not) | .21 | −.34* | .19 |
| Verbal IQ | −.17 | −.32* | −.21 |
| Performance IQ | −.31* | −.37* | −.17 |
| Full Scale IQ | −.31 | −.43** | −.14 |

*p < .05
**p < .01

seemed that the fewer the restrictions imposed by parents, and the earlier such restrictions were imposed, the more positive the effect on children's motivation and skill development (Baumrind, 1970; Winterbottom, 1958).

Black adoptive mothers imposed significantly more restrictions on their children's behavior (13.5 versus 8.9 restrictions), and imposed these restrictions significantly later (6.3 versus 5.1 years) than reported by the white adoptive mothers. Neither the age of the child, the sex of the child, nor the educational level of the mother were found to relate to their attitudes toward the imposition of restrictions.

Adoptive mothers' attitudes toward independence training, and the imposition of restrictions on their children's autonomous strivings, were found to be significantly related to their children's WISC performance. Table 6.2 shows the observed correlations between the family demographic characteristics expected to influence mothers' child-rearing attitudes and the children's WISC achievement.

TABLE 6.3
Effects of Adoptive Mothers' Race on Ratings of Autonomous
Achievement, Social Comparison Achievement,
and Independence Scale Items

| Variable | Hypothesis Univariate | | |
|---|---|---|---|
|  | Mean Square | F | p-Level |
| Autonomous Achievement Motivation Scale | 0.0010 | .0024 | .9614 |
| Independence Scale | 7.4027 | 23.7294 | .0001 |
| Social Comparison Achievement Scale | 2.3989 | 8.1814 | .0073 |

Mothers with more children may require early independence to accommodate the needs of all, and may be more comfortable in their motherhood role, given their greater experience in parenting. Working mothers, because they must be away from children a good deal of time, may impose more restrictions to satisfy their safety concerns. As can be seen, the number of children in the family is not significantly related to the mothers' independence training practices. However, mothers' employment did result in a higher number of imposed restrictions. Significant negative relationships were observed between children's verbal scale and full scale performance; age, when restrictions were imposed, showed no significant relationship to the children's achievement.

## Adoptive Mothers' Attitudes Toward Achievement Qualities in Their Children

It was hypothesized that the apparent lack of achievement motivation of black children observed by other investigators may result from the fact that black parents encourage a greater social comparison achievement orientation in their children. When conditions are not met to evoke this achievement orientation, as in the standardized testing situation, the child fails to strive. To test this hypothesis, the mean ratings of importance provided by the mothers for each the independence, autonomous, and social comparison scales were transformed to multivariate logits and submitted to multivariate analysis of variance, with sex of the child, education of the mother, and adoptive status, as independent variables in the test model. No significant interaction effects were observed, and the only main effect was for adoptive status.

Table 6.3 shows that significant race differences were observed for adoptive mothers' ratings of independence scale and social comparison achievement items, though not for the autonomous achievement scale items by sex of child, mothers' education and adoptive status. White adoptive mothers rated independence qualities as significantly more important. However, black adoptive mothers rated social comparison qualities as more important. Both groups of mothers rated autonomous achievement striving in their children as very important.

Results obtained for the two groups of adopted children's achievement orientations were not consistent with their mothers' expressed values. Twelve of the traditionally adopted children were rated as high autonomous. The observed frequencies of the two groups ratings were significantly different for autonomous achievement, (chi-square = 7.7, df=1, p < .01). However, no significant differences were observed between the two groups in social comparison achievement motivation. Based on parental ratings for these types of achievement qualities, one would have predicted differences in children's achievement orientations in the opposite direction.

These data are also inconsistent with the Ruhland and Feld (1977) finding of no significant differences between black and white working-class children (grades one and four) in level of autonomous achievement striving, but significant differences between the races in social comparison achievement. This inconsistency may be due to the uniqueness of the present sample. However, it could also be related to the nature of the task, requiring that the children memorize objects. The social comparison task was a relatively neutral one, since the children did not know what was inside the envelopes. Of course, Ruhland and Feld used similar tasks in their study and obtained different results.

## CONCLUSION

The data presented here show that when black children are socialized in the white middle-class normative system, their performance on standardized intelligence measures is comparable to, if not better than, that of similarly socialized white peers. The data also show that when socioeconomic status is controlled, significant differences in the child-rearing practices of black and white adoptive mothers are observed. These differences are related to the differential achievement of their black children on standardized intelligence tests.

The tradition in American social science is to interpret findings on black families and their children in terms of the Anglo-American, middle-class definitions of competence (such as IQ), and appropriate socialization procedures. Were this tradition followed here, one might conclude that the black middle-class families in this study suffer the cultural deprivation syndrome. However, to draw inferences about the functioning of black families based on their deviation from the middle-class white normative system is invalid. It has yet to be documented that competence is, can, or should be defined in the same way for both groups. Erickson (1968) states that in attempting to interpret cultural differences in child-rearing we must remember:

> There is . . . some intrinsic wisdom, some unconscious planning . . . in the seemingly arbitrary varieties of child training. But there is also a logic—however instinctive and unscientific—in the assumption that what is "good for the child", what *may* happen to him, depends on what he is supposed to become and where. (p. 99)

Ogbu (1978) posits that black Americans have historically occupied lower caste positions in a racially stratified society where the distribution of socially valued statuses is skewed to favor the white upper caste. It would therefore be illogical to expect that competence would be defined by the two groups in the same way. As Ogbu notes, we have little information about the attributes and qualities necessary for black children to function competently in this, a racist society. More research aimed at illuminating the logic of black families' child training is needed.

All that can be safely concluded from the present investigation is that ethnicity of the rearing environment affects the development of competence *as defined by intelligence test performance*. If this is to be taken as the operational definition of competence for black children, then transracially adopted children show a greater level of competence than their traditionally adopted peers. However, the transracially adopted children are still identified as black by the larger society. We know so little about the qualities and attributes necessary for black children to become competent black adults.

It is not clear that the socialization processes contributing to higher test performance among transracially adopted black children will also make them more effective in their adult roles (than are traditionally adopted black children). An agency study of these children at age four, including data on social and emotional functioning, as well as cognitive achievement, offers some clues on this point. Results indicate that black children adopted by black families displayed higher levels of social and emotional adjustment than did black children adopted by white families. More research will be required to determine the effects of ethnic childrearing environment on black children's social, emotional and cognitive development into adulthood.

# 7 Towards a Model of Teacher– Child Transactional Processes Affecting Black Children's Academic Achievement

Bertha Garrett Holliday
*Peabody College of Vanderbilt University*

Black children's low academic achievement has been a persistent concern of contemporary child development research and intervention. There was a time, in the not too distant past, when child developmentalists were certain of the solutions for black children's academic achievement problems. Local school districts would be desegregated—thus eliminating racial isolation and inequitable school financing policies. Developmental and learning theories, social intervention strategies, and modernized instructional technology would be deployed simultaneously with the assistance of massive governmental funding. The deficits of educational organizations and practices, along with those of black children, would be radically altered.

But now, that era seems so very distant, and our certainties are shaken. It is not that past solutions were without effects. It is simply that those effects had neither the magnitude, nor duration, initially envisioned (e.g., Gray, Ramsey, & Klaus, 1981). And child developmentalists, witnessing increasing urban school resegregation and legal/legislative action against busing, and declining black achievement scores and federal support of education, must now acknowledge the audacity of earlier visions. Black children's school experiences and social, institutional and educational change processes are not as simple, nor as insular, as earlier experimental research findings suggested.

In this paper, an attempt is made to empirically explicate the complexities of black children's achievement as experienced in the classroom. This explication is informed by a transactional, theoretical perspective, which emphasizes the interrelationships among the psychological characteristics (e.g., attitudes and perceptions) of black children and their teachers, and the effects of these interrelationships on achievement. In support of these emphases, implications for change processes are discussed.

Why do black children tend to demonstrate low levels and rates of achievement? In responding to this question, researchers generally adopt one of two major theoretical perspectives. The individual difference perspective emphasizes analysis of black children's personal attributes. Examples of such attributes include: genetic intellectual deficits (Jensen, 1969; Shuey, 1966); low self-esteem (Clark & Clark, 1947; Dreger, 1973); social linguistic deficits (Hunt, 1969; Riessman, 1962); depressed need for achievement (Katz, 1969; McClelland, 1961); external locus of control (Battle & Rotter, 1963; Gurin, 1969); and resistance to delaying of gratification (Lessing, 1969; Sarbin, 1970). The social learning perspective emphasizes analysis of teachers' attributes and teacher-child interaction patterns. Examples of this perspective include studies of racial and social class bias both in teachers' attitudes, and in the type and frequency of their interactions with black students (Brophy & Good, 1974; Leacock, 1969; Rist, 1973).

Both perspectives lend themselves to somewhat narrow descriptions of the school experience. The individual difference perspective, in suggesting that the sources of black children's low achievement is primarily within the children themselves, fails to acknowledge the potential influence of other actors in the school experience. The social learning perspective, while recognizing that both teacher and child are primary actors, does not necessarily lead the researcher to explore the specific effects of deleterious teacher attitudes and behaviors on children's achievement.

This paper argues that the transactional perspective facilitates more complex description by focusing on the perceptions of settings by their inhabitants, and related effects on behavior. Specifically, the transactional perspective recognizes that: (1) behavior is a function of the reciprocal interaction of person and environment; (2) environments may be conceptualized as bounded spaces having social qualities (i.e., settings for action of self and other); (3) psychological processes (e.g., perceptions, expectations, attributions) mediate relationships between behavior and environment; (4) individuals and groups differ in perceptions of the content and meaning of any given social setting (Barker & Wright, 1949; Lewin, 1954; Stokols, 1977).

As a procedure, the transactional perspective allows us to understand black children's school experience as a set of attributes, attitudes and behaviors which are embedded in a distinct cultural and social status. We also are led to recognize that teachers' professional roles are embedded in a differing cultural and social status (Ogbu, 1978). But most significantly, the transactional perspective suggests that teacher and child are both components of the other's perception of, and action on, the social environment of school (Dewey & Bentley, 1973). These joint perceptions of teacher and child must be understood as a unitary segment of experience, and analyzed as such. Accordingly, in this paper, children's achievement is analyzed as an outcome of such joint experiences.

## THE LARGER STUDY

The analyses in this paper reanalyze the school data subset of a larger study (Holliday, 1978, 1981) concerning black children's behavioral competencies. These competencies refer to the frequency and effectiveness of black children's use of (1) functional life skills, e.g., communication, mobility and independence; (2) interpersonal skills with peers and adults; and (3) problem solving skills related to personal, interpersonal, technical, and social predicaments. The study investigated competence skills in the three settings of home, neighborhood (as reported by mothers) and school (as reported by teachers) and related physical and psychological environmental factors. Such factors included indicators of structured home environment, family size, crowding, family intactness, parental expectations, and children's self-esteem and locus of control.

No significant relationship was found between the children's total competence (scores on all three skills across three settings) and the physical and psychological environmental factors ($F = 1.25$; $p = .31$). There were no significant relationships between the children's home–neighborhood competence and their academic achievement ($F = .46$; $p = .71$). These results are compatible with Achenbach and Edelbrock's (1981) finding of minimal relationships between demographic variables and the reported social competence of 2600 children. Slaughter's (1977) finding of discontinuities between the early childhood home experiences and later school experiences of the 56 black children in her longitudinal study was also corroborated.

Findings of the larger study also indicated that the children changed their behavioral styles between home-neighborhood and school. At home and neighborhood, the children reportedly demonstrated greatest competence in problem solving skills. But at school, the children reportedly demonstrated greatest competence in interpersonal skills. One must remember that a child is not put out of school for being dumb, but for being disruptive and failing to get along with others. The children's school interpersonal skill scores (which were the highest of the study's nine skill-by-setting competence scores) suggest that school is an arena where demands for academic excellence compete with those for interpersonal excellence.

These, and other findings of the larger study, suggest that we can enrich the substantive interpretation of our findings about black children's achievement by attending to the ecological and behavioral structure of these children's lives in multiple settings (Bronfenbrenner, 1979a & b). As Ogbu (in this volume) notes, these structures and the behaviors they dictate contribute to the unique cultural imperative of black development.

Lewin (1951, 1954) has characterized the structure of person-environment interactions as a "lifespace". An urban black child's lifespace can be conceptualized as consisting of seven hierarchical lifespheres: (a) the child; (b) the family or home; (c) the neighborhood; (d) the black community; (e) the service or reference community (i.e., predominantly white administered and/or owned services, businesses, and institutions located in the black community); (f) the broader community; and (g) social structure. Each of these spheres is distinguished from the others by differing socializing agents and differing opportunities for role-taking and accomplishment.

Within the lifespace framework, the overall task of human development is to ease the transitions between spheres, and thereby, to facilitate progressive personal differentiation and integration. Such transitions occur along the dimensions of time (affective, cognitive, and social experiencing of the past, present, and future) and space (physical and social settings) (Berger & Luckmann, 1966; Erickson, 1968; Riegel, 1976). To affect transitions, it is necessary to gain facility in various developmental-socialization skill areas.

However, for black children, such transitions are fraught with historically rooted barriers which limit access to large portions of the lifespace as one proceeds upward through the spheres. These barriers result from beliefs and practices of the institutional and social structural levels, and result in inequitable distribution of status, income, power, and wealth. In response to such barriers, black children must attempt to develop skills appropriate for meeting both the social demands of black and white communities, and negotiating transitions between these communities (Peters, 1978).

The school is the major social institution confronting all black American children by age six. For many of these children, the school presents them with their first (and frequently devastating) encounter with the values of the broader society. Thus, for black children, school is not only a setting for learning basic academic skills and knowledge—it is also a setting for significantly demonstrating one's ability to negotiate transitions between black and white communities through the use of bicultural strategies. And, as previously noted, mastery of these strategies is complicated by the school's competing demands for academic and interpersonal excellence. Indeed, one might speculate that these competing demands are the central focus of black children's negotiation and bicultural efforts.

The analyses that follow elaborate the structure and impact of the school's competing demands by investigating the effects of teacher-child transactional processes on achievement.

## METHOD

### Subjects

The 44 black children (22 male, 22 female) of the study were from low and moderate income families having a 1978 modal gross income in the range of $5000 to $8900. The children were 9 (N = 29) and 10 (N = 15) years of age, and enrolled in integrated, but predominantly minority, public schools located in their neighborhoods in a medium size southwestern city.

The study's sampling procedures facilitated the selection of children experiencing similar ecological worlds. U.S. Census Block Data (1970) were used to identify a geographic area (2 miles by 1 mile) inhabited predominantly by low and moderate income black families. We then identified within this area, all moderate income government subsidized housing units. A 14-item screening questionnaire was administered on a door-to-door basis to determine if households included children who met the study's social and environmental criteria. Interviews and tests were administered orally to the children and their mothers in their homes by trained black female examiners. School data were collected from the children's classroom teachers and their cumulative school records.

## School Data Instruments and Indicators

Teachers of the study children completed a newly developed two part 48-item Teacher Rating of Behavior Competence (Spearman-Brown reliability: r = .84). Part A consisted of five point rating scales for the eight school activities of reading, arithmetic, oral language, written language, spelling, handwriting, classroom behavior, and playground behavior. On each of these activities, teachers rated the study children's behavior ''compared to other children of this age.'' Part A scores were viewed as highly reactive to personal judgement and served as indicators of teachers' *attitudes* towards the children.

Part B consisted of 40 items assessing children's functional life, interpersonal, and problem solving skills at school. Each item was rated on a three point scale of frequency or effectiveness of skill demonstration. In comparison to Part A items, these items were far more focused and structured. Consequently, Part B scores served as indicators of teachers' *perceptions* of the children's school competence. Part B items were drawn from varied sources (Doll, 1947; Gesten, 1976; Lambert, Windmiller & Cole, 1974; Mercer & Lewis, 1980; Stott & Sykes, 1967). Other items were newly developed. All items were submitted to a panel of judges for skill area assignment, and assessment of content and wording.

We then obtained the children's grade point averages and California Achievements Test scores in math and reading. The former served as indicators of teachers' *evaluations* of children, and the latter served as the study's dependent variable. Children, individually and orally, were administered the Coopersmith (1975) Self-Esteem Inventory, Form A, and the Bialer-Cromwell (Bialer, 1961) Children's Locus of Control Scale.

## Analysis

Descriptive analysis of the school variables involved statistics of mean tendency and variability. Analyses of variable effects and relationships were accomplished through use of correlation, partial correlation, two way ($2 \times 2$ fixed effects with equal cells) analysis of variance, and two way analysis of covariance. In the latter two procedures, the effects of sex and competence groups (high and low) were assessed on each of the school data indicators. The major study variables' joint effect on achievement was assessed through multiple regression analysis.

## RESULTS

### Descriptive Analyses

Descriptive statistics for the school variable indicators are presented in Table 7.1. The children were characterized by positive self-esteem and internal loci of control. Although the children exhibited relatively low percentile scores on math

TABLE 7.1
Descriptive Data on the Study's Major Variables

| Variables | Minimum Sample Score | Maximum Sample Score | Mean | SD |
|---|---|---|---|---|
| *Child Generated* | | | | |
| School of Self-Esteem | 2.00 | 8.00 | 5.32 | 1.39 |
| Locus of Control | 9.00 | 16.00 | 12.80 | 1.98 |
| Math Achievement[1] | 1.00 | 69.00 | 32.30 | 19.32 |
| Reading Achievement[1] | 1.00 | 86.00 | 34.10 | 22.81 |
| *Teacher Generated* | | | | |
| Total-Teacher Attitudes (ratings) | 8.00 | 34.00 | 21.39 | 6.86 |
| 1) Reading | 1.00 | 4.00 | 2.76 | .88 |
| 2) Arithmetic | 1.00 | 4.00 | 2.79 | .81 |
| 3) Oral Language | 1.00 | 4.00 | 2.83 | .70 |
| 4) Written Language | 1.00 | 4.00 | 2.60 | .80 |
| 5) Spelling | 1.00 | 4.00 | 2.81 | .83 |
| 6) Handwriting | 1.00 | 4.00 | 2.81 | .77 |
| 7) Classroom Behavior | 1.00 | 5.00 | 2.92 | .86 |
| 8) Playground Behavior | 1.00 | 5.00 | 3.10 | .82 |
| Total School Competence (perception)[2] | 46.00 | 91.00 | 70.60 | 9.40 |
| 1) Functional Life Skills[2] | 42.00 | 91.00 | 67.30 | 11.86 |
| 2) Interpersonal Skills[2] | 48.00 | 97.00 | 74.03 | 12.38 |
| 3) Problem Solving Skills[2] | 45.00 | 93.00 | 71.43 | 9.68 |
| Grade Point Average[3] | 1.80 | 3.60 | 2.94 | .36 |

[1]Achievement scores are reported in percentiles

[2]Competence scores are reported in recoded form (i.e., a uniform 100-point scale) to facilitate ease of comparison.

[3]Grade point averages are on a 4-point scale

achievement ($\bar{x} = 32.30$, $SD = 19.32$) and reading achievement ($\bar{x} = 34.10$, $SD = 22.81$), they obtained relatively high grade point averages ($\bar{x} = 2.94$ on a 4 point scale, $SD = .36$). Means on teacher ratings of the eight school activity areas were generally in the "below average" to "average" range.

## Effects and Relationships Among Variable Indicators

*Correlation and Partial Correlation Analyses.* As expected from the larger study's findings, scores on mothers' reports of children's competencies in the home and neighborhood, fail to correlate significantly with any school indicator. With the single exception of a significant correlation between sex and locus of control ($r = -.31$, $p < .05$, boys > girls), child indicators (school self-esteem, locus of control, and sex) neither correlated significantly with each other, nor with any other school indicator.

However, as expected, children's achievement test scores in reading and math correlated significantly ($r = .71$, $p < .001$). In addition, math and reading scores each correlated significantly with teacher ratings (attitudes) ($r = .37$ and .43, $p < .05$), and grade point average ($r = .54$ and .51, $p < .001$). Reading achievement alone correlated significantly with teachers' reports of children's school competence ($r = .34$, $p < .05$). All teacher indicators (teacher ratings, reports of children's school competence, grade point averages) significantly intercorrelated, with the strongest relationship occurring between teachers' ratings and teachers' reports of children's school competence ($r = .82$, $p < .001$).

Since numerous significant correlations were found, the data were submitted to partial correlation analyses to determine the extent to which the observed correlations were spurious. A series of partial correlation matrices were computed in which the effect of one of the study variables on the associative relationship among pairs of other variables, was controlled. When the effects of teacher ratings were controlled, the resulting partial correlations represented significant reductions (i.e., 10% or more in $r^2$) from zero-order correlations for the following variable paris: 1) school competence and grade point average (from $r_{xy} = .45$ to $r_{xy.z} = .17$), 2) school competence and reading achievement (from $r_{xy} = .45$ to $r_{xy.z} = -.07$), and 3) grade point average and reading achievement (from $r_{xy} = .51$ to $r_{xy.z} = .40$). Because it was assumed that teacher attitudes (ratings) causally precede all the affected partial correlation variables, the observed decrements are viewed as indicative of spurious correlations. The patterning of the zero-order correlations matrix substantiates the inference about the common dependence of the affected variable pairs on teacher attitudes.

*Analysis of variance (ANOVA) and analysis of covariance (ANCOVA).* As a means of exploring the effects of the two child status indicators of sex and competence, a series of two way ($2 \times 2$ fixed effects with equal cells) ANOVA's were performed. The children's high or low competence status was determined by a median score split on the sample's total competence score (i.e., composite scores of mothers' and teachers' reports).

As indicated in Table 7.2, significant effects were found on the teacher variable of school competence. However, no significant effects were observed on the other teacher variables (i.e., teacher attitudes and grade point averages). There also were no significant effects on the child variables of school self-esteem and reading achievement. However, a significant sex effect was evidenced on locus of control ($F(1,40) = 4.36$, $p < .05$), with boys being significantly more internal than girls. A significant sex by competence level interaction ($f(1,36) = 4.93$, $p < .05$) is shown on math achievement. Low competence boys demonstrate significantly higher math achievement than both low competence girls and high competence boys.

The previously reported partial correlation results suggested the need to explore the effects of the child status variables through analyses of covariance

TABLE 7.2
Significant Two-Way Analysis of Variance Effects

| Dependent Variables | df | MS | F | p |
|---|---|---|---|---|
| *School Competence* $MR^2 = .19$ | | | | |
| Main Effects | 2 | 1805.76 | 5.07 | .01 |
| Comp. Level | 1 | 2075.16 | 5.82 | .02 |
| Sex | 1 | 1699.80 | 4.77 | .04 |
| Interaction | 1 | 1056.94 | 2.96 | ns |
| Explained | 3 | 1556.16 | 4.37 | .01 |
| Residual | 40 | 356.32 | | |
| *Math Achievement* $MR^2 = .03$ | | | | |
| Main Effects | 2 | 241.50 | .70 | ns |
| Comp. Level | 1 | 369.14 | 1.07 | ns |
| Sex | 1 | 180.49 | .53 | ns |
| Interaction | 1 | 1694.09 | 4.93 | .03 |
| Explained | 3 | 725.69 | 2.11 | ns |
| Residual | 36 | 343.93 | | |
| *Locus of Control* $MR^2 = .10$ | | | | |
| Main Effects | 2 | 8.29 | 2.18 | ns |
| Comp. Level | 1 | .01 | .00 | ns |
| Sex | 1 | 16.57 | 4.36 | .04 |
| Interaction | 1 | .66 | .18 | ns |
| Explained | 3 | 5.74 | 1.51 | ns |
| Residual | 40 | 3.80 | | |

TABLE 7.3
Significant ANCOVA Effects with Teacher Attitudes as a Covariate

| Dependent Variable | df | MS | F | p |
|---|---|---|---|---|
| *School Competence* | | | | |
| $MR^2 = .75$ | | | | |
| Covariate | 1 | 14038.04 | 120.05 | .001 |
| Main Effects | 2 | 87.58 | .75 | ns |
| Comp. Level | 1 | 80.69 | .69 | ns |
| Sex | 1 | 117.34 | 1.00 | ns |
| Interaction | 1 | 147.65 | 1.26 | ns |
| Explained | 4 | 3590.21 | 30.70 | .001 |
| Residual | 39 | 116.93 | | |
| *Reading Achievement* | | | | |
| $MR^2 = .20$ | | | | |
| Covariate | 1 | 3075.20 | 7.85 | .008 |
| Main Effects | 2 | 332.50 | .85 | ns |
| Comp. Level | 1 | 400.90 | 1.02 | ns |
| Sex | 1 | 154.61 | .40 | ns |
| Interaction | 1 | 1643.48 | 4.20 | .05 |
| Explained | 4 | 1345.92 | 3.22 | .02 |
| Residual | 35 | 391.69 | | |
| *Math Achievement* | | | | |
| $MR^2 = .14$ | | | | |
| Covariate | 1 | 1944.00 | 6.56 | .02 |
| Main Effects | 2 | 66.07 | .22 | ns |
| Comp. Level | 1 | 101.10 | .34 | ns |
| Sex | 1 | 52.86 | .18 | ns |
| Interaction | 1 | 2111.58 | 7.12 | .01 |
| Explained | 4 | 1046.93 | 3.53 | .02 |
| Residual | 35 | 296.31 | | |

Note: Reading & Math Achievement data were not available for four subjects.

(ANCOVA) in which the effects of teacher attitudes as a covariate, were assessed and controlled.

As indicated in Table 7.3, teacher attitudes emerged as a significant covariate of teachers' reports of school competence ($F(1,39) = 120.05, p < .001$). Indeed, inclusion of this covariate in the prediction model for school competence resulted in both a marked increase, over the ANOVA model, in the variance accounted for (from $MR^2 = .19$ to $MR^2 = .75$), as well as elimination of the significant main effects. However, teacher attitudes is a nonsignificant covariate of grade point average.

On the child variables of both reading and math achievement, teacher attitudes emerged as a significant covariate ($F(1,35) = 7.85$ and $6.56, p < .05$). The addition of the covariate to these respective predictive models resulted in a

TABLE 7.4
Standard Multiple Regression
(DV = Total Academic Achievement)
Multiple $R$ = .678
$R^2$ = .460
$F(6,33)$ = 4.960***

| Independent Variable | Beta |
|---|---|
| Grade Point Average | .554*** |
| Total Teacher Attitudes | .478* |
| School Competence (Perceptions) | −.306 |
| Child School Self-Esteem | −.176 |
| Child Locus of Control | −.150 |
| Child's Sex | −.113 |

*p < .05
***p < .001

marked increase in the variance accounted for over the ANOVA models (from $MR^2$ = .06 and .03 to $MR^2$ = .20 and .14). For both models, inclusion of the covariate did not affect a change in the nonsignificance of the main effects. But a significant sex by competence level interaction effect did emerge on reading achievement ($F(1,36)$ = 4.20, $p < .05$; low boys > low girls; high girls > high boys), while the significant interaction on math achievement was maintained.

*Joint Variable Effects of Achievement.*    Multiple regression analysis was used to explore the study variables' joint effect on the children's academic achievement. For purposes of this analysis, total achievement (a composite of children's math and reading achievement scores) served as the dependent variable. This composite variable was constructed with consideration of the relatively high correlation ($r = .71$) existing between reading and math achievement. It should be noted that the dichotomous indicator of children's total competence (i.e., high or low group) was not included in the regression analysis because it is neither empirically nor conceptually independent from the school competence indicator.

The relationship between the six independent variables and academic achievement was highly significant ($MR^2$ = .678, $F(6,33)$ = 4.96, $p < .001$). Two of the six independent variables exhibited significant beta weights, indicating that high grade point average and highly positive teacher attitudes were significantly related to children's high academic achievement. Interestingly, the other independent variables (child's sex, school self-esteem and locus of control, and teacher's perceptions) were negatively and nonsignificantly related to high achievement (Table 7.4).

## DISCUSSION

### Data Interpretation

Empirical data are best interpreted with the assistance of a theory that suggests the causal order of observed relationships. In this study, such assistance was provided by Stokols' (1977) typology of human-environmental transactions. Stokols identified three kinds of functional transactions: orientation, operation, and evaluation. As postulated, these transactions assume causal ordering—that is, orientation precedes evaluation.

In relating Stokols' typology to the variables of current interest, it was assumed that teacher attitudes were representative of the orientation function; teacher perceptions (school competence) were representative of operation; grades given (GPA) were representative of the evaluation function. Consequently, teacher variables were assumed to be causally ordered as follows: Attitudes → Perceptions (School competence) → Grade point average. For the child variables, it was assumed that sex is an orientation variable, school self-esteem is representative of evaluation. Thus these variables were assumed to be causally ordered as follows: Sex → Locus of Control → School Self-esteem.

The analyses revealed the following major orientation effects: (1) correlation and ANOVA suggested that black boys when compared to black girls, had more internal locus of control, and were the objects of more negative teacher attitudes; (2) correlations suggested that positive teacher attitudes were associated with teachers' positive perceptions of children, high grade point averages, and children's high math and reading achievement scores; (3) partial correlations and ANOVA suggested that positive teacher attitudes predicted in part the relationship between positive teacher perceptions and high grade point average, positive teacher perceptions and high reading achievement, and high grade point average and high reading achievement. Major operation effects were indicated by significant correlations between teacher's positive perceptions, high grade point average and high reading achievement. Major evaluation effects were indicated by correlations which suggested that high grade point average was associated with high math and reading achievement.

A causal interpretation is further elaborated by the differential outcomes of the correlation and multiple regression analyses. These analyses suggest that the direction (positive and negative) of variable relationships differ according to whether one views these as bivariate or multivariate. Correlational analyses revealed primarily positive bivariate relationships between achievement indicators and the other school indicators. However, multiple regression analysis suggest that after controlling for the effects of more powerful predictors of achievement, high scores on the remaining school indicators are related to low achievement. Results of partial correlation and covariate analyses suggest that the differences in the direction of relationships result from the critical moderating influence of teacher attitudes.

Findings of the larger study on black children's competence illustrate the significance of the direct and moderating effects of teacher attitudes. The data suggest that mothers perceive the study of children as demonstrating highest competence in problem solving skills at home and in the neighborhood. These, and other findings of the larger study, suggest that black children are socialized to assume a posture of persistence, assertiveness, and problem solving. Numerous other studies of black child socialization validate this assumption (Baumrind, 1971, 1974; Halpern, 1973; Young, 1970).

But at the age of nine and ten, children studied apparently had not yet developed the maturity and resilience necessary for withstanding their day-to-day encounters with teachers' moderately low attitudes toward their assertive style of problem solving. We speculate that the effects of teacher attitudes transform young black children's achievement efforts into learned helplessness. One should remember that some of the achievement scores of the children in this study were as low as one percentile—indicating a total lack of effort.

One might further speculate that this transformation is facilitated by the school's competing demands for academic and interpersonal excellence. Numerous studies suggest that high academic achievement in black children is related to these children's positive interpersonal relationships with teachers, parents, and other adult significant others (e.g., Silverstein & Krate, 1975; St. John, 1971). Thus, high achieving black children are successfully meeting both of the school's demands. But low achieving black children, as indicated by the high level of their reported school interpersonal skills, choose to meet only the demand for interpersonal excellence. It is this demand which is most directly linked to these children's survival at school. Thus, the transactional processes of the classroom (e.g., teacher attitudes) along with institutional transactional processes (competing demands) jointly encourage academic incompetence.

A more theoretical explanation for the observed incompetence effects is provided by Dewey's (1967) admonition that intelligence is not individual, but social in character. As a social phenomenon, intelligence arises from those processes through which people attempt to actively adjust and shape their needs and resources to those prevailing in their environment. Thus people are guided in their actions by various meanings and norms which are internalized through transactional processes, and communicated through rules and regulations, expectations and attitudes, and verbal and nonverbal behaviors. The current study's findings suggest that the school's norms can militate against attaining recognized institutional goals when those norms are ambiguous and discontinuous from children's present and prior experience.

In general, the study's findings support a transactional perspective of black children's achievement. Teachers' attitudes and perceptions both affect and moderate children's academic achievements. Children's psychological processes are relatively insignificant predictors and moderators of both academic achievement and teachers' attitudes, perceptions, and evaluations. Child attributes (e.g., gender) directly influence both child and teacher attitudes, but minimally influence children's academic achievements. One can conclude that black children's academic efforts are minimally influenced by their own transactional processes, and significantly influenced by teachers' transactional processes.

## Implications

It should be emphasized that the small size of the study sample imposes inferential limitations on some of the reported findings. In particular, the causal interpretation of observed variable effects should be viewed as heuristic rather than definitive.

Several major studies have indicated that black children's school achievement is significantly influenced by such factors as cognitive style, intelligence, socioeconomic status, and linguistic competence. In light of such findings, it is somewhat surprising that the multiple regression analysis, which included no cognitive or intellectual indicators, accounted for 46% of the variance in these children's achievement. This finding suggests that social, developmental, cognitive, and other types of school interventions affecting black children might be most successful if buttressed by processes and procedures which effectively assess and re-engineer the role expectations and behaviors of teachers and children. Attempts in the direction of such role assessment and re-engineering are represented by Moos' (1979) ecological school social climate scales, and Plas' (1981) transactional school liasion intervention procedure. Of course, effects on teacher–child transactional processes resulting from such attempts should be monitored and reinforced at the classroom level.

The school's competing demands influence black children's academic achievement. In this regard, the effects of institutional racism cannot be minimized. Institutional racism is not characterized by the widespread prevalence of individual racist attitudes, but rather by policies, and the role behaviors they dictate (Knowles and Prewitt, 1969). Such policies probably account for much variance in teacher attitudes unexplained by the study's teacher-child variables. If this is indeed the case, attitude change among teachers cannot by itself be expected to significantly improve black children's achievement.

Teacher attitudes and teacher-child interactions operate in the context of institutional policy. For example, teachers with high expectations of, and sensitivities to, black children are typically unable to implement the institution's demands for academic excellence by refusing to promote significant proportions of their classes. Institutional policies such as those on student promotion and retention, tracking, teacher tenure, and dismissal, all too often facilitate incompetence in both teacher and black child outcomes.

In attempting to elaborate the effects of institutional policy on black children's achievement, any future research might explore transactional models of schools and school systems. Models at these more complex levels of analyses would incorporate indicators of institutional processes and related policy and behavioral outcomes.

## CONCLUSION

In this paper, transactionalism was used as a conceptual guide for analyzing and interpreting empirical indicators of processes occurring within natural settings. When used in these ways, the transactional perspective is distinguished by its focus on those behavioral and psychological mediators of relationships between persons and environments. These mediating processes lend meaning to human interactions and transform them into human experiences.

School experiences of black children are profoundly human experiences. Unfortuantely, they are also, all too often, destructive. The issues related to black children's school achievements are complex; so, too, will be their solutions. Child developmentalists must increasingly utilize those methods and theoretical perspectives which encompass complexities into our research and intervention designs. This paper suggests that the transactional perspective can provide significant directions towards that end.

# 8 The Coping Personality: A Study of Black Community College Students

Yvonne Abatso
*Bartlesville Wesleyan College*

There has been a great deal of research in the behavioral sciences on breakdown and maladaptation. Consistent with this larger trend, during the last decade, black student populations have frequently been studied in order to discover reasons for academic failure and underachievement. The focus of this study is the reverse; it is concerned with success. Why have some black students from lower socioeconomic levels overcome well-documented obstacles to succeed academically?

Those obstacles most frequently include social, economic, political, and psychological realities which result in limitations in choice of employment, schools, and residence. As members of a negatively valued minority group, these young people must learn a sense of self-competence within a societal framework which views their ethnic group members as incompetent, dependent, and powerless. Realistically, they must always consider the possible effect of their minority status on their risk-taking, expectations, and decision making. It is likely for them that the two major socializing institutions in their life—family and the school—will be overburdened with problems which complicate the implementation of their culturally assigned tasks.

In the midst of these kinds of environmental obstacles, how do some young people persist through secondary school, enter college, and achieve academic success? In the predominantly black community college setting where I taught, there were always minority students who appeared to share similar backgrounds and prior school experiences but who overcame the predictions of failure and excelled in their scholastic efforts. Conversations with these students suggested that the differences in their academic experiences were not exclusively a result of greater aptitude, but were often associated with nonintellectual personality characteristics and coping behavior differences.

The population under study reflects a demographic shift which has occurred in the last decade among black college students. These students are enrolled in a northern urban community college system which educates more than half of the minority status college students in Illinois (Holleb, 1972).

There has been very limited research on characteristics of community college students and their relationship to achievement (Bushnell & Zagaris, 1972). Cross (1968) described students in "open door colleges" as a new college population which differs from traditional college students in orientation toward achievement. This suggests that traditional predictors of success may need re-examination for this population. The interaction between nonintellectual factors, namely personality, motivational, and situational variables in predicting academic performance has been a useful framework in research (Gurin & Epps, 1975; Raynor, 1974; Brown, 1974).

This study suggests that an additional behavioral dimension—coping—should be explored in developing a predictive model for the attainment/achievement process among black community college students. Coping is conceptualized within the general framework of adaptation including the most causal and realistic forms of problem-solving.

The theory of achievement motivation proposed by Atkinson & Feather (1966) and the theory of coping developed by Lazarus et al (1974) provide a framework for looking at background constructs found to be correlates of achievement and coping. Four of these constructs appear to be particularly relevant when examining the psychological factors related to mastering academic demands and the ability to handle one's environment. These will be discussed in relationship to the inquiry undertaken in this study. The four constructs are: achievement motivation; expectancies; sense of self-competence; and achiever personality.

## Achievement Motivation

Achievement motivation based on an affective arousal model has been suggested as the most important personality characteristic related to achievement for all students (McClelland & Atkinson, 1953). The achievement motive was defined as a capacity for taking pride in accomplishment when success is achieved. In distinguishing the achievement motive from other motives, the McClelland team proposed that the expectations are built out of universal experiences in problem solving as well as involving the students' perception of performance in terms of standards of excellence. In their view, the achievement motive grew out of expectations which were influenced by the outcomes of prior experiences.

For this reason, it may also be an important variable in coping. However, because these achievement motives do not take into account social factors affecting the lives of black students, this construct alone is not sufficient for understanding achievement among black students. Therefore, successful achievement among black students must be examined by looking at broader societal perceptions and the cluster of personality characteristics and attitudes which characterize these students.

## Expectations

Two competency based expectations, the students' sense of personal control and academic self-confidence, were found to be significantly related to individual achievement as well as to educational/occupational aspirations by Gurin and Epps (1975). This research includes similar variables, but also attempts to specify some of the processes by which students seek to master the demands of the achievement/attainment process.

## Sense of Self-Competence

White (1959) has written extensively on the motivating quality of the concept of competence. He refers to the concept as the organism's capacity to interact effectively with the environment. Competence is attained by humans through prolonged years of learning. Smith (1968) describes competence as that inner-personality core which furnishes a person with the basis for feelings of hope and self-respect, resulting in positive interaction with the environment. Brookover et al's (1967) self-concept of ability represents an aspect of this overall sense of competence which should be related to academic coping.

## Achiever Personality

Miller and O'Connor's (1969) study shows that the best predictor of academic success for black college students at a midwest state university is the presence of an "achiever personality." Epps' (1969) study indicates that the high school student's perception of his own competence, as measured by Brookover, is a major correlate of academic achievement. Both studies found personality variables to have stronger positive correlations with black student grades than traditional aptitude measures.

Many studies have focused on isolated traits in attempting to understand the relationship between personality and achievement. This research sought to understand the multifaceted coping personality by attempting to discover personality attitudes which contribute to it, and by discovering the concrete ways it expresses itself. The study also examined the relationship between coping personality variables and achievement. The study's significance lies in its potential contributions to the development of a model of the educational achievement/attainment process for black students.

This research project involved three interrelated inquiries which sought to contribute to the achievement literature by explaining the components and correlates of coping. The three inquiries under investigation were:

1. What are the personality correlates of high coping? Are there significant age, sex, and socioeconomic differences in coping level?

2. What are the coping strategies of high coping students versus low coping students?
3. What is the relationship between coping personality/ability variables and achievement?

## CONCEPTUAL FRAMEWORK AND HYPOTHESES

The study assessed such broad coping properties as flexibility, reality orientation, future direction, problem solving, and appropriate handling of affect. These properties were examined as they related to a specific adaptive area—student problem solving efforts during the freshman year in a community college.

Lazarus and associates (1974) contend that three aspects of appraisal must be distinguished when seeking to understand coping. Primary appraisal concerns a judgment of the possible threat of a situation's outcome. Secondary appraisal is an assessment by the individual of the range of coping options through which the situation can be mastered. Thirdly, reappraisal refers to any change in the original perception based on the changing flow of external or internal conditions. Both productive and unproductive coping attempts are products of this mediating perception of expectancies. When the stakes are appraised as being high, stronger emotions are evoked and the probability is increased for ineffective coping strategies.

Since aptitude and verbal ability measures are insufficient for predicting achievement in black students (Temp, 1971), the coping variable was explored here as an additional variable which might yield more accurate prediction. The intention was to realize a more precise prediction of achievement, because existing formulas were unsatisfactory. An essential consideration was, that if coping proved to be significant, it offered promise for intervention since it represents learned behavior.

The attitude/personality constructs, achievement motivation, and expectancies, are a direct measure of Atkinson's tendency to achieve assessed by the Mehrabian instrument described later. The constructs, self-concept of ability and locus of control, relevant aspects of self-competence, are other dispositional variables upon which the appraisal process depends. These personality variables, along with the perception of the opportunity structure and expectancies, appear crucial in judgments related to answering the appraisal questions—What is required for success and do I possess what is necessary for mastery?

The essential goals of this research were to identify, with a view toward predicting, personality attitudes and perceptions which characterize high coping black college students. Previous research using similar conceptual models would lead one to expect certain personality variables to be positively related to coping. After establishing specific personality variables which correlate with coping, behavioral strategies were assessed. Lastly, it was questioned whether these characteristics were also related to high academic achievement for these community college students.

Based upon the conceptual models of Atkinson and Lazarus, the following hypotheses were proposed:

1. There is a personality syndrome associated with high coping for black community college students. Among the selected personality variables, self-concept of ability, locus of control, and expectation of success and failure (Mehrabian achievement motivation), will be, in that order, the most important discriminators between high and low copers.

   a) High copers will possess higher self-concepts of ability than low copers.
   b) High copers will express a greater sense of internal control than low copers.
   c) High copers will have more positive expectations about academic outcomes and employ more alternatives in obtaining their goals.

2. There will be a sex difference in coping levels with females being higher than males, but no difference in pattern across the personality variables which discriminate between high and low copers.

3. There will be a difference in coping levels between the older and younger age groups, the older student having a higher level than the younger, but no difference in pattern across the personality variables which discriminate between high and low copers.

4. There will be a difference in coping levels between the social classes. The middle socioeconomic class will be higher than the lower, but no difference in pattern across the personality variables which discriminate between high and low copers.

5. There will be differences in coping strategies between high and low copers. Within the high coping group, there will be a greater variety of profiles of coping strategies than in the low coping group.

6. High coping will be positively correlated with high achievement and will, along with verbal ability, contribute to the discriminating function.

## METHODOLOGY

The research plan consisted of an in-depth sample survey of 120 black community college students in which the personality variables were assessed. Differences within (rather than between, i.e. black vs. white) ethnic groups were explored.

Three coping groups (low, average, high) were separated out. Academically related coping strategies were examined to determine whether common patterns existed within coping groups and whether different strategies were used by high and low copers. Three achievement groups, based on total grade point average, were also studied to see if personality variables operated in relationship to varying achievement groups in the same manner as they functioned among coping groups. Since successful college work is usually highly correlated with verbal ability, a verbal ability measure was given and used in the analysis to determine whether this ability influenced coping or achievement level.

Demographic characteristics, age, sex, and socioeconomic status information were gathered and viewed as possible intervening variables. The following age groups were determined: 18–22, 23–27, 28–24, and 35 and over. Social class was based on the occupational/educational level of the father and mother according to the Duncan (1961) two-factor classification system.

The sampling plan was designed to obtain a reasonably representative sample of this urban community college population. The sample, consisting of six intact social science classes, was drawn from Social Science 101 because this course was required of all freshmen in the baccalaureate, technical, and vocational programs. The sample of 120 students was a subsample from a larger research study consisting of approximately 1500 Chicago City College students who were randomly selected from all the social science classes offered by the colleges.

Data collection procedures involved a self-report battery of instruments administered to the sample in two sessions within the social science classrooms. Students in the complete N took the complete battery of instruments. Students in the incomplete N missed one or two of the four instruments in the study. Comparison of the complete and incomplete samples failed to reveal any significant differences; therefore, the full N of 120 was used throughout data analysis except where indicated.

Discriminant function analysis with coping as the predicted variable, were used to test research hypothesis number one. The following ordering of personality variables was determined a priori in discriminating between low and high coping groups: Verbal Ability, Self-concept of Ability, Locus of Control, Menrabian Academic Motivation, and Perception of Opportunity Structure. Discriminant analysis is an efficient way to examine group differences on many variables in order to determine: whether groups differ significantly and, the combination of variables which best accounts for observed group differences. A Fortran IV program of multivariance was used for the discriminant analysis. The verbal measure was entered first in order to adjust for any ability differences within the coping groups. Analysis of variance was used to test the effects of four independent variables; coping (low, average, high), age (18–22, 23–27, 28–34, 35 and over), SES (low, low-middle, upper-middle and highest), and sex. Chi-square and contingency coefficients were used to examine coping strategies among the three coping groups. Finally, discriminant analysis of the achievement variable, grade point average, yielded insight into the relationship between coping personality/ability variables and achievement.

## Operational Definitions and Instrument Description

The following operational definitions of variables in the study and the instruments used to assess them will be described.

1. Coping (operational definition)—Behavior related to how students attempt to master the academic demands of the classroom; namely, the conditions which they set up and the ways in which they attempt to learn and study.

Coping instrument[1]—This instrument was used in the study to assess the outcome of the appraisal process proposed by Lazarus. It was designed by the researcher as a set of situational—if-then, open-ended questions. The instrument required that students imagine themselves in a realistic, problematic situation and describe how they would respond and why they would behave in such a way.

The coping instrument was content analyzed using coping criteria from Haan (1963), and was written in a manner which permitted students to use their own terms to explain attempts to cope with academic requirements and to report problem solving processes and strategies. The selected coping criteria follow:

1. Behavior involves choice and it is flexible and purposive.
2. Behavior is pulled toward the future and takes account of the needs of the present.
3. Behavior is oriented to the reality requirements of the present situation.
4. Behavior involves secondary process thinking, and is highly differentiated in response.
5. Behavior operates within the organism's necessity of "metering" the experiencing of disturbing affects.

Questions were asked about the following categories generally considered to be important in freshman year adjustment: (1) study skills and practices; (2) test preparation; (3) classroom participation; (4) relationship to instructor; (5) use of supportive services and college facilities; (6) resources for course advisement and support; and (7) relationship to peers.

Sample items from the coping instrument follow:

If an assignment is returned with a D grade on it, what do you usually do? What do you do when you get worried about an important examination coming up?

The coping construct was conceived of as a continuous variable. Therefore, responses to all questions were rated on a three point scale within each of the five coping criteria areas listed above. The three point scale used for rating varied

[1]Validity and reliability information is available from the investigator.

from little, to moderate, to high evidence of coping. Respondent scores were averaged and then grouped into three predetermined coping categories: low copers (mean score 0–1.6), average copers (1.7–2.3), and high copers (2.4–3.0).

A subsample of responses were content analyzed to establish categories of specific behaviors and practices and to determine whether patterns emerged which could be described as coping strategies. Behaviors were coded numerically to create profiles of various coping strategies, characteristics of different coping groups. This served as a criterion related validity test as well.

In addition to coping, the other variables are defined below:

2. Achievement—Measured by the student's total grade point average in major subjects at the end of freshman year in community college. Grades from academic courses, only, were included. These included from three to six courses. Three predetermined levels of low (GPA less than 2.0), average (2.0–2.99), and high (3.0 or higher) performing students, based on a four point scale were created.

3. Verbal Ability—The College Qualification Test by Bennett, Bennett and Wesman was used as a verbal ability measure. It consisted of 75 multiple choice vocabulary terms. Established junior college percentiles and norms are available.

4. Personality Variables

a. *Self-concept of ability*—an individual's subjective feelings about academic capabilities.

b. *Locus of control*—an individual's sense of personal control in relationship to environment. The concept of internality or externality relates to whether one believes one personally has impact on what happens to oneself or whether it is determined from outside.

c. *Achievement motivation*—a behavior disposition based on Atkinson's theory of achievement motivation which differentiates between high and low achievers. Specifically, high achievers have more positive feelings aroused by success than they have negative feelings aroused by failure.

d. *Perception of the opportunity structure*—a concept based on an individual's perception of whether the opportunity structure is open or closed to one. Perceptions are related to educational opportunities as well as occupational openings and advancement.

## RESULTS

The results of the data analysis will be discussed in relationship to the three main inquiries of the research.

### What Are the Personality Correlates of High Coping?

Coping groups differed on three personality variables—academic motivation, locus of control, and self-concept of ability. High copers were distinguished from average and low copers by a higher self-concept of ability and more internality in their locus of control. There were no significant differences among the three coping groups on the other personality variables. The high copers' strong sense of their academic capabilities and even stronger sense of internal control over their lives evidently moderated and contributed to their high coping performance. High copers were higher on all variables except perception of the opportunity structure.

Discriminant analysis was used to distinguish between coping groups. Two discriminating functions were identified. The first was a competency function with two major components—self concept of ability and locus of control. This function summarizes student feelings about self, namely confidence in academic capabilities and the ability to control events affecting one's life. Function one accounted for 85% of the variance explained by the discriminant analysis among the three groups. Function two, an expectancy function, had two contributing variables—perception of the opportunity structure and academic motivation. It reflects beliefs about how responsive the society will be to the individual's efforts. The predictive power of the discriminant analysis was 69% of cases correctly grouped. Because of the relative importance of function one, the competency function, the two personality variables which best characterized the high coping personality were a high self-concept of ability and an internal locus of control.

Problem one, which focused on a personality description of the high coping personality, proposed subsidiary issues related to whether these personality variables formed a common pattern across sex, age, and socioeconomic groupings. The results indicated no significant socioeconomic variation among the personality ability measures. The upper middle-class student who chooses a community college may have a lot in common with students from lower classes in personality and ability. At least once having enrolled in college, it appears that socioeconomic status has no significant influence on a student's personality/ability functioning.

It had been hypothesized that females would score higher than males on the personality/ability variables, this, however was not supported. The level of personality/ability variables, with two exceptions, were generalizable within both sexes. Males scored significantly higher on two of the variables, verbal ability ($\bar{X}=.5$ vs .3, $p<.01$) and self-concept of ability ($\bar{X}=7.3$ vs 6.6, $p<.05$).

Significant age differences were found, older students scored higher on the verbal ability and achievement measures. Older students also expressed greater internality as measured by the locus of control instrument. No significant age differences were found on the other four variables; self-concept of ability, coping, academic motivation, and perception of opportunity structure.

Verbal ability mean scores were highest among the oldest age group, students thirty five and over ($\bar{X}=.56$). This age group also had the highest ratio of men, the sex group which scored highest on verbal ability. The F ratio was significant at the .09 level. Grade point average, the achievement criterion, increased with advancing age, thus the oldest age group again had the highest mean.

Locus of control reflected the greatest age variation of all the personality variables. Older students expressed more internality in their locus of control. The greatest externality was evidenced among the youngest age group, 18–22 years olds ($\bar{X}=13.1$); externality was lowest in the oldest age group ($\bar{X}=11.3$).

The concept of a coping personality was supported as hypothesized and was generally constant across socioeconomic status, sex, and age. The personality variables which best separated high from low copers, high self-concept of ability and internal locus of control, are related to internal dispositions which are shaped by social interaction.

## Do High Copers Differ From Low Copers in Their Behavioral Strategies?

This study attempted to specify behavioral processes by examining the ways that varying copers actually responded to the expectations and demands of college. The open-ended coping instrument requested that students indicate how and why they engaged in certain academic practices in order to reveal the strategies employed in coping.

High copers, as predicted, employed more coping strategies with greater flexibility. Coping strategies were analyzed by assessing the extent to which each student indicated (on the coping instrument) practicing or using a particular skill or technique in the attempt to meet classroom demands.

High copers did indeed utilize different coping strategies than low copers. Differences between them are significant for academic expectancies, selection of courses, study skills, time management, exam preparation, classroom learning, and handling competition. High copers expressed more confidence in their ability to perform well academically. They were more often involved in conversations with teachers, at their own initiation, over subject matter under study. Better study skills were employed, which assisted the students in organizing their work and time and internalizing their subject matter. Scheduling on a daily and weekly basis occurred more frequently among high copers. Breaks of more than 15 minutes before class were utilized for review and study. Examination preparation included, not only extra reading, but review techniques. Skills related to gaining the most from lectures and class projects were developed. The behavior of high copers was characterized by persistence and an on-going attempt to engage structure for the propose of mastery. It was an active orientation toward life which utilized choices and decision making.

Not only did high copers prefer using certain techniques, but they possessed a larger repertoire of behaviors designed to accomplish specific tasks. While all students tried harder when faced with academic competition or failure, the high copers showed greater resourcefulness and flexibility, such as also studying with better students.

There were differences even in how courses were selected. High copers utilized many more people, including other teachers, in determining which courses to take. They had learned who to contact in the school organization for obtaining accurate information and getting personal recommendations.

Differences among the groups indicated that high copers had a more positive orientation, greater knowledge about concrete ways of achieving academic success, and more discipline in their study habits. It appears that the high copers bring to the academic situation a positive sense of their ability to perform academically and a belief that they can control the events in their own lives. This orientation expresses itself in specific skills designed to bring about desired ends.

## What Is the Relationship Between Coping, Personality/Ability Variables and Achievement?

The purpose of investigating coping was to lead eventually toward a better prediction of achievement. It was hypothesized that coping would be positively correlated with achievement and would be part of a linear combination that would contribute significantly to distinguishing high achievers. Correlations indicated that there was a positive relationship between coping and achievement. To explore these relationships further, discriminant analysis was computed using the personality/ability variables on the achievement criterion, and grade point average. Three variables, verbal ability, perception of the opportunity structure, and coping formed the significant combination that discriminated among achievement groups.

Verbal ability was the strongest component of discriminating function one, but high coping, as well as an open perception of the opportunity structure, composed the combination of variables which best separated the achievement groups. Since verbal ability was such a strong factor in function one, a partial correlation of grade point average and coping holding constant verbal ability was performed. It yielded a coefficient of .20. Coping is a construct positively related to achievement. When combined with an understanding of the language and a view of the opportunity structure as open and responsive, it inclines toward higher achievement.

## CONCLUSIONS AND IMPLICATIONS

The findings in this study support the hypothesis that group differences in coping for black community college students can be related to how they view themselves academically and their sense of control over events which affect their life. Self-concept of ability, locus of control, and academic motivation all have high positive correlations with academic achievement. All are variables influenced by learning and social impact. There does exist in these data a definable coping personality which distinguishes high copers from low copers. These same personality variables have been found in other research to be positively correlated with high achievement among black students. A high self-concept of ability and internal locus of control may therefore represent important components in the achievement/attainment process for black students.

High copers had confidence in their academic abilities. This attitude, combined with the belief that they had control over the events which affected their lives, resulted in a higher investment of time and energy in academic pursuits. Their expectation of success reflected their assessment of the effectiveness of their efforts to meet standards of excellence. It suggests the important cyclical relationship between the nature of one's social interaction and personality. Achievement motivation was a weaker contributor to the aggregate of personality correlates of high coping, thereby illustrating the need for more refined measurement of Atkinson's theory before determining its contribution to a conceptual framework for investigating coping.

The two more crucial aspects of personality, academic self-confidence and autonomy have been shown to be related to a person's level of behaving purposively and decisively toward the fulfillment of future goals. For this, in essence, is the summary of the central properties of coping. Results from this research go beyond linking these personality variables to academic achievement, as has been done in the past. Our findings suggest that these traits may be viewed as correlates of specific ways of behaving, with implications for academic achievement as well as other areas of challenge or opportunity in life.

The data confirm the importance of internal and external factors for understanding the coping achievement syndrome among black college students. The role of expectation common to both Atkinson's achievement and Lazarus' coping models was assessed by three kinds of expectations—locus of control, self-concept of ability, and the student's estimate of the chances for success. These different aspects significantly differentiated between coping groups. Instrumental behavior was a product of the mediation of expectancies as proposed in both models.

The sex differences observed did not support a theory of black females as more ambitious, or dominant, than black males. Although higher proportions of females attended the college, males measured higher on self-concept of ability and verbal ability measures. Nevertheless, there was a high ratio of females among the high copers which questions the implications of Horner's (1968) theory for black women from lower socioeconomic classes.

Older students reflected a pattern of higher self-concept of ability, higher verbal scores and higher grades. These mutually reinforcing traits may be due to increased opportunity for learning gained through the experience of living. They may also reflect the decline in secondary academic standards, or may be indicative of a trend for better qualified older persons to return to school in order to improve their occupational options. Females in the older age groups expressed a high level of internality in their personal control.

The assessment of coping strategies provided insight into what these personality constructs mean behaviorally. They represented significant differences among the coping groups in the areas of: academic expectations, amount of student–faculty interaction, course selection, level of study skills, time management, examination preparation, classroom learning techniques, and the way in which one handles competition.

The study clearly indicates the importance of academic coping strategies and positive expectations in assuring continued persistence. The low copers, as compared to the higher copers, often relied on a system of trial and error which may account for a pattern of drop-out and return prevalent among this group. Atkinson, Lens and Malley's (1976) revised theory of achievement motivation takes into account the effect of strength of motivation on the proportion of time spent in the activity. The more strongly motivated student would typically spend more time actively listening in class, as well as more time studying outside of class.

The coping strategies specified the varying routes by which students attempted to master the academic demands of their college life. They also pointed out areas of possible intervention since they appeared to be learned (and therefore teachable) skills. High copers employed multiple coping strategies, sought out side help more often, and persisted longer. They thereby increased the possibility of reappraisal which Lazarus proposed as so important in successful coping. High copers, initiated more contact with the teacher and were positively reinforced. Almost all students who initiated contact reported receiving some form of help. Obviously, the cycle of lack of confidence which leads one to a sense of passivity or helplessness, has to be broken if change is to occur. It would appear that the role of the school and the teacher—nature of the curriculum and the quality and amount of the teacher/student interaction, can build positive self-attitudes around academic competence and coping strategies.

The analysis of achievement yielded three components—verbal ability, perception of the opportunity structure, and coping, which operate together in distinguishing achievement groups. Verbal ability as assessed in this study, actually measures a student's familiarity with terms generally used in school. Perception of the opportunity structure implies not only whether one views the opportunity structure as open or closed, but open or closed to one as a member of a particular group. Changes in these perceptions should be predicated upon change in the state of the particular group within the society.

The coping personality, then, is not just a set of stable personality characteristics, but is mediated by expectations based on an appraisal of self in relation to the realities of the social situation. The appraisal process described by Lazarus appears to be supported by the data in this study. Achievement motivation, as defined by Atkinson and as measured in this study, appears not to be a primary factor in coping or achievement. Positive expectations can be accomplished by a change in self-appraisal which will need reinforcement through a change in societal attitudes and opportunities. These students are much too reality-controlled and reality-conscious to be influenced by anything less than this. Undoubtedly, part of their enhanced capacity to cope, in spite of multiple obstacles, comes from being reality-oriented.

# Summary

John Dill
*Memphis State University*

Ewart A. C. Thomas
*Stanford University*

The area of social competence made a dramatic entrance into developmental psychology only a few decades ago. The strategies used by children in acquiring social functioning along with the idea that children can—and do—influence their own world views became fertile topics of inquiry. Theorists and researchers alike endorsed new perspectives of what the child's true make-up was. As such, minority group psychologists became especially interested in social competence for at least two reasons. First, the traditional, almost exclusive, concern with intellectual competence has led to an underestimate of the ability of minority group members to cope with the challenges of the society at large. Second, and more important, it is only when an analysis includes the social and environmental bases of behavior that one can hope to construct a reasonably comprehensive psychology of the experience of minority group members. The researchers in the preceding section offer new data, theories, and methodologies, which not only contribute to understanding developmental determinants for a special group of children, but also significantly improve the quality of behavioral research as it applies to all children.

Since social competence is a complex area, the reader quickly learns of the diversity of theoretical perspectives necessary for comprehensive understanding of the domain. It has become apparent that most research on the development of behavioral competence in black children has focused on themes among the disadvantaged. This perspective has been challenged by the preceding papers. More importantly, each of the four authors contributes seminal ideas useful in future study of this complex topic.

The paper by Vonnie McLoyd provides an expansive analysis on the area of pretend play among low-income black children. Her study is significant since earlier investigations ignored or misinterpreted black children's capabilities in this area. McLoyd's analysis of this literature highlights its equivocal and contradictory attributes: some investigators report a lower quality of play among black children, while others have found parallels to middle-income white children's play behavior. In an attempt to reduce such ambiguities, McLoyd conducted a study of pretend play among low-income, black children with "high" and "low" structure play materials. McLoyd's careful approach to correcting the methodological flaws of past research sharpens the meaning of her investigation. Indeed, McLoyd points out that pretend play may not be the only, or even most important, influence on social and cognitive development. There may be other influences; therefore, information about alternate expressions of imagination and creativity is desirable.

Certain developmental trends were observed which appear to challenge previous claims that the play of low-income children is primarily nontransformational and shows no progress with age. Although this important study was able to glean critical differences in pretend play according to structural contexts, the role of the developmental-cognitive-racial nexus is left unanswered. Of course, this is a complex problem and as McLoyd appropriately asks: "How then, do we decide which is the preferable outcome and under what circumstances . . . ?" This question may never be answered in our exploration of play behavior. However, one immediate task for our exploration of play is to follow McLoyd's leadership in attempting to unravel the complexities of black children's social competencies.

Bertha Holliday's paper adopts a transactional perspective on black children's development within the context of teacher-child interactions. Her study provides a novel approach for establishing the origins of black children's school achievement. The attitudinal and perceptual processes of teachers are shown to profoundly influence children's school achievement. Holliday's study identifies the salience of the teacher's transactional behaviors over the child's own transactional processes. It attempts to implement change in the child's behavioral repertory which needs to be supplanted (or complemented) by increased concern with changing teacher behaviors. "Children's psychological processes are relatively insignificant predictors and moderators of both academic achievement and teacher's attitudes, perceptions, and evaluations." One implication which Holliday draws is that school intervention programs affecting black children are likely to be most successful if attempts are made to monitor, and change if necessary, the role expectations and behaviors of teachers and students. The identification of this factor provides a renewed opportunity to examine current educational theory and practice. Until—and unless—this is accomplished, Holliday warns us, old mistakes will continue and new remedies will fail. Transactionalism provides a promising framework within which to consider all persons and processes which mediate and impact on the black child.

The academic context of social competence is also addressed in Yvonne Abatso's paper "The Coping Personality: A Study of Black Community College Students." This study is unique because of the subjects' ages and its conceptual framework. Community college students as a target population have received scant attention in the developmental literature. Abatso's conceptual framework incorporates the interplay of four constructs which, she contends, contribute to improved academic functioning: achievement motivation, expectancies, sense of self-competence, and the "achiever personality" syndrome. Her findings about differences in coping orientation and strategies portray the salient distinctions between "high copers" and "low copers." For example, high copers were more involved in conversations on the subject matter with their instructors; were more likely to use daily and weekly work schedules than were low copers. Abatso concludes that it "appears that the high copers bring to the academic situation a positive sense of their ability to perform academically and a belief that they can control the events in their own lives, which expresses itself in specific skills designed to bring that about." Since the various strategies used by high copers appear to be acquirable skills, these findings suggest areas of possible intervention in order to improve the efficacy of low copers. High copers in Abatso's study had regular and substantive interactions with the instructor. This suggests that the frequency and quality of teacher-student interactions are important factors in the development of academic competence.

In all three of the chapters summarized so far, mention was made of the influence of situational variables (type of playthings in McLoyd's study, and teacher-student interactions in the studies by Abatso and Holliday). Probably the most fundamental of situational variables is ethnicity. Moore, in the remaining paper in this section, views ethnicity as "a process variable which begins to have its effect in the earliest interactions between mother and child, and continues to have its effects" as the child becomes socialized by parents to become a competent member of the group. According to the author, the effect of ethnicity can be assessed in terms of children's test performance. The author views both the heredity and environment views of black children's test performance in a balanced fashion. The exclusion of a third perspective—"interactionism"—may not have been deliberate, although a brief mention would have helped to clarify and better focus the parameters of this ongoing debate. In Moore's study, black children adopted by whites (transracial) and by blacks (traditional) were compared on several dimensions. Special emphasis in these comparisons was placed on two areas—test performance and parenting strategies.

It was found that there were significant differences in the childrearing practices of black and white adoptive mothers. There were also significant differences in the test performances of the two groups of children. There are, of course, many possible explanations of these two findings, and a more detailed study would be necessary to establish a causal link between them. Furthermore, her discussion on the nature of adaptive functioning or competence illuminates the necessity for new interpretive perspectives. The paper contributes to our understanding of the interaction between parent ethnicity, economic status, and childrearing strategies as these affect definitions of appropriate childrearing goals. And more important, Moore's work demonstrates the necessity of examining social-emotional as well as cognitive development in any assessment of competence.

In summary, there are important unifying factors that one can identify in these papers. In most cases, careful attention was given to identifying and operationalizing situational (or ecological) variables. Thus it can be assumed that any assessment of social competence has to take into consideration specific environmental factors. While the role of the developmental-social-cognitive-racial nexus is basically left unanswered in all four papers, the reader is persuaded to consider the need to address that role if an understanding of the black experience is sought. Further, as can be implied from the papers, social competence spans the whole of human development and requires functioning in multiple environmental settings (e.g., Moore's question regarding high test performance at 8 years old and subsequent competent adult status; or Abatso's "high copers" in community college settings). The challenge for future investigators is to unravel the interplay between dimensions of socially competent behavior, the standards used to judge competence, and the socio-cultural realities of blacks in contemporary America. This challenge will have its foundation in the four creative studies presented in this section.

# Section B: Identity

# Introduction

The papers in this section explore aspects of black children's identity formation. Because they highlight the unique historical problems of the literature and present alternative empirical approaches, the papers collectively offer a special perspective. There is an overall concern with conceptual, political, and methodological issues.

Proshansky (1966) and others have noted the significant attention accorded negative intergroup attitudes and their origins. However, the plethora of studies during the previous 50 years have contributed minimally to the understanding of the negative intra and intergroup attitudes of oppressed groups. The studies seldom addressed these issues as related to: (1) the perceptual development of race as a concept; (2) the politics of science; (3) the self system (i.e., both personal and group); and (4) a broader conceptualization of minority child development. The identity section attempts to address each of these issues.

The general treatment of identity and its development for black and minority children makes assumptions about the nature of the relationship between, or connectedness of, the child and the broader society. Rather than majority, white society, it is the child's own family and community that provide "significant others" or the primary reference group for the child's self–other comparisons (Barnes, 1971). The tasks of identifying significant others, measuring their influence, and determining the relative importance of black vs white institutions has yet to be satisfactorily addressed in the study of black children's identity development. Given the qualitative variations in children's rates of development and the different contexts where that development occurs (all of this over time), a broader perspective of black children's identity formation is required. As with any modality of the child's being, identity development is not a static process.

Changes, as the child ages and moves into different settings, are critical determinants of the directions and content of identity development.

Identity formation has been most often approached from the perspective of personality dynamics. However, it is critical to look at the child's affective development in relation to his or her cognitive development. Such an approach is likely to provide an improved understanding of:

1. Children's racial awareness
2. Their developmental patterns (i.e., encompassing both transitions and continuities)
3. The relationship between racial values, attitudes, and child development
4. The role of race in the ontogeny of personal beliefs and reference group orientation
5. The consequences of racial identity for performance in achievement situations
6. The place of racial identity in theories of black child development

Together the papers in this section address these and related issues relevant to the study of identity formation among black children.

Marguerite Alejandro-Wright's paper, "The Child's Conception of Racial Classification: A Socio-Cognitive Developmental Model," examines prominent conceptual transformations which characterize the child's knowledge of racial categories with increasing age. The innovative use of multiple measures of race awareness and descriptive vignettes produce a vivid representation of the child's conception of racial classification. The paper entitled "Black Identity: Rediscovering the Distinction between Personal Identity and Reference Group Orientation," by William Cross, offers a clear delineation of personal identity from group identity. A large volume of empirical literature is reviewed during the process of "rediscovering" the distinction between personal and group identity. This review encourages alternative interpretations of myriad empirical research findings generated over the past 50 years.

Leachim Semaj's paper, "Afrikanity, Cognition, and Extended Self-Identity," examines the issues of race and identity within the context of revolutions in paradigms and alternative research strategies in science. His examination of personal and group identity goes a step further than the previous chapter by examining developmental implications within an Afrikanist perspective. His analysis of the individual's identity (personal identity) and the group oriented identity or the "we" (extended self-identity) is examined from an African worldview and stresses the implication of the two components for the socialization of black children and the liberation of black people.

Hare's and Castanell's paper, "No Place to Run, No Place to Hide: Comparative Status and Future Prospects of Black Boys," is a prophetic statement. The authors investigate the comparative self-perspective and achievement of a sample of pre-adolescent black boys. The study's goal is to determine whether there are early indicators of a black male's future.

The final paper of the identity section by Margaret Beale Spencer—"Cultural Cognition and Social Cognition as Identity Correlates of Black Children's Personal-Social Development"—offers a dynamic theoretical approach to the identity literature on the child's evolving cognitive structures. The paper's goal is to offer a synthesis of the literature by interfacing the cognitive and affective modes and examining their unique consequences for minority group (black) children who are reared in a majority group (white) environment.

# 9 Black Identity: Rediscovering the Distinction Between Personal Identity and Reference Group Orientation

William E. Cross, Jr.
*Cornell University*

Perhaps as many as 200 investigations have been conducted on black (and white) identity development in children and adults. The first task one confronts when attempting to review this literature is a meaningful system to reduce the data. Such a system reveals the methodological issues and hypothetical constructs that are stressed in describing, classifying, and analyzing each study.

In previous reviews, Proshansky and Newton (1968) emphasized the constructs, racial conception (how the child learns to make racial distinctions at a conceptual level) and racial evaluation (how the child evaluates his own group membership). Banks (1976) differentiated racial preference from racial self-identification studies; Williams and Morland (1976) looked at studies of racial attitudes, racial acceptance and racial preference. The five methods used to operationalize self-concept (doll studies, participant observations, unscaled interviews, projective tests, personality or self-esteem inventories) in studies of black identity, provided the point of departure for three recent commentaries (Gordon, 1976, 1980; Baldwin, 1979).

In the current review of 161 studies of black identity published between 1939 and 1977, it is argued that students and scholars of black identity have lost sight of the key constructs which have guided practically every study of black self-concept, i.e., personal identity, and group identity or reference group orientation. In rediscovering the distinction between personal identity and reference group orientation, a particular perspective has evolved. This perspective facilitates the development of highly plausible responses to questions about black identity development that have not, as yet, been adequately addressed.

155

## EMPIRICAL STUDIES ON BLACK IDENTITY:
## DIFFERENTIATING PERSONAL IDENTITY (PI) FROM
## REFERENCE GROUP ORIENTATION (RGO)

The Horowitz (1939) and Clark and Clark (1939, 1940) studies have been significant in establishing the doll technique as the dominant method for assessing
group identity in children. In addition, both reveal the variables upon which
identity studies continue to pivot. Each study affirmed that the concept of self
(first variable) is extremely important to the study of human behavior. It is then
suggested that information on how persons orient themselves toward their socially ascribed group, i.e., reference group orientation (the second variable), can
provide accurate information on how they feel about themselves at the personal
level (the third variable). While these first three variables are readily identified, it
should be emphasized that a fourth variable is implied, if not always explicitly
discussed. Clark and Clark in effect suggested that the relationship between PI
and RGO (the PI/RGO interface, the fourth variable) shows a positive linear
correlation.

The four variables set forth by studies of black identity are self-concept (SC);
group identity or reference group orientation (RGO); personal identity (PI); and
the relationship between PI and RGO. A two factor model (SC=PI+RGO) of
black identity is revealed in the seminal works of Horowitz and the Clarks. It is
the purpose of this paper to demonstrate that the two factor model can assist in
the classification and analysis of black self-concept research for the simple
reason that PI and RGO are its central foci. We now need to determine whether
researchers have consistently operationalized the two constructs in a way that
makes them readily discernable.

*Criteria for Defining RGO Studies.*    Much has been made of the Clarks' use
of dolls in their operationalization of the construct "group identity" (RGO).
Gordon (1976) has argued that this method is distinctive in requiring "forced
choice" behavior; however, neither issue addresses the central feature of RGO
studies. Horowitz and the Clarks were not studying children's reactions to dolls
per se: They were concerned with the most effective way of presenting explicit
symbols of "race or color" to subjects who happened to be children. Had they
been working with adults, race or color would have remained a central property
of the stimulus condition; however, the nature of the choices offered adult
subjects would have reflected objects more typical of adult life.

In the assessment of RGO, race or color is usually an explicit property of the
stimulus condition and it is always a factor in the scoring technique. In some
projective devices or open-ended interviews, the researcher may not present race
or color as a stimulus, but will search the protocols for race explicit attitudes,
feelings, etc., elicited spontaneously by the nondirective stimulus. Generally
speaking, explicit race or color information is a part of the dependent measure in

every RGO study. In most instances, it is also a salient component of the stimulus situation or items. The subject, in turn, must make a particular type of preference or relate particular types of attitudes toward his or her socially ascribed group in order to achieve a high in-group score, the obverse resulting in an out-group or self-hatred score.

We note that race or color explicit stimulus-scoring techniques are direct measures of one's "group identity" (Lewin, 1948; Porter, 1971), "racial attitudes" (McAdoo, 1977), "racial orientation" (Goodman, 1952) or "reference group orientation" (Cross, 1978; 1979). The latter term is preferred for two reasons. First, it binds these studies to the sociological literature on reference group theory (Hyman and Singer, 1968). Second, the students and scholars of this technique have been concerned with the creation of valid measures which reliably demonstrate how children or adults orient themselves toward their socially ascribed group. In this light, studies of racial attitudes, racial identity, racial self-esteem, racial evaluation, racial preference, or racial self-identification are subcategories of the domain "reference group orientation" (RGO).

*Criteria for Defining PI Studies.*    We could take the easy path and describe a PI study as any investigation of identity where race or color is not a dimension of the stimulus condition and/or the dependent measure. However, this definition does not adequately capture the primary concern of such studies. PI studies attempt to investigate how "universal elements" of behavior vary in intensity, or are more likely to be present or absent across different racial groups. In effect, PI studies assume that, at least for Western cultures, one's self-concept, personal identity, or generalized personality consists of certain universal human tendencies, traits, behavioral elements or capacities. How then does race enter into the equation of PI research on blacks? The answer is that race is always treated as an independent variable or subject variable in PI research. The researcher:

1. Locates some personality scale, inventory, or questionnaire (MMPI, self-concept scales, Rorschach Test, locus of control scale, anxiety scale, etc.) which purports to tap universal elements of personality and which contain no reference to race, nationality, gender or religion.
2. The device is administered to black and white subjects (in the case of scales standardized on whites, the white control group may not be incorporated in PI studies and comparisons are made on the basis of normative data).
3. The researcher then determines whether race as an independent variable is statistically significant.

Consequently, objective criteria can be used to discern PI from RGO studies. PI studies treat race as a subject variable/independent variable, while race or color is excluded from the stimulus conditions and the dependent measures. In PI studies, the dependent measure operationalizes some universal personality element; therefore, with the exception of projective techniques and open-ended interviews, most devices associated with PI studies preclude the possibility of race or color. In most RGO studies, on the other hand, the graphic presentation of color or some other explicit race related symbol constitutes a salient dimension of the stimulus. In all RGO studies, race related information is always an important, if not paramount, element of the dependent measure.

The information needed to determine whether a study has assessed for PI or RGO can generally be found in the methods section. The titles of such studies and information contained in the discussion sections can often be very misleading. We pointed out earlier that researchers may clearly set out to assess for RGO and then in the discussion section, results are presented as if the study had actually assessed for level of self-worth (a PI variable). Consequently, low ingroup preferences, orientations or attitudes are pointed to as evidence of self-hatred.

## Classification of Empirical Studies on Black Identity by the Constructs PI and RGO

A total of 161 studies were identified for classification, and it was determined that the list was inclusive of the types of empirical studies that are referenced in a number of critical reviews (Baldwin, 1979; Banks, 1976; Cross, 1979; Gordon, 1976, 1980; Pettigrew, 1964; Proshansky & Newton, 1968; Rosenberg & Simmons, 1971; Taylor, 1976). The list systematically excludes "Field studies which relied on case study and participant observation techniques . . ." and studies which used an ". . . unscaled or informal questionnaire or interview for gathering data" (Gordon, 1980 pp. 60–61). Such studies have played a minor role in documenting the alleged negative Negro identity from 1939 to 1967 and documenting the apparent change in black identity from 1968 to the present.

The studies were relatively easy to classify which attests that researchers have generally operated with either a PI or RGO related construct. With the exception of the Draw-A-Person technique (clearly an RGO device), studies using projective devices were frequently problematic. For example, the TAT has figures usually identified as depicting white people; consequently such studies, it could be argued, assess black themes engendered by white stimuli (Williams, 1980, personal correspondence). While the Rorschach Test is a race free or race neutral stimulus, Kardiner and Ovesey (1951) apparently used as many RGO units as universal behavior units in establishing the case for a negative Negro identity. Technically it might be classified as one of the first studies to measure both PI and RGO on the same sample; however, the failure to systematically isolate group identity dependent measures from PI measures precludes its being so classified. Their study provides a glaring example of how willing researchers

TABLE 9.1

The Superordinate (PI & RGO) and Subordinate Hypothetical Constructs Associated with Studies of Black Identity, and the Frequency of PI, RGO Studies Across Two Time Periods: 1939–1960 & 1968–1977

| | Superordinate Constructs | Subordinate Constructs | Documentation of Negative Negro Identity: 1939–1960 | Documentation of Black Identity Change: 1968–1977 | Total # of Studies: 1939–1977 |
|---|---|---|---|---|---|
| | Reference Group Orientation (RGO) | racial attitudes, group identity, race awareness, racial ideology, race preference, race evaluation race-esteem, racial self-identification, race image esteem for group, in-or-out group orientation, etc. | 17RGO studies & all (100%) showed negative Negro identity. | 22RGO studies, 15 (68%) showed a positive, 6 (27%) a negative and 1 (5%) a varied Black Identity pattern. | 47 |
| Self-Concept (SC) = | Personal Identity (PI) | self-esteem, self-worth, self-confidence, personal-self, self-concept, general personality, personality interpersonal competence, primary-self, personality traits, anxiety level, unconscious-self, hidden personality dimensions, etc. | 1 PI study | 84 PI studies, 61 (73%) showed positive, 13 (15%) negative self-esteem in Blacks. 10 PI studies reported varied results (12%) | 101 |
| | PI × RGO Association (PI/RGO) | (generally an implicit factor in Black identity research in which PI & RGO constructs are discussed ''as if'' empirical studies demonstrated the PI × RGO association follows a positive linear correlation of considerable magnitude [r = .40?]) | 0 (zero) | 12 PI/RGO studies, *none* of which have been discussed in recent critical reviews on Black identity with one exception (Cross, 1979). | 13 |

159

have been to treat PI and RGO as highly correlated variables despite the paucity of supporting empirical evidence.

Table 9.1 shows the classification of 161 studies of black identity published between 1939 and 1977. The marginals on the far right show that 47 (29%) were classified RGO, 101 (63%) as PI and 13 (18%) as having assessed for both PI and RGO on the same sample. More importantly, the last two columns show (1) which types of studies contributed to the empirical documentation of negative Negro identity; and (2) which have played a role in empirically documenting a change toward a positive black identity.

*Negative Identity Trend: 1939–1960.* Self-hatred among Negroes was a well documented trend of empirical studies on black identity by 1954 and an assumed fact by 1960. During this interval, there were about 18 empirical studies reported and as shown in Table 9.1, 94% were RGO studies. In other words, the self-hatred argument, which would appear to be a PI related hypothesis, was developed on the accumulation of evidence from RGO studies. In fact, studies of personal identity played a minor role in discussions of black identity occurring between 1939–1960. For example, in their now classic work Proshansky and Newton (1968), on the "Nature and Meaning of Negro Self-Identity," not one personal identity study is cited as empirical evidence on the "development of self-identity in the Negro" pp. 182–192. All of the evidence cited came from studies of reference group orientation, i.e., racial preferences—forced choice identification studies. Similarly, Pettigrew's (1964) important overview of black American life contains a section on self-esteem and identity based primarily on reference group/racial preference studies (in it he cited only *one* personal identity study).

The irony is that when each of the RGO studies for this period is reviewed, the experimenter clearly specifies in the methods section that a blatantly related RGO construct was assessed. In the various discussion sections, however, the distinction between PI and RGO information is blurred and the construct self-hatred is injected as if PI and RGO data had been collected or as if it was established fact that PI and RGO are highly correlated. Between 1939–1960, in no study was PI and RGO data collected on the same sample in order to test the presumed association. What can be found are extremely influential, highly speculative, and polemical works asserting the PI/RGO connection (Lewin, 1948).

Before moving on to the period of identity change, a summary would state that for the studies on black identity conducted between 1939–1960, evidence was accumulated from the results of RGO research which suggested:

1. Black children, as compared to whites, tended to be out-group oriented.
2. Black children evidenced a considerable attraction to symbols representative of the white perspective. Black in-group preference usually accom-

panied the tendency of blacks to select white symbols (Cross, 1978, 1979).

3. No significant number of PI studies were conducted during this period; consequently, conclusions about the negative or positive nature of the personal identity of blacks from 1939–1960 were purely speculative.

The tendency of researchers from this period to use reference group terms in labeling dependent variables and psychoanalytic/self-concept constructs in explaining results remains a puzzle to most students of black identity.

*Evidence of Identity Change: 1968–Present.*    The Black Social Movement had two phases: (1) the Civil Rights Phase, which lasted from 1954–1967 and (2) the Black Power Phase, which began to take hold from 1965–1967. Black identity change has been linked with the second, not the first phase; consequently, studies assumed to reflect this change were thought to have been conducted between 1968 and the present (Cross, 1978; 1979; Butler, 1976). We noted that of the 161 studies reviewed in Table 9.1, 118 or 73% were conducted during the period 1968–1977. Of these, 22 (19%) were RGO oriented, 84 (71%) were PI related and 12 (10%) applied PI and RGO measures on the same sample. A significant number of both RGO and PI studies from this period show blacks with an increased in-group orientation (RGO trend) and adequate to above average levels of self-esteem (PI trend).

Strictly speaking, the only evidence documenting change in black identity comes from RGO studies for which there is a past and present trend. On the other hand, the number of PI studies conducted when the "negative black identity notion" was being documented, was not large enough to constitute a trend. Since, PI studies did not contribute to the establishment of the negative pattern, there is no reference point for comparing trends in PI studies since 1968. The most highly publicized study of "negro personality" (Kardiner & Ovesey, 1951) conducted during the initial period, used RGO and some PI related dependent variables, to support the finding of "negative self-worth" among Negroes. The modest number of PI studies conducted before 1968 and the larger number conducted after 1968 both show blacks having average to above average levels of self-esteem (Taylor, 1976). Since studies of the third type, PI × RGO investigations, were not conducted before the 1970s, no past versus present trend can be compared. The PI × RGO studies have not contributed to documentation of black identity.

Thus, those who would call attention to the large number of PI related studies conducted after 1968 as evidence of black identity change have mistakenly assumed that PI studies were conducted in the distant past and that PI has been shown to correlate with RGO (in which) case the nonexistence of a previous PI trend would be irrelevant). Ironically, from 1939–1960 RGO studies dominated the field and affiliated researchers argued that self-hatred (a PI variable) had been demonstrated. Today, PI studies are predominant and researchers point to the PI data as proof of group identity change. Both have been guilty of mixing apples with oranges because the empirical evidence supporting the presumed PI × RGO link has been nonexistent.

## Research Strategies in the Study of Black Self Concept

Let us underscore three research strategies intrinsic to the two factor model of black (and white) self-concept which have guided previous and current research on black identity. Strategy I involves the exploration of the construct personal identity and its associated methodology. Strategy II deals with the analysis of the construct reference group orientation or group identity and its associated methods. Finally, Strategy III is concerned with the relationship between personal and group identity through the simultaneous application of both assessment methods. We examine the consequences of Strategy I, referencing an important literature review of RGO studies (Banks, 1976); and the consequences of the other two strategies in terms of information revealed by our own review.

## Strategy I
## RGO Studies: The Group Identity Component
## of Self-Concept

Trends in the 47 RGO studies identified in the current review have already been articulated in an earlier section. We have noted that (1) between 1939–1960, RGO studies provided almost all of the empirical evidence used to support the negative black identity notion; (2) RGO studies do not measure self-esteem, they produce evidence on the esteem one holds toward his/her group; (3) only RGO studies provide a basis for comparison between past and current trends in black identity; (4) RGO studies show blacks having an out-group orientation before 1967, and an increasingly in-group orientation after 1968.

We now turn to a study which calls into question whether RGO studies, past or present, have actually produced statistically significant findings in support of either trend.

Banks (1976) recently reviewed 20 of the prominent investigations of evaluative preference and 12 studies of preferential self-identification, all of which fall under the RGO classification. The Chi-square statistic was applied to the choice frequencies for black subjects only, resulting in the assignment of each study to one of the following categories:

1. *White-preference,* as represented by responses which depart significantly from chance in favor of White stimuli, on all or a majority of the choice tasks.

2. *Black-preference,* as represented by responses which depart significantly from chance in favor of Black stimuli, on all or a majority of the choice tasks.
3. *No preference,* as represented by responses which do not deviate from chance on all or a majority of the choice tasks.

The results showed that 69% of the reviewed studies revealed no race preference in black subjects; 25% were found to have demonstrated black preference, while only 6% indicated a pattern of white preference. Considering that black self-hatred was thought to be a fairly clear cut finding in the research literature for over thirty years, Banks' findings are certainly unexpected if not startling. How then did the notion of black self-hatred evolve from these studies? Banks offered the following explanation:

> Reliance upon White comparative frames has largely perpetrated the notion of black self-rejection in the absence of definitive evidence of preference behavior in blacks. Even in those investigations which employed only black samples, implicit a priori standards tended to reflect presumptions about the desirability of such highly ethnocentric response sets as are common only in White samples. The fact that blacks failed always to prefer black stimuli evaluatively, or as objects of self-identification, has generally been interpreted as a failure to adopt positive racial self-regard. [p. 1185]

As will be seen shortly, "reliance upon a white comparative frame" is problematic only in RGO related black identity studies. In the other major cluster of studies where self-esteem is measured directly, the majority show blacks and Whites to have comparable levels of self-worth. It is curious to note that use of Whites as a comparison group in one instance (RGO studies) results in a picture of "low Black self-esteem," while in studies where self-esteem is measured directly, blacks appear to have adequate self-esteem, even when compared to whites (Cross, 1978; Gordon, 1980).

## Strategy II
## Studies of Personal Identity: The
## Direct Assessment of Self-Esteem

The literature was reviewed for studies comparing black and white personal identity, generally these used self-esteem inventories, which did not incorporate race related anchor points. The primary sources for the studies reviewed were *Psychological Abstracts* and *Dissertation Abstracts International* covering the period between 1960 and 1976. Most of the studies involved black and white subjects; a few used only black subjects but reported normative data for the inventory in question. A total of 101 studies were reviewed and each was placed into one of four categories based on the reported results:

1. B=W: Fifty-one studies (51%) showed blacks with the same level of self-esteem as whites.
2. B>W: Twenty-one studies (21%) showed blacks with higher levels of self-esteem as whites.
3. B<W: Sixteen studies (16%) were found in which the level of self-esteem reported for whites was higher than that reported for blacks.
4. Varied: Thirteen (13%) of the 101 studies reported mixed results.

Seventy-two percent of the studies showed black self-esteem to equal or exceed that recorded for Whites; this compares to 54% in the review conducted by Gordon (1980). Taylor's (1976) review, which cited only those studies involving large sample sizes, also showed black personal identity matched white self-esteem levels.

Gordon (1980) attributes conflicting findings about black self-concept produced by doll (RGO) versus self-esteem (PI) studies to the theoretical complexity implicit in each type of study. She notes that many self-esteem inventories have numerous subscales, underscoring complex or multidimensional approaches to self-concept. Doll type (RGO) studies concentrate on the elicitation of rather limited information (i.e., racial preferences or race awareness), thus apparently revealing a monadic, simplistic unitary concept of self. Baldwin (1979) also favors this interpretation.

Most RGO studies have been conducted with very young children; consequently, the level of cognitive complexity demanded by the doll task is low. Self-esteem studies make use of paper–pencil inventories which clearly require more complex competencies. Not surprising, most self-esteem studies have been administered to black subjects who, on the average, were considerably older than the subjects included in the typical doll study. When complex self-esteem scales are administered orally to young children, the results are generally far less reliable than when administered to older children. In fact, many experts in child development have argued that only direct observation techniques can be counted on to provide valid and reliable information about the social-emotional aspects of early childhood behavior.

In short, RGO studies have produced limited information because the construct has been explored with children at an age when RGO patterns are just beginning to emerge. Likewise, the self-esteem literature is rich in complexity because the assessment devices have been able to take advantage of the mature adult mind. In recognizing that PI and RGO related studies have conflicted over the nature of black self-concept, one need not turn to venturesome explanations before asking the first logical question: "Are these two sets of studies actually measuring related variables?" This question can only be answered by studies where separate measures of RGO and PI are administered to the same subjects.

Scholars who used reference group assessment strategies have not felt compelled to also administer direct measures of self-esteem, *for the RGO measures were viewed as offering accurate indirect insight into the level of one's self-esteem.* Conversely, studies of personal identity did not incorporate RGO measures since this information was assumed to be redundant. An entire people have been burdened with images of their children's self-hatred even though no empirical link between racial preference behavior and direct measures of low self-esteem has been demonstrated.

## Strategy III
## Testing the Lewinian Hypothesis: Applying PI and RGO Measures on the Same Samples

In the later 1960s and early 1970s, studies interfacing PI and RGO measures began to appear. These studies represented direct tests of the assumed positive linear correlation between self-esteem and group identity (Lewin, 1948). We now turn to a review of the few studies of this genre reported.

1. *Studies Accepting the Null Hypothesis.* Porter (1971) examined the self-concept/personal identity and group identity of 400 black and white Boston preschoolers, ages four and five, enrolled in Head Start. She found that among the poor and working class, there was a greater instance of black children having both low self-esteem and negative attitudes toward other blacks. However, for black children of higher socioeconomic status, Porter discovered one group of children with a pro-black attitude and another with pro-white attitudes—although each could be characterized by high self-esteem.

In a longitudinal study of the development of racial attitudes (RA) and self-esteem (SE) in black children, McAdoo (1977) administered separate measures of SE and RA to black children in 1969 when they were ages four and five, and again when the same children were ages nine and ten. Her sample included chilren from several Northern urban ghettos and an all black town in Mississippi. Analysis of her first wave of data indicated high self-esteems for all the children, although the children from the all black southern town had higher self-esteem levels. When evaluated as a group, the children from all areas tended to have an out-group racial orientation. Further, individual scores for SE and RA were not correlated. Children from intact middle-class homes were the most out-group oriented, although their self-concept was equal or higher than children from lower income homes.

When the measures were re-administered in 1975, McAdoo (1977) reported that self-esteem remained high for all groups; however, the average self-esteem score for the Northern children increased to the point where it approximated the Mississippi group. The most dramatic change was in racial attitudes, all groups became more in-group oriented. As was true in the first dataset, no significant correlation was found between self-esteem and racial attitudes. McAdoo's study is significant because it also showed that black children from a variety of home environments and regions of the country had high self-esteem before and after being influenced by the Black Power Movement. The same children had a predominantly out-group orientation before the Black Power Movement and an increasingly in-group orientation as the Black Power Movement progressed.

Similar findings suggest the absence of a positive linear relationship between group identity and self-esteem in black preschoolers (Spencer, 1977), black elementary school age children (Dulan, 1978; Williams-Burns, 1977) and black high school and college students (Slade, 1977). When comparing black adults, Williams (1975) found similar self-concept levels for those with "old (Negro) identity" and those with "new (black) identity." Where the groups differed was on "world view" or reference group orientation, with the latter being more in-group oriented.

We found two studies where personal identity and reference group orientation measures were administered to both black and white subjects. Bennett and Lundgren (1976) studied 42 black and 42 white boys, ages three to five, were attending either segregated, semi-integrated or fully integrated day care classes. While a significant negative correlation was found between self-concept and racial attitudes for boys attending the fully integrated setting, no such relationship, negative or otherwise, was found for the children in the other settings. Storm (1971) found no association between racial attitudes and self-concept in a study involving black and white first graders.

2. *Studies Rejecting the Null Hypothesis.* Results from five studies appeared to support the PI/RGO relationship. However, upon closer inspection only one shows unqualified support (Ward & 8raun, 1972); two present qualified evidence (Fouther-Austin, 1978; Vaughan, 1977), and another two have been misrepresented in that a re-analysis of data from these studies (Mobley, 1973; Butts, 1963) clearly did not confirm a PI/RGO connection.

Ward and Braun (1972) studied the PI/RGO relation among 60 black boys and girls, between the ages of seven and eight, making use of the Piers-Harris Children's Self-Concept Test and a modified Clark and Clark doll task. The authors found few subjects with either low self-esteem scores or low doll task scores. The results of a Mann-Whitney U Test indicated subjects who expressed more black color preferences had higher self-concept scores than those who expressed fewer black preferences. The number of subjects with low doll test scores was, in fact, very small. Seventy to 80% of subjects made black preferences on three of the four doll task questions. Paradoxically, this, the only study to date which showed a general relationship between PI and RGO, had a problem with constricted variance on each dependent measure.

Fouther-Austin (1978) administered a self-esteem (Tennessee Self-Concept Scale) and race awareness scale (Banks Black Consciousness Scale) to 392 black tenth grade students across six test cities. She reported a significant correlation (r=.32) between PI and RGO for all subjects. The correlation fluctuated greatly across test sites (r-range = .07 to .50) and was only significant in three cities. In effect, her data showed support for a PI/RGO relationship under certain circumstances, but not as an overall trend. This was also true of a study by Vaughan (1977) who investigated the PI/RGO association with 33 third grade and 42 seventh grade black children from predominantly low income working class families, making use of the Piers-Harris Self-Esteem Scale and the Cheek (race-awareness) Scale. The correlation between the two instruments across all subjects approached significance (r=.22, $p<.065$). The self-esteem/race-esteem correlation for girls was statistically significant, again supporting the interpretation that only under certain circumstances is the PI/RGO correlation significant.

The studies by Mobley (1973) and Butts (1963) present questionable evidence to support the PI/RGO relationship, either as a main effect or interaction. The Butts (1963) study, applied a self-esteem and two factor race awareness measure to 50 children. The actual analysis, however, was conducted using only the 14 students who misidentified on the race awareness measure. Of the 14, six scored high on the PI measure and eight placed low on PI. The eight/six split for 14 cases showed one could not predict, beyond chance, the PI level for an associated RGO level. Butts also had direct observation ratings as another measure of PI; when the observation data failed to show a significant relationship to the misidentification data (again, the N=14), Butts questioned observer reliability. Finally, while Butts did not analyze his self-esteem by racial preference data, he nevertheless concluded that many of the other 36 subjects (with high self-esteem) were demonstrating an out-group preference. Mobley (1973) also inappropriately interpreted her data as demonstrating a PI/RGO relationship for a study conducted with 163 college students. The Tennessee Self-Concept Scale and a 101 item Black Identity Index were applied to the sample. Ninety one of the items failed to show a relationship. To report such findings as support for the PI/RGO relationship is simply not acceptable.

In brief, one is pressed to find any study that demonstrates the PI/RGO connections except under circumscribed conditions (i.e., interaction effects). RGO variables, then, are not indirect measures of PI variables, and conversely, PI devices are not indirect measures of RGO. The speculation about the link between doll studies and estimates of self-esteem turns out to be more a myth than reality.

## Reference Group Orientation and Black Identity

The independence of self-esteem and reference group orientation means that even if all evaluative preference/self-identification studies showed blacks to have an out-group orientation, such information would offer little knowledge about the personal identity of blacks. In fact, several studies have reported average to above average levels of self-esteem in black children manifesting a clear-cut, out-group orientation (McAdoo, 1977; Rosenberg & Simmons, 1971; Spencer, 1977). Elsewhere, Urry (1973) has emphasized that the concept of reference group was developed to help account for the fact that actors may manifest attitudes generally associated with groups where they are not members. Urry continues by stating "it is because of man's ability through symbols, language, and communication to take on the role of the other that he is able to orient himself to groups other than those with which he is directly and continuously implicated" [p. 18].

Are blacks subject to have either an all black or all white reference group orientation? If the racial preference studies demonstrate anything, it is that the black perspective incorporates both black and white anchor points (Teeland, 1971), while the white perspective is governed almost entirely by white anchor points. Recall Banks' finding that white children typically exhibited a monadic (white) orientation. In contrast, black subjects showed white preference in 6% of the studies, black preference in 25% and no preference in 69%. Perhaps the no preference category reflects the existence of a dual consciousness, rather than subject confusion or ambivalence.

Forced choice methodologies allowing for only two options (select either black or white) are inherently insensitive to dual worldviews. Dual perspectives can best be unmasked by repeated measure on triadic comparisons (select white, black or yellow); triadic preferences may best be derived from repeated measures on quadratic options (select black, brown, yellow or white) and so on. Be that as it may, the concept of a dual reference group orientation in blacks seems credible in light of several recent studies.

Banks and Rompf (1973) asked a group of black and white children to view and reward the performance of two players (one black, one white) in a ball tossing game. Each game consisted of five trials for which the outcomes were controlled: (a) white wins by slight margin; (b) white wins by large margin; (c) black wins by small margin; (d) black wins by large margin; and (e) one trial ends in a tie. Consistent with past research, white children showed preference for the white player by rewarding him more for his performance and by more often selecting him as the overall winner. Although black children showed preference for the white player by rewarding him more often after each trial, the same black children showed preference for the black player by choosing him significantly more times as the overall winner. To repeat, the same black children showed preference for whites and blacks as a function of the task within which they were asked to make evaluations.

Rosenberg and Simmons (1971) found black children to have self-esteem equal to or higher than that of whites even though the black children also showed a clearcut preference for light skin. And yet, 73% of the black children (65% for the whites) said that they were very good looking or pretty goodlooking. In fact, they found that on the whole, the black children were more enthusiastic about their looks than white children. In response to these findings, they concluded that blacks probably use other blacks as the comparative other.

Tentative results from a longitudinal study show black parents present both the black and white worlds to their children, while white parents tend to convey the world as being primarily white. For example, in black homes, one is as likely to find white dolls or human figures as black ones, while black dolls are seldom, if ever, found in white homes. Black children, and perhaps black people in general, have a dual reference group orientation. It is interesting to note that the "multiple anchor point notion" corresponds to a variety of constructs used to describe the black perspective: "double-consciousness" (DuBois, 1903), "double-vision" (Wright, 1953), "bicultural" (Valentine, 1971), "diunital" (Dixon & Foster, 1971) and "multidimensional" (Cross, 1978a).

## The Black Movement

The proposition that black self-esteem was already adequate before the Black Movement has been strengthened by several independent literature reviews (Gordon, 1976; 1980; Taylor, 1976). Most of the studies show blacks with levels of self-esteem which match or surpass self-esteem in white comparison groups. After reviewing the empirical literature on the Negro-to-black identity shift, which occurred within the context of the contemporary Black Movement, Cross (1978a) remarked that "the conversion experience radically modified the values, ideologies, reference group orientation and priorities of black people, but did not alter their basic personality and/or self-concept" [p. 26].

While the findings of self-esteem studies are consistent with the hypothesis that black personal identity/self-esteem was not changed by the Black Movement, Banks' (1976) re-analysis of key evaluative preference studies failed to show a change in black reference group orientation. Banks' conclusion does not hold for evaluative racial preference studies, the studies most often cited in discussions of black identity development. Twenty-one evaluation preference (RGO) studies were classified as indicating white, black or no preference in blacks. As was mentioned earlier, evidence of black negativity was reported from 1939–1967, while the trend toward positive black group identity was present in studies conducted after 1967. If Banks' assertion is correct, then the trend of the studies conducted from 1939–1967 should be identical to the trend for 1968 to the present.

Before the Black Power Phase of the Black Social Movement, blacks displayed a decidedly dualistic worldview. After 1968, a trend toward a black perspective, which is almost as significant as the dualistic frame, becomes apparent. In point of fact, all of the clearcut black preference manifestations are evident only in RGO studies conducted after 1968, the apex of the Black Power era (Cross, 1978a). A reactionary, extreme prowhite position is seldom advocated: The dualistic, integrationist ethic was perhaps stronger in the past than it is today, although it is probably still the dominant ideology among blacks. Finally, over the past 10 years, a nationalistic black oriented ideology has become increasingly important in discussions of black affairs.

## SUMMARY AND IMPLICATIONS

In looking at the black identity literature, this paper reaches the following conclusions:

1. Blacks have consistently had a high sense of personal worth. The Black Movement probably had a less dramatic effect on the personal identity as opposed to the reference group orientation of black people.
2. Blacks have had, and continue to have, a multifaceted reference group orientation such that black and white anchor points may determine behavior depending upon the situation being confronted. The Black Movement probably increased the number of black anchor points in a person's worldview.
3. While identity is context bound, the Black Movement has increased the probability that more blacks will superimpose a black orientation upon a greater variety of situations.
4. An out-group perspective may measure the extent to which the world view of the mainstream group (Americanism) has been internalized by a minority member and not self-rejection. This suggests racial preference studies measure more of a *political-cultural* propensity rather than a *psychological trait*.
5. Contrary to the long held Lewinian hypothesis, reference group orientation does not predict personal identity, but it does predict the extent to which a person, neurotic or otherwise, will join in collective struggle and cultural propagation.
6. Knowing that a person has a strong black identity will not inform us about the nature of his/her personal identity; however, it gives us considerable insight into the person's value system, political posture, and cultural stance.

Although the data investigated in this paper were descriptive rather than prescriptive, there are implied problem solving strategies. It is clear that the many problems faced by blacks require sustained collective action. The black community needs programs that increase the probability of black children developing into adults who will identify and participate with other blacks in political action. Similar conclusions are also likely to be true for other minorities. Consequently, while the individual black person may enhance his/her self-esteem through activities shared with other than black people, the political/cultural needs and problems of the black community require that a critical mass of black people strongly identify with black people and black culture.

## ACKNOWLEDGMENT

This paper was produced as part of a larger research venture (Cross, Bronfenbrenner, & Cochran, 1977) supported by a research grant from ACYF #90C1254/03.

# Afrikanity, Cognition and Extended Self-Identity

Leachim Tufani Semaj
*University of the West Indies*

## PARADIGMATIC REVOLUTIONS

At the core of what we call science is a particular worldview, set of normative assumptions, and frame of reference. These combine to form a paradigm (Nobles, 1978a). Thomas Kuhn (1970) defines paradigms as "universally recognized scientific achievements that for a time provide model problems and solutions to a community of practitioners" (p. viii). These theories, applications, and instruments together provide a model for scientific research by defining the lines of inquiry (Harris, 1979). For example, in the area of black children's identity, the predominant paradigm has been derived from the work of the Clarks (Clark & Clark, 1939, 1940) who established a methodology involving forced choice between racially different dolls or pictures. The results of these studies defined attributes of the identity of black children.

However, Kuhn points out that "the greatest scientific discoveries . . . are not those made during the period of normal science (when everyone is following the same paradigm) but rather during periods of paradigmatic revolutions" (Harris, 1979 p. 19). We have seen this most clearly in the areas of physics—"when, for example, Copernican astronomy replaced Ptolemaic astronomy, or Newtonian dynamics replaced Aristotelian dynamics, or quantum mechanics replaced classical electrodynamics" (Harris, 1979, p. 19). Today we are experiencing a similar paradigmatic revolution in the area of race and identity. The shift is from a social learning/symbolic interaction model to a socio-cognitive one in which the child's ability to process social cues is seen as a critical construct. In addition, we are also experiencing the growth of a cadre of black scholars who are rejecting exocentricity, and thus Eurocentricity. This has resulted in a greater

173

willingness to acknowledge the legitimacy of their perspective, own Afri-
centricity (Asante, 1980).

In Harris' (1979) exploration of "Research Strategies and the Structure of
Science" we see that when paradigms clash, scientists resort to strange behaviors. During this time opportunities are provided for the development of new
theories (and paradigms) because solutions cannot be found for a growing
number of conceptual problems. But new theories often talk past each other
because often they do not share the same paradigm (Feyerabend, 1970). However, the sophisticated falsificationist position of Lakatos (1970) shows us that old
theories do not just fade away or die natural deaths because of being subjected to
criticism. A new theory must first better explain the old facts, as well as the new
facts, within the context of a holistic system. As Harris (1979, p. 24) stated,
"there is no falsification before the emergence of a better theory." An example
of this phenomenon is the IQ measurement. Despite the negative criticisms
leveled from many quarters, the IQ measurement is still widely used to label
black children because no new theory has yet subsumed it. Many black psychologists have also been caught up in this dilemma. They have been busy reacting to
assertions made from the Euro-American psychological position about low self-
concept and negative racial identity in black children. However, since their
efforts (with few exceptions) have not resulted in a better theory, the old deficient theories have not yet been superceded. The objective of this work then is to
attempt to contribute to the development of such a theory and to further articulate
a better paradigm, which is grounded in Afrikanity. This perspective recognizes
that in order to understand the behavior of Afrikans in the New World, one has to
understand the interaction between (1) "the Afrikan nature or basis for (the)
behavior," and (2) the conditions imposed by the alien culture and the ways in
which it "influences the development and/or expression of such behavior"
(Nobles, 1978b, p. 685).

## WHAT IS THE SELF?

From the Euro-American worldview the self is that which distinguishes and
separates the individual from everyone else. Rosenberg and Simmons' (1971)
survey of some of the literature includes the following definitions of self: "the
inner nature"; "the essential nature of man"; and "the experience and content
of self-awareness".

This situation contrasts with the Afrikan world view in which the self has a
broader frame of reference; namely, the collective representation of one's identity. For example, the Akan perceive the self as represented by seven concentric
circles. The smallest, innermost, and least important represents the individual.
Moving outward we find the family, clan, tribe, nation, people, and ultimately,
the world. Young children and imbeciles are expected to have a small self, but

with maturity and responsibility the self is expected to expand. The first four levels of self are called mogya meaning blood ties, while the outer three are called kra (soul or spirit). One is not considered a whole person until one knows where one's blood is coming from and where one's soul is going. Wade Nobles (1973) presents a more condensed model of the Afrikan concept of self using only three referents, "I," "Me," and "We." The "I" is self perception. The "Me" is attitudes about self which develop as a result of the incorporated perception of others. The "We" is the most important component of self in the Afrikan ontology; it represents the feelings and perceptions one has towards one's group. William Cross (1979) further condenses the self so that the "I" and "Me" are conceptualized as personal identity (PI) and the "We" as reference group orientation (RGO). However, concerning this "We" component, Nobles (1976) suggests a better term, the extended self:

. . . in terms of self-conception, the relationship of interdependence (and oneness of being) translates to an "extended" definition . . . One's self-definition is dependent upon the corporate definition of one's people. In effect, the people definition TRANSCENDS the individual definition of self, and the individual conception of self EXTENDS to include one's self and kind. This transcendent relationship (that between self and kind) is the "extended-self" (p. 21).

We therefore concur with Nobles' (1973) position that it is only through full understanding of the Afrikan concept of self that we can understand the self concept of black people—adults or children.

## THE STATUS OF PERSONAL IDENTITY (PI) AND EXTENDED SELF-IDENTITY (ESI) IN BLACK CHILDREN

The works of Rosenberg and Simmons (1971), Taylor (1976), Gordon (1976) and especially Cross (1979) provide convincing evidence that there is no problem with regard to the individual, I/me or personal identity (PI) component of self in black children. "Blacks have consistently had a high sense of personal worth " (Cross, 1979) [p. 42]. This is because black children do not passively internalize negative definitions or assessments provided by aliens. The child's interaction with the alien culture is filtered through the Afrikan frame of reference provided by the community, thus protecting and maintaining personal identity (Taylor, 1976). Personal identity develops as a result of self-perceptions with respect to one's own community, family, and peers, not the alien society.

With regard to extended self-identity (ESI) the situation is quite different. ESI has been conceptualized in the literature as racial awareness, preference or identity. Beginning with Clark and Clark (1939, 1940), many studies have described black children as self-rejecting and assumed them to be lacking in racial pride (e.g., Ascher & Allen, 1969; Coles, 1965; Morland, 1958; Richardson & Green, 1971; Sciara, 1971). Some researchers have reported opposite findings which they attribute to rising black awareness and racial pride as a result of the events of the 1960s (Epstein, Krupat, & Obudho, 1976; Gregor & McPherson, 1966; Hraba & Grant, 1970; Mahan, 1976; Ogletree, 1969; Ward & Braun, 1972). Criticism of the research supporting both of these views has been made from conceptual and methodological perspectives (Baldwin, 1979; Brand, et al., 1974; Jones, 1972; Nobles, 1973); "for example, gross stimulus-response ambiguities, uncontrolled experimenter effects, and demand characteristics are to be found virtually everywhere in this body of research" (Baldwin, 1979, p. 69). In addition, Banks' (1976) review of the literature reveals that there may be no phenomenon of past black self-rejection or present rising awareness, since the overwhelming evidence suggests either no preference or, a simple change responding on the part of black children because of contrasted racial stimuli. (These categories correspond to the levels of Alien, Collective, and Diffused ESI, respectively.) Cross (1979) expands on this finding. He suggests that "perhaps the 'no preference' category reflects the existence of a dual consciousness rather than subject confusion or ambivalence" (p. 35). He therefore concludes that ". . . if the racial studies demonstrate anything it is that the black perspective incorporates both black and white anchor points while the white is governed almost entirely by white anchor points" (p. 35). Cross however makes the argument that the events of the 1960s were associated with a transformation in Extended Self Identity. These issues suggest that the status of ESI in Afrikan-American children is not clear. It is hoped that this analysis will shed more light on the situation.

## Theorized Levels of Extended Self Identity (ESI)

The three levels of ESI, Collective, Alien, and Diffused, are summarized from Semaj (1980).

*Collective ESI.*    In children this is represented by in-group racial preference and evaluation and identification with black culture. To this, adults add a consistent orientation to an Africentric worldview and a commitment to the collective survival of black people.

*Alien ESI.*    In contrast, these children show anti-black preference and evaluation and identification with an alien culture. Adults "consistently demonstrate a Eurocentric worldview, are concerned with individual needs over collective good, denigrate or deny Afrikanity . . . and may even be willing to work against the collective survival of their own (people) [p. 29]. This level is characterized by exocentricity (Armah, 1980).

*Diffused ESI.* This level is between the Alien and the Collective. Here children attempt to balance the black and Alien values and culture by identifying with both sides. Adults further intensify this balancing act; for example, "They *believe* that black is beautiful but *know* that white is powerful. They are aware that changes are necessary but have strong doubts that changes are possible." (Semaj, 1980, pp. 30–31).

Asante (1980) proposes five levels of awareness leading to Afrocentricity (and out of diffusion):

1. *Skin recognition:* The person recognizes that his/her skin and heritage are black, but that is the extent of the reality.
2. *Environmental recognition:* "The person sees the environment as indicating his or her blackness through discrimination and abuse."
3. *Personality awareness:* The person expresses positive affect towards black cultural artifacts. However, a person may talk black, act black, dance black and eat black, although he does not THINK black.
4. *Interest concern:* At this level the "person accepts the first three levels and so demonstrates interest and concern in the problems of blacks and tries to deal intelligently with the issues of Afrikan people. However, it lacks Afrocentricity in the sense that it does not consume the life and spirit of the person."
5. *Afrocentricity:* At this the highest level, the person becomes totally changed to a conscious involvement in the struggle for his or her own mind liberation and becomes aware of the collective conscious will. Now the person is consumed. "Once you have Afrocentricity no one needs to tell you that you have it or ask you if have it"; it is consciously revealed in everything you do, say, think or feel.

These levels therefore represent a series of concentric circles leading out of diffusion and into collectivity. The main developmental question is "When can children begin moving on this path?"

## MODELS FOR THE DEVELOPMENT OF ESI

The following four models are characteristic of the various explanations provided for the development of ESI in children in general.

### Goodman

Goodman (1964) divides the development of racial conceptions into three over-lapping stages: (1) racial awareness, (2) racial orientation, and (3) racial attitudes. Using these categories, Proshansky (1966) concluded that the evidence for black and white children indicated that, as early as age three, both groups are aware of racial differences in people. By the time the child enters grade school, the awareness of racial differences is said to be quite advanced.

In the next stage, between ages four and eight, the child is said to enter a period of racial orientation. Here the child learns the phrases and concepts associated with racial grouping, without necessarily understanding the meanings attached to them. Preference is shown for some groups over others at this stage.

The third stage includes development of racial attitudes. During this period, the child's beliefs, feelings and behavioral tendencies toward the members of different ethnic groups become differentiated, resembling those of an adult. Proshansky (1966) concludes that:

> There is evidence that the cognitive and behavioral components of such attitudes become more differentiated as the child matures. It seems pretty clear that the prejudice among American youth increases with age, and that such prejudice is directed at a number of minority groups (p. 327).

## Katz

Katz's (1976) review of the literature delineated some of the major processes associated with the acquisition of attitudes, including direct instruction, reinforcement, personality factors, childrearing techniques, cognitive development, and perceptual factors. She also attempted to synthesize diverse findings within a developmental context. Believing that Goodman's three-stage approach to the development of racial identity was oversimplified, Katz proposed a developmental sequence consisting of at least eight overlapping but separate steps which span approximately the first 10 years of the child's life. Briefly, the stages are as follows:

1. *Early observation of racial cues.* Little is known about this stage except that it is present by age three.

2. *Formation of rudimentary concepts.* This stage occurs in many children prior to three years but generally is completed by age four. Here the child begins to "express a differential response to an individual from another group," (p. 148) and begins to learn group labels. The process by which this is acquired can either be direct or indirect.

3. *Conceptual differentiation.* Here the child learns both "group boundaries and defining characteristics" [p. 149]. This stage elaborates on the skills acquired above as the child encountered more examples of out-group members and received additional feedback explaining some possible contradicting or ambiguous cues.

4. *Recognition of the irrevocability of cues.* The child learns that racial classi-fication is immutable, despite conflicting and confusing evidence.

5. *Consolidation of group concepts.* The child now understands both the positive and negative stereotypes attached to the group classification. This phase begins by age five and may continue over a long period of time.

6. *Perceptual elaboration of racial cues.* Perceptually the child reduces intra-group differences while increasing intergroup differences resulting in the belief that "they all look alike." Some evidence suggests that this stage begins in preschoolers; however, further development is presumed to occur throughout grade school.

7. *Cognitive elaboration of racial cues.* This is the process by which "con-cept attitudes" become racial attitudes during middle childhood years. Katz uses the term concept attitude to describe the young child's response, since it differs in complexity from what we classify as attitudes in older children and adults. The relationship between these two are not clearly understood.

8. *Attitude crystalization.* This stage is similar to Goodman's third stage (Goodman, 1964) and represents the formation of fairly stable racial attitudes during later grade school years.

## Porter

Porter (1971) tested some hypotheses in a doll study with preschoolers. The aim of the study was to "elicit racial attitudes held by children without arousing suspicion of the test's purpose." Porter's conclusions were as follows.

> By the fifth year, the connection between color and race becomes clear and vague preferences have developed into real social attitudes (though not fully developed as adult attitudes). The child is, however, beginning to develop strong preference and indicates reasons for them. This response is more complex than has formerly been supposed. Negro children manifest ambivalence toward their own race and some hostility toward the opposite race, while whites begin to show internalization of the American creed as well as anti-Negro feelings (p. 85).

The Goodman, Katz, and Porter models indicate that there is a fairly stable ethno-racial identity and out-group attitude by the end of the primary school years.

## Williams and Morland

The Williams and Morland (1976) model suggests that since visual orientation, satisfaction of child's activity needs, human interaction, and contact comfort all occur in light, these early experiences lead children to prefer light over dark.

This results in a pancultural tendency for light to be associated with good and dark with bad. So from a non racial origin we have the origins of black/white racial evaluations. This situation is then further polarized by cultural and subcultural influences such as mass media, children's literature, Judeo-Christian religious symbols, and idiomatic speech in which Europeans are called white and Afrikans called black. The major flaw with this model is its ahistorical perspective, which assumes that whites have always and will always dominate the lives of people of color and ignores the mechanisms by which this situation developed.

## The Socio-Cognitive Model

The socio-cognitive model was developed by integrating the theoretically sound constructs from the four preceding models. The evidence accumulated from the works of Piaget (Ginsburg & Opper, 1969; Inhelder & Piaget, 1964) and Kohlberg (1969) show the "qualitative and quantitative changes in the cognitive functioning of children, especially in the first ten years of life" (Semaj, 1979a, p. 9). Central to this approach is the realization that the acquisition of operational skills, especially classification and conservation abilities, should impact on the development of Extended Self Identity. This phenomenon has been demonstrated in the area of gender identity and sex-role development (Kohlberg, 1966, Emmerich, et al., 1977; Marcus & Overton, 1974). In this area of racial conception, Katz (1976) postulates that such a construct should be relevant. This is stage four in her model. There have been a number of independent empirical confirmations of this construct (Alejandro-Wright, 1980; Clark et al., 1980; Semaj, 1979a, 1979b).

The socio-cognitive model proposes that the development of classification and conservation skills regarding inanimate objects (impersonal cognition) precede and facilitate such skills in the area of race and ethnicity (social-cognition). This means that before the child can understand "that one's racial identity could not be altered by wishing and that racial classification was immutable despite conflicting and confusing evidence" (Semaj, 1979c, p. 2), the child must first acquire these abilities regarding inanimate objects. Thus, the child is first "capable of coordinating all the dimensions and aspects of a stimulus irrespective of transformations performed" in the impersonal domain before being able to do so on the social domain of race and ethnicity.

The relationship between impersonal and social cognition has been substantiated (Semaj, 1979a, 1980). It was found that children acquired the ability to conserve mass and weight before racial constancy. However, even though the presence of conservation did not guarantee that the child would have racial constancy, the absence of conservation usually indicated an absence of racial constancy.

Social cognitive skills of racial classification and constancy are differentially associated with the development of Extended Self Identity. Elsewhere (Semaj, 1980) this stage/phase is summarized as follows:

By age four or five, children understand that people are categorized into various ethno-racial groups, but they do not yet understand the bases for these groupings. They have some understanding of the group to which they belong, but do not understand the permanence of this classification. They also have problems differentiating between black and white as colors and the concepts "black" and "white." Nonetheless, they are beginning to learn the evaluation of and the connotations associated with these colors and concepts in the form of stereotypes. At this stage, any expressed ethno-racial evaluation will not be much more than a regurgitation of the input received from the social environment on both the dominant and subcultural levels. The child's ethno-racial evaluations are independent of self-evaluations since self-group interaction is not fully comprehended (p. 76).

However, with the achievement of racial constancy, black children age four to seven most often demonstrate collective ESI. This is because their cognitive maturity enables them to better understand the interrelatedness of self and group which is inherent to the Afrikan concept of self. This is a small group because most children under seven do not have racial constancy. For this precocious few "self-evaluations and group evaluations become related, and so, irrespective of what the dominant culture says, his/her group is better than the out-group" (p. 76).

For black children over seven and without racial constancy, experiential maturity enables the majority to demonstrate a quasi collective ESI. They, like the 4- through 7-year olds with racial constancy, are able to integrate positive individual and group evaluation and filter negative out-group influence. But since they lack the cognitive underpinning, one can not be certain of the stability of their ESI. With racial constancy, however, they demonstrate a different behavior. Now the modal ESI becomes diffused. The combination of cognitive and experiential maturity further facilitate the child's perception of the social reality. Perhaps due to the cumulative effects of the dominant cultural perspective, the child begins to lose some of the naturally positive identification with black culture and people achieved at an earlier age. The child still believes that black is beautiful, but now knows that white is powerful. The results are a relatively equal evaluation of both sides (black and alien).

Evidence supporting these relationships can be provided by re-analyzing some of the data presented elsewhere by Semaj (1979a, 1979b, 1980). From these data we can examine the relationships between age and racial constancy (independent variables) and three measures of the child's evaluations and preferences regarding racial cues (dependent variables). These dependent measures are the Preschool Racial Attitude Measure (PRAM), the Social Affect to Black measure (SAB) and the Racial Reference Group Test (RRG).

On all three measures there were significant interactions between age and racial constancy. With the achievement of racial constancy, pro black and in-group racial preferences increased for 4- to 7-year-olds but remained constant or decreased for the 8- to 11-year-olds. This relationship is best summarized by the children's response to the question, "Which is better, black or white?"

TABLE 10.1
Responses to Question, "Which is Better, Black or White?" by
Children With and Without Racial Constancy

|  | (n) | 4–7 year olds | | |  |
|---|---|---|---|---|---|
|  |  | Black | White | Neither |  |
| Racial Constancy |  |  |  |  |  |
| With | 12 | 9 | 3 | 0 |  |
| Without | 28 | 19 | 9 | 0 | N.S. |
|  |  | 8–11 year olds | | |  |
| Racial Constancy |  |  |  |  |  |
| With | 20 | 8 | 3 | 9 |  |
|  |  |  |  |  | $\chi^2 = 8.64$ |
| Without | 20 | 17 | 1 | 2 | $p < .001$ |

Among the 4- to 7-year olds, racial constancy was associated with pro black evaluation going from 68% to 75% and pro white showing a reciprocal decline. However, among the 8- to 11-year olds racial constancy was accompanied by a reduction in pro-black preference from 85% to 40% and a neutral response increase from 10% to 45% (see Table 10.1).

Further empirical research is being conducted to elucidate the role of the primary socializing agents and environments such as the home, school, and mass media (Semaj, 1979).

## IMPLICATIONS FOR SOCIALIZATION

The developmental trends in the socio-cognitive model are obviously toward what for Banks (1976) was "no-preference," for Cross (1979) was "dual-consciousness" and what we are defining as diffused Extended Self Identity. Consistent with the Afrikan concept of self, cognitive and experiential maturity is initially associated with movement toward collective ESI. This would be manifested by an identification with black culture and a positive evaluation of black people. The primary socializing agents of a black child (e.g., parents, relatives, teachers) would have to actively and continuously struggle to present evidence confirming the worth of black culture and people for the child; and against the entire arsenal of an alien and oppressive culture in order to maintain collective ESI. Since most black adults, who live within an anti black, dominant culture, are themselves diffused in their ESI, this struggle is often absent. So either by their example or by default to the wider alien cultural apparatus, the result is a diffused ESI child. This perspective would not necessarily indicate a negative evaluation of non black culture and people, but more likely, indifference. However, the imperatives of the wider alien cultural milieu often necessitates accommodation on the part of the black child, resulting in a reduction in the level of identification with black (Afrikan) values and people, and an incorporation of alien values and people into the extended self-identity. This results in a diffused ESI which the collective ESI socialization process suggested here would minimize.

Euro-American children growing up in a dominant culture which is pro white and anti black generally do not face this situation. Their collective ESI becomes more intense with cognitive and experiential maturity. Even in the absence of the appropriate socio-cognitive capabilities, the quasi ESI of these children is still likely to be collective due to mimicking of the social cues experienced. This is because independent of individual desire, the mechanisms for cultural transmission (e.g., mass media) provide continuous propaganda regarding the superiority of Euro-American culture and people. The primary socializing agents of a white child would not need to do anything extra to maintain the child's collective ESI. The dominant position of Euro-American culture enables these agents to draw from other cultures at will without fear of cultural domination. This is because they, on their own terms, filter alien influences through their own cultural mechanisms and discard what they no longer have use for.

In summary, it appears that Cross' (1979) statement is still appropriate: Liberation is contingent on more black children being socialized for a collective extended self-identity. Collective extended social identity is a socialization for liberation among black children.

# 11

# The Child's Conception of Racial Classification: A Socio-Cognitive Developmental Model

Marguerite N. Alejandro-Wright
*Yale University*

It is widely recognized in the research literature that by age five, children have achieved a basic, adult-like concept of race (Horowitz, 1939; Clark and Clark, 1947; Proshansky, 1966; Katz, 1976). The consistency of this finding is remarkable in light of the elusiveness of race as a concept. As the *Encyclopedia Britannica* points out, the term race has variously referred to linguistic, national, cultural, social, and even political groupings. Although anthropologists and ethnologists have uneasily settled on the notion that race implies genetically transmitted differences, they continue to have considerable difficulty in differentiating among races, in agreeing about classification criteria, and in reaching consensus on the number of distinct racial groupings (Dunn & Dobzhansky, 1952).

One need only peruse the many definitions of race to discover that race is a complex category, based not only on physical characteristics, but also on ancestry, geographic origin, and cultural and political alliances. How then is it that the preschool child has a basic grasp of what is demonstrably so complex, ambiguous, and elusive a concept?

To answer this question it is necessary to point out that although researchers have extensively studied the child's knowledge of race, their research has been primarily limited to racial attitudes and to racial self-identification. Suffice it to say that their findings are consistent with what is perceived as the societal norm, that is, negative black and positive white values and images. Since the 60s, there has been an increasingly positive valuation of blackness among both black and white children (for excellent reviews of this literature see Brand, Ruiz, Padilla, 1974; Katz, 1976). By showing the child's adult-like evaluations of race, this

185

literature infers, with only sketchy empirical data, that the child comprehends the criteria for racial classes.

In recent years, a new body of research has emerged that challenges many of the claims of the preferential-identification literature on methodological (see Brand, Padilla, Ruiz, 1974), analytical (Banks, 1976; Cross, 1980) and interpretative (Taylor, 1976; McAdoo, 1973) grounds. However, a more obvious and fundamental issue is whether the young child truly demonstrates a basic knowledge of race as this literature maintains.

This exploratory study uses a socio-cognitive developmental perspective to study the child's construction of racial classification. The study's major aim is to identify and describe prominent conceptual transformations that characterize children's knowledge of racial categories as they age. Knowledge of racial classification is predicted as evolving from a vague, undifferentiated awareness of skin color differences to knowledge of the cluster of physical-biological attributes associated with racial membership and eventually to a social understanding of racial categorization. Newly developed methodological procedures (including innovative materials representing a broad range of skin colors, hair colors/textures, and facial features) are employed in testing this hypothesis. The sample is 32 black girls, ranging in age from three to 10.

## THE PROBLEM

To adequately address children's race awareness, one must examine the definition of race used by most researchers. This definition holds that race awareness is "knowledge of both the visible difference between racial categories and the perceptual cues by which one classifies people into these divisions" (Porter, 1971, p. 22). Although investigators agree that race awareness entails knowledge of the different perceptual cues (e.g. skin color, hair texture, and color), most incorporate only one physical index—skin color—into their research instrument for examining the child's knowledge of race. As a further limitation, the skin color categories are usually restricted to two, brown and white. One study, after extending the choices by only one color (Greenwald & Oppenheim, 1968), established that the black child's rate of self-misidentification significantly decreased.

There is little, if any, evidence that skin color is the primary criterion employed by preschoolers for distinguishing between people of different races. In fact, two recent studies (Gitter, Mostofsky & Satow, 1972; Sorce, 1977) found that physiognomy may be more frequently employed by preschoolers than skin color in assigning race. Sorce suggested that the "hair and eye category" is a more salient racial cue than skin color. Indeed, he flatly asserted that "color discrimination is not a valid measure of racial awareness."

In light of conceptual weaknesses in research on the formation of racial knowledge, it is not surprising that conventional wisdom maintains that the young (5 year old) child has achieved a basic, adult-like concept of race. Although several researchers have vigorously asserted that color discrimination is not a valid measure of race awareness (Sorce, 1977; Williams & Morland, 1976), this basic assumption remains entrenched. We consider this misconception a logical extension of the theoretical perspective tacitly embraced by investigators. Few of these studies are informed by a coherent theory. Rather, their inferences are loosely and often implicitly based on social-learning theory. Thus, the child is viewed as passive, "absorbing," "internalizing," or "acquiring" a knowledge of race which differs only in degree from that of the adult.

In contrast, socio-cognitive developmental theory, based principally on the work of Piaget (1960–1972), maintains that the child's thinking differs from that of the adult not only in degree, but most fundamentally in kind. This theory holds that the child's knowledge is actively constructed, rather than passively acquired. Cognitive development is seen as a gradual process of reconstructing reality at progressively more advanced stages of understanding as a result of the child's increasingly complex interactions with the environment.

The research literature urgently invites a reexamination of children's development of the concept of race guided by a theory which allows the child's own construct of race to emerge in the empirical investigation unfettered, as much as possible, by adult preconceptions. In a few recent studies, the socio-cognitive developmental perspective in investigating the child's knowledge of race has been productively and revealingly applied (Alejandro-Wright, 1976; Katz, 1976; Semaj, 1979b; Clark, Hocevar & Dembo, 1980). This paper builds on and extends the investigative traditions of these studies.

## A MULTIFACETED VIEW OF THE CHILD'S CONCEPT DEVELOPMENT OF RACE

This study is part of a larger research project which takes a multifaceted view of the child's development of race conception by using four dimensions to assess the child's knowledge of race—racial self-identification, racial constancy, comprehension of the genetic basis of racial identity, and racial classification/phenotype. This paper restricts its focus to one of the four identified dimensions that comprised the indices of race awareness. By focusing exclusively on the component of racial classification, we are better able to show the richness, diversity, and novelty characterizing the child's evolving knowledge of racial categories.

In the literature, racial classification is examined rarely, and then usually perfunctorily. Racial classification is defined by most researchers as the child's ability to employ accurately racial terms i.e., Negro, black, white, colored (Clark & Clark 1939, 1947; Goodman, 1964; Porter, 1971). On examination, it is difficult to view this as a proper classification task, mainly because classification involves the act of grouping similar things, whereas this task usually requires the child to make identifications (e.g., "Give me the white/Negro, etc. doll").

A grouping procedure would be more consistent with Piaget's view. He defines classification as the "fundamental act of the logic of classes, systemically putting together things that belong together on the grounds that they share the same property or properties" (Bruber and Voneche, 1977) [p. 359]. Proper assessment of it necessitates an examination of the child's spontaneous classification, that is, how the child groups people without the provision of the investigator's term or label.

There is a strong consensus among developmental psychologists that preschool children do not have a "genuine grasp of classification" as embodied in verbal labels (Allport, 1958; Piaget, 1972). While a word or label may be used by older children with classificatory skills to symbolize or indicate a category or class, the young child's ability to use a label, in and of itself, does not indicate a true sense of classification (Piaget & Inhelder, 1964; Brunner, Goodnow & Austin, 1956; Vygotsky, 1962).

Unless children understand that race is a group category based on physical as well as socio-biological dimensions, it cannot be persuasively argued that they have a basic conception of race. To identify the child's true understanding of racial classification, a valid classification task must be used.

## Methodology

*Subjects.*    Thirty-two black females, primarily from working-class and lower middle-class backgrounds, aged 3–10 years (four subjects at age 5; five subjects each at 4 and 10 years; six subjects each at 3 years; 6 years and 8 years, including one set of twins), were studied. Also included were 31 parents (mothers of the participants). All the participants resided in New Haven, CT. Places of residence included a predominantly black and a predominantly white area in the city.

*Procedure and measures.*    The measurement instruments were newly developed especially for this study and extensively pilot tested.

The instruments consisted of four interviews. The first, the Introductory Interview, sought to determine the child's knowledge of and ability to discriminate and to classify colors and textures. Two Piaget-like, clinical, semi-structured interviews directly examined the child's concept of race by using props.

Interview I used; (1) six cutouts of oval-shaped faces, which varied in skin color tone from dark brown to a light pink tone; (2) crescent-shaped cutouts of seven types of hair textures (from a tightly curled, coarse type of the Afro variety to straight type hair, in three colors—black, brown, and blonde); and (3) facial features including (a) lips—three sizes varying from thin lips associated with whites to medium lips to the fuller lips associated with blacks; (b) noses—three sizes ranging from the narrow nose to medium nose to the wider nose associated with blacks; (c) eyes—three types, two oval-shaped varing in color, blue and brown, and one of a shape commonly associated with Asians. The child was encouraged to manipulate these materials in order to respond to the tasks posed in the interview questions.

The second interview examined the child's concept of race using photographs of babies, elementary school children, and adults of different racial backgrounds (black, white, and Asian) in an interview format similar to that employed in Interview I. The photographs showed five gradations of skin color ranging from dark black to medium black to tan and ivory and including three racial groups— black, white and Asian.

The photographed individuals were identically attired in a blue cape. A systematic attempt was made to elicit spontaneous explanations of the child's responses to the various dimensions of the child's concept of race, namely, racial identification, knowledge of racial terms, as well as more specific judgments on the proposed dimensions of race awareness (i.e., racial classification, constancy, understanding of the biological basis of race). Although the interview questions were sequentially ordered, the interview was open-ended so as to allow the investigator to pursue important aspects of the child's responses in order to evaluate the structure or form of the child's thinking about race. For the younger children, ages three to five, the two interviews usually required four 30 minute sessions. Older children typically required two 1-hour sessions.

## Specific Classification Tasks: Photo Interview

Children were presented with 10 photos of elementary school children matched in gender and complexion, with one boy and one girl varying on the following dimensions: two dark complexion blacks, two medium complexion blacks and two light complexion blacks; two whites and two Asians. The photos were presented in random order and scrambled after each response. The classification task was threefold in nature:

1. *Spontaneous Task.* The respondent was shown the group of photos and requested to ''put the people together (in a group) who belong together or who are the same.'' Verbal justification of the child's grouping pattern was elicited. These instructions were repeated until the child had exhausted her repertoire of ways to group the photos.
2. *Structured Tasks.* The child was requested to categorize different members of the array of pictures according to individual racial labels: ''Put all the children together who are black, white, Negro, colored, Chinese.''

3. *Probing Task.* This task introduced the child to the photo of an indeterminate child (of interracial parentage) and requested that the photo be added to the most appropriate of the child's previously assembled groups (see classification task #2). The child was also requested to explain her response.

Children were also asked to draw self-portraits (after the Photo Interview) and family portraits (after the Cutouts Interview).

The final interview, the mother's interview, contained questions concerning the way mothers approached the issue of race in the rearing of their children and their observations of memorable moments in their children's development of an awareness of race. All of the interviews were administered in the respondents' homes.

## Hypothesis

An age-related progression will be observed in children's performance on the racial classification tasks. Younger children will perform at the lower stages of racial classification (do better on the easier tasks) while, conversely, the older children's performance will be scored consistently at the higher stages of racial classification.

## Results

The results of this study provide substantial support for the hypothesis that there is an age-related developmental progression to children's conception of racial categories. The presentation of the results is organized as follows: (1) a brief examination of children's spontaneous classification responses; (2) performance on the individual indices of the structured classification items (e.g., black, white, Chinese, child of indeterminate race); and (3) a general model of racial classification that emerges from this analysis will be reviewed. An examination of children's notions of the nonphysical indices employed to distinguish members of different racial classes will also be explored.

### I. *Spontaneous Classification Task*

There is a discernable age-related pattern in children's response to "put the people together who belong together/are the same." Children in the youngest (3–4 years) and middle (5–6 years) age groups tended to use criteria other than color or race as a basis of their spontaneous groupings. Children in the older group (8–10 years) initially tended to follow this pattern but were more likely to group spontaneously by color prior to the investigator's introduction of the structured classification tasks (i.e., the racial terms). Even older children, who used color in spontaneous groupings, eschewed the use of common racial terms black, white, Chinese to describe their groups. Rather, there was a tendency to label spontaneous groups by relative color labels ''brown,'' ''light white,'' or to use ethnic categories (e.g., ''Puerto Rican,'' ''Italian''). In sum, the spontaneous classification results suggest that a child's propensity was to use categories other than color or race to group people. However, with age there is a slight but discernable tendency toward grouping people by color/ethnic or even national group, though not necessarily using conventional racial terms to describe these groups.

## II. *Structured Classification Task*

Children's responses to each of the structured classification tasks (''Put the people together who are black, Negro, white, Chinese.'') showed a distinctive age-related developmental pattern reflective of children's evolving knowledge of racial classes.

A. *Black.*   In response to the classificatory item black: ''Put all the people together in the same group who are black,'' results showed a pronounced age trend in children's response patterns, with majorities in the youngest (3 and 4 years) and middle (5 and 6 years) groups interpreting the term black in other than a racial manner. Most of the children in these age groups viewed black as a reference category for only the darkest people (fewer than four photos correctly grouped as black) or a reference group for darker individuals referring to the medium as well as the dark complexion people (four photos correctly grouped as black). With the exception of the 4 year old, none of the children below age eight correctly categorized all of the six photographs of blacks.

An analysis of children's explanations of their grouping pattern for the term black revealed that this term was interpreted literally—as the color black—for children in the youngest age group who showed knowledge of color identification and possessed basic classification skills. For children in the middle age group (5 to 6 years) the category black broadened to include both dark and medium complexion blacks. However, they preferred the label brown as a reference term for medium complexion blacks in the category black. They shared the color orientation of younger children in their preoccupation with skin color as the single criterion used to determine group membership. References to hair or phenotype were generally absent from these children's justifications of their grouping patterns. Thus, it was not surprising that light complexion blacks were systematically excluded from the black group. Overall, these children's response pattern to the categorization of blacks reflected a fundamental limitation in their grasp of the racial class black. At most, they interpreted this category as physical, and devoid of socio-biological meaning.

The response pattern of most 8 year olds to the category black bore some resemblance to that of younger children. However, their inability to form a group of all the blacks was fundamentally dissimilar to that of younger children. Not until age 10 do children show a sophisticated understanding of black as a physical, social and biological category. Eighty percent of 10 year olds correctly classified all blacks in the group black, regardless of skin color, hair and phenotype variations. Justifications of their groups/classes revealed the knowledge that there is a wide variation in black's skin color and phenotype and a recognition that a certain cluster of physical characteristics, as well as inferred ancestral heritage, imbue the term black with a special sociobiological, even historical, meaning.

Children's knowledge of racial classification as tapped by the term Negro closely parallels that of the term black. However, the majority of younger children (3–6 years) displayed unfamiliarity to the point of perplexity with this term. Although there is a gradual progression with age to an adult-like understanding of the class Negro, it is not until age 10 that the majority of children group appropriately.

B. *White.*    Children's approach to the task of forming the racial category white reflected the underlying organizational pattern demonstrated in their classification of blacks. Younger children conceptualized white in strict color terms whereas older children progressively imbued the term with socio-biological meaning. Of those children up to age six who showed a discernable pattern in their groupings, most formed a white group which was composed of light complexion people regardless of race. Specifically, their white group included whites as well as Asians (Chinese) and light complexion blacks. An analysis of the explanations of their responses revealed the group to be exclusively based on skin color similarity.

By age eight, the majority of children were beginning to grasp the socio-biological implications of the term white. By age 10, a majority (80%) of the children displayed an adult-like understanding of the term white as inferring both socio-biological and physical properties. This white group was composed exclusively of white members on the basis of skin color, hair and phenotype as well as inferred socio-biological characteristics (e.g. children make reference to whites as having white ancestry and European national origin). Asians were considered a distinct group based on phenotype as well as national origin.

C. *Chinese.*    Children's concepts of the category Chinese did not follow the gradual age-developmental pattern established in classifying other racial groups. With the exception of 3 year olds, the majority of children, regardless of age, correctly grouped Chinese. Interestingly, most of the children in the youngest and middle age groups were unable to elucidate the criteria employed to assemble members of the Chinese group. Their response pattern contrasted with that of black and white groups where children immediately pointed to skin color to justify their grouping patterns. A typical explanation was, "I just know that's what it is." Curiously, a high proportion of 6 year olds spontaneously labeled the

Chinese people as Puerto Rican. Although the majority of children age four and higher could accurately form a Chinese category, most demonstrated a limited knowledge of this racial class. They viewed Chinese as a subclass of the white group because of the skin color similarity of the two races. Indeed, not until age eight did the children begin to conceptualize that Chinese belonged to a racially distinct group from whites.

D. *Child of "Indeterminate" Race.* In order to assess the child's reliance on skin color as the primary index of racial class membership, a task was introduced requiring the determination of racial class membership in the face of ambiguous stimuli. A picture of a girl of indeterminate race was presented (the girl pictured, who was actually of interracial parentage, was characterized by an olive complexion and curly hair). The respondent was requested to place the girl pictured in one of the previously constituted groups. The majority of children in the youngest and middle age groups categorized the indeterminate child as white, consistently justifying their responses on skin color similarity with whites. In the older age groups (8–10 years), there was a striking shift in children's response pattern with a high proportion of these children (50% of the 8 year olds and 80% of the 10 year olds) classifying the indeterminate child as either black or other (usually Puerto Rican or a half and half [interracial]).

An examination of children's responses revealed that hair and phenotype figured more prominently in their determination of the indeterminate child's racial category than did skin color. Only a small minority of the children, all in the older age groups, made inferences pertaining to the racial ancestry of the indeterminate child. Even those who accurately guessed the interracial parentage of this child differed in their assignment of racial class membership to the indeterminate child—some constructed a distinct group of half and half while others included them in the group of blacks.

Pearson R was used to measure relationships between the various racial classification indices. The individual indices correlated significantly with each other (ranging from r=.31, p<.10 to r=.58, p<.01) and very significantly with chronological age (r=.58, p<.01 to r=.81, p<.001).

## Stages of Racial Classification

A Guttman scalogram analysis (Green, 1956) was employed in the assessment of whether a developmental sequence was observable in children's knowledge of racial classification. A summary of this analysis is presented in Table 11.1. Scores were dichotomized so that a child was assigned a + for accurate comprehension and a − for inaccurate or partial understanding on the three main classificatory items: Chinese, black/Negro/colored and white. The majority of the children (94%) fit into one of the four stagelike patterns of response (Coefficient of Reproducibility = .96; coefficient of scalability = .85). The rela-

## TABLE 11.1

### Guttman Scalogram Analysis of (P) Classification

Scalogram Analysis of the Percentage of Children in Each Age Group
Passing and Failing Items on (P) Classification Component
(Based on Five Questions Set)[1]

| | Question Set | | | Proportion of Children Age Group | | | | | | |
|---|---|---|---|---|---|---|---|---|---|---|
| Type | "Chinese" | "Black" "Negro" "Colored" | "White" | 3 (n = 6) | 4 (n = 5) | 5 (n = 4) | 6 (n = 6) | 8 (n = 6) | 10 (n = 5) | N (n = 32) |
| **Stage** | | | | | | | | | | |
| Old Idiosyncratic | | | | | | | | | | |
| Color | − | − | − | 1.00 | .40 | 0 | 0 | 0 | 0 | .25 |
| I Sublimnal | | | | | | | | | | |
| Awareness | + | − | − | 0 | .40 | 1.00 | .67 | .17 | 0 | .34 |
| II Preconceptual | + | + | − | 0 | .20 | 0 | .17 | .50 | .20 | .19 |
| III Conceptual | + | + | + | 0 | 0 | 0 | 0 | .17 | .80 | .16 |
| **Non-Stage** | | | | | | | | | | |
| A | + | − | + | 0 | 0 | 0 | .17 | .17 | 0 | .06 |
| B | − | + | − | 0 | 0 | 0 | 0 | 0 | 0 | 0 |
| C | − | + | + | 0 | 0 | 0 | 0 | 0 | 0 | 0 |
| D | − | 0 | + | 0 | 0 | 0 | 0 | 0 | 0 | 0 |

Coefficient of Reproducibility = .96
Minimum Marginal Reproducibility = .73
Percent Improvement = .23
Coeffcint of Scalability = .85
[1] + = passing, − = failing

tionship between the child's assessed stage of racial classification and chronological age was highly significant ($r = .55$, $p < .001$). These data indicated an identifiable age-related developmental stage sequence. As suggested, the developmental path of race conception progressed through four stages, beginning with idiosyncratic knowledge of color categories at Stage 0 and culminating with conceptual awareness of racial categories at Stage III.

Twenty-five percent of the sample, all 3 and 4 year-olds, responded at the idiosyncratic (Stage 0) level of racial classification. Few of these children understood the notion of class or were consistent in their use of color labels. A few even had their own private labels (e.g., pink, vanilla, chocolate) for referring to groups of people. Generally, these children's approach to the task was characterized by a marked reluctance to categorize people into large groups, conveying the impression that the act of grouping individuals according to physical characteristics was an alien, uncomfortable, unfamiliar, and therefore forced one. Upon the investigator's introduction of the color/racial labels (black, white, Chinese), children at Stage 0 generally responded by attempting to comply, grouping the photos according to these terms but eventually abandoning the interviewer's labels and substituting their own terms.

For example, in the following dialogue between a 3 year old and the interviewer, the child initially assembled a mixed group of people as black. Upon in-depth questioning about the blacks in the group, she decided that the separate category of brown should be made for the medium complexion blacks. Children at this stage generally have difficulty with their own color self-identification, as illustrated in this excerpt, so it was not surprising that they showed confusion with the more abstract skill of racial classification.

I (Interviewer): . . . give me the children who are black . . .
C (Child; 3 yrs.): Child? [Groups photos of black, Asian and white children together]
I: Any other little kid who's black. . . They're all black?
C: [shakes her head]
I: But they're not all black?
C: This is brown, we call them brown. He's not black, she's not black. [Later in the same line of inquiry]
I: . . . What color are you. . . What color is your skin?
C: Red.
I: Who told you you were red?
C: [Points in the direction of her mother, who is in an adjacent room]

The largest percentage of children (34%) ranging widely in age from 4 to 8 years, with the majority at ages five and six, was found at Stage I (Subliminal Awareness). Children at this stage showed a greater propensity to assemble, with a little encouragement from the interviewer, categories based on physical characteristics, than did children at the elementary stage. Generally, Stage I children based their categories on global skin color groups (black, white) and their under-standing of color categories was accurate and consistent. They appeared unaware of the cluster of physical characteristics which help to distinguish racial mem-bership, leading them mistakenly to group both light complexion blacks and Chinese as whites. Moreover, a high proportion of them did not view skin color as a stable characteristic:

> I: Put all the black people here. . .
> C: (5 yrs.) [Groups the dark- and medium-complexion people together]
> I: How can you tell they're all black?
> C: They've been in the sun.

These children's unawareness of color/racial terms as connoting socio-biolog-ical categories implies at best only a rudimentary knowledge of racial classes. However, unlike children at Stage 0, Stage I children could appropriately group Chinese children once the label was provided, although they were unable to articulate the basis of their reasoning for this categorization.

Nineteen percent of the sample, primarily 8 year olds, displayed a Stage II (Preconceptual) level of understanding of racial classification. The global and amorphous quality that characterizes the earlier stages yields at this stage to differentiated categories embodying subtler distinctions associated with racial group membership. Stage II children demonstrated an awareness that racial group membership was based on not only skin color but also on other physical characteristics. In the following excerpt, an 8 year old justified her categorization of the light complexion blacks as black.

> I: Put all the people together who are black. . .
> C: (8 yrs.) [Groups photos of the dark, medium and light complexion people together].
> I: [Points to the photos of light complexion blacks]. How did you know they were black?
> C: Cause most black people have this kind of hair.
> I: . . . What kind of hair do most black people have?
> C: I don't know what it is called but . . . like nappy.

Stage II children's justifications of their grouping patterns suggest an emerging awareness that the dimensions used to distinguish different color/racial groups were not only physical but also biological.

Only 16% of the sample, predominantly 10 year olds, demonstrated a Stage III (conceptual) knowledge of the basis of racial classification. These children understand that the color/racial categories used to distinguish different people are based on physical and biological properties. Unlike younger children, Stage III children began to transcend the superficiality of the physical dimension by assigning a more prominent role to the biological dimension of racial identity. Moreover, these children were *beginning* to recognize that the social dimension was a salient, if not crucial factor, in racial classification. The following comments by a 10 year old illustrate Stage III:

I: [Question asked in a follow-up inquiry] . . . But how could a person tell [if someone is really black]?
C: (10 yrs.) Maybe you couldn't tell.
I: . . . I don't understand that.
C: Cause you were born that way.
I: And you can't change at all?
C: Yea, you can change.
I: But you said I would still be black if I changed.
C: I mean you would be white. Your skin color would be white but for real, you were born black.
I: What does it mean to be born black? . . .
C: Being brown like your skin color. That is your race. . .

Children at Stage III showed an emerging awareness of the social subtleties underlying racial classification. This awareness allowed them to avoid the conceptual confusion evident in younger children's classification responses.

Not until this final stage (Stage III) was there semblance between children's racial categories and the conception of race as denoting separate and distinct groups characterized by a specific cluster of physical attributes, ancestral origin, and social alliance. However, most children at this stage are not fully able to comprehend the socially derived meaning of racial classes, which can transcend physical and biological realities and encompass culturally specific realities. Racial distinctions are demonstrably inconsistent across different societies. Racial identification may vary; given environmental conditions, a light complexioned black may be identified as white or black depending on environmental signals. Only a couple of children at the highest stage appeared to be cognizant of the possible flexibility of racial classification as evident in their allusion to the expression of blacks "passing" for whites. Thus the adult-like standard that views racial categorization as sometimes ambiguous, vague, inconsistent, and possibly culturally-specific, was at best only minimally appreciated in Stage III construction of rigid racial categories.

To summarize, the color/racial classification data revealed an identifiable developmental sequence: Initially lacking knowledge about racial classification (Stage 0), children then show a rudimentary, even subliminal, awareness (Stage I) of race-like categories as suggested by their ability to accurately group Chinese. Nevertheless, children at this stage did not fully understand racial categories to be mutually exclusive, or based on multiple dimensions. In the next stage (Stage II) the child's concept of racial categories became more differentiated and less diffused. It was not until the final Stage (III) that there was some semblance to the adult-like notion of race as denoting separate and distinct classes defined by a specific cluster of physical attributes and ancestral origin.

## III. Knowledge of the Non-Physical Dimension of Racial Classification

In addition to an examination of the child's knowledge of the definable physical cues (i.e. skin color, hair color/texture, facial features), this study sought to identify other cues children relied on to categorize people into groups. Table 11.2 summarizes the distribution of responses of the major categories of differences identified. The basic inquiry was deliberately open-ended: "Are black people different from white people?" and follow-up probes: "Do blacks act/speak/dress differently from whites?" Children's responses to this inquiry provided rich and intriguing data and revealed an age-related progression to their knowledge of the varied and multi-faceted subtle cues used to group people into various categories.

Given the scope of this paper, these data can only be examined briefly. Not surprisingly, children in the youngest age groups (3–4 years) showed little com-

TABLE 11.2
Children's Understanding of Differences Between Blacks and Whites:
Proportional Distribution of Responses by Age Group

| | Age Group | | | | | | |
|---|---|---|---|---|---|---|---|
| Response | 3 (n = 6) | 4 (n = 5) | 5 (n = 4) | 6 (n = 6) | 8 (n = 6) | 10 (n = 5) | All (n = 32) |
| No Differences | .67 | .60 | 0 | 0 | 0 | 0 | .21 |
| Yes Differences Without Explanation | .33 | .40 | .25 | 0 | 0 | 0 | .16 |
| Yes Differences With Physical Explanation | 0 | 0 | .75 | .83 | .17 | 0 | .28 |
| Yes Differences Physical Explanation and Limited Socio-Cultural Explanation | 0 | 0 | 0 | .17 | .33 | .40 | .16 |
| Yes Differences Physical Explanation and Elaborated Socio-Cultural Explanation | 0 | 0 | 0 | 0 | .50 | .60 | .19 |

prehension of this question. However, this limitation cannot be attributed primarily to underdeveloped verbalization but fundamentally to limitations in their understanding of the categories black or white. Since many of these children interpreted black and white strictly in terms of color categories, devoid of sociobiological connotations, they were puzzled by the term black or white people. Again, they preferred their own idiosyncratic terms like brown or pink people. By the middle years (5–6 years), children consistently relied on physical cues (primarily skin color) as a basis of differentiating between blacks and whites. It was not until age eight that a sizeable proportion of children began to identify nonphysical cues perceived to differentiate blacks and whites, such as style of dress, speech patterns, culinary tastes, musical preference, socioeconomic status, lifestyle, history, and ancestry. These children distinctly sensed that something other than physical cues was crucial in revealing racial class membership.

In sum, this examination of the child's conception of racial classification reveals the process of comprehending racial group membership to be very complex. These results suggest that not until age 10 does the child begin to grasp an adult-like conception of racial classes as encompassing multifaceted, sometimes arbitrary and contradictory cues.

This exploratory work challenges conventional views of the child's race awareness as differing from an adult's primarily in degree. In contrast, the child's concept of race was qualitatively different from that of the adult; the child had his/her own unique way of thinking about color and racial categories. This work revealed the developmental process of racial classification to be more complex and gradual than had been previously proposed. These initial findings indicated the child's construction of racial categories to follow an ordered developmental pattern, suggestive of a hierarchical, invariant sequence. The primary determinant of stage differences in race classification appeared to indicate how the child's thinking about color/physical/socio-biological categories was structured or organized.

This study suggests that it is critical to examine the child's spontaneous response patterns of color/racial classification, knowledge of racial subclasses, and understanding of the properties by which racial categories are defined. Four stages of racial classification were identified: (0) Idiosyncratic, (I) Subliminal, (II) Preconceptual and (III) Conceptual. The child's progress through these stages is characterized initially by an increasing awareness of the physical, later the biological, and finally the social cues commonly used to ascribe racial membership (for a more detailed discussion of this stage sequence, see Alejandro-Wright, 1980).

We recognize limitations of this exploratory study, particularly as relates to generalization of findings. At this point, our research emphasis was on stage construction rather than a stage verification. Future research, particularly longitudinal, is required to substantiate our findings. A major question is whether the developmental sequence of racial classification, sketched in this preliminary work, holds for larger, more varied samples.

A crucial task of further research is to follow the developmental course of race awareness to its conclusion with the inclusion of a more extended age range. As previously stated, the 10 year old's knowledge of racial categories bears only some semblance to that of the adult. It is critical that we follow the child's racial concept, from the preschool years to, at least, middle adolescence to document the major changes in the child's awareness over this span of years. Impressionistic data (primarily anecdotal material) suggest that a sophisticated concept of race, in its multifaceted manifestation, is not realized until adolescence.

Moreover it is equally important to examine the affective, experiential, and environmental factors which impact on the ontogeny of the child's conception of race. Given that race is a particular, socially determined category, it is important to identify factors (e.g. popular media, school, family, environment, etc.) which contribute building blocks to the child's construction of racial categories. The anthropologist Brace observes that ''The reality of races as biological entities . . . is to be found in the human conviction that they exist. . . They are real because people believe they are. . .'' (Williams and Morland, 1976). Thus, we need to examine how these nearly elusive categories of race become a shared basis of reference in spite of their inherent ambiguities.

Finally, future research should examine whether the developmental stage sequence of racial classification identified in this study is characteristic of a coherent universal system of thought. Cross-cultural studies are necessary to correct this deficiency in the literature. Because racial typologies vary across societies, there may be differences in the content of children's racial categories. However, we speculate that the socio-cognitive developmental view will remain consistent across cultures, with the structure of the child's reasoning progressing from an idiosyncratic, to a physical, to a biological, and finally, to a social conception of race.

# 12 No Place to Run, No Place to Hide: Comparative Status and Future Prospects of Black Boys

Bruce Robert Hare
*State University of New York—Stony Brook*

Louis A. Castenell Jr.
*Xavier University of Louisana*

> *Something happens when the son knows that the father cannot do anything about it. Something happens to the father too.*
> —James Baldwin (1981).

## INTRODUCTION

Recent reports on mortality rates in the United States indicated that black males were the only race/sex group for whom the average life expectancy actually declined between 1960 and 1970 (Staples, 1978). They also have the shortest life expectancy and the highest high school dropout rate. Current unemployment rates among black youth in major cities in the United States are reported to be as high as 47%. While black males were approximately 6% of the population, they constituted over 42% of the inmates, and as of 1978, 47% of those on death row. Black males have traditionally entered predominately black colleges at lower rates than black women (Gurin & Epps, 1975).

Little has been offered to explain the uniquely endangered status of the black male in America or the forces that have historically acted to limit his possibilities. To be sure, he has not been ignored, which the abundance of negative literature will attest. However, the socialization processes and the educational and occupational structures that create and perpetuate these conditions have scarcely been addressed. The disjunction between role expectations and reality must also be addressed.

The simultaneous existence of normative male role expectations and the "fact" of black male underachievement provides "proof" of the inadequacy of black men. Consequently, while both the black man and those for whom he is supposed to provide, may intellectually understand racism as the cause of his relative inability to provide, the reality of his failure will impact on his life. Both

201

his self-image and his dependents' view of him will be affected. The existence of an aracial provider role stereotype, along with racial inequality, and the black man's inability to successfully play the role, makes for a racial stereotype most attainable by middle and upper class white men. In short, while he shares the burden of racism with black women, the black male's structured failure to meet the normative male cultural standard as a successful bread winner, protector, father, and husband increases his vulnerability in the general society, his own home, and his own mind. He has no place to run, no place to hide.

While cultural stereotypes regarding his shiftlessness, laziness, or innate inferiority, are easy explanations, they fail to address the conditions against which he must struggle from childhood. Clearly, the preceding information, at the very least suggests that the prospects for black boys, as an aggregate, are relatively dismal. The need to investigate the mechanisms through which they are brought from assumed equal potential at birth, to a disadvantaged adult status, becomes urgent.

It is the intent of this paper to investigate the comparative self-perception and achievement of a sample of 10 and 11 year old preadolescent black boys. The objective is to ascertain their current status and whether there exists early indicators of their future precarious status. The attempt is to identify black boys' shared characteristics with their two general membership groups (i.e., blacks and males), their unique characteristics, and potential connections between their characteristics and future prospects. Data for the paper are from a 1977 study of 500 fifth grade students in Champaign, IL.

There have been few studies comparing black boys and girls. Most studies of black children have been race studies which failed to provide information on sex differences. Most studies of sex differences have been on white middle-class children and adults (Maccoby & Jacklin, 1974). Thus the specific comparison of black boys and girls, and black and white boys offers an opportunity to study black boys in a more systematic way, and raises the possibility of eliciting a clearer picture of their relative status. The study of sex differences among white children has proven to be a poor predictor of sex differences among blacks (Lewis, 1975). So too has the general study of race difference proven a questionable means of assessing within-sex race differences (Hare, 1980a).

This study raises three questions for investigation:

1. Do black boys and white boys differ significantly in self-perception and achievement?
2. Do black boys and black girls differ significantly in self-perception and achievement?
3. Does the relative self-perception and achievement of the black boys shed any possible light on their future status?

The dimensions on which comparisons are made are general self-esteem, area-specific (i.e., school, peer, and home) self-esteem, self-concept of ability, achievement orientation, general anxiety, sense of control, importance of social abilities, and performance on standardized reading and math achievement tests.

## OVERVIEW

Because of the scarcity of literature directed to the study of black boys, the following overview will be presented within the context of what is known about sex and race differences in general.

### Sex Difference

Most of the psychological work on sex differences has been done with white middle-class American children and adults. Maccoby and Jacklin (1974) reported no significant sex differences among children in general self-esteem, confidence in task performance, achievement orientation, sense of control or verbal (reading) and math ability, although they reported a tendency for girls to score higher in verbal abilities than boys. They also reported boys to be more independent; to have more positive peer interaction, possess a higher self-concept of strength and potency; and to have lower anxiety scores than girls. There is little comparative sex data on area-specific (school, peer, and home) self-esteem. However, recent area-specific research (Hare, 1977a) on black and white children of varying socioeconomic backgrounds, revealed no significant sex differences on these dimensions when race and SES were controlled.

Although we would generally expect similar sex findings for black boys and girls, the possibility of varying patterns of sex differences across racial groups must be considered. Arguing an egalitarian character of black culture, some researchers have hypothesized fewer sex differences among black children and adults (Gutman, 1976; Lewis, 1975; Willie, 1976).

### Race Differences

There is a long tradition which reports lower general self-esteem among black children than among white children (Clark & Clark, 1947; Grier & Cobbs, 1968; Kardiner & Ovesey, 1951). The theoretical premise of this school of thought was succinctly stated by Kardiner and Ovesey (1951) when they postulated, "the basic fact is that in the Negro aspiration level, good conscience and even good performance are irrelevant in face of the glaring fact that the Negro gets a poor reflection of himself in the behavior of whites, no matter what he does or what his merits are" (p. 297). The foundation of this assumption is that as a people in a predominately white culture, blacks are incapable of rejecting the negative images of themselves that are held by whites. This tradition has been based on interpretive analysis of why black children chose white dolls over black dolls, and studies that often used psychiatric patients to make generalizations about the black population at large. Such research also frequently ignored the effect of socioeconomic background on self-esteem. Because such studies often compared lower-class blacks and middle-class whites, and attributed all differences to race, their results are highly questionable.

In contrast, more recent studies with larger and more representative samples, and SES controls, have ranged from finding no significant differences among white and black boys (Edwards, 1974; Calhoun, Kuriffs & Warren, 1976) to finding blacks scoring higher (Bachman, 1970; Hare, 1977a). There has been little cross-race research on area-specific (school, peer and home) self-esteem. Coopersmith's (1967) major work in this area used a restricted sample of white, male, middle-class children. However, more recent research by Hare (1977a) reported a significant race difference only in school self-esteem, although a subsequent study by Hare (1980b) showed no significant race difference on any of the area-specific self-esteem measures.

Significant race differences also have been reported on other variables germane to this article. Blacks were reported having a higher self-concept of ability than whites (Hare, 1980b); lower achievement orientation (Hare, 1980b; Rosen, 1959); lower sense of control (Battle & Rotter, 1963; Hare, 1980b); higher concern with social abilities (Dreger & Miller, 1968; Hare, 1980b); and lower scores on standardized reading and math achievement tests (Coleman, Campbell 1966; Hare, 1980b). However, these findings are from studies which did not compare the black and white boys separately, but rather analyzed a pooled sample of black and white children of both sexes.

## METHODS

### Sample

This study was conducted in the Champaign, IL school system in the spring of 1977. The complete sample of over 500 subjects included all fifth graders (10–11 years old) in the district who participated with parental approval and were in school on the days of the survey. Over 90% of the total fifth grade population completed questionnaires. The literature supports the belief that both in stability and ability, children at this age are an ideal sample for such a study (Simmons, Rosenberg, & Rosenberg, 1973).

### Instruments

A 30 item general and area-specific (school, peer, and home) self-esteem scale developed by Hare was used to measure self-esteem. School, peer, and home self-esteem were the three 10 item subscales of this general measure (Hare, 1975; Shoemaker, 1980). A seven item general self-esteem measure by Rosenberg

(1965) was also included as an additional general self-esteem measure. Self-concept of ability was assessed by five of Brookover's (1965) items, and general anxiety by Sarason's et al. (1964) scale. Academic achievement was measured by performance on the math and reading sections of a standardized metropolitan achievement test administered district wide in the fall of 1976. Sense of control was measured by Coleman and Campbell's (1966) three item internal versus external control measure. Higher scores on this measure indicate a greater belief in internal control. Finally, achievement orientation was measured by Epps' (1971) 13 item scale, and social abilities by a scale developed by Hare (1975).

Socioeconomic divisions were developed from the Blau and Duncan (1967) index of occupational status. The index was divided into thirds based on head of household's occupation. The index is divided such that the first point approximated the separation of manual from nonmanual labor, and the second division approximates the point of separation between nonprofessional and professional workers. Educational background of parents was used as an additional social class indicator.

## Analysis

To investigate the questions, a set of separate 2×3 (black boys versus black girls and white boys by blue collar, lower white collar, upper white collar) analyses of variance were used. The test reported for each main factor effect (race and sex) is equivalent to the test for the unique proportion of the variance accounted for by each factor in a hierarchical multiple regression analysis. As such, it is a conservative test of the importance of race and sex, since the variance accounted for jointly by race and SES (or by sex and SES) is removed before assessing the significance of race and sex.

## RESULTS

### Sex Differences Between Black Boys and Black Girls

Whereas literature reviewed on sex comparisons between white children reveal few differences, black boys and girls in our sample differed on a variety of important dimensions (see Tables 12-1 and 12-2). Our results were consistent with the literature for similar aged whites in reporting no significant sex differences among blacks in general self-esteem or sense of control. The results were also consistent with the literature on whites in reporting black boys scoring lower than black girls in general anxiety (means 11.84 and 14.54, respectively) and reading achievement (means 25.90 and 34.31 respectively), and in showing among black boys a tendency toward higher peer self-esteem, and significantly higher ratings of the importance of social abilities. However, our results differed

TABLE 12.1
Analysis of Variance for Compared Groups
(Significance of "F Values" From Two
by Three ANOVAs for Compared Groups)

| Variables | Black Boys vs. Black Girls Sex differences within race | Black Boys vs. White Boys Race differences within sex |
|---|---|---|
| Rosenberg General Self-Esteem | .354 | .196 |
| Hare General Self-Esteem | .768 | .275 |
| School Self-Esteem | .082 | .060 |
| Peer Self-Esteem | .067 | .789 |
| Home Self-Esteem | .654 | .397 |
| Self-Concept of Ability | .194 | .183 |
| Achievement Orientation | .042*g | .000***w |
| General Anxiety | .042*g | .691 |
| Sense of Control | .713 | .031*w |
| Social Abilities | .012*b | .000***bl |
| Read Ability | .004**g | 0.000***w |
| Math Ability | .026*g | 0.000***w |

*p ≤ .05; **p ≤ .01; ***p ≤ .001
g = Girls higher; b = Boys higher; bl = Blacks higher; w = Whites higher

from the literature on white children, in that black boys score significantly lower than their female counterparts in math ability (means of 24.48 and 31.96, respectively), achievement orientation (means of 32.82 and 34.55), and tended toward lower school self-esteem.

It should be noted that separate comparison of white boys and girls did not differ significantly on these dimensions. There were no significant differences between black boys and girls in home self-esteem or self-concept of ability. It should also be noted that none of the sex by socioeconomic interaction values were significant. In short, our data suggest some very important sex differences between black boys and girls, particularly with regard to the school related dimension of achievement (and achievement orientation), in which girls hold a clear advantage. The only dimensions where the boys scored higher, were the non school dimensions of social abilities, and peer self-esteem.

## Race Differences Between Black Boys and White Boys

Consistent with more recent studies of race differences in general and area-specific (school, peer, home) self-esteem, the results indicated no significant differences on any of these measures between the black and white boys. Nevertheless, as previous studies of race differences have reported, the black boys scored significantly lower than the white boys on sense of control (means 8.98 and 9.88), achievement orientation (means 32.82 and 37.49), performance on

TABLE 12.2
Group Means and Standard Deviations

| Variable | Black Boys | | Black Girls | | White Boys | |
|---|---|---|---|---|---|---|
| | Mean | S.D. | Mean | S.D. | Mean | S.D. |
| Rosenberg General Self-Esteem | 21.20 | 3.37 | 20.87 | 4.02 | 22.63 | 3.53 |
| Hare General Self-Esteem | 88.40 | 11.39 | 88.85 | 12.05 | 91.86 | 11.59 |
| School Self-Esteem | 27.70 | 5.27 | 29.45 | 5.33 | 30.05 | 5.07 |
| Peer Self-Esteem | 29.04 | 4.53 | 27.42 | 4.36 | 28.76 | 4.94 |
| Home Self-Esteem | 31.66 | 5.54 | 31.99 | 5.01 | 33.05 | 5.13 |
| Self-Concept of Ability | 18.54 | 3.85 | 19.39 | 3.06 | 18.52 | 3.19 |
| Achievement Orientation | 32.82 | 5.28 | 34.55 | 5.21 | 37.49 | 5.74 |
| General Anxiety | 11.84 | 6.54 | 14.54 | 6.89 | 10.38 | 6.44 |
| Sense of Control | 8.98 | 2.04 | 8.76 | 1.68 | 9.88 | 1.70 |
| Social Abilities | 33.66 | 3.89 | 31.43 | 5.05 | 31.06 | 4.41 |
| Reading Ability | 25.90 | 15.23 | 34.31 | 18.72 | 51.40 | 26.24 |
| Math Ability | 24.48 | 13.87 | 31.96 | 18.22 | 48.70 | 26.46 |
| | n = 50 | | n = 67 | | n = 241 | |

standardized reading (means 25.90 and 51.40) and math tests (means 24.48 and 48.70). The black boys, however, scored significantly higher on social abilities ratings (means of 33.66 and 31.06, respectively), and showed a tendency toward higher peer self-esteem (see Table 12.2).

## Black Boys Current Status and Future Prospects

Although the data were of limited value for projecting the future status of these black boys, they nevertheless painted an illuminating picture. A picture which was not at all inconsistent with the contemporary status of black men as outlined at the beginning of this paper.

The existence, for example, of standardized test performance differences which place black boys at the bottom of the reading and math hierarchy is consistent with their lower rates of college attendance. Their lower achievement orientation scores and trends toward lower school and higher peer self-esteem were consistent with the higher high school dropout rates of black boys, as well as was the reportedly greater role of peers and nonacademic activities, in influencing their general self-esteem. The absence of significant differences in general self-esteem between black boys, and either the black girls or white boys, further suggested that whatever academic liabilities black boys suffer may already be compensated for by their perceived social assets. In short, while projections about their relative future are tenuous at best, these black boys do appear to currently hold an attainment position, which, if not altered during adolescence, will ultimately deliver them to the same relative disadvantaged status currently outlined for black men.

## DISCUSSION

In this discussion we attempt to theorize regarding some reasons for the contemporary comparative status and future prospects of black boys. We look at the nature of their interactions at home, in schools, and with peers. Theoretically, these three arenas may be considered the child's universe. It is further assumed that the quality of interactions here, as well as the level of consensus or conflicts among the significant others across these arenas, are critical to the self-perception and performance of children (Hare, 1977b).

## Black Boys at Home

The existence of sex differences in academic performance as well as attitudes toward school among black children, suggests a need to investigate sex role socialization practices in black homes. To be sure, the absence of differences in self-esteem at home by sex among black children suggests that they feel equally adjusted. Nevertheless, unless the school is to receive *total blame* for the achievement differential, both the home and the peers deserve attention. Some authors have, in fact, begun to theorize about the characteristics of black child socialization that might shed light on these findings. For example, Kunkel and Kennard (1971) argued that "mothers are apt to be strong disciplinarians, particularly toward daughters, from whom they expect more responsibility than sons" [p. 46]. McAdoo (1979) also reported more fathers expected their daughters to be independent and assertive in relation to their sons. Lewis (1975) concluded in a study of black families that "while mothers have high expectations for their daughters they do not expect as much from their sons" [p. 236]. Allen (1978c) concurred by suggesting that black parents are likely to be harder on their same sex children, since they have responsibility for teaching the specifics of the future role. Thus, since fathers are likely to be out of the home more often, daughters are more likely to be under the more stringent continuous discipline of their mothers. Reid (1972), in a survey of over 200 black women, noted that many felt their brothers received preferential treatment, got away with more, and were generally raised differently. It is tenable then to conclude that black boys are treated differently at home than black girls.

The combination of the Allen notion, more restrictive socialization of black girls than boys by mothers, and the possibility of a better fit between the black girls and school, probably accounts for reported sex differences in attitudes and academic achievement among black children. The implication for the rearing of black boys is that lessons from the more effective academic socialization and control of black girls by black families should be applied toward black boys.

The effects of the presence or absence of fathers, and successful male role models as they condition the socialization of black boys should also be studied. Specifically, given the preponderance of athletes and entertainers over academically successful black male role models that these boys are exposed to through the media, one must wonder if these boys are in fact being *led* to the unrealistic view that nonacademic pursuits are higher probability roads to success. This possibility becomes even more tenable when one considers that they are likely to be exposed to educationally unsuccessful male role models in their real world.

## Black Boys in School

Given gender performance and attainment differences, there exists a dire need to investigate schools as potential contributors to this pattern. While conventional wisdom would have us believe that every child begins the great quest for status at the same starting line, there is ample evidence to suggest that such egalitarian theories are myths (Hare, 1977b). For example, Cicourel and Kitsuse's (1963) study of educational decision makers, after examining the egalitarian assumption, concluded that quite the opposite is true. Lavin (1965), in a study predicting academic performance concluded, ". . . some evidence suggests that implicit subjective criteria are involved in teacher grading practices . . . the more the student's atttitudes and values coincide with those of the teacher, the higher the student's academic performance will be'' (pp. 20 and 150). Thus these studies suggest that the greater the commonality of characteristics and attitude between student and teacher, the higher the possibility of positive outcome. Conversely, the lower the commonality, the greater the possibility for conflict and failure. Other authors, such as Parsons (1959), Smith and Brache (1962), Greeley and Rossi (1966), and Hare (1977b), have posited that the quality of teacher/parent interaction also varies by their commonality of characteristic and values, with direct implications for the academic socialization and performance of children.

This phenomenon may both explain why middle-class, white children are most effectively educated in the American public schools, and why lower class, nonwhite children are least effectively educated. The latter are, in theory, less likely to share the middle-class, white oriented values of their teachers. Such a possibility, needless to say, does not argue well for the schooling prospects of black children in general, or black boys in particular.

With specific reference to teacher behaviors and student race, Epps (1975) concluded that ''turning from student characteristics to the learning environment provided by the school, there is ample evidence that teachers perceive minority students differently than they perceive white students'' (p. 311). The belief among black children that they can succeed, ''but that someone or something is blocking their progress'' (Hare, 1980b, p. 687), and the greater discrepancy between their expected and actual achievement scores (West, Fish & Stevens, 1980), suggest that black children may know this themselves. Rubovitz and Maehr (1973) reported a surprising race difference in patterns of gifted student treatment, with black gifted children experiencing *more* discrimination than those labeled nongifted. Katz (1967) concludes, in an analytic study of teacher attitudes, that:

> the meaning of these teacher differences is that on the average, children from low income homes, most of whom are Negro, get more than their fair share of class-room exposure to teachers who are really unqualified for their role, who basically resent teaching them and who therefore behave in ways that foster in the more dependent students, tendencies toward debilitating self-criticism. (p. 177)

Given suggested sex differences in student treatment, it seems logical to investigate whether there also exist within race sex differences in teacher treatment of black children. If the idea that commonality of characteristics is conducive to support and differences conducive to conflict, is sound, then black boys, and especially lower-class black boys, would theoretically experience the greatest potential conflict, in a middle-class, white female dominated public elementary school system. Black males might also be theorized to have the greatest difficulty in the middle-class, white male dominated postelementary schools. The assumptions here are that shared sex might prove slightly beneficial to the relationship between black girls and their white female teachers, and that black girls may also be perceived as less threatening by white males.[1]

While there are no data to confirm these speculations, it is the authors' opinion that these factors are urgently in need of investigation. The work of Grant (1984) may fill some of this void. The findings of her study about the relationship of race-sex status to schooling experiences indicate that, black boys are privately rated lowest in educational ability by teachers, although most often praised. They have the least "personal chit chat" with the teachers and are least likely to approach the teacher if failing. They are most often threatened by the teacher, sent to the principal or guidance counselor, and disciplined by calling in the parents. Additionally, Rosenberg and Simmons (1971), and Hare (1977a, consistent with the Maccoby and Jacklin (1974) finding of a sex difference among whites) found black girls receiving significantly higher grades than black boys. Interviewed teachers have also reported that black girls receive better conduct ratings, and behave better (more passively?) than black boys. However, black boys are not without school success and are most likely overrepresented in school athletic achievement. This further suggests that the "non-academic but athletically gifted" stereotype of black males may also condition school personnel to route black boys toward athletic activity at the possible expense of academics, both creating and reinforcing the stereotype (Braddock, 1980).

Existing evidence concerning race and sex differences in the quality of the school experience, suggests that the lower attainment, greater negative attitudes, and higher attrition rates of black boys may, in part, be due to the unique problem that they present to the schools. Put simply, black males are probably the most feared, least likely to be identified with, and least likely to be effectively taught group. If this is true, then the responsibility for their lower attainment should be shifted from them, their families, and peers, to the alien, indifferent if not hostile, climate of the schools. Furthermore, their reportedly more negative attitude toward school should be seen, not as the cause of their low attainment, but as a consequence of their mistreatment.

It should also be noted that the school plays a unique role in allocating people to different positions in the occupational system through routing and grading practices (Anderson, 1968). Relative success in school is, in fact, the major avenue through which discrimination in the job market is justified. People in lower status jobs are said to *deserve* them, being the losers in a "fair" competition.

[1]It should be emphasized that whatever slight advantage in treatment black girls might accrue relative to black boys, they also remain significantly behind Whites of both sexes in attainment. The fact that black girls are also least likely to attend professional schools, leaves them most underrepresented in many of the highest status occupations. Thus, sex role socialization to traditional female typed occupational choices (nurse, teacher, social worker, etc.) also serves to discourage higher attainment, by conditioning them to "self-select" out (Cole, 1981).

Given racism and classism in America, it can be argued that the disproportionate allocation of black males to the lowest male labor slots is intended and
functional. It goes without saying that their relative academic failure is essential
to getting the job done. Their failure feeds the lowest ranks of the military, fills
the unskilled labor pool, and provides necessary unemployed workers. Furthermore, the myth of equal educational opportunity increases the probability that
these black men will blame themselves for their failure, accept their low status,
and be seen as getting what they deserve.

## Black Boys and Peers

Although our sample of preadolescent boys, at ages 10 and 11, are probably too
young to be fully entrenched in a peer culture, they are already showing a trend
toward higher peer self-esteem. It may be theorized that as black boys age and
progressively lose in school evaluations, they shift toward peer evaluations, in
search of higher possibilities of success and ego enhancement. As indicated by
Castenell (1983) in a recent study of area-specific achievement motivation, if an
adolescent is discouraged by significant others, or through repeated failure, to
perceive achievement within the school environment, then that adolescent may
choose to achieve in another arena. Cummings (1977) reported that as black boys
grow older, their values are more influenced by peers than is true for other
groups; and that the maintenance of ego and self-respect increasingly requires
peer solidarity. These authors further support the possible existence of a progressive shift in motivation and attachment from the school to the peers among
black boys, and particularly urban, lower-class black boys. They also suggested
that such a shift is a logical pursuit of "achievement" and positive "strokes,"
and a flight from failure and ego damaging experiences. Given this possibility
and the relative failure of black males in the American educational system, it is
plausible to discuss black adolescent peer culture as a short term achievement
arena, but a long term wash-out plan.

Although the benefits are short term, and unlikely to pay off in the adult
occupational structure, the black male adolescent peer culture may also be
viewed as an achievement arena. Consistent with Castenell's (1984) area-specific achievement motivation notion, Maehr and Lysy (1978), also questioned
traditional restricted cultural and academic notions of achievement motivation.
They posit that contextual conditions are important in expressions of achievement motivations, and that the particular form in which achievement is expressed
is determined by the definition that culture gives to it. They further indicated that
motivation is manifest in a broad range of activities, and that motivational
questions are questions of the ways in which, rather than whether, people are
motivated. It would take no more than the observation of a serious basketball
game in a lower-class black community playground, to observe the need to
achieve. Other abilities such as mastering the streets, sexual conquests, supple-

menting family income, and taking on aspects of adult roles at early ages, also provide opportunities to demonstrate competence (Hare, 1977b). It should be noted that although the larger culture views these patterns as maladaptive and strange, they are, within the cultural milieu, perfectly realistic, adaptive, and respected responses to reality (Davis, 1948).

The black boy's peer culture may be regarded as a dead end mainly because, even though it succeeds in providing alternative outlets for achievement through the demonstration of competence, it offers little hope of long term legitimate success. The real dangers are that it often drafts young boys into the self-destructive worlds of drugs and crime. The notion of "peer solidarity" (Cummings, 1977) also suggests an anti intellectual strain between peers and the schooling experience. It should be re-emphasized, however, that the collectively negative schooling experiences of black boys produce this anti school sentiment, rather than the opposite. The apparent contradiction between "being cool and doing school," becomes more a necessary affirmation of the possibility of being cool without suffering school, and a self-protection, rather than a purely anti school ideology.

In summary, given the presence of negative schooling experiences, the availability of positive peer experiences, and the inability of adolescents to perceive the long term consequences of youthful decisions, these boys can be said to be making a logical decision in shifting from school to peers. In the long run, of course, they are disproportionately washed out of legitimate occupational success possibilities.

## CONCLUSION

The data presented here document black boys' (and by inference, black men's) uniquely precarious status and suggest that, even if a conscious conspiracy does not exist, normative individual and institutional processes are operating to their disadvantage. These processes disproportionately deliver black males to the lowest rungs of the educational, and subsequently, occupational ladder. Perhaps the most surprising finding is that compared to black girls and white boys, black boys do not generally feel any less good about themselves, either as preadolescents, or adolescents (Castenell, 1981). A plausible explanation may reside in Epps' (1975) conclusion of a stronger connection between school grades and self-esteem among whites than blacks. He argued that the finding could be "attributed" to the fact that the two groups base self-esteem on different attributes [p. 306]. The process may also have been well described by Rosenberg (1965) when he stated that,

> In the long run, we would expect most people to *value those things at which they are good* [emphasis added], and try to become good at those things they value.

They may still consider themselves poor at those things which to them are unimportant, but this is likely to have little effect on their global self-esteem. (p. 250)

They appear to increasingly value the nonschool areas in which they feel they are good and have control over, and to devalue their negative schooling experiences. This is not, however, meant to imply that school ceases to matter. Hunt and Hunt (1977), in a study of black youth, found a high sense of control to be associated with low school attachment and nonschool factors. They suggest a pattern of self-image maintenance among black boys not so much through rejection of conventional values and institutions as clear substitution of compensatory terms of self-respect.

The implications for home relations are that socialization practices must encourage black boys to exert greater school effort, despite negative experiences. The implication for schooling is that the community must exercise greater influence over the process, in order to reduce the incidence of their children's miseducation (Woodson, 1933). The implications for peers reside in the assumption that if home and school are consonant, there will be less room or reason to devalue school. Greater parental control will also reduce negative peer influence.

Finally, and most importantly, none of these goals will be attained without the strengthening of a collective sense of identity and mission. This will defend and preserve the community, and inform black children of the community's definition of the situation, and their role in the resolution of problems. These actions are commonly engaged in on behalf of their children by other racial, ethnic and cultural groups. Black parents cannot trust the schools—or streets—to tell the children their story, or to do their job. Nor can black people expect an alien structure to have their, or their children's, best interests in mind. The motto during the "community control" of schools movement in New York City in the late 1960s is still necessary:

We are engaged in a struggle over the control of the minds (and the futures) of our children.

# 13 Cultural Cognition and Social Cognition as Identity Correlates of Black Children's Personal-Social Development

Margaret Beale Spencer
*Emory University*

A preoccupation with identity themes and issues concerning black people has characterized research on minorities during the previous four decades. The motivation for the focus has its etiology in the literature concerned with black children's white-choice behavior (Clark & Clark, 1939, 1940). Generally, the focus on identity research is paralleled in volume only by black/white comparative studies of IQ and achievement. This paper's focus is on the black child's understanding of societal values and attitudes. Specifically, the child's implicit knowledge of culture, along with the more general social cognitive abilities, are seen to shape group identity.

Cultural cognition specifies the child's limited although evolving awareness of race as a biological and social phenomenon. The child's basis for judgements concerning culture are relative, differing, for the most part, according to events, persons, patterns of feedback, and contexts. The capacity to "step out of self" is related to the child's ability to make explicit interpretations using implicit knowledge about related cultural and racial issues.

Social cognition as described by Shantz (1975) refers to the way in which children conceptualize other people: How children come to understand the thoughts, emotions, intentions, and view points of others. Social cognition refers to the child's intuitive or logical representation of others, that is, how he characterizes others and makes inferences about their covert, inner psychological experiences. Although not usually conceptualized as such, identity is assumed to be influenced by underlying cognitive structural characteristics. This particular cognitive-developmental perspective, or "child as constructivist view," offers as a basic proposition the notion that the expected developmental course of identity

215

formation for black children is toward identity imbalance, unless an intervention occurs.

For black children, the ontogenetic course, from an undifferentiated to a more differentiated view of self, appears to require that a cognitive shift from an egocentric to a decentric view of culture occurs. This change necessitates that the child overcome socially acquired cultural egocentrism. Cultural egocentrism implies that the young child takes in information *without* an awareness or an understanding of its implications for self as a member of a specific, identifiable ethnic group. Variations in the child's construction of the world across developmental stages suggests that race dissonance research should not assume identity as stable: Rather identity is in constant transformation. Thus, our use of the term group identity formation implies 1) organismic plasticity as a response to, or an awareness of, discontinuous sociocultural factors (i.e., cultural cognition); and 2) underlying cognitive structural characteristics of the organism's social perception for any particular developmental period (i.e., social cognition).

The last several decades have suggested specific research themes in the area of identity formation among minority group members—most frequently Black Americans. Generally, these data suggest that, if given a choice, young black children demonstrate consistent race dissonance. Young black children frequently show white biased preferences or attitudes when offered the choice between black and white color concepts or persons. Race dissonance findings have been consistently documented and carefully reviewed (see Brand, Ruiz & Padilla 1974; Porter 1971; Spencer 1977). These data have promoted the maintenance of old controversy with little or no substantive progress in how black identity originates and evolves (McCarthy & Yancey, 1971; Powell, 1974).

Research and theory on black children's identity formation is problem ridden (Spencer, 1982a). The literature lacks coherence, is not developmental, and focuses more so on pathological, than normal developmental processes. Perusal of 40 years of research on this topic suggests a dire need for synthesis. Synthesis is both imperative and basic to the generalization process (Wolf, 1980). Without generalization, or the process of obtaining clear statements about principles underlying a phenomenon, science stagnates, leaving us unable to comprehend natural phenomena.

This paper raises issues intended to influence debates surrounding identity formation in black and minority children. Several points require consideration in the search for important influences:

1. Identity needs to be examined from a *developmental perspective*. Black children have historically been studied in a static manner, as mere reactors to 20th century racism.
2. The lifespan (developmental) view is a more inclusive perspective for examining identity issues. The approach emphasizes biological, historical, sociocultural, and psychological factors that provide a context for explaining human behavior from birth to death.

3. There have been few attempts to interface the cognitive with the affective domain, rather the consistent focus has been on the cognitive domain (Piaget, 1967; Piaget and Inhelder, 1969). There is a need to consider the self, or the child's identity, as a cognitive construction of his or her social experience. Dependent upon the child's developmental stage, experiences and underlying cognitive structures, different categories of self should emerge and disappear over time (Lewis & Brooks-Gunn, 1979; Mead, 1934).

4. Finally, it should be noted that without personal/psychological, or extrinsic/sociocultural intervention, the expected course of black child identity is toward identity imbalance. An identity imbalance characterized by a nonfit between personal and group identity.

The four topical areas delineated provide an integrative framework for the examination of black children's senses of self. For each area of concern research is reviewed which sheds light on the significance of that topic. Table 13.1 summarizes sample demographics and measures from three empirical studies which address the topic areas.

## A DEVELOPMENTAL APPROACH TO RACE
## DISSONANCE FINDINGS: THE ACQUISITION
## OF CULTURAL UNDERSTANDING

As black children develop an awareness of self and other objects, this awareness includes content which reflects knowledge of black people and their world. Furth (1978) noted that the child's growth of societal understanding is best conceptualized as a continual process of exploration and testing. In Piagetian theory, objects are primarily a construction on the part of the person rather than imposed from without. This constructivist view is obviously more dynamic than that advanced by traditional identity theorists. According to Furth (1978), it is necessary to regard the child's socialization, not as the impact of a given societal system on the child's mind and behavior, but instead as the child's construction or understanding of his or her social world. Further, the way the child comes to perceive self or other persons will take on different meanings dependent on whether one considers the "objects" as given from the outside, as construed from within the child, or as an interaction between behavior, cognitive/internal events and the external environment (Bandura, 1978, p. 345). In accepting Furth's more radical constructivist view, it is assumed that children construct social and societal reality as much as they construct logical and physical reality.

Recent research suggests that society's perceptions of minorities have remained essentially unchanged, although these perceptions may have varied in form (Spencer, 1982a). While blacks are no longer lynched physically, forms of economic lynching (i.e., rampant black unemployment) are still commonplace.

TABLE 13.1

| | Sample Demographics | | | | | Measures | | |
|---|---|---|---|---|---|---|---|---|
| Study | N | Age | Race | SES | Sex | Cultural Values | Self-Concept | Parental Strategies |
| I (1973, Midwest) | 48 | 3–5 | 24W 24B | MI LI | 24B 24G | Attitudes/preferences | — | — |
| II (1976, North) | 130 | 4–6 ½ | B | MI | 64B 66G | Attitudes/preferences attitude/preference | All subjects | — |
| III (1982, South) | 384 | 3, 5, 7, 9 | B | 192MI 192LI | 192B 192G | Attitudes/preferences attitude/preference | All subjects | Subsample n = 45 |

Irrespective of the forms which discrimination and disrespect take, the consequent influences remain oppressive for what Bronfenbrenner (1977) would term black children's ecosystem experiences. Black children and their families experience an at-risk sociocultural status. The biological fact of racial differences, coupled with societal responses to ethnicity, generates socialization experiences and identity conflicts specific to black children.

Aspects of children's socialization experiences are manifested either in practice or knowledge: as social behavior or as social awareness. Either aspect of socialization (behavior or awareness) is considered to be covert (i.e., an internal process of construction). Although internal, the socialization process is responsive to the person's experiences of the world. It must be viewed as a gradual life-course process which is neither static nor unidirectional. The notion of reciprocal determinism goes one step further, conceptualizing the dynamic (and reciprocal) interaction of manifested behaviors with cognition, other internal processes, and the environment (see Bandura, 1978).

The young child's concept of self is actually primitive and undifferentiated. This affective state reflects the general egocentric state of young children with respect to concepts. Young children often construct and use concepts before they acquire logical and functional character: This includes the child's understanding of race. Thus, studies reporting race dissonance among young children (i.e., finding early Eurocentric values or white-choice behavior of black children) reflect, in fact, the child's egocentric constructs.

The view of child as constructivist is consistent with Piaget's (1952) views of an organism who responds to the environment in ways consistent with his or her understanding of its essential features. Viewing intelligence as a basic life function for environmental adjustment, Piaget sees intellectual content as what the child thinks about the world. Intellectual structures serve as the organizational components of intelligence, the modes of thinking that determine intellectual content. Finally, intellectual functions are the processes through which intellectual structures are created, organized and changed. It is critical, then, for researchers to re-examine earlier work on race dissonance from a constructivist perspective.

It is clear that the interaction between early intrinsic social knowledge and identity quests held by society's children produce significantly different developmental outcomes as a consequence of the status of the (minority) group. Further, it is suggested that within racial groups, lower income children experience greater discordant information than their black middle-income cohorts. Specifically, European values concerning class and caste must be reordered or modified to insure that positive identity elements are incorporated into the self system. The child's evolving understanding of society must be conceptualized as a continuous process of constructing, exploring, and testing out personal encounters and interests as hypothetical theories. Several research findings illustrate the salience of a developmental perspective for race dissonance findings.

### Developmental Perspective: Research Findings

Findings from a recently reported study demonstrate the importance of a developmental perspective on black child development (Spencer, 1982b.). One hundred and thirty black preschool children (4–6.5 years) were administered a set of measures which assessed the development of social cognition. Piagetian theory formed the basis for exploring the relationship between social cognition (i.e., the ability to take the perspective of another) and cultural cognition. Cultural cognition, includes both the awareness of race and socially acquired knowledge concerning racial stereotypes. The study's purpose was two-fold: First, to propose possible cognitive structures for the development of race awareness and subsequent racial attitude formation; and second, to offer a developmental interpretation of this social phenomenon during the preoperational stage of thought.

One hypothesis suggested the prediction of race awareness from social cognition. Two measures of social cognition were used: conceptual decentering ability and an affectual differentiation task. Race awareness was predicted by several subtests of the social cognition construct ($p < .001$). Data analysis indicated that knowledge of social stereotypes (i.e., Eurocentrism or race dissonance) was not predicted by social cognition. The child's developing structures, which aided the self/other distinction, were not related to the child's knowledge of social stereotypes. Although the awareness of race as a socio-biological phenomenon was related to developing cognitive structures, knowledge of racial stereotypes was unrelated to social cognition (i.e., either decentering measures or a measure of interpersonal competence). It was concluded that progressive conceptual or affectual differentiation is unrelated to knowledge of racial stereotypes, which are assumed to reflect social learning.

These findings and their implications are important to the interpretation of personality theorizing (e.g., Thomas Pettigrew, *Profile of the Negro American*). During the preschool developmental period, values concerning race (i.e., race dissonance) are seemingly unrelated to conceptual issues involving self and others. They appear to reflect unchallenged exposure to racial epithets or stereotypes. Racial stereotyping in black children should be viewed as objectively held information about the environment and not as manifestation of personal identity. A developmental view reflects a more sophisticated view of black child development. The application of this model to the study of minority status people clearly elevates discussion of life course events to a new theoretical level.

## LIFE SPAN DEVELOPMENTAL PSYCHOLOGY: ADVANTAGES FOR MINORITY CHILD RESEARCH

The characteristics of a life span perspective are both specific and appropriate for the issue under review: black child development. Brim and Kagan's (1980) conceptualization of human nature suggests a capacity for change across the entire life span. They question the validity of the traditional notion that early life experiences, which have demonstrated contemporaneous effect, necessarily constrain the characteristics of adolescence and adulthood. Baltes and Willis' (1979) lifespan developmental perspective also offers the unique conception of continuous development and change across the life course. They, with Riley (1979), maintain that aging is a lifelong process that is properly and necessarily studied as an outcome of lifelong experiences. During the lifecourse, the individual as a member of a "cohort," experiences "aging" which implies both growing up and growing old.

Of importance for the study of minority group members, this lifespan developmental perspective is concerned with aging processes at the microlevel (i.e., the ontogenetic individual level) as influenced by biological, social-cultural and historical changes. A life-course perspective underscores the notion that the forms of developmental change are not unitary, but instead, display diversity both within and between individuals—as well as cohorts (Baltes and Willis, 1979). The race dissonance literature seldom examines the phenomenon multidimensionally and certainly not in terms of multidirectionality. In fact, rather than assuming or accepting possible intraindividual variability as the life course unfolds, most researchers assume a static state across the life course. In addition, sociocultural, biological, and historical influences are seldom carefully analyzed as significant influences in individual lives.

## Lifespan Developmental Perspective: Research Findings

The intra individual variability of race dissonance is illustrated by the abrupt changes in racial attitudes and racial preferences occurring after the preoperational stage of cognitive egocentrism (Spencer, 1982a). Previous research has illustrated white-biased choice behavior in preschool children between the ages of three and six, in both the Midwest and North (Spencer & Horowitz, 1973; Spencer, 1977). These findings were replicated with a Southern sample of preschool children (Spencer, 1982a). Older children in the concrete operational stage were also included in the Southern study. Blacks were more often valued and preferred as friends by older children, who were more own-race biased, than by younger preschoolers. The one consistent finding across age groups for both the Midwestern and Southern studies was the white-biased choice behavior for color connotations. Irrespective of age (preschool, kindergarten or primary grade), stage (preoperational or concrete operational) or region (Midwest or South), the connotations associated with color appear both consistent and strong: The color white is valued and the color black is devalued. Given the increasingly strong effect of mass media on the lives of black children, these findings for color evaluation are not unexpected.

The data support a view of race dissonance as multidimensional, encompassing racial attitudes, racial preferences, and color connotations. Further, the findings presented also suggest the construct's multidirectionality. The pervasive, unchallenged color connotations extant in western culture undoubtedly impact color values. On the other hand, subjectively experienced racial attitudes and preferences appear to be more influenced by the child's own evolving cognitive structures along with specific socialization experiences.

Recent research in process (Spencer, 1984) demonstrates the unique contributions of a lifespan perspective. Much on the order of Elder's (1974) *Children of the Great Depression,* the research explores the follow-up effects of a major life course event for 150 black children: Atlanta's child murders. Research findings (Spencer, 1982a) were expanded to assess the effects of the killings on the original sample of children. Preliminary data analyses indicate minimal effects of the child killings. Pre and post comparisons for personal identity measures (i.e., self concept) and group identity measures (i.e., race dissonance) show that irrespective of age group, children and early adolescents appeared to have adapted to this specific life stressor event. It may well be that children who are constantly exposed to mundane stressors adapt more adroitly to exotic stresses, such as the Atlanta child murders.

The self concept measure employed for reassessment on children 9 years or younger was *The Thomas Self Concept Test* (Thomas, 1967). The advantage of the measure is its inclusion of four referents: self as seen by self, mother, teacher and peer. Fourteen attributes are included. One attribute concerns the child's affective response to men. Others include feelings about size, cleanliness, friendliness, etc. The one finding of significance was the less positive response to men after the crisis. The period of reassessment (Time 2) occurred 3 months after a (male) suspect was charged and imprisoned. Clearly, sociocultural contexts and historical factors in America must be considered when attempting to design and interpret research on black Americans.

## COGNITION AND AFFECTIVITY: COGNITION AS THE MEDIATOR OF AND "INTERVENTION" FOR COGNITIVE IMBALANCE

Knowledge about self and others develops simultaneously (Lewis & Brooks-Gunn, 1979). Neither could exist alone, since the two develop in response to social interaction. Through gestures and language, the child is provided with the means to interact with others, to anticipate the reactions of others, to take the role of the other, to perceive self as object, and finally to differentiate self from others (Cooley, 1912; Mead, 1934). Play and games are the mechanism by which roles are learned and through which the self becomes differentiated. Thus, the self is a cognitive structure resulting from the child's interaction with the world.

## Social Cognitive Perspective: Research Findings

Personal identity (i.e., self-concept) and group identity (i.e., race dissonance) have been assumed to be synonymous. Only recently have researchers examined both constructs in the same sample (i.e., Spencer, 1977, 1982a, Semaj, 1981). These data are important for demonstrating the independence of personal esteem and ethnic group esteem for young preschool children.

Studies of preschoolers in the North, and preschoolers and primary grade children in the South, found that irrespective of the region or grade, black children obtained positive self-concept scores (Spencer, 1982a). The reported mean scores for the North and South were 49.78 and 49.62 respectively. The standardized mean score for the measures is 50.00 (Thomas, 1967). These data clearly refute the assumption of low self-concepts among black children.

Although theorists would suggest otherwise (e.g., Pettigrew, 1964), only 13% of the sample obtained low self-concept scores. However, 10% of the sample obtained both low self-concept scores and showed race dissonance. The study was replicated for the Southern preschool sample and showed that 81% of the sample had positive self-concepts. Forty-seven percent showed both positive self-concepts and race dissonance (as compared to 63% of the Northern sample). Fourteen percent of the preschool sample demonstrated both positive self-concepts and black choice behavior (as compared to only 5.4% for the Northern sample). The pattern for the Southern primary grade children varied significantly. Almost 94% of the total sample had positive self-concepts. Approximately one third of these positive self-concept youth also showed race dissonance or a white-bias. Another one third obtained positive self-concepts, although neutral with regard to racial values. The final third were not only positive about self, but they also were black-biased, or lacked race dissonance.

For both the Northern and Southern samples, race dissonance and self-concept were not significantly correlated. In light of developmental patterns, race awareness and race dissonance were related for cognitively egocentric preschool children. The child's developing social cognition was related to race awareness, although *not* racial stereotyping (i.e., race dissonance). These data suggest a relationship between race awareness and evolving cognitive structures. The development of more complex cognitive structures during the primary grade years appears to be associated with a shift to own-race, or black-biased responses— race dissonance progressively diminishes.

## SOCIALIZATION OF MINORITY STATUS CHILDREN: THE ACQUISITION OF SOCIETAL MEANING

Outside writings on the development of meaning by theologians (e.g., Fowler, 1981), few essays have focused on the development of the young child's understanding of the world. In a notable exception, Furth (1978) states that young children develop the first glimmer of awareness of self and objects between 1 and 2 years. They encounter persons (one of whom is the self) and not merely concrete and natural events. As a result of this new object capacity, the child begins to produce, to use, and to understand symbols. This process occurs variously in the form of external play or gestures, speech, or internal images of fantasy. Later, the child's interaction with others takes on forms which earn the labels of adult, mature, and logical.

The child's evolving object capacity requires an attempt to fit social experiences with existing knowledge. Without intervention on the personal/psychological or extrinsic/sociocultural level, the expected course of identity evolution for black children is toward identity imbalance. Implied here is a nonfit, or unbalanced state, between personal identity (i.e., the self-concept) and group identity (i.e., cultural values, beliefs). The probability of identity imbalance is expected to be greatest for those individuals who least demonstrate or who minimally epitomize, European values and/or physical characteristics.

When using the term European, Russell Means (1980) does not necessarily refer to skin color or a particular genetic structure. Instead, his referent is a world view that is a product of the development of European culture. The acquisition of this outlook is due to specific socialization experiences. In Means' parlance, American Indians sharing European values are termed Apples—red on the outside (genetic) and White on the inside (their values). For other groups there are similar terms: blacks, of this persuasion are termed Oreos, Hispanics are termed Coconuts, Orientals are termed Bananas and so on. In Means' view, to function mentally as a European does not necessarily involve racism, but instead, is an acknowledgement of the mind and spirit that makes up (American) culture. Means' discussion implies a better person–environment fit for Americans (regardless of race or ancestry) who manifest a European outlook.

The socialization of minorities in a Europeanized context and the implication for identity development is an important issue. Serious research efforts on minorities began at the century's onset in response to the largescale migrations from Europe. Although much of the new IQ research during that period had the hidden agenda of stemming the tide of immigrants (Kamin, 1974), one significant observation of these ethnic minorities is that they passed swiftly from secondclass citizens to Americans.

Missing from many historical and sociological analyses of this voluntary migration pattern is the fact that the operation of the American opportunity structure differed for certain non White groups (e.g., black and Native Americans). Given this historical variance, it would be expected that the cognitive operations or structures by which each group's children construe, or come to have meaning of, the world would necessarily vary. These structures will likely differ on the basis of implicit knowledge that becomes explicitly interpreted in the course of cognitive maturation and accumulated social experiences. Referred to here are the negative stereotypes and values about non whites which are communicated as incipiently and saliently as the gender stereotypes inculcated beginning from the first day of life.

American culture and social institutions produce diverse psychological outcomes for different groups and individual members. European values central to American heritage have potentially deleterious effects for excluded or unassimilated minorities in America (e.g., blacks, Hispanics and American Indians). It is not surprising that these groups have remained outside the mainstream. They share several characteristics with each other: characteristics which distinguish them from EuroAmericans. Each group: (1) is racially different; (2) has attempted to maintain aspects of their own cultural heritage; and (3) did not become Americans by choice.

Given these major differences between minority group children and children of European ancestry, specific child-rearing strategies require careful scrutiny.

## Socialization Perspective: Research Findings

Parental interviews focused around child-rearing attitudes and values illustrate the importance of child-rearing strategies for child development (Spencer, 1983). Forty-five interviews with Southern black parents were conducted in the home by two female same-race interviewers, Table 13-2 summarizes the results from these interviews. The subjects were equally divided by socioeconomic status. These interviews were conducted as a pilot study which was part of a larger project. There were several unexpected findings on the socialization of cultural values.

Parents stated that their own parenting style was significantly influenced by that of their own parents (66%). A listing of child-rearing informants in the order of importance suggested that one's own ideas and religion were ranked first and second before the "own parent" category. As expected, parents perceived the primary function of the maternal role as the teacher of life skills. Middle-income parents were twice as likely as lower-income parents to characterize the maternal role in this manner. Parents more often viewed the father's role in child-rearing tasks as egalitarian with, or supportive of, the maternal role. The role of grandparents in child rearing was seen as equal to that of parents across social class.

Regardless of social class, when asked whether the roles of parents and grandparents would be different if the child were of the opposite sex, 73% of the sample said there would be no difference. When asked whether socialization approaches would differ if the child were white, 91% reported that the content of socializing goals would not be any different.

Parents varied in regard to what they would tell their children upon entrance into a new class or school. Consistent with previous research on ethnic minorities, the primary response, independent of SES, indicated that discipline is stressed. The expectation was that the child "should behave." Twice as many middle-income parents also noted the value to "strive for academic success" as

## TABLE 13.2
### Parental Stressed Values and Child-Rearing Strategies:
### Study III, Southern Sample

| Parental Response Category and Individual Response | Percentage Response |
|---|---|
| Differentiation of child characteristics | |
| (1) No change in child rearing if child were of opposite sex | 73 |
| (2) No change in child rearing if child were white | 91 |
| Views of and preparation for "new" environments | |
| (3) Integrated school *would* change child's experiences | 47 |
| (4) White schools would broaden child's social experiences | 22 |
| Perception of improved racial climate | |
| (5) Raising a child in the late 1970s is different from the 1950s and 1960s | 56 |
| (6) Perceived current change in racial climate is due to a more tense, polarized, earlier period | 56 |
| (7) The 1960s had no impact on parental child rearing | 27 |
| (8) The 1960s transmitted black consciousness in child-rearing efforts | 25 |
| Optimism of child's future | |
| (9) Optimism about the child's future would not vary if child were of the opposite gender and race (white) | 85 |
| (10) The greatest problem in raising a minority child is racism and discrimination | 36 |
| (11) No problems specific to raising a black child | 22 |
| Child qualities stressed | |
| (12) Reinforced qualities would not change if child were white | 71 |
| (13) Reinforced qualities would not change if child were opposite sex | 100 |
| Cultural beliefs stressed | |
| (14) Children taught that all people are equal | 51 |
| (15) No discussion of race unless child asks specifically | 33 |
| (16) No discussion of sex-role issues | 35 |
| (17) Children taught that social class is not important | 33 |
| (18) Teaching children about race is not important | 50 |
| (19) Teaching children about race is important | 50 |
| Views of race as asset/deficit | |
| (20) Children will have no problems in school because of race | 60 |
| (21) Children will have no problems in school because of gender membership | 93 |
| Black history knowledge | |
| (22) Child knows "some" black history | 25 |
| (23) Child knows "a lot of" black history | 25 |
| (24) Child knows "no" black history | 25 |
| (25) Parent knows "a lot" of black history | 50 |
| (26) No discussion of civil rights | 47 |
| (27) Civil rights are discussed | 33 |

a secondary response. Respondents ranked "parent" virtually equal with "teacher" and "child" as an important person in the educational process. In addition, most rated their child's current school as "good." The most prevalent response (47%) was "yes" to the question "Would attendance at an integrated school change your child's experiences?" Of the 21 reporting "yes," 11 stated that white schools were better staffed and equipped. The remaining 10 stated that white schools would broaden children's social experiences. Parents did not view an all black school as necessarily inferior to attendance at a predominately white school. Parental responses suggested that education in a predominately black school would provide a different set of child experiences (36.4%).

Many parents noted (55.6%) that raising a child in the late 1970s is different from raising a child in the 60s or 50s. Fourteen of the 25 who answered "yes" (i.e., it is different) stated that the racial situation was much different, i.e., more tense and polarized, during the earlier period. These responses suggest that black parents perceive a much improved racial climate. Further, 27% of the parents responded that the 60s had no impact upon their child-rearing patterns. Another 25% stated that, for themselves, the 60s had resulted in an increased transmission of black consciousness in their child rearing efforts.

Many parents were optimistic about their child's future (34%) because of specific child attributes (e.g., talent, intelligence, etc). Of the total sample, almost 85% reported that they would feel the same way if their child were of the opposite sex or race. Only four parents noted that race does make a difference and stated that their optimism would be greater if their child were white. Further, three out of 45 suggested that their optimism would vary since gender is important. Thirty-six percent of parents noted that the greatest problems in raising a minority group child are racism and discrimination. Another 30% stated economic pressures as the greatest problem. Importantly, it was the perception of 22% of parents that there would be no problems in raising a black child.

The majority of black parents interviewed noted personal qualities (e.g., confidence, ambition, respect) as those which they primarily reinforced. Educational values were listed as the second most frequently reinforced value (34%). All respondents noted that the personal qualities reinforced would not change if the child were of the opposite sex. In addition, 71% stated that the values reinforced would not change if the child were white. Those parents who noted that the values would be different if the child were white usually stated that whites have more opportunities.

When asked what their child is taught concerning people of other races, over half reported that they taught their children to believe that all people are equal. Middle-income parents tended to respond in this manner more frequently than did lower-income parents. Approximately one third of all parents noted that there is usually no discussion of race unless the child asks specific questions. Relative to sex or gender membership, 36% noted no discussion of the issue. However, approximately one fourth stated that sex-role differences are occasionally discussed. A third of parental respondents reported teaching that social class is not important (e.g., money is not important). This response was most frequently made by middle-income parents. Lower-income parents most often reported teaching their children that being "rich" is better than being poor (31% of respondents).

When asked whether or not teaching children about race is important, 50% responded "no." Of the 23 responding "no," 17 specifically stated that race is not important. Forty-seven percent of the respondents replied "yes," noting that race is important. Only seven of the 22 "yes" respondents specified that it is important to prepare the child for possible racial discrimination. Three out of the 22 "yes" respondents noted that it is important to instill self-pride and cultural awareness. However, 12 of the 22 "yes" respondents (i.e., it is important to prepare children for possible discrimination) answered "yes" for "other" non-racial discrimination related reasons.

Approximately 60% of parental respondents noted that children would have no problems in school because of race. No respondents believed there would be many problems and 18% responded "yes," there would be a few. Surprisingly, given the increasingly visible feminist movement, and perhaps as a result of its success, 93% of parents stated that children would have no problems due to gender membership.

Parents were generally split when asked about their judgments of their child's knowledge of black history. Almost one fourth noted that their child knew "some" black history, although 25% stated that their child either "knew a lot" or "none at all." Not unexpectedly, one half of parental respondents noted that they themselves knew a lot about black history, although an additional one fourth noted "maybe they knew a lot" about black history. Most parents (75%) had told their children about famous black people. Parents rated the home first (76%), the school second (51%), and books/periodicals third (44%) as the most important sources for learning about black history. Further, almost half noted an absence of discussion of civil rights with their child although another one third responded "yes"—civil rights are discussed.

These findings suggest that many black parents tend to **transcend race** in their socialization efforts. The goal appears to be the rearing of racially "neutral" children, or "human beings" irrespective of the continued salience of race on the macrostructural level. The most important predictors of black children's, black-biased choice behavior for color connotations and racial preferences was age and whether the child had knowledge of black history. Older children and those knowing more black history showed less race dissonance for color connotations and racial preferences.

Forty-six percent of the variance for children's white-choice behavior, or race dissonance was predicted by several independent variables in a stepwise regression: (1) parents who do not teach children about civil rights; (2) parental beliefs that integration is an enriching experience; (3) child's lack of knowledge concerning black history; (4) parental knowledge of black history, (5) parental belief that current racial climate is better than the 50s or 60s; and (6) no parental discussion of racial discrimination. Accordingly, for nearly one half of the time, child race dissonance findings for racial attitude are predicted from specific parental child rearing strategies. It appears that the "race transcendence" of some black parents is not compatible with the psychological intervention required to nullify black children's sociocultural at-risk status. The "humanistic" or race-neutral emphasis of black parental child-rearing efforts appears to be offset by other events in the child's own life.

## DISCUSSION AND CONCLUSIONS

Research and theory in the area of group identity formation has assumed that personal identity (self-conception) and group identity (racial attitudes) are inextricably linked in a consistent fashion over the life course. By integrating the cognitive and affective domains with the race dissonance literature from a life-course developmental perspective, an alternative perspective on black children's identity formation was presented. It appears clear from the empirical findings that definite links exist between the cognitive and the affective domains. More specifically, it is suggested that changes in personal and group identity are expected given variations in the child's developing cognitive construction of the world.

Society's traditional socialization of children is consistent with an achieved, differentiated white, European child. Among majority children, cognitive construction of reality along with specific child rearing strategies represent the interventions which allow for identity differentiation and a healthy ego. The goal of this paper was to examine both theoretical and empirical aspects of similar processes among black children—with special reference to culture. Advanced was the idea that the child treats culture as an object of knowledge which is influenced by the available cognitive structures and social history. In conjunction, cognition and social context influence behavior. Thus, as supported by the empirical findings, personal identity is not assumed to necessarily be in accordance with group identity for a given developmental period. Specific variations are expected in the child's capacity to step out of self and to interpret implicit knowledge appropriately in a contextually consistent manner. It would be anticipated that identity is in transformation or metamorphosis across the lifespan.

In sum, this paper suggests a view of individual (i.e., ontogenetic) development as the product of forces (both internal psychological and external sociocultural) which are interactive and bidirectional. This synthesis is different in that it considers more than social-structural and socioeconomic concerns. It also considers the interactive influences of the developing organism. One conclusion drawn is that these questions and variable relations are more complex than previously speculated. Further examination is required with a broader age range of children, adolescents, and adults. The inclusion of identity variables with cognitive performance measures would also be required. An improved understanding of the relationship should enhance educational programs and elevate the quality of theoretical and empirical research on black children and youth.

## ACKNOWLEDGMENTS

An earlier version of this paper was presented during the 1981 Society for Research on Child Development meetings, Boston, April 2–5, 1981. The author acknowledges helpful comments from Study Group members. The research reported was funded by the National Institutes of Mental Health (MH-31106) and the Foundation for Child Development.

# Summary

Morris Rosenberg
*University of Maryland*

The noxious effects of racism on the self-concepts of black people have concerned social scientists at least since the 1940s. Yet few areas of investigation have yielded such genuinely baffling findings. Results yielded by one research method have contradicted results yielded by another method; and conclusions based on sound theory have contradicted conclusions based on sound research.

Although certainly not unknown, it is comparatively rare in social science for different research methods to yield such diametrically opposed conclusions. Most of the early research on black children's self-concepts, based on the use of dolls, pictures, or puppets, concluded that black children had damaged self-esteem. This finding, of which the Clark and Clark (1952) study was the prototype, was consistently replicated by subsequent investigators (Goodman, 1952; Porter, 1971). On the other hand, sample survey research on the topic, begun in the 60s, clearly indicated that black self-esteem was at least as healthy as white self-esteem (Wylie, 1979; Gordon, 1977; Rosenberg & Simmons, 1972).

What was one to believe? Although projective methods had enjoyed favor at an earlier period, more systematic evaluation (e.g., Wylie, 1979) had called into question the validity of these procedures. The sample survey, to be sure, was also not immune to criticism. Nevertheless, it had a number of methodological advantages over the doll studies. First, the sample surveys employed probability samples rather than samples of convenience, thus enabling one to generalize with specified degrees of confidence to broader populations. Second, the doll studies, although offering evidence of damaged self-esteem among black children, failed to show that this damage was any greater than that suffered by white children. Sample surveys, on the other hand, were more likely to make such comparisons. Third, whereas the doll study measures of self-esteem were inferential and unvalidated, the survey self-esteem measures could be, and occasionally were, subjected to more systematic tests of validity. Fourth, as William Cross observes, the survey studies made it possible (though admittedly not usual) to study personal identity and reference group orientation independently—the doll studies tended to *infer* individual self-esteem on the basis of racial attitudes. Finally, the probability sample tended to study a broad age range, whereas the doll studies focused on preschool, kindergarten, and early grade samples. Nevertheless, some investigators favored the doll studies, and the appearance of contradictory results stemming from different research traditions spawned a confusing and contradictory literature.

The second source of bafflement stemmed from the fact that sound theoretical principles suggested one conclusion, while sound methodological principles suggested its opposite. Sample survey studies showed black self-esteem to be at least as high as white self-esteem and at least three principles suggested that racism, in its diverse manifestations and expressions, would be injurious to self-esteem. One of these was the principle of reflected appraisals. As Mead (1934) and Cooley (1912) had suggested, we learn about ourselves in large part by seeing ourselves through the eyes of others. If, as research demonstrated, blacks as a group were held in lower regard in the society as a whole, then, viewing themselves from the perspective of the broader society, they would be expected to develop negative self-attitudes.

A second principle is social comparison. Festinger (1954) observed that, in the absence of objective evidence, people draw conclusions about themselves by comparing themselves with others. Since the heritage of racism was to produce damaging comparisons—in educational achievement, occupational prestige, income, and academic achievement scores—one would expect self-esteem to suffer as a consequence. The third principle is self-attribution (Bem, 1967; Kelley, 1967; Rosenberg, 1979a), which holds that people draw conclusions about what they are like on the basis of observations of their overt behavior and its outcomes and the associated circumstances under which it occurs. Unfortunate economic outcomes would be expected to damage self-esteem.

Theory suggested one conclusion; research another. When I first undertook sample survey research on adolescent self-esteem in the early 60s (Rosenberg, 1965), I was familiar with the doll research and was implicitly guided by these theoretical principles. Imagine my astonishment, then, when my data showed that the self-esteem of black adolescents differed little from that of whites. How was it possible for a group subjected to so many and such severe assaults on the self to maintain such a healthy level of self-respect?

Today we have a much better understanding of these matters. This improvement can be attributed to theoretical advances made in recent years, advances so well exemplified in the papers in this section. The most important theoretical development is the increased awareness of the self-concept as a complex, intricate, multifaceted structure. The early research had viewed self-esteem as virtually the only dimension of interest and importance in the self-concept. Today we know that self-esteem, though important, is only one of many self-concept components. For example, Kurt Lewin (1948) had treated group self-hatred and individual self-hatred as virtually identical, but the paper by William Cross makes it strikingly clear that these two variables are distinct. Far from being identical, Cross demonstrates that they are scarcely even related. The reason is not that the black child's race is unimportant to him or her—on the contrary, it is extremely important (Rosenberg, 1979)—but a very large number of other self-concept components, such as various traits, social statuses, and ego-extensions are also important influences on self-esteem. Race is but one of a large number of important factors that mold the child's feelings of self-worth.

A second theoretical refinement represented in this section is the awareness of the distinction between specific and global self-esteem. Global self-esteem, it should be recognized, is a disposition (Rosenberg, 1979b)—a general tendency to respond. When we say that someone has high global self-esteem, we do not mean that this person will invariably hold a favorable self-view but, rather, will do so in general. It thus follows that one cannot reason from the general to the specific, for example, from global self-esteem to school self-esteem nor vice versa.

The paper by Hare and Castenell thus represents a signal theoretical contribution in separating area-specific (school, home, peer) self-esteem from global self-esteem. In so doing, it underscores the point that self-esteem in one institutional realm may be quite different from self-esteem in another, and that it is essential to study the specific and the global separately.

The paper by Alejandro-Wright makes another important theoretical point, namely, that we shall never gain an understanding of racial self-concepts until we are able to understand the world as seen by the child. When some black children said they liked to play with the white doll or that they looked like the white doll in doll studies, the attribution of low self-esteem rested on two adult presuppositions: that the self-concept was fully formulated and salient and that the social-biological concept of race was understood. What the Alejandro-Wright research so clearly demonstrates is that adult and children's modes of thought are decidedly different. The young child's racial awareness, it is evident, is extremely dim. Her research demonstrates that children are chiefly responsive to skin color, not to race, as adults understand the concept.

It may appear astonishing that it has taken so long to develop awareness of this fact. But what makes it doubly astonishing is that Clark and Clark (1952) explicitly stressed the child's responsiveness to skin color in their research. In pointing out that many of the black children said that they looked like the white doll, they noted:

> The results suggest further that correct racial identification of these Negro children at these ages is to a large extent determined by the concrete fact of their own skin

color . . . only 20 percent of the light children, while 73 percent of the medium children, and 81 percent of the dark children identified themselves with the colored doll. (p. 555)

In other words, many of the children who said they looked more like the white doll probably actually did look more like the white doll. It was the adult, fully cognizant of the widespread racism in the society, who interpreted the child's response as evidence of racial misidentification and, by implication, low self-esteem. The child, on the contrary, was responding to skin color. As both Semaj and Spencer demonstrate, racial identification is highly correlated with and strongly influenced by children's relative levels of cognitive development.

In sum, it is imperative that we see the world, not from the perspective of the objective social scientist, but from the viewpoint of the child. The principles of self-esteem formation described here appear very different from this viewpoint. The reflected appraisals that shape the black child's self-concept are not the reflections of the broader society but of the child's significant others—mother, father, siblings, friends, etc.; these reflected appraisals are every bit as favorable as those received by white children. Similarly, the comparisons that children make are not comparisons with distant and unknown others but with those who enter their immediate experience; like white children, black children's socioeconomic and academic comparisons tend to be with their peers. Finally, the self-attribution principle is supported by the fact that blacks are aware that many of the observed socioeconomic outcomes are attributable to external causes— racism in its diverse expressions—rather than to personal deficiencies.

The self-concept, as Lecky (1945) once expressed it, is the basic axiom of the individual's life theory. It is the most constant feature of the individual's experience and the most important basis for human action (McGuire & Padawer-Singer, 1976). Although black self-concept has been a subject of research for at least four decades, the fact is that we know remarkably little about it. This meager knowledge is surely not attributable to lack of interest but to narrowness of vision. During most of this period the focus of research has been either on global personal self-esteem or on reference group identification. But the self-concept, as the papers in this section clearly reveal, is a complex structure, and we are only beginning to gain an idea of what it includes and how to measure it. These articles suggest that, in the years to come, we may expect to obtain a much clearer, deeper, and truer understanding of the self-concepts of black people.

# SECTION C: FAMILY

# Introduction

This section could easily have been titled "Family: Developmental Contexts and Consequences." Each paper examines an aspect of black child development in relation to family patterns. The authors were also concerned with determining how different institutional contexts influenced parent-child relationships and children's eventual paths of development.

The ecological perspective, as elaborated by Urie Bronfenbrenner (1979b), provides an appropriate framework for the introduction and organization of papers in this section. This perspective focuses on the developing person, the environment, and the evolving interaction between the two. It adopts a dynamic view of developing persons, whose perceptions and actions are seen as having real consequences for their experiences and responses.

The ecology of human development perspective also adopts an encompassing view of environment. A person's ecological environment is conceived as a set of interconnected concentric circles or nested structures, each inside the other. Innermost is the immediate setting where the developing person finds herself. At the next level are relations between settings in which the developing person participates. The third level of the ecological environment involves settings where the developing person is not necessarily a participant, but where events occur that have consequences for settings with which the developing person is routinely involved. Bronfenbrenner labels these levels of the ecological environment respectively as the *micro, meso,* and *exo* systems. Together these systems form the normative and organizational patterns characteristic of a particular culture or subculture.

Bronfenbrenner (1979) argues that:

. . . by analyzing and comparing the micro, meso, and exo systems characterizing different social classes, ethnic and religious groups, or entire societies, it becomes possible to describe systematically and to distinguish the ecological properties of these larger social contexts as environments for human development [p. 8].

Papers in this section do just that: They examine differences in developmental contexts and consequences for black children created by race, socioeconomic status and kinship system differences.

Velma LaPoint, et al., are concerned with parent–child interpersonal relationships as influenced by a particular institutional context in their paper, "Enforced Family Separation: A Descriptive Analysis of Some Experiences of Children of Black Imprisoned Mothers." The paper describes characteristics of the children and their relationships with their mothers as affected by maternal incarceration, the prison setting, extended family patterns, and length of separation.

The paper by Geraldine Brookins, "Black Children's Sex-Role Ideologies and Occupational Choices in Families of Employed Mothers," directs attention to the world of work. The central concerns are the egalitarian sex-role ideologies and range of perceived occupational choices among black children. These characteristics are expected to vary with maternal employment history, family socioeconomic status, sex of child, and father's sex-role ideologies.

Finally, the paper by Walter Allen, "Race, Income, and Family Dynamics: A Study of Adolescent Male Socialization Processes and Outcomes," looks at black teenage male developmental outcomes in relation to their families. Race, family socioeconomic status, parental child-rearing practices, and parent–son relationships are all investigated as potentially influential ecological factors.

# 14 Enforced Family Separation: A Descriptive Analysis of Some Experiences of Children of Black Imprisoned Mothers

Velma LaPoint
*Howard University*

Marilyn Oliver Pickett
*National Institute of Mental Health*

Beverly Fairley Harris
*Prince George's County Public Schools*

There are approximately 30,000 incarcerated women in jails and prisons in the United States, representing 6% of the incarcerated population (National Coalition of Jail Reform, 1984; U.S. Department of Justice, 1983). Black women comprise at least half of all women in jails and State and Federal correctional institutions (Green, 1981; U.S. Department of Justice, 1983; National Coalition of Jail Reform, 1984).

It is estimated that 225,000 children have incarcerated mothers and that almost 50 to 80% of all incarcerated women in federal, state, and local facilities are mothers (Glick & Neto, 1977; McGowan & Blumenthal, 1978; National Coalition of Jail Reform, 1984; Rosenkrantz & Joshua, 1982). Black children are disproportionately affected by maternal incarceration due to the disproportionate percentage of black imprisoned mothers. The experiences of these children, confronted with maternal imprisonment, provide another example of the many harsh realities that black children and their families must face in this society.

As mothers progress through the various stages of the criminal justice system, children have corollary experiences. Imprisonment labels the mother as bad and in need of punishment. Such stigmatization often becomes associated with the mother's identity and subsequently, the child's identity. In addition, the process of imprisonment often contributes to feelings of degradation which affect the mother–child relationship.

## BACKGROUND

Professionals in research, service delivery, and social policy contexts have generally ignored this family crisis and type of parent–child separation. Only recently have individuals begun to focus on this particular family circumstance (LaPoint & Mann, in preparation). The lack of research on black children whose mothers are incarcerated allows this population to be viewed with unfounded suspicion and stereotypes. Research that is questionable, biased, and unrepresentative of black children and their families exaggerates this problem (Boykin, 1979; Myers, Rana, & Harris, 1979). In addition, criminal justice officials do not compile detailed data on the family characteristics of incarcerated individuals. More data are available on incarcerated mothers and their childen than can be found on incarcerated fathers.

Theories concerning the overrepresentation of blacks in the criminal justice system are controversial, ranging from biological to sociological interpretations. Conditions of poverty and discrimination in the judicial system are frequently cited explanations of incarceration rates among minority groups (National Minority Advisory Council on Criminal Justice, 1982). Substantive theories concerning the overrepresentation of black women in correctional facilities do not exist. Several scholars have suggested that there is a relationship between racial discrimination in the judicial system and socioeconomic factors (Chapman, 1980; Klein, 1976; Rafter & Natalizia, 1981).

These issues have implications for social policies and programs affecting the lives of black families confronted with maternal imprisonment. Successful programs and policies must be based upon factual data and knowledge of the experiences of children and their families. It is imperative that data be collected on this population.

## THE STUDY

This study focuses on incarcerated mothers and their children. It includes two comparison groups—mothers on probation and mothers not involved in the criminal justice system. These comparison groups will facilitate an examination and understanding of conditions confronting incarcerated mothers and their children in the broader context of parenting and child rearing.

This paper addresses phenomena unique to imprisoned mothers and their children. The conditions of separation, restriction, and stigmatization inherent in maternal imprisonment strain the relationships between mothers and children. We will examine the following major questions: (1) What is the nature and quality of relationships between children, their mothers, and primary caregivers preceding and during maternal imprisonment? (2) What is the nature of children's exposure to facets of mothers' socially-defined deviant activities and the criminal justice system? The implications for social policies, service delivery programs, and legal issues affecting black imprisoned mothers and their children will be discussed in light of this study's findings.

## Studies of Parent–Child Separation Due to Maternal Incarceration

Demographic studies and reports indicate that incarcerated mothers are typically single parents, poor, and from a minority group. Incarcerated mothers typically have limited education and vocational skills which may result in unstable life circumstances and employment (Chapman, 1980; Crites, 1976; Female Offenders Resources Center, 1976).

The psychological impact of parent–child separation on incarcerated mothers resembles other forms of loss such as death and divorce. Responses and behaviors of incarcerated mothers are characterized by remoteness, emptiness, helplessness, anger, guilt, fears of loss of attachment, and rejection (Baunach, 1982; Bonfanti et al., 1974; Lundberg et al., 1975). Children's experiences in this situation have also been problematic. Findings indicate children display poor academic performance, aggressive and withdrawal behaviors, and strained interpersonal relationships with parents, guardians, and peers (Baunach, 1982; McGowan & Blumenthal, 1978; Stanton, 1980).

A majority of mothers plan to reunite with children after incarceration (Lundberg, et al., 1975; McGowan & Blumenthal, 1978; Stanton, 1980). Maternal reports have indicated mixed expectations relating to reunion. Some mothers felt secure in their relationships during incarceration and anticipated no difficulties upon reunion. Others anticipated rejection, loss of respect, lack of intimacy, problems with authority and discipline, and custody battles over children. Findings from a study of the mother–child relationship during and after incarceration indicate that many mothers did not resume care of their children upon release (Stanton, 1980). The incidence of separation after release was related to the mothers' inability or unwillingness to assume care for children. Such decisions were associated with financial and housing problems, as well as with personal adjustment problems.

The needs of incarcerated mothers and their families have been virtually ignored until recently (LaPoint & Mann, in preparation). Several factors account for this. Children of incarcerated mothers cannot necessarily be categorized as neglected, abused, or delinquent. Thus, their needs tend to be overlooked by professionals (McGowan & Blumenthal, 1978). The demographic characteristics of this population (predominantly minority and poor) also serve to minimize the concern, services, and funding directed to their needs (French, 1976; LaPoint, 1980). Such neglect is part of a larger pattern where the needs of minority group children are generally ignored and disregarded (Billingsley & Giovannoni, 1972; Edelman, 1980).

Little effort has been made to determine, at a national level, the effects of criminal justice policies and programs on the family life of incarcerated individuals (LaPoint, 1980; McGowan & Blumenthal, 1978). The problems confronting incarcerated mothers and their families include institutional policies affecting child care and visitation; legal and custodial rights of parents and children; economic needs of families; and psychological service needs of families (Buckles & LaFazia, 1973; Chapman, 1980; Daehlin & Hynes, 1974; Dubose, 1977; Goldstein, Freud & Solnit, 1979; LaPoint & Mann, in preparation).

## Research Procedures

The project was conducted at the Maryland Correctional Institution for Women, Jessup, MD, located approximately 20 miles from Baltimore City. It is the only prison for women at the state or federal level in Maryland. During the period of data collection, approximately 230 women, of which 80% were black, were imprisoned at the facility.

In general, incarcerated mothers and their families are not readily accessible to research. First, as researchers from an outside agency we were external to correctional goals, functions, and personnel. Correctional goals and research goals are different. These differences had to be overcome. Second, the conditions of maternal imprisonment, as a highly stigmatizing and stressful family crisis, created a particularly sensitive social environment in which to conduct research. Third, the purpose and intent of research, which includes psychological assessment, have been questioned by members of the public as well as the scientific community (American Psychological Association, 1982; Anastasi, 1982). In addition, more sensitive issues have been raised concerning research in both low-income and black communities (Boykin et al., 1979; Gary, 1974; Myers et al., 1979).

Strategies which emphasized staff participant–observer methods were employed in both recruitment and data collection procedures. Furthermore, to maximize familiarity between participants and staff, black female staff members were utilized to facilitate rapport, trust, and comfort among research subjects. Staff members were similar in age to prisoners and worked to minimize visible differences between themselves and participants (e.g., by dressing casually, using nontechnical language, and sharing common interests).

The research project was advertised in the prison to all mothers through the use of posters and individual letters inviting them to participate. An explanation of project objectives, procedures, and criteria of eligibility was given:

1. mothers with children between 4 and 12 years of age.
2. residence of children in Baltimore City, MD.
3. children being in the care of nonagency appointed caregivers.

4. mothers' parole or release data at least 4 months distant.
5. mothers having an appropriate grade status within the institution as stipulated by prison officials.

The letter indicated that participants would be paid to participate in the project. Prospective volunteer mothers were given an overview of project goals, objectives, and procedures at these meetings. Signed consent forms were obtained from each mother. After these consent procedures, mothers communicated with their families about the project. Contact by mothers with other family members greatly facilitated subsequent staff contacts. Written project information was given to mothers to assist them in explaining the research to their families. A staff member telephoned each caregiver for an appointment to gather data. Caregivers usually had sufficient information in advance and were quite receptive to staff contact. The participation of the child involved obtaining consent from the child, the mother, and the caregiver.

## Subjects

The sample consisted of 40 primarily low-income black mother–child–caregiver family units, from Baltimore City, MD. There was no attempt to select families on the basis of ethnicity or socioeconomic status. The demographic characteristics of the prison population, which was 80% black and mostly low-income, and the volunteer selection criteria determined the final social composition of the sample.

Black imprisoned mothers were between the ages of 19 and 42 with an average age of 26 years. The educational status of mothers was generally between grades nine and 12. At least 85% of the mothers were single parents, with the largest subgroup having never been married. Approximately 40% of the mothers had one child. Of the remaining 60%, approximately 40% had two children.

Mothers included 23 first and 17 repeat offenders. Offenses ranged from shoplifting to homicide. The most common offenses were property related, some of which included armed or physical assault. The length of sentences were from one to over 45 years. Although length of current mother–child separation ranged from 1 month to 4 years, most mothers and children had been separated for 1½ years at the time of their participation in the study.

The 40 black children in the study ranged in age from 4 to 12 years with an average age of 8.5 years. There were 20 girls and 20 boys. Only one child per family participated in the study. With few exceptions, the oldest child in the family who met the age criterion was included in the sample. Children were divided into two groups: "young children" were between the ages of four and eight, while "old children" were between the ages of nine and 12 years old.

The caregivers of children during maternal absence were 40 black extended family members related to the imprisoned mothers. Eighty-five percent of the primary caregivers of children were maternal grandmothers. Fathers, aunts, great grandmothers, or great-aunts assumed the primary caregiver roles in the remaining cases.

## Data Collection Procedures

The primary focus of this study was the social interaction between incarcerated mothers and their children during the period of mother–child separation. Systematic naturalistic observations and self-reports from participants were principal methods of data collection.

Data were collected by trained black observers using the following procedures: (1) mother discussion groups; (2) home visits with the child's caregiver and child; (3) mother–child prison visits; (4) child–peer groups at a facility in the community where children lived; (5) follow-up telephone discussions with caregivers of children after procedures with children; and (6) official school records of children's academic and behavioral competencies.

All data collection procedures at the prison were conducted in a modular double-width trailer unit. This unit was specifically designed to provide a laboratory setting for the conduct of naturalistic and standardized research procedures. All data collection procedures involving child–peer groups were conducted in the recreation room of a large community church in Baltimore City.

## Mother Discussion Groups

Mother discussion groups were designed to obtain self-reported information about: (a) the nature of the mother–child relationship prior to and during incarceration; (b) the impact of conditions of separation on the child; and (c) their general experiences in prison. Pilot tests of procedures indicated that individual maternal interviews would possibly be perceived as too threatening to mothers. The private setting of interviews would create suspicion among mothers and would be similar to interrogations with all their negative connotations. The group forum was therefore chosen as one of the primary research procedures. The small discussion groups resembled quasiclinical support groups where mothers engaged in discussions and provided support to one another.

Mothers were grouped in four-person groups according to the ages of their children and the mothers' approximate parole or release data. Such groupings provided mothers with common bases to discuss child related topics and helped to maintain stable group membership which facilitated comfort and trust among mothers. Mothers in the small groups were mixed, however, in the histories of their experiences in the criminal justice system and kinds of convicted offenses.

Mother discussion groups were conducted by the principal investigator, who, as a group leader set the framework for the topics. Group meetings were held once every 2 weeks over a 3 month period and lasted 2 hours each time. Group sessions were tape recorded with prior participant knowledge and consent.

## Home Visits

Home visits were designed to: (a) ascertain interest of caregivers and child for participation in the project; (b) observe home conditions; (c) observe interactions between caregiver and the child; and (d) establish rapport and trust between the staff and the research participants. At the beginning of the project, two staff members made an initial 2 hour visit with the caregiver and child. The principal investigator and one research assistant comprised the team. Caregivers invariably used the visit and subsequent contacts to disclose additional information about mothers, children or themselves. Home visits were also tape recorded.

## Mother–Child Prison Visits

Mother–child visits at the prison were designed to provide an opportunity for observation of social interaction between incarcerated mothers and their children. The visits included: (a) unstructured free interaction between mothers and children; (b) organized group game activities and lunch; and (c) structured interaction between individual mother–child pairs.

The principal investigator and three observers conducted mother–child observations. Each staff member was responsible for the observation of individual mother–child pairs during designated periods of unstructured activity. Observations consisted of ongoing narrative accounts of mother–child interaction, parental role functions, and emotional affect.

Within the two mother–child prison visits, individual mother–child dyad sessions were conducted, one in each of the prison visits. Their purpose was to provide a private setting where staff could more closely observe the dynamics of the relationship between individual mother–child pairs.

The first dyadic session was structured to include: (a) a period of informal conversation; (b) a period when the investigator exits the room in order to facilitate mother and child intimate interaction; (c) a quasi-clinical projective technique for children involving painting faces of significant others on stones; and (d) closure of the session by the investigator. The second dyadic session was structured to include: (a) a period of informal conversation; (b) a follow-up discussion about the stone paintings in the projective technique made in the first session; (c) a picture-taking session in which the investigator took two pictures with an instant camera of mother and child and then left the pair alone to discuss the pictures as they developed; and (d) closure of the session by the investigator. Prior to the mother–child visits, mothers were informed about the dyadic session and were instructed to interact freely with their children, discussing the child's experiences during separation and other self-initiated topics.

## Measures and Data

Data were collected in various settings over a 3 month period from mother–child–caregiver units. Following each mother–child prison visit and child peer group, followup telephone discussions with caregivers of children were conducted. After both sessions which involved children, the research team convened to analyze events or to observe social interactions of mothers and children. Information was recorded at this time to supplement data gathered on site in natural field settings. Reliance on subject self-reports and observations of subject social interactions across the various data collection settings served to corroborate and validate the research data. Inter-rater reliability among raters was 84% in naturalistic observations and 88% in coding of raw data.

Three sets of measures were developed to assess the characteristics and social interactions of imprisoned mothers, their children, and children's caregivers (variables and measures can be obtained from the senior author). The measures were categorized into the following areas: (1) maternal dimensions which included personal background variables and mother–child relationship variables; (2) child dimensions which included personal background variables and variables relating to the child's experiences with stages of maternal involvement in the criminal justice system; and (3) caregiver dimensions which included personal background variables and caregiver–child relationship variables.

## Mother–Child Relationships Before Incarceration

Data reveals the important role of extended family relationships of black children *before* mothers' incarceration. Prior to mothers' imprisonment children were generally reared by both their mothers and maternal grandmothers. When analyzed in terms of amount of primary care, residence of child, and quality of child's care from mother, data reveals significant relationships among these factors.

Thirty-one children (78%) were the receipients of shared childrearing in which both mothers and grandmothers provided for the primary needs of children. In contrast, the primary needs of nine children (23%) were provided by mothers only. Children received care from mothers within three types of residential settings: (a) twenty-five children (62%) resided with their mothers in residences of extended family members; (b) twelve children (30%) resided with mothers in mothers' own residences; and (c) three children (8%) resided with extended family members in residences separate from mothers. Regardless of residential patterns, all children were a part of extended family networks. However, it appears that children who received most of their primary care from mothers typically lived with mothers only. In some cases, where children resided with both mothers and caregivers, children still received most of their primary care from mothers.

Eleven children (28%) were rated as receiving a high degree of quality care from mothers and eight children (20%) were rated as receiving a medium degree of quality care. In contrast, twenty-one children (52%) were rated as receiving a low quality of care.

Analysis reveals significant relationships among specific variables relating to children's care prior to mothers' imprisonment. Data reveals that quality of primary care is related to the amount of shared childrearing ($r=.820$, $p \leq .000$), the amount of primary care ($r=.968$, $p \leq .000$) and residence of child ($r=.635$, $p \leq .000$). Thus, those children who received a high overall quality of care from mothers prior to mothers' imprisonment were likely to have resided with mothers only, received most of their primary care from mothers, and were the receipients of little shared childrearing.

The low quality of children's care from mothers prior to imprisonment reflects mothers' limited involvement in childrearing. One reason for this limited involvement relates to mothers' ages at birth of their first child. Thirty-four mothers (85%) had their first child between the ages of 13 and 18 years with 28 mothers (70%) having their first child between ages 16 and 18 years. These mothers described problems associated with adolescent parenthood. Included among these were disruption of high school (and/or vocational training), limited employment opportunities, lack of child care knowledge, and economic dependence on outside sources. These concerns and problems suggest severe alterations in the life cycles and personal development of parents.

Thus another reason for the mothers' limited involvement in childrearing was related to the disruption of her own personal development by adolescent pregnancy and parenthood. Some mothers reported continued excessive participation in social activities typically characteristic of the adolescent period. These activities competed with and reduced the mothers' childcare responsibilities. In some instances, mothers reported having idle time as a consequence of being unemployed and not in high school. Some mothers purposefully chose to live away from their children to prevent exposing them to negative aspects of their lifestyles. In these cases, weekend visits, special occasions, and limited financial support constituted the levels of responsibility assumed by these mothers.

In some instances, mothers and caregivers reported that the grandmother assumed primary care of the child from birth. This was because of the mothers' perceived youth and inexperience. Maternal negligence was seldom mentioned as the cause. Many grandmothers reported strong attachments to their grandchildren and informed the research staff that these children were "like their own." Two final reasons for limited childrearing involvement by mothers included previous separations due to out-of-state visitation with family and friends (often to seek improved employment opportunities) and shortterm incarcerations in local detention facilities.

## Mother–Child Relationships During Incarceration

Based on their self reports, mothers were assessed on the frequency of visits, telephone calls, and written communication with their children. Mothers rated as high (35%) reported frequent visits from children (e.g., one to three visits per week); frequent telephone calls to children (e.g., two to four calls per week); and frequent written communication with children. Mothers rated as medium (43%) or low (23%) had less than half the frequency of all forms of communication with their children. In addition, these mothers received far fewer visits per week from their children than did mothers who were rated high. In extreme cases, mothers saw children one or two times per month.

Children's contact with mothers is largely a function of two important factors: (a) institutional policies which govern the frequency and duration of mother–child visitation and telephone calls (e.g., children are not permitted to initiate calls to mothers; visits are a function of mothers' conduct status in prison) and (b) familial factors (e.g., caregivers' ability and willingness to provide transportation for children to visit; the kind of relationships between children, mothers, and caregivers; mothers' or caregivers' concerns about psychological effects on children as a result of visiting mothers in a prison setting).

When communicating with children, mothers typically express concern for children's health status, academic performance, relationships with family members and friends, and the possible negative influences of the mothers' prisoner status on children (e.g., loss of respect for mothers, teasing of children by peers who are knowledgeable of mothers' imprisonment). Mothers' concern and care for children is also expressed in mothers making practical gifts, and sending money to caregivers, and facilitating social service benefits for children.

During prison visits children were observed interacting with mothers in various social activities: playing games, doing schoolwork, and conversing about current life experiences. Mother-child pairs were rated on defined types of mother-child role models. These models are: Adult-Child Role Model, Child-Child Role Model, Adult-Adult Role Model, and Child-Adult Role Model. Although most mother-child pairs displayed some behavior characteristic of all models, ratings reflect the predominate behavioral role model.

Six pairs (15%) were rated as displaying the Child-Child Role Model. These pairs were characterized by mothers behaving submissively, frequently deferring to children, and lacking in maintaining general management of their children. Mothers in this model expressed having peer-like relationships with their children and exerting little authority and leadership. Children in this model were observed seeking guidance and nurturance from mothers. In some cases children expressed having a sibling-like relationship with their mothers.

Four pairs (10%) were rated as displaying the Child-Adult Role Model. In these pairs, children were observed giving directions and maintaining general control over mother child interactions. Some children expressed themselves authoritatively, "talking back" to mothers, and behaving belligerently. Mothers, on the other hand, tended to defer to children's authority and directions and behaved submissively. Mothers expressed feelings of powerlessness in their ability to manage and influence their children's behavior.

Seven pairs (18%) were rated as being the Adult-Adult Role Model. In these pairs, children were discouraged from participating in games and activities with other children and were expected to engage in "adult-like" conversations with mothers. In one case, a child was mother's partner and confidant and was given "parent-like" responsibilities for other children. Children displayed assertive, independent, and authoritative behaviors similar to behaviors of mothers.

Twenty-three mother-child pairs (58%) were rated as displaying the Adult-Child Role Model. In these pairs, children were observed seeking direction and nurturance from mothers. They tended to defer to mothers as authority figures. Mothers were observed displaying complimentary behaviors of providing direction and nurturant behavior. Mothers expressed a basic knowledge of parenting and age-appropriate behaviors and expectations for children.

The observed mother-child behaviors in the four role relationship models seem to reflect mothers' knowledge and awareness of basic methods, techniques, and attitudes toward parenting during imprisonment. Twenty-one mothers (52%) were rated medium, while eleven mothers (28%) were rated high, and eight mothers (20%) low on knowledge of basic childrearing practices. A strong relationship appears to exist between the types of mother child role models and mothers' knowledge of basic childrearing practices ($r = .483$, $p \leq .001$). It appears that mothers with the greater amount of knowledge of basic childrearing practices during imprisonment are more likely to be mothers who are a part of mother-child relationships displaying behavior characteristic of the Adult-Child Role Model.

Mothers and children were observed displaying both positive and negative emotional affect toward each other. Twenty-three pairs (58%) were rated as being mostly high on overall affect of the mother-child pair during imprisonment. The remaining pairs were rated as mixed in their overall affect. In these pairs, mothers and children tend to display equal amounts of positive and negative affect toward each other. A strong relationship appears to exist between types of mother-child role models and the overall affect of mother-child pair during imprisonment ($r = .606$ $p \leq .000$). Therefore, mother-child pairs who display behaviors characteristic of the Adult-Child Role Model are more likely to also display mostly positive emotional affect toward each other. In most cases, mother-child relationships were harmonious. However, some conflicts and problems existed particularly where role reversals occurred in models other than the Adult-Child Role Model.

As indicated earlier, children reside with extended family members during the period of maternal incarceration. Most often, maternal grandmothers assume the roles of primary caregiver during mothers' imprisonment. In many cases, these grandmothers *continue to assume* the role of primary caregiver as it had existed prior to mothers' imprisonment. Thirty-one caregivers (78%) provided at least half of the primary care for children prior to mothers' imprisonment. It was usually shared with mothers. Of the remaining nine caregivers (23%), most provided intermittant care for children. Thus, there is the existence of continuity of care and caregivers for many children prior to and during mothers' imprisonment.

The nature of caregiver-child relationships during mothers' imprisonment is generally positive. Thirty-three caregiver-child relationships (82%) were rated as high on their overall affect. These pairs were characterized as having positive emotions (e.g., happiness, satisfaction) for each other as observed and reported during home visits and in mother discussion groups. Remaining caregiver-child pairs were rated medium to low. These relationships were characterized by the absence of positive emotions and the presence of little warmth.

Caregivers, in general, provide a high quality of care for children during mothers' imprisonment. Thirty-three caregivers (82%) were rated as providing a high quality of care. They more than adequately provided for children's basic needs for food, shelter, clothing, and psychological security. The remaining seven caregivers (18%) provided a medium to low quality of care for children. In these situations children's basic needs were provided for adequately, or in some cases, less than adequately as observed and/or as reported by caregivers themselves or mothers. In most cases this low quality of care was related to a lack of resources.

Mothers reported and displayed varying degrees of distress related to separation from children. Distress due to maternal incarceration was defined as psychological and/or physical strain and stress arising from the separation experience and perceived loss of parental role functions. Examples of this state included statements of mourning and grieving and extreme preoccupation with thoughts and feelings regarding their children.

Ten mothers (25%) were rated as low on degree of distress due to separation from children while the remaining mothers (75%) were rated as expressing and displaying a high degree of distress as a consequence of separation from children. Mothers who expressed high distress reported several coping strategies. These included sharing events and feelings with other mothers and, to a lesser degree, with institutional staff; channeling such responses into work, recreational, or artistic activities at the prison; and relying on family members for emotional support. A majority of mothers perceived their participation in the research project as providing a forum to discuss their children, parental role functions, and coping strategies.

## Experiences of Children with the Criminal Justice System

Children of imprisoned mothers have unique socialization experiences in the criminal justice system. The seven characteristic stages of this system include the: (a) deviant activity stage where the mother may have been associated with a socially defined deviant activity; (b) arrest stage where mother was apprehended and/or arrested by law enforcement officials; (c) court proceedings stage where the mother's case was adjudicated; (d) offense stage where the mother was convicted of a specific socially defined deviant activity; (e) *jail/detention center stage* where the mother was incarcerated in a short term facility; (f) *prison stage* where the mother was incarcerated in a long term facility; and (g) halfway-house stage where the mother resided in a community based facility, serving the remainder of a sentence. All mothers were not necessarily involved in all seven stages of the criminal justice system. Therefore, all children were not exposed to all stages of the system.

For each stage, children were rated on their information about and their direct experience in that stage. Information about a stage refers to whether children have or do not have information about a given stage of the system. Direct experience in a stage refers to whether children are absent or present with their mothers in a given stage. Assessments of the nature of children's exposure to maternal involvement in stages of the criminal justice system are not measures of children's understanding of their experiences in these stages.

Most children of black imprisoned mothers are exposed to analogous events as their mothers progress through stages of the criminal justice system. In general, mothers experience unpredictable stressful events in these stages which may include arrest, prosecution, and involuntary confinement in correctional facilities. These events are likely to be characterized by emotions of sadness, anger, fear, and shock for mothers. Thus, children are exposed, either through information or direct experience, to these potentially traumatic events involving their mothers.

Several accounts of children's responses in stages of the criminal justice system were reported. One child ran and hid in fear in the aftermath of a homocide which occurred in the home. Another child cried profusely at seeing her mother behind a metal screen and talking by telephone during visitation in a jail. Finally, in one extreme case, a child was hospitalized for prolonged periods of crying and refusal to eat upon initial separation from mother.

More children have information and direct experience with the jail/detention center stage and prison stage than with any other stage. Two reasons may account for this: (1) the jail and prison stages are places where children visit mothers (over an extended period of time) and (2) mothers are in more transition in other stages, progressing from one stage to another. Thus, children are more likely to be present in the jail/detention center and prison stages.

Children have information about an average of four stages of the criminal jusice system in comparison to having direct experience in an average of two stages. These different patterns of exposure reflect differences in (1) children's opportunities in obtaining information and having experiences with stages of the criminal justice system and (2) maternal and caregiver childrearing practices in relation to children's exposure to the criminal justice system. For example, most socially defined deviant activities typically occur outside the home, away from the presence of children. In addition, mothers and caregivers display behaviors which indicate strong beliefs that children's exposure to stages of mothers' involvement in the criminal justice system may have negative influences on children. They actively monitor children's information about and direct experience in stages of the criminal justice system. Although children's direct experiences could be limited, mothers and caregivers reported an inability to monitor the amount of information concerning the status of mothers from numerous sources (e.g., peers, neighbors, newspapers, or television).

A statistically significant direct relationship exists between children's information about the number of stages of the criminal justice system and age of children. However, in describing the direct experience of children in stages of the criminal justice system, age of children is found to be significant only among the younger group of children ($r=.3893$). Thus, within this age group, the older the child, the more stages of the criminal justice system the child experiences as a consequence of a mother's involvement.

## DISCUSSION AND IMPLICATIONS

Our overall analysis revealed strong interdependence of relationships among black imprisoned mothers and their children, and childrens caregivers. The caregiver role was found to be of particular importance in maternal role functioning prior to and during incarceration. Although the dynamics of relationships and attachments among mothers, children, and caregivers were not thoroughly examined, such relationships are crucial in the interpretation and understanding of relationships between incarcerated mothers and their families. Research on black families suggests a high degree of extended family involvement in childrearing during crisis as well as noncrisis periods (Billingsley, 1968; Hill, 1972; Stack, 1974). High degrees of maternal distress indicate that separation and imprisonment affect the mothers' enactments of maternal roles. High maternal cognizance of the potentially negative impact of separation on children serves as one index of maternal concern for children. Other areas where maternal concern over children's well-being was often expressed included: provisions for meeting children's basic needs for food, shelter, clothing, safety, and health; children's academic performance and interpersonal relationships (with peers and adults), and involvement in criminal activity as a direct consequence of maternal incarceration.

Data revealed definite attitudes and practices among mothers and caregivers regarding children's knowledge and participation in the seven stages of maternal involvement with the criminal justice system. They were concerned over the possible negative effects of children's knowledge, exposure, and involvement. Distinct practices which reflect this belief include: (a) limiting the amount of information children receive about mothers' socially defined deviant activities; (b) limiting mother–child visitations in correctional facilities; and (c) disguising the true custodial residence of mothers.

Whether the focus is on providing services to black imprisoned mothers, to their children, or to extended family members who care for children during maternal incarceration, knowledge of the actual experiences of individuals and families in these circumstances should be the basis for policy and program development. Caution should be used in generalizing findings from this study. This particular prison's proximity to children and caregivers (20 miles distance) and the institutional policies must be considered. The distance of correctional facilities from prisoners' home communities and institutional policies governing visitation vary greatly across the country.

Our data indicate heterogeneity among black imprisoned mothers prior to and during incarceration. The experience of adolescent parenthood among some, along with related problems, suggests the necessity for education in parenting skills and child development. Motivations to acquire such skills and training are apparent for many mothers in this insitutional setting. For some, mother–child relationships were of low quality prior to and during imprisonment. For others, the conditions of imprisonment (e.g., sporadic contact) foster romanticized views of mother–child relationships. Motivations are also an issue when participation in such programs is related to parole decisions and conditions of release. Ironically, the cultural appropriateness of program curriculum, training materials, and staff to the needs and experiences of low socioeconomic status black parents and children is often questionable.

Verbal and behavioral indices of maternal distress due to separation from children suggest a need for specialized therapeutic services. Given the relatively short duration of sentences assigned mothers, and their probable reunion with children, such psychological distress could later become problematic for both mothers and children.

Visitation policies at local, stage, and federal correctional institutions should be examined to determine their influence on the frequency and quality of communication between mothers and children. The remoteness of prisons from the communities of prisoners' families obviously influences the nature and frequency of visits. The physical structure and atmosphere of visitation facilities, and policies with regard to the mothers' institutional status (e.g., general grade level, disciplinary procedures), further impact on interactions between incarcerated mothers and their children.

Black extended families provide a support system for children during maternal incarceration. Although this support is evident, some problems tax or extend beyond caregivers' capabilities. Caregivers may also be nonsupportive towards mothers and/or children because of their own values or antagonisms toward the mother. Legal issues with regard to child custody and other mother–child–

caregiver relations often arise in this situation particularly in the case of social agency-appointed caregivers. Such issues are also evident even when children reside with extended family members. Thus, a need for legal services may exist for this group of families and children.

Data suggest that some children may encounter difficulties in handling facets of maternal incarceration. Our observations indicated that most of the children were significantly attached to their mothers. Yet, many children also displayed confusion, fear, and shame as reported by mothers and caregivers or as observed by staff. The embarrassment, stigmatization, and trauma surrounding maternal incarceration proved burdensome for children. Our data indicated that some children had behavioral problems, apparent to school, psychological, and legal service personnel. Such problems may have been caused or exacerbated by maternal incarceration. Therapeutic interventions may be required for the children of incarcerated mothers.

Policies intended to alleviate separation problems between incarcerated mothers and their children, or to rehabilitate mothers by permitting children to reside with them in community based and traditional/modified prison settings, need to be carefully assessed. The rationale underlying such policies is that children can assist in the rehabilitation of mothers. Some correctional personnel believe that children have a positive influence on mothers' behavior during maternal incarceration and its aftermath. Although we recognize some beneficial effects of children's behavior on parents, we have questions concerning the use of children in treatment strategies. Children have their own developmental tasks to handle, without the additional responsibility of rehabilitating mothers. Undoubtedly, children need responsible care of parents or significant adults. Institutionalized conditions of child-rearing and parenting are facets that need to be thoroughly examined in terms of benefits and costs to both mothers and children.

National statistics on caregiving arrangements for children during maternal incarceration do not exist. Published reports of certain locales indicate that a significant number of children reside with extended families. Removing children from their families to institutional settings should be carefully examined with respect to the impact on the family unit. Questions can also be raised about the desire of mothers and caregivers to have children reared in institutional environments.

Data from many sources document that a majority of women in prison (including those who are mothers) are convicted and sentenced for property and drug related offenses. Given the negative conditions of imprisonment and its impact on the individual and family members, alternatives to incarceration (e.g., community facilities, probation, fines, restitutions) have been proposed for certain less severe offenses (Hinds, 1980; Watts, in preparation). In addition, many scholars have raised critical issues concerning deviance, social control, punishment, and rehabilitation, given the highly political nature of the criminal justice system. Major changes in the social, political and economic systems will be required to redress societal inequities leading to the greater definition of certain groups as deviant. These same inequities lead to these groups' greater involvement with the criminal justice system (National Minority Advisory Council on Criminal Justice, 1982; Owens & Bell, 1977; Woodson, 1977; Wright, 1973).

Underlying these policy and program areas are philosophical issues concerning: (1) the use of family relationships in the rehabilitation or control of individuals; (2) the extent of permissible state intervention into family relationships; (3) responsibility for the needs of family members resulting from such intervention; (4) the relationship between individual and environmental factors leading to individual incarceration; (5) minority representation in policy/program development and implementation; and (6) prevention issues. Social policies and interventions temptingly lend themselves to focusing on a single dimension of benefits. Dangers exist if the range of consequences to black mothers, children and families are not considered. These implications for social policies and programs suggest the need for a coordinated effort by allied mental health and service delivery professionals.

## ACKNOWLEDGMENTS

The senior author and two co-authors were formerly a research fellow and assistants, respectively, in the Laboratory of Developmental Psychology, National Institute of Mental Health, Department of Health and Human Services when this study was conducted.

The authors are grateful to this agency and other sponsoring agencies: the Maryland Department of Public Safety and Correctional Services; the National Institute of Justice, Department of Justice; and Center for Studies of Minority Group Mental Health, National Institute of Mental Health. This research does not necessarily represent the official position of sponsoring federal or state agencies.

# 15

# Black Children's Sex-Role Ideologies and Occupational Choices in Families of Employed Mothers

Geraldine Kearse Brookins
*Jackson State University*

This paper investigated black children's sex roles and occupational aspirations in families of employed mothers. The study is discussed within a developmental, historical, and contextual framework.

In our society, the organization of one's life is significantly influenced by sex role and occupational role. Sex-role orientation influences one's interests, attitudes, overt behavior, emotional reactions, and cognitive functioning. Occupational role influences leisure time, colleagues and friends, place of dwelling, and life pace. There is also a strong relationship between the two roles: Sex-role ideology often governs occupational choice.

Given the centrality of these roles in individuals' lives, it is crucial to understand how sex roles and occupational roles are acquired. It is not entirely clear how occupational and sex roles develop; however, parents apparently influence that development. Major theories of sex-role acquisition postulate important roles for parents as models, identification objects, or role reinforcers (Freud, 1949; A. Freud, 1946; Kagan, 1958; Mischel, 1966, 1970; Kohlberg, 1966). Theories of occupational-role acquisition also stress the importance of parents (Ginzberg et al., 1951; Super, 1953; Roe, 1956). Mothers' and fathers' sex roles, occupational roles, and behaviors toward their children thus become important determinants of children's role acquisitions. Children therefore acquire sex roles and occupational roles differently, depending on family configuration and the role enactments of various family members. Different family settings represent distinct contexts in which the child interacts, processes information, and constructs notions of the social world.

## REVIEW OF RESEARCH

It stands to reason that children in families where the mother is employed outside the home and the father shares in general household tasks, will acquire sex roles and occupational roles differently than will children whose mothers and fathers exhibit "traditional" sex-role and occupational-role behaviors. Among whites it has been demonstrated that maternal employment specifically facilitates egalitarian sex-role beliefs and attitudes (Douvall, 1955; Hartley 1960, 1961a, 1961b; Miller, 1975) and affects children's career aspirations (Banducci, 1967, Almquist & Angrist, 1971; Tangri, 1972).

Numerous studies have attempted to determine the relative influence of various agents on individuals' occupational choices (Sewell et al., 1957; Stewart, 1959; Steinke & Kaczkowski, 1961; Bennett & Gist, 1964; Kuvlesky & Bealer, 1966; Pallone et al., 1970; Peters, 1971). While most of these studies have focused on the adolescent or young adult, they are of interest because their findings have direct relevance to factors in the current study. In general, the findings identify parents as most influential of adolescents' occupational choices. Also, girls tend to rank mothers as the most important influencers of occupational aspirations.

Little is known about black children's sex-role and occupational-role behavior and/or beliefs in relation to maternal employment. Since black women have historically combined the roles of wife, mother, and employee (Feagin, 1970), their participation in the labor force has undoubtedly resulted in some displacement of traditional sex-role behavior of parents. Earlier research findings suggested that black families are characterized by an egalitarian pattern in decision making and performance of household tasks (Blood & Wolfe, 1960; Middleton & Putney, 1960; Hyman & Reed, 1969; Hill, 1972). It is reasonable to assume that this pattern emerged partially in response to maternal employment outside the home. Given the stability of black mothers' labor force participation and the egalitarian interactional patterns of black families, it is important to understand black children's perceptions and beliefs concerning appropriate roles for males and females.

Among blacks, women have long participated in the workforce. In Africa, women were significant contributors to the economy of the family and the community, serving as entrepreneurs, controlling industries, and raising crops. These economic activities coexisted alongside women's traditional nurturing functions for their children (Rodgers-Rose, 1980). During slavery, black women were required to work long hours in the fields (or elsewhere) and then to care for their families at day's end (Lerner, 1973). This duality of responsibility continued after emancipation. Around the turn of the century, one could discern an emerging pattern which remained extant for nearly 80 years. A higher proportion of black wives, than any other group of married women, were earning wages (Pleck, 1970). Comparing the income earnings among married Italian and black women, Pleck (1970) found that despite similar economic circumstances, black wives were more likely to engage in paid employment.

In an attempt to account for these differences, Pleck (1970) advances three explanations. She notes that following slavery both black women and men accepted the traditional model of men as breadwinners and women as homemakers. In spite of these attitudes, black wives had an unusually high rate of wage employment. Pleck (1970) suggests (1) that black wives came to see it as their responsibility to "help out" and subsequently persuaded their husbands to accept their employment; (2) that black mothers were more disposed to train their children for independence and thus did not view good parenting as requiring their constant physical presence; and (3) black mothers viewed education as an important stepping stone to a better life and therefore could justify their labor force participation in terms of sacrificing for their children.

This is the historical background for the existence of an egalitarian pattern among black families. Nobles (1976) found that black parents did not specifically teach their children sex roles but rather encouraged them to be flexible enough to compete and survive in this society. Such egalitarian patterns and teachings influence sex role perceptions of children in black families.

Findings have been mixed regarding social class status as a factor in maternal employment studies (Hoffman, 1974). As such, there is a need to explore its role in black families with employed mothers. How does class status influence children's sex role beliefs and occupational choices?

## PROBLEM

The following study investigated relations between maternal employment, sex-role ideologies, and occupational choices for middle- and working-class children in black families. The specific objectives of this study were to:

1. examine the relationship between maternal employment and egalitarian sex-role ideologies among middle- and working-class black children.
2. examine the relationship between maternal employment and the perception of the range of occupational choice among middle- and working-class black children.
3. determine if girls of employed black mothers have higher occupational aspirations than do girls of nonemployed mothers.
4. explore the relationship between social class and black children's egalitarian sex-role ideologies.
5. explore the relationship between social class and black children's occupational choice.
6. explore the father's influence on the sex-role ideologies and occupational choices of children of employed mothers.

Literature on sex-role acquisition indicates that children establish gender constancy around the age of five or six (Kohlberg, 1966). Similarly, sex-typed behavior is fairly well established by this age (Maccoby & Jacklin, 1974). Findings suggest that maternal employment may influence sex-role beliefs and occupational aspirations beyond the preschool years due, in part, to changing cognitive structures (Seegmiller, 1980). It seemed reasonable, therefore, to study children between the ages of six and eight since the influence of maternal employment would probably be more apparent than at an earlier age.

## METHODS

### Subjects

This study investigated 36 black families in a Northeast metropolitan area with a mother, father, and one child, 6 to 8 years old, serving as participants. The children in the sample included 20 males and 16 females. Ages ranged from 6.1 to 8.8 years. The mean IQ score on the Peabody Picture Vocabulary Test was 117.7. The mode for number of children per family was two, with a range from one to eight. Mothers' ages ranged from 25 to 50 years (mean = 34.4 years). Mothers' years of education ranged from 10 to 22 years (mean = 14.5 years).

Discrepancies between employment self-ascription and actual practice convinced the author that the mother's current employment status might have less impact on the child than would her employment history. Consequently, each mother was asked to report employment history for three developmental periods: from the child's birth to 3 years of age, from 3 to 5 years, and from 5 years to the present time. Maternal employment history during the third developmental period was judged to be critical. At this stage children were more cognitively sophisticated, thus they were better able to make the adjustments in attitudes and distribution of household chores made necessary by maternal employment. Analyses were done using the percentage of time the mother worked from when the child was 5 years of age.

Fathers' ages ranged from 26 to 50 years (mean = 36 years). The number of years of education ranged from 11 to 23 years with a mean of 15.7 years. The average number of years these men had been in their current jobs was 6.5 years, the range was 1 to 21 years. Most fathers reported that they were in their current jobs for either the money or the challenge it presented. As judged by the Hollingshead Scale, applied to fathers' education and occupation, 18 families were determined to be middle-class and 18 working-class.

### Measures

Three instruments were used to measure children's sex-role ideology, occupational choice, and intelligence. Four instruments were used to measure parents' demographic characteristics, employment status, sex-role ideologies, occupational satisfaction, and maternal employment history.

*Child Sex-Role Ideology Measure.*   In order to assess children's beliefs about roles for men and women with particular reference to household tasks and activities, an 11 item Sex-Role Ideology Instrument was devised. In this instrument, children were presented with a picture of "neutral" hands performing a task, such as washing dishes. They were then asked to state who should perform that task, "the man," "the woman," or "either one". Items were stated in such a way that the children were required to determine who had ultimate responsibility for a given activity (e.g. "It's after dinner and the dishes need to be washed, but both the man and the woman are tired. Who should wash the dishes, the man, the woman or either one?). Each child received an egalitarian score, a counter-traditional score, and a traditional score. For this study only the egalitarian scores were analyzed. An egalitarian score was the total number of egalitarian responses each child made on the 11 items.

*Occupational Choice Interview.*   In order to assess children's occupational choices, Looft's (1971) occupational interview was modified and employed. In Looft's interview, the child is asked what she would most like to be when she grows up and what she will be when grown. In modifying the interview, a third question was added which asked about the range of occupations the children perceived to be of interest and available to them. In addition to range of occupational choice, measures of occupational aspirations, occupational expectations, and specificity of occupational knowledge were derived from interview responses. Several scoring procedures were developed for the various dimensions of occupational choice (see Brookins, 1977 for details).

*Peabody Picture Vocabulary Test.*   The third measure for children, the Peabody Picture Vocabulary Test (PPVT), was used to determine the relative intellectual functioning of the sample. The PPVT's relatively high correlation with the Weschsler Intelligence Scale for Children and the Stanford-Binet (Buros, 1965), as well as easy administration, made it a suitable measure of intelligence for the purpose of this study.

*Demographics and Employment Questionnaire.*   This instrument was utilized to elicit background information on the families. The basic data gathered from this instrument included the parents' ages and education, the sexes, ages, and number of children in the family, and abbreviated work histories for both spouses.

*Adult Sex-Role Ideology Scale.*   In order to assess parental beliefs regarding roles for men and women, an adult sex-role ideology scale was devised to parallel the children's measure. The scale consisted of 20 items related to tasks and activities in the areas of housework, children, employment, and family functioning. According to adult judges' views of societal conventions, 10 of the items were traditionally ascribed to men and 10 to women. Respondents were asked to indicate on a 5-point scale whom they thought should perform certain activities, with the end points of the scale being labeled as "the man" and "the woman". Due to the low variability of scores, this instrument was collapsed into a three-point scale with codes "1" and "2" combined and "4" and "5" combined. The final scoring procedure allowed for traditional, counter-traditional, and egalitarian response scores. For these analyses, only the egalitarian scores were utilized. Mothers and fathers were categorized as highly egalitarian, moderately egalitarian or minimally egalitarian.

*Occupational Satisfaction Scale.*    A 30-item Likert scale was devised to assess how parents felt about their work. For purposes of this study, work was defined as both employment outside the home and full-time household responsibilities. The items were in the form of statements about work to which respondents were required to indicate strength of agreement, disagreement or uncertainty. Due to the low variability of scores, this instrument was collapsed into a three-point scale. Final scoring was based upon satisfaction scores, thus mothers and fathers were categorized as evidencing high satisfaction, moderate satisfaction, or minimal satisfaction with their work.

*Employment History Instrument.*    In order to determine the amount of time each mother had devoted to employment since the birth of the participating child, a detailed history was taken. Information from this instrument was used to determine the percentage of time mothers worked outside the home during various stages of the children's lives. A formula was derived to calculate the percentage of available employment time the mother utilized at three developmental stages of the children: zero to 3 years, 3 to 5 years and over 5 years of age (see discussion of formula in appendix). It was believed that children would be most affected developmentally by maternal employment during the over 5 years age span. Consequently, calculations for that age span were primarily used for this study. Table 15.1 presents information on the mothers' employment patterns from when the child was 5 years old to now. Mothers' stated employment pattern are by sex of subject and SES of family.

## Procedures

After it was determined that a family was eligible to participate in the study, an appointment to interview the participating child was made. All participants were interviewed in their homes. It was assumed that rapport could be more quickly established with child participants in the home setting where they would feel more comfortable. Each child was administered the PPVT following procedures

## TABLE 15.1
### Mother's Employment Characteristics by Sex of Child and SES of Family

| | Mother's Designation of Her Employment At Time of Recruitment | | | Percentage of Employment From Five Years to Present Age of Subject | | |
|---|---|---|---|---|---|---|
| | Nonemployed | Full-time | Part-time | Minimal (0–16) | Moderate (17–58) | High (59–100) |
| *Male* | | | | | | |
| Middle Class | 5 | 3 | 3 | 5 | 4 | 3 |
| Working Class | 3 | 3 | 3 | 0 | 4 | 4 |
| Subtotal | 8 | 6 | 6 | 5 | 8 | 7 |
| *Female* | | | | | | |
| Middle Class | 3 | 4 | 0 | 2 | 1 | 4 |
| Working Class | 6 | 1 | 2 | 7 | 2 | 0 |
| Subtotal | 9 | 5 | 2 | 9 | 3 | 4 |
| TOTAL | 17 | 11 | 8 | 14 | 11 | 11 |

in the test manual. In order to minimize any order effects, the administration order of the Sex-Role Ideology measure and the Occupational Choice Interview was rotated. The children were tested in a separate room to avoid possible familial influences and interference. The entire procedure required approximately 35 minutes. While children were being interviewed, parents were asked to complete the Adult Sex-Role Ideology Scale, the Occupational Satisfaction Scale, and the Maternal Employment History form. Generally, the Demographics and Employment Questionnaires were completed prior to the home visit.

## RESULTS

Correlations between IQ and sex-role ideology ($r = -.04$) and IQ and social class ($r = .18$) were examined. Since these correlations were not significant, IQ was excluded from further analyses.

In order to determine the relationship between maternal employment and egalitarian sex-role ideologies among middle- and working-class black children a sex by employment analysis of variance was computed. Interactions between sex and employment levels failed to reach significance. The main effect of employment did, however, approach significance ($F = 2.7$, $p = .08$). As mothers' participation in employment increased so did children's egalitarian sex-role scores.

To examine the relationship between maternal employment and the child's perception of his or her range of occupational choices, a sex by employment analysis of variance was employed. This analysis showed a significant main effect by employment ($F = 4.8$, $p = .02$). As maternal employment increased so did children's range of choices. Sex approached significance ($p = .08$), with clear interactions occurring between sex and employment )$F = 4.4$, $p = .02$). Boys' range of choice was greater than girls' for both minimal and high maternal employment levels; boys' range of choice was less than girls' for moderate maternal employment. The only significant difference, as indicated by the Dunn Multiple Comparison Test (Kirk, 1968), was between boys with mothers in the high-employment group and girls with mothers in the minimal-employment group ($p < .01$).

The occupations to which girls most aspired were significantly affected by maternal employment, as indicated by a one-way analysis of variance ($F = 5.96$, $p = .02$). Girls with mothers in the high-employment group evidenced higher levels (i.e., white collar) of occupational aspirations than did girls of mothers in minimal and moderate-employment groups. Maternal employment affected neither the aspirational levels of what girls ''think they will really be'' nor their total aspirational levels.

Egalitarian sex-role scores were subjected to a sex by social class analysis of variance, which indicated no main effects. Interactions between sex and social class approached significance ($F=3.3$, $p=.08$): Working-class boys had higher egalitarian scores than working-class girls. Middle-class girls had the highest egalitarian scores of all the four sex/class groups. A Dunn Multiple Comparison Test indicated the absence of significant differences amont the four means.

A social class by sex analysis of variance indicated no effects on children's degree of occupational specificity and no significant interaction. The pattern of the interaction showed, however, that working-class boys evidence more occupational specificity than all other sex/class groups.

To determine the relations among maternal employment, maternal job satisfaction, maternal egalitarian sex-role ideologies, and the dependent variable children's egalitarian sex-role ideologies, a stepwise regression analysis was done. The total amount of variance accounted for by these variables was 16%, with the standardized regression equation being: Egalitarian Ideology = .47 (Employment) + ($-.28$) (Maternal Sex Role Ideology) + ($-.20$) (Sex) + ($-.20$) (Job Satisfaction). A stepwise regression analysis was also used to examine the relationship between father variables, maternal employment, and children's egalitarian sex-role ideologies. Twenty-seven percent of the variance in children's egalitarianism was explained by these variables with the following standardized regression equation: Egalitarian Ideology = .42 (Fathers' Job Satisfaction) + .37 (Maternal employment) + .20 (Fathers' year in Job) + .19 (Sex). Finally, stepwise regression was used to determine the combined relations among father variables, maternal employment, and children's occupational choices. In this case, 26% of the variance in the dependent variable was explained with the standardized regression equation being as follows: Occupational Choices = .36 (Maternal Employment) + .24 (Sex) + ($-.49$) Social Class + .35 (Fathers' Education).

## DISCUSSION

Children's egalitarian sex-role ideologies and occupational choice were examined in relation to maternal employment and other parental variables. It was expected that maternal employment would affect children's egalitarian ideologies; and it seemed reasonable to expect that girls would be affected somewhat more than boys. While an examination of the means suggests trends in that direction, the results only support a main effect of maternal employment with no significant sex differences and no significant sex by employment interaction.

More maternal employment, less maternal egalitarian sex-role ideology and maternal job dissatisfaction contributed to children's increased egalitarian sex-role ideologies. Why maternal egalitarian sex-role ideology and job satisfaction were negatively associated with the children's egalitarian ideologies is intriguing. One possible explanation emerges. As has been suggested in the culture at large, many working women experience role conflict (Bardwick & Douvan,

1972). In keeping with less egalitarian ideology, some women feel that they should be able to perform all the duties required to run a household effectively, and at the same time, hold a job outside the home. The failure to be effective or successful in either—or both—of these "jobs," probably gives rise to job dissatisfaction. It is quite possible that the chilren studied here were aware of their mothers' job dissatisfaction and their mothers' less egalitarian ideas about how to divide household chores. They, then, might have come to believe that the mothers' predicament could have been ameliorated if there were a more suitable and equitable distribution and sharing of tasks in the home. Hence, their more egalitarian sex-role ideologies.

On the other hand, given the historical and cultural basis of maternal employment among blacks, the preceding statement appears more contradictory than explanatory. One could advance the notion that, while black families have enjoyed an egalitarian approach to household and family economy functioning, heretofore, the women's movement and associated attitudes has transformed black women's perceptions of work. No longer do black women see themselves as working solely to fulfill family economic needs, but issues of self-fulfillment have also emerged. This pattern would hold whether the black women are homemakers or a combination of homemakers and employees. This coexisting set of attitudes, behaviors, and beliefs necessitates different kinds of expectations about father/husband participation in household and family responsibilities. Thus, we see egalitarianism of a different magnitude than the prevailing mainstream standard.

Fathers' job dissatisfaction, more maternal employment and fathers' years on the job contribute to children's egalitarian sex-role ideologies. In fact, these variables accounted for more of the variance than did solely maternal variables. It is quite possible that as fathers work longer, they become less satisfied with their jobs and as a result of mothers' participation in the labor force, they spend more time engaged in activities around the home. This could influence their children's sex-role ideologies. If this were the case, then obviously there may be a discrepancy between what mothers view as ideal and what fathers actually contribute with regard to household and family activities. If so, the question becomes: Do the children then move toward an egalitarian sex-role ideology in order to process discrepant cues in their own families?

With regard to children's occupational choice, maternal employment has a significant influence. Boys, in general, nominated more occupational choices than did girls, which is consistent with other findings (Clark, 1967; Looft, 1971; Kirchner & Vondracek, 1973; Siegel, 1973). While not significant, girls of moderately employed mothers tended to have a wider range of mean occupational choices than did girls of highly employed mothers. A possible explanation is that moderately employed mothers had more contact with females representing a variety of occupations than did highly employed mothers and somehow conveyed to their daughters information about the different kinds of jobs females hold. It is equally possible that mothers who were highly employed had just as much contact with females representing a variety of occupations as did moderately employed mothers but spent less time talking to their daughters about the world of work. While girls' range of occupational choice was more restricted than boys', the evidence supports the assumption that maternal employment tends to widen that range. It is reasonable to assume that moderately employed mothers provided a different model for their daughters than did either minimally or highly employed mothers.

Maternal employment, fathers' education, social class, and sex contributed significantly to children's range of occupational choices. The negative relationship between range of choice and social class indicated in the regression analysis suggests working-class boys had a wider range of occupational choice than did middle-class boys. This seems to be reasonable. Working-class boys tended to choose occupations at the lower end of the status spectrum. These lower-status occupations are more visible within the community than are professional ones. Working-class boys are also more likely to view this wide range of occupations as open to them than are middle-class boys, whose occupational choices tend to be restricted to professional jobs (Galler, 1951). Since professional occupations are less visible within black communities, middle-class boys are likely to have a more narrow range of occupational choice.

Finally, the nomination of 120 different occupations suggests that these children possessed considerable awareness of the existence of different occupations. Occupational knowledge is generally believed to be a function of age (Wehrly, 1973). Data from other studies (Clark, 1967; Looft, 1971; Kirchner & Vondracek, 1973) also imply that the number of different occupational nominations increases with age, ranging from a composite number of 13 for 3 to 5 year olds, to a composite number of 60 for 12 year olds. Our findings reveal children in this study to evidence greater sophistication of occupational awareness than would be expected for children their age, not only in terms of numbers, but also in terms of the status spectrum. There is little question that maternal employment was a primary contributing factor in this high degree of occupational knowledge.

The assumption that middle- and working-class girls' occupational aspirations would increase as the level of maternal employment increased was partially supported by the data. A Dunn Multiple Comparison Test indicated that girls whose mothers were highly employed had significantly higher aspirations than did girls whose mothers were moderately employed. There were no statistically significant differences between girls whose mothers were minimally employed and girls of moderately employed mothers; nor between girls of highly employed mothers and girls of minimally employed mothers. The trend for girls of moderately employed mothers as evidenced by the means is difficult to assess. Pallone et al., (1973) found that black, white and Puerto Rican high school girls perceived their mothers as having the greatest influence on their occupational aspirations. It has also been noted that black mothers generally have high aspirations for their children (Scanzoni, 1971). Moderately employed mothers in this study tended to hold low-status jobs. Perhaps their daughters were more influenced by the status of their mothers' jobs than by the aspirations their mothers held for them.

Social class did not prove to be a significant factor, which is somewhat surprising. There are three possible explanations: (1) Black children are less affected by social class than are other groups; (2) Social class is mediated by maternal employment with respect to the dependent variables in this study; (3) Social class was not a distinguishing variable because it was based on the traditional measures, that is, fathers' educational levels and occupational titles. In this latter case it would appear that a more appropriate method would be to take into account both the mothers' and fathers' levels of education and occupation. This method would probably provide a more accurate index of black family socioeconomic status since status is generally achieved and maintained by both the husband's and wife's occupational and educational status. Had an expanded measure been employed in this study, perhaps social class would have been a more significant variable in relation to the dependent variables.

In summary the major findings from this study are:

1. Maternal employment is positively associated with children's egalitarian sex-role ideologies.
2. Maternal egalitarian sex-role ideology and job satisfaction, in conjunction with maternal employment, is negatively associated with children's egalitarian sex-role ideologies.
3. Fathers' job dissatisfaction and fathers' year on the job, in conjunction with maternal employment, contribute significantly to children's egalitarian sex-role ideologies.
4. There are no significant social class differences for children's egalitarian sex-role ideologies relative to maternal employment, but SES by sex interactions approach significance.
5. Children's range of occupational choice is significantly associated with maternal employment with differential effects for boys and girls relative to the mothers' level of employment. Boys of mothers in the high-employment group evidenced a wider range than did girls of mothers in the minimal-employment group.
6. Maternal employment, fathers' education, and social class significantly contribute to children's range of occupational choice.
7. Girls' occupational aspirations are differentially associated with levels of maternal employment with girls of mothers in the high-employment group evidencing higher levels of occupations than girls of mothers in minimal- and moderate-maternal employment groups.

This study was conducted, in part, because there were virtually no data on how maternal employment affects children within black families. It was expected to provide data somewhat different for black children of employed mothers than for white children of employed mothers. Further investigations are required before this expectation can be confirmed.

## IMPLICATIONS

More information on how different levels of employment affect the attitudes of children is necessary. Some women are turning to part-time employment as a solution to the conflict of maintaining a career and raising a family; others are choosing full-time employment as an answer to their own personal and professional needs. It would be important for a mother at the point of decision to know how level of employment might affect her child and whether those effects would differ by sex of the child. Ultimately, of course, these decisions would have to be made within the context of the mother's own value system and financial situation.

It has been noted that a mother's assessment of her employment pattern and the pattern found when she details her employment history do not always coincide. In those cases, it is possible that the mother's assessment represents either how she really sees herself or what she feels her employment status should be. This employment self-concept is important to understanding the total impact of maternal employment on children. It may be that her *perceived* employment pattern or status affects the child more than her actual status.

There was considerable variability in mothers' employment patterns from the children's birth to their present age. Discontinuous patterns over a child's lifetime may have differential effects on the child, depending on his/her developmental stage and the mother's level of employment at each stage. It is suggested that research on the impact of maternal employment take into account (1) the mother's employment self-concept; and (2) her employment history, with particular emphasis on the variability of that history over the young child's life.

Finally, it is rather clear that fathers are integral to understanding the impact of maternal employment on children in black families. This study was different from others because it explored the impact of maternal employment on children in the context of family units. It is apparent that more research of this nature needs to be conducted examining triadic rather than dyadic parent–child relationships.

## CONCLUSION

This paper has examined maternal employment influences on black children in a social, historical, and cultural context. Given this, the study raises issues that go far beyond its scope. However, these issues are pertinent to future research on black children whose mothers are employed and on black women in the labor force. It is clear that economic pressures and household needs tend to structure the work life of black mothers. In addition, employed mothers' social, personal, and professional needs interface with those of their spouses and, in turn, these combined needs of the mother and father impact on the socialization of children. To ignore this complex and interactive process is to do disservice to the very questions for which researchers in this area seek answers.

We suggest that black mothers' participation in the labor force can be viewed historically as an extension of their role in the family economy, not unlike that of white mothers during the Depression (Bennett & Elder, 1979). The primary difference is that for black mothers, economic pressures, household needs and agenda are ongoing and transcend major social and economic changes in mainstream society. History has given rise to cultural imperatives; thus the expectation of a worklife for black women has been transmitted between generations. As such, maternal employment becomes a process linking historical continuities to the perceptions, decisions, and options of the younger generation. It is therefore important to note that independent variables, such as maternal employment, when related to black families are inherently invested with socio-historical meaning which must be acknowledged in order to accurately interpret their impact on specific dependent variables.

Finally, it is important to acknowledge that black children actively engage and construct their environments and subsequently derive meaning from them at different developmental periods. Consequently, data regarding black children and their employed mothers must be interpreted from a developmental perspective along with the social, historical, and cultural perspectives. Only when all these factors are considered will black children be properly understood.

## APPENDIX: EMPLOYMENT TIME UTILIZATION FORMULA

It was assumed that there are 2520 hours per year that could be utilized for fulltime employment (40 hrs./week, plus 2 hrs./day for transportation). This figure was calculated in the following manner: Months were converted to weeks by multiplying by 4.2, the approximate number of weeks in a month; this number was then converted to days by multiplying by five, the normal number of work days in a week. Finally, the resultant figure was mlutiplied by 10, the number of hours during the day that a mother would be outside her home—8 hours for employment and 2 hours for transportation.

Using the figure 2520 as the yearly amount of available employment time, the proportion of that time each mother utilized was derived from the following formula:

$$\frac{\text{Yrs. employed during Span}}{\text{Age Span of S}} \times \frac{\text{Ave. } \#\text{mos. } (4.2) \times [\text{hrs./wk. } + (\text{hrs./wk./8})2]}{2520}$$

## ACKNOWLEDGMENTS

The completion of this chapter was facilitated by a grant from the Charles Stewart Mott Foundation. Gratitude is also extended to James Smith of Jackson State University for his able assistance with data analysis.

# 16 Race, Income and Family Dynamics: A Study of Adolescent Male Socialization Processes and Outcomes

Walter Recharde Allen
*University of Michigan*

The 1970s represented the most productive period of black family research in history. More than 50 books and 500 articles about black family life were published during the decade. This production represented a 500% increase over the black family literature published in all years prior to 1970 (Staples & Mirande, 1980). The widespread recognition of the limitations in our knowledge concerning the organization and function of black family life led to a resurgence of scholarly interest in this area.

Given its importance in the hierarchy of assigned family functions, childrearing is a particularly important dimension of the black family to investigate. A perusal of the literature shows considerable misrepresentation in discussions of black child socialization. One is literally inundated by visions of domineering mothers; absent fathers; disorganized families; abusive, neglectful interpersonal relations; routine psychological self-defamation; and, frustrated, hopeless, intellectually barren lives. Black families are characterized as essentially pathological.

How is it that such hostile familiy environments have not lead to the complete decimation of black life in this society? To what can we attribute the monumental, documented accomplishments of black Americans? These and similar questions formed the basis for this study of adolescent socialization patterns in a sample of black and white families. Convinced that prior conclusions about parent performance, childrearing practices and child outcomes in black families did not ring true, this research sought to explore these issues.

The study's primary goals were to:

1. Propose an alternative, ideological perspective for the study of black child socialization.

2. Provide baseline data of an exploratory nature on several dimensions of black family characteristics, dynamics and outcomes.

3. Present a framework for the systematic assessment of black child socialization processes and outcomes.


## IDEOLOGICAL PERSPECTIVE AND THE STUDY OF BLACK CHILD SOCIALIZATION

We are trained to subscribe to ideas of scientific objectivity, thus our ingrained expectation is that researcher biases will not affect research findings or interpretations. Accumulated experience shows, however, that despite genuine efforts and commitments, the goal of immaculate perception remains an elusive one. Researcher biases and values continue to intrude on the scientific process and to color study conclusions. Perhaps in no area of scientific inquiry is the impact of ideology more apparent than in studies of black family life. The historically perjorative tradition which dominates the black family literature results largely from researcher biases in favor of conventional family patterns, i.e., Anglo-Saxon, middle-class, Protestant.

Three distinct ideological perspectives have been identified in the black family literature (Allen, 1978a). They are the cultural deviant, cultural equivalent, and cultural variant perspectives. These perspectives form a continuum ranging from negative to positive assessments of black family organization and process. The cultural deviant perspective is by far the more common in the literature, having been the dominant view into the early 1970s. Under this rubric, black families are viewed as pathological deviations from the "healthy" norm represented by white, middle-class families.

During the decade of the 1970s, black family research took a dramatic turn toward the cultural equivalent perspective (Haynes & Johnson, 1980), making it the second most common in the literature. This perspective's emphasis is on characteristics shared by both black and white families, the implication being that black family lifestyles are legitimate only insofar as these parallel white, middle-class family lifestyles. While the emphases of equivalent and deviant perspectives are different, the end result is the same. The culturally defined attributes of black families are devalued through an expressed, or implied, preference for the normative, white family model.

The cultural variant perspective continues to be most underrepresented in the literature on black family life. Using a cross-cultural, or culturally relative framework, this perspective treats black families as different, but legitimate, functional family forms. This approach is valuable because it focuses attention on empirical issues rather than on normative issues.

This study will use a cultural variant perspective to examine black child socialization. Although socialization processes and outcomes for white adolescents were also studied, these were not treated as normative. Rather, the intent was to explore cultural variations in family characteristics, dynamics, and outcomes across racial lines.

## BLACK CHILD SOCIALIZATION: CHARACTERISTICS, DYNAMICS AND OUTCOMES

The factors believed central to the determination of adolescent socialization outcomes are: 1) Parent and Family Background Characteristics; 2) Parent Child-rearing Goals; 3)Parent Child-rearing Practices; 4) Parent–Son Interpersonal Relationships; and 5) Child Socialization Outcomes.

### Parent and Family Background Characteristics

Research findings have led us to expect considerable variation in adolescent socialization processes and outcomes by race (Allen, 1978b; Bartz and LeVine, 1978). Adolescent socialization processes and outcomes have also been shown to vary with differences in family socioeconomic status, structural composition, and parental characteristics such as sex or age (Bronfenbrenner, 1958; Walters & Stinnett, 1971; Gecas, 1979; Walters & Walters, 1980). While the consequences such variations hold for black child development are not always clearly understood, researchers recognize the important influence of parent and family characteristics.

### Parent Childrearing Goals

Parent values are central in the socialization process, for values mediate between situation and behavior. Nevertheless, few systematic studies of the relationship between black parent values and child-rearing practices have been done (Bronfenbrenner, 1980). Four important studies have, however, examined links between parent child-rearing values and the socialization process. Data from the Lynd's (1929) *Middletown* community study showed great differences by class in reported maternal childtraining values. Middle-class mothers placed greatest value on "independence" and "frankness" in children while lower-class mothers felt "strict obedience" and "loyalty to the church" to be most important (pp. 143-144). In her categorization of Chicago mothers as either traditional or developmental in their conceptions of parental roles, Duvall (1947) revealed similar class distinctions.

In an attempt to link changing childrearing practices with changes in the U.S. occupational structure, Miller and Swanson (1958) studied middle-class mothers in Detroit. These mothers were from two groups, those involved in small business (entrepreneurial) and those who worked in large organizations (bureaucracies). They found that entrepreneurial mothers required their children to develop more manipulative stances toward life, while bureaucratic mothers encouraged their children to adopt more accommodating approaches to life.

The most thorough study of parents' social class and child-rearing values to date revealed that middle-class parents treated internal dynamics as the highest priority in childrearing, and for working-class parents, the highest primacy was behavioral conformity (Kohn, 1969a). Kohn found that class differences in parent child-rearing values were clearly related to the characteristically different occupational milieus of middle- and working-class parents.

The research is consistent in its definition of parent child-rearing goals as important components in the overall child socialization process. Parent child-rearing goals are clearly influenced by characteristics such as occupation, class, race, and sex.

## Parent Childrearing Practices

Davis and Havighurst's 1946 Chicago study concluded that lower-class and black mothers were more permissive in their child-rearing practices than middle-class and white mothers. Class differences in parental childrearing, it was concluded, were more pronounced than color differences. Maccoby and Gibbs (1954) disputed the Chicago conclusions. They suggested that lower status mothers were less permissive in childrearing than upper status mothers. In addition, they argued that class differences in childrearing occurred independently of color or ethnic differences. The consensus of several studies published later (see Bronfenbrenner, 1958 for detailed list and reviews) was that middle-class and white parents were indeed more permissive in childrearing than their lower-class and black counterparts.

Bartz and Levine (1978) compared parent child-rearing practices in three ethnic groups (Anglo, black and Chicano) with class controlled. While there were ethnic differences vis-a-vis general beliefs about childrearing, few differences in specific childrearing practices were revealed. Bartz and LeVine defined black parents as authoritative in their childrearing practices, that is, reflecting a combination of high support/high control, open communications, and demands for maturity in their approaches to childrearing.

In assessing the child-rearing literature from the decade of the 1970s, Walters and Walters (1980) criticized it for simplistic discussions of causal systems in parent–child relationships; failure to explore ethnic and racial differences in sufficient detail; tendencies to ignore father–child relations and paternal roles in socialization; overreliance on deficit theorizing, coupled with careless matching of comparison groups; and the absence of complex models of child socialization and development. While Gecas (1979) simply chose to characterize the literature as "messy and chaotic" [p. 365].

## Parent-Child Interpersonal Relationships

Numerous researchers have found child development to be strongly influenced by parental patterns of control and support. (See Rollins and Thomas, 1979 for a detailed review and discussion of this research tradition.) Although parental control and support behaviors are often viewed as orthogonal (i.e., on opposite ends of a continuum), black parents have been shown to score high on both the control and support dimensions in relating to their children (Allen, 1978b; Bartz & LeVine, 1978).

The exercise of parental power is another influence in parent-child interpersonal relationships. Democratic authority relations with parents have proven to be conducive to high achievement goals and positive development in youngsters (Rehberg, et al., 1970; Walters & Stinnett, 1981; Walters & Walters, 1980). There is also reason to believe that sons require more autonomy from fathers than mothers in order to develop properly (Allen, 1975; Rollins & Thomas, 1979). Finally, in their exhaustive review of the literature concerning the effects of parent-child interpersonal relations on child socialization outcomes, Rollins and Thomas (1979) specified parent-child power, support, and control relations as central, connected factors in the child development process.

## Child Socialization Outcomes

Various studies have concluded that black children are socialized by their families into poor academic motivation; under achievement; confused sex-role identities; poor self-concepts; and delinquency (Coleman, J. S. & Campbell, E. et al. 1966; Jencks, 1972; Heiss, 1975; Kardiner & Ovesey, 1951; Rosen, 1959; Rainwater, 1970). Recent research challenges the assumption that black children experience primarily negative outcomes from the socialization process. For example, studies show that contrary to accepted views, black youngsters have high self-esteems and positive self-concepts (Brookover, et al., 1965; Hare, 1980b; Rosenberg & Simmons, 1971). Moreover, black children's levels of achievement aspirations, cognitive complexity, sex-typed adjustment, and coping skills have all been found to be characteristic of normal, healthy, well-adjusted, positively-oriented individuals (Allen, 1975, 1978b; Gurin & Epps, 1975; Lewis, 1975; Gordon, 1972; Thomas & Sillen, 1972).

## The "Socialization Complex": A Model of Child Socialization Outcomes

This study also sought to organize the maze of factors and relationships shown by past empirical research to be correlated with child socialization outcomes. The model presented in Figure 16.1 diagrams these key factors and their interconnections. The socialization complex model attempts to specify, systematically arrange and casually link the major variables intervening between social context

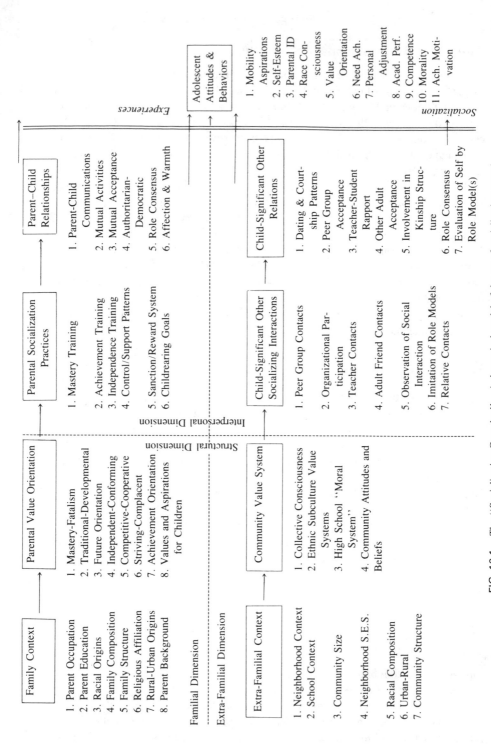

FIG. 16.1. The "Socialization Complex"—A theoretical model of the set of socialization experiences believed to determine adolescent personality and behavior outcomes.

and adolescent socialization outcomes. In the socialization complex, the antecedents of adolescent solialization outcomes are conceptualized in terms of four dimensions of adolescent socialization experiences; the structural and interpersonal dimensions and the familial and extrafamilial dimensions. The resulting four-fold paradigm is then further partitioned into eight general blocks of variables, each containing a set of similarly focused and correlated individual variables. The majority of prior research in the area has tended to focus on some combination of these individual variables.

Listed below each block variable are examples of the individual variables that it encompasses. The block variables are linked in antecedent–consequence patterns to convey the causal relationships believed to systematically link social context with adolescent socialization outcomes. For analytic purposes, the model interprets causal relationships as being undirectional. Thus, social context is thought to determine parent world views (or values) which condition parental styles of interpersonal interaction. Parental interactional styles in relation to the child act, in turn, to shape adolescent attitudes and behaviors. In each instance, block variables are expected to simultaneously exert direct (unmediated) and indirect (mediated) effects on adolescent socialization outcomes.

## FOCUS OF STUDY

The socialization complex model establishes the general parameters of this inquiry into adolescent socialization outcomes. Needless to say, full investigation of all factors and relationships postulated in the model are beyond the scope of any single study. Thus, our attention focuses on a simpler model for which the socialization complex provides the context. Briefly, this derived model assumes parent child-rearing goals for the son to be shaped by the immediate family context (i.e., family structure, socioeconomic status, and race of parents). Parental aspirations for the son (i.e., child-rearing goals for the son) are further thought to determine their modes of interacting with him (i.e., child-rearing practices, interpersonal relationships). Finally, it is assumed the son's socialization outcomes (i.e., personality and behaviors) are influenced by parental child-rearing goals and parent–child interaction in combination.

This study was originally conceived as an attempt to approximate the richness and detail of an ethnographic study using survey research methods. The result was a 1500 variable per case (each family represents one case) dataset. During the last 7 years, much time has been spent sorting through these data. This paper presents the final edition in our assessment of these data. Since the exploratory thrust of this research and its limited sample size, long ago consigned it to a heuristic exercise, we attempted here to delineate relationships of sufficient promise for future, largescale investigation. In this connection, the rich data from the families studied are used to demonstrate the viability of research into black child socialization. Culturally relative perspectives, systematic attention to process, and detailed assessment of family and child characteristics are emphasized.

## DATA AND METHODS OF STUDY

Data for this study are from a 1974 survey of Chicago, IL male adolescents and their families. A city-wide, stratified cluster sample of 120 two-parent families, with sons aged 14 to 18 in the home, was drawn using the following procedures: City census tracts were stratified by race, income level, and educational attainment using 1970 Census data. This information was then used to create four major tract groups: black or white, working-class or middle-class neighborhoods. Thirty blocks were selected from each of the four tract groups using a probability of selection proportional to size of cluster sampling design (Kish, 1965). A random, door-to-door sampling design was used at the block level to identify specific households qualified for the study.

In each household, interviewers sought to complete separate, 2-hour interviews with each of the three concerned family members. Information on individual and family characteristics, values, and relationships was obtained and then combined with record data of two types: 1) Census Bureau statistics on the family's neighborhood (Census Tract); and, 2) Chicago Board of Education data summarizing the characteristics of the high school that the son attended. Copies of measures may be obtained by writing the author.

Of the 360 respondents originally sought (father, mother and son in each family), 211 or 59% were interviewed. For these analyses, the sample breaks down as follows: blacks—sons (31), fathers (18), and mothers (35); whites—sons (47), fathers (35), and mothers (45). The small number of cases available for analysis restricted the range of statistical techniques which could be validly used. We were, for example, prevented from testing the variety of implicit and explicit multivariate hypotheses apparent in our conceptualization of the problem. Instead, we primarily relied on contingency table analysis and comparison of means tests to draw inferences about these complex interrelationships. While conclusions drawn from these data are tentative, this exploratory study does address, in a preliminary fashion, issues important to the systematic assessment of adolescent socialization outcomes.

## FINDINGS

Selected comparisons of the black and white families in this sample (Table 16.1) show them to be comparable in terms of our indicators of socioeconomic status. Our sample is restricted to what are essentially middle-class (or more appropriately, middle-income) families. Proportionately, whites had been in their neighborhoods longer and were more frequently buying (or owned) their homes than was true for blacks. However, these differences were more a matter of degree, since both groups were clearly well-established in their neighborhoods. Roughly 70% of the blacks owned their homes and had been in their neighborhoods for 6 or more years.

Predictably, average statuses for whites across education, occupation, and income were higher than those for blacks. These differences were significant, however, only in the cases of maternal educational and paternal occupational prestige. Reflecting the character of Chicago's population, our sample consisted largely of black Protestants and white Catholics. The significant race differences in years married to present spouse appear to be an artifact of older mean ages for whites and younger childbearing ages for blacks.

## Parent Childrearing Goals

Parent child-rearing goals were measured by a revised version of Kohn's (1969) index of parental values for children. In identifying goals stressed in their own childrearing, parents most frequently mentioned honesty, irrespective of race or sex. For black parents and white fathers, obedience was the second most frequently mentioned goal. Slight race differences were apparent in that whites most often cited individual-centered goals (e.g., good student, independent), whereas blacks tended to more often cite group-centered goals (e.g., consideration). In an apparent sex difference, independence was a frequently reported maternal goal, while few fathers invested it with major importance.

Parent ratings of the five most and least important child-rearing goals, from a list of 20 goals, showed striking unanimity. Black parents rated ambition and obedience as the most important goals, while white parents assigned these spots to honesty and happiness. Sex and race aside, parents agreed that popularity and athletic ability—peer oriented traits—were least important among their child-rearing goals. For black mothers, self-concern was the next least important goal, while for white mothers, it was the trait of seriousness.

Parent importance rating of the 20 identified child-rearing goals revealed several interesting patterns. Fathers and blacks, for example, tended to claim that more of the goals were important in their child-rearing than did mothers and whites. More than 50% of black fathers rated 17 of the 20 goals as important or very important. By contrast, only 10 goals for white fathers, 12 for black mothers and nine for white mothers were reported as important by more than 50% of the respondents.

## Parent Childrearing Practices

Data were collected on five aspects of parent childrearing practices in this study; (1) attitudes toward child-rearing experts; (2) husband involvement in childcare;

## TABLE 16.1
### Family Socio-Economic Characteristics by Race and Sex

| Family Social or Economic Characteristics | Race and Sex Percentage Distributions in Sample [Due to rounding rows may not add to 100.00] | | | | | | Tests of Significance / Measures of Association | |
|---|---|---|---|---|---|---|---|---|
| | 5 or less | 6–15 years | Over 15 | N | | | | |
| 1. Years lived in present neighborhood† | 36.4 | 51.5 | 12.1 | 33 | | | CHI = 9 | p = .01* |
| | (17.8) | (40.0) | (42.2) | (45) | | | V = .34 | G = .52 |
| | Rent | Own | | | | | | |
| 2. Home Ownership† | 29.0 | 71.0 | | 31 | | | CHI = 5 | p = .08 |
| | (6.8) | (93.2) | | (44) | | | V = .29 | G = .69 |
| | 8 years or Less | Some H.S. | H.S. Grad | Some College | College Graduate | N | | |
| 3. Educational Attainment | | | | | | | | |
| Men: | 27.8 | 16.7 | 22.2 | 27.8 | 5.6 | 18 | CHI = 7 | p = .25 |
| | (5.7) | (22.9) | (22.9) | (28.6) | (20.0) | (35) | V = .35 | G = .36 |
| Women: | 9.4 | 40.6 | 21.9 | 21.9 | 6.2 | 32 | CHI = 15 | p = .01* |
| | (0.0) | (11.1) | (42.2) | (33.3) | (13.3) | (45) | V = .45 | G = .49 |
| | Level One | Level Two | Level Three | Level Four | Level Five | Level Six | | |

## 4. Occupational Prestige Level†&‡

| | Less than $9000 | $9000–$12000 | $12001–$15000 | $15001–$18000 | $18001–$24000 | over $24000 | | | |
|---|---|---|---|---|---|---|---|---|---|
| Men: | 16.7 (2.9) | 27.8 (14.7) | 5.6 (20.6) | 33.3 (17.6) | 16.7 (23.5) | 0.0 (20.6) | 18 (34) | CHI = 11 V = .46 | p = .09 G = .44 |
| Women: | 23.8 (5.3) | 28.6 (13.2) | 19.0 (34.2) | 19.0 (21.1) | 9.5 (23.7) | 0.0 (2.6) | 21 (38) | CHI = 9 V = .38 | p = .19 G = .46 |

## 5. Annual Family Income†

| | Less than $9000 | $9000–$12000 | $12001–$15000 | $15001–$18000 | $18001–$24000 | over $24000 | | | |
|---|---|---|---|---|---|---|---|---|---|
| | 22.2 (9.3) | 29.6 (16.3) | 18.5 (11.6) | 14.8 (23.3) | 7.4 (16.3) | 7.4 (23.3) | 27 (43) | CHI = 8 V = .34 | p = .16 G = 45 |

## 6. Religious Preference†

| | Protestant | Catholic | Other | | | |
|---|---|---|---|---|---|---|
| | 90.6 (20.0) | 9.4 (73.3) | 0.0 (6.7) | 32 (45) | CHI = 37 V = .70 | p < .001* S = .95 |

## 7. Years Married to Spouse†

| | Less than 15 | 15–20 | 21–24 | 25 or More | | |
|---|---|---|---|---|---|---|
| | 15.2 (2.2) | 30.3 (44.4) | 30.3 (20.0) | 24.2 (33.3) | 33 (45) | CHI = 6.5 V = .29 | p = .09 G = .14 |

( ) = White Respondents    CHI = Chisquare Statistic    V = Cramer's V Statistic    G = Gamma Statistic

* = Relationship significant at .05 level or beyond

† = Wives represent calculation base

‡ = Representative occupations by level: *One*—Janitor, Steel Worker, Common Laborer; *Two*—Auto Mechanic, Tailor, Bus Driver; *Three*—Electrician, Machinist, Optician; *Four*—Secretary, Nurse, Salesperson; *Five*—High School Teacher, Draftsman, Manager and *Six*—Engineer, Attorney, Physician.

(3) sources of child-rearing advice; (4) independence expectations; and, (5) patterns of child punishment and reward.

In this sample, black fathers were least likely of all parents to have sought advice on childcare and childrearing from books and magazines. Seventy-eight percent reported not having read any type of child-care publications while their sons were growing up. At the other extreme were white mothers, where 73% reported having consulted child-care books or magazines in the rearing of their sons. In general, mothers were more likely than fathers to have read child-care publications. Not too surprisingly, over three quarters of black fathers believed parents knew as much about childrearing as "experts", while white mothers expressed greatest confidence in the knowledge of these experts. Significantly, only two of the total 133 parents believed unequivocally that experts knew more than parents about childrearing. None of the observed race, sex differences in attitudes toward experts were statistically significant.

Black wives rated husband involvement in childcare and childrearing slightly higher. A fifth of the white wives claimed their husbands gave less than ordinary assistance, as compared to only 6% of black wives. Further, a sizeable 63% of black mothers, versus 47% of white mothers, reported that their husbands had given more help than average in rearing the son.

Parents received advice on childrearing from a variety of sources. When asked to identify the person(s) who had given the most helpful advice, white parents and black fathers most commonly cited the spouse (all 60% or higher). Black mothers broke this pattern by citing their own mothers first (41%), followed by husbands (33%). On the average, larger percentages of blacks than whites, and mothers than fathers, reported having received child-rearing advice. In both races, husbands seemed to rely more heavily on wives for advice than the reverse. No major race differences were seen in sources of advice for fathers. Black mothers, by contrast, relied much more on advice from "other relatives" and "friends" than was true of their white counterparts (respectively, $\chi^2=2.1$; s=.15; and, $\chi^2=4.4$; p=.04). On the other hand, white mothers more frequently reported reliance on doctors, teachers, social workers, and other professionals for child-rearing advice.

Race and sex differences in parent independence age expectations were striking. Fathers and blacks tended to expect independence in the behaviors identified at much older ages than did mothers and whites. In this sample of parents, white mothers claimed to make the earliest demands for independence in the identified behaviors, followed by their spouses, black mothers and black fathers.

It seems that fathers punished sons considerably more frequently than mothers at each of the three periods of childhood specified (blacks: $\chi^2=45$; whites: $\chi^2=42$; both p<.001). There was also a pronounced tendency for whites, more so than black parents (2 to 1), to claim that they rarely punished the son. Several other interesting patterns are apparent in the data (See Table 16.2). For instance, the majority of parents (34% or higher for each race-sex subgroup) rarely used

## TABLE 16.2

### Race, Sex and Parent Methods and Frequency of Child Punishments and Rewards (Mean Comparisons)†

| Methods of Punishment and Reward | Sex Means and Comparisons | | | | Race Means and Comparisons | | | |
| --- | --- | --- | --- | --- | --- | --- | --- | --- |
| | Fathers | | Mothers | | Blacks | | Whites | |
| | Black | White | Black | White | Fathers | Mothers | Fathers | Mothers |
| **Punishments** | | | | | | | | |
| Scolding | 4.47 | 3.48* | 3.49 | 3.08 | 4.64 | 3.79 | 3.43 | 3.15 |
| Spanking | 4.74 | 5.1 | 4.02 | 4.92* | 4.74 | 4.67 | 5.1 | 4.99 |
| Isolation | 4.58 | 5.19 | 4.73 | 4.94 | 4.58 | 4.88 | 5.13 | 4.97 |
| Privilege Denial | 4.26 | 4.65 | 4.1 | 4.22 | 4.16 | 4.20 | 4.59 | 4.28 |
| Discussion | 2.98 | 3.45 | 3.6 | 2.81* | 3.04 | 2.84 | 3.44 | 2.86* |
| **Rewards** | | | | | | | | |
| Kissing, Hugging | 5.13 | 4.09* | 3.54 | 3.09 | 5.13 | 3.6* | 4.03 | 3.14* |
| Gifts, Special Privileges | 3.47 | 4.24* | 4.11 | 4.24 | 3.53 | 3.89 | 4.21 | 4.21 |
| Praise | 2.98 | 3.03 | 2.73 | 2.13* | 3.01 | 2.77 | 3.02 | 2.12× |
| Good Behavior Self-Rewarding | 3.93 | 4.36 | 4.54 | 3.9 | 4.05 | 4.02 | 4.45 | 4.06 |

† = Frequency of use for each punishment/reward method across three ages (8, 12 and now) were averaged.

* = t-test statistic for comparison of means significant at the .05 level or beyond.

Note: Cases for analysis were as follows: Black fathers (17); White fathers (35); Black mothers (33); White mothers (45).

the most indirect strategy, discussion, in their punishment of sons. On the other hand, a sizeable majority (57% or higher for each race-sex subgroup) used the most direct punishment, spanking. Few statistically significant race differences for specific punishments were found. In terms of sex differences, fathers reported significantly more frequent use of all the various punishment strategies. (All chi-square values for father–mother comparisons were significant at the .01 level or beyond.)

A majority of parents reported it was not their practice to take special notice of good behavior in rewarding their sons. Similarly, most said that they rarely complimented or praised the son as a reward. Of all parents, fathers in general, and white fathers in particular, seemed most likely to reward the son. At the other extreme, white mothers seemed to least frequently reward their sons.

Other important differences were also seen. Fathers, for instance, were more likely than mothers to ignore good behavior by the son (blacks: $\chi^2 = 17.2$, p<.01; whites: $\chi^2 = 21.3$, p<.001). Mothers were much more likely than fathers to praise the son as a reward (blacks: $\chi^2 = 17$, p<.01; whites: $\chi^2 = 19$, p<.001). Material rewards were given to the son significantly more often by black fathers than mothers ($\chi^2 = 25$; p<.001). Surprisingly, given the traditional roles assigned parents by sex, fathers were significantly more likely than mothers to report having rewarded the son during his childhood by kissing and hugging (blacks: $\chi^2 = 21$; whites: $\chi^2 = 30$; both p<.001). In what are noteworthy race effects, black fathers more often rewarded good behavior by kissing and hugging, whereas white fathers preferred to give gifts. White fathers and black mothers were more likely than their spouses to allow good behavior to go unrewarded.

## Parent–Child Interpersonal Relationships

Several measures were used to assess the nature of parent–son interpersonal relations; (1) shared leisure time activities between parent(s) and son; (2) perceived closeness between parent(s) and son; (3) son identification with parent(s); (4) parent(s) approval of the son; (5) parent(s) control of son's decision-making; and, (6) parent(s) control of son's social relationships.

Several interesting race-sex differences in parental interpersonal relationships with sons were found. For instance, black mothers and white fathers, according to the adolescents, shared significantly more activities with sons than did white mothers and black fathers (respectively, $\chi^2 = 14$; p<.001 and $\chi^2 = 5$; p<.10). When compared with spouses, white fathers were reported to have spent sizeably more leisure activity time with son as he was growing up. Black mothers and fathers apparently spent about the same amount of time in shared leisure activities with the son.

Race differences were also found in sons' reported emotional closeness to parents. While 60% of black adolescents claimed above average closeness with parents, only 47% of white adolescents did so. More strikingly, although the majority of white sons believed themselves to have the most in common with their fathers, just the reverse was true for black sons. Black sons felt they had more in common with their mothers ($\chi^2 = 12$; $p < .02$).

Important race-sex differences also emerged when parent approval and acceptance of the son was compared. Black mothers were reported by their sons as being significantly less approving than were white mothers ($\chi^2 = 10$; $p < .02$). In general, sons viewed white parents and mothers, as more approving than black parents and fathers. It is important to note that while black sons felt "outsiders" (friends, teachers) were more approving, white sons felt them to be less approving relative to parents.

Parents in this sample, according to sons' reports, exercised considerable control over the adolescents' decision-making and social relationships. White mothers kept closer tabs on their sons' friendships than was true for black mothers ($\chi^2 = 7$; $p < .001$). Similarly, mothers were significantly more aware than fathers of who their sons' friends were (blacks: $\chi^2 = 42$, $p < .001$; whites: $\chi^2 = 52$, $p < .001$). White fathers knew more about their sons' friends than did black fathers (69% versus 48% knew most or all), although the differences were not statistically significant. When parents control over son's decision making was compared, no major differences between fathers were revealed. In both races, however, fathers were significantly more authoritarian and controlling than mothers (blacks: $\chi^2 = 28$, $p < .001$; whites: $\chi^2 = 18$, $p < .01$). White mothers also exerted much less control than black mothers over the son's decision making.

## Son Socialization Outcomes

The following measures of son socialization outcomes were included in this study: (1) parent(s) reported satisfaction with son's overall behaviors; (2) son's educational expectations; (3) son's occupational expectations; (4) son's self-esteem; (5) son's academic self-concept; (6) son's achievement values; and, (7) son's mastery orientation.

Several differences were found in parents' levels of satisfaction with sons' overall behaviors. Black parents expressed considerably more desire for change(s) in the sons' activities than did white parents. They were significantly more likely to wish that the son would either do more or less of an activity. Black fathers were also less satisfied with socialization outcomes, than was true for black mothers. Interestingly, no sizeable differences in general satisfaction with the son were revealed between white spouses. In considering these findings, it is important to note that rarely did parents of either sex express extreme dissatisfaction with the socialization outcomes reflected in their sons' behaviors and personality. The 20% of black fathers was the highest proportion of parents expressing major dissatisfaction with sons' behaviors of all race-sex parent subgroups.

Numerous black–white differences were found in sons' attitudes and expectations for the future (see Table 16.3). White sons reported significantly higher

TABLE 16.3

Adolescent Socialization Outcomes by Race

| Adolescent Socialization Outcomes | Race Percentage Distributions in Sample [Due to rounding rows may not add to 100.0] | | | | | N | Tests of Significance Measures of Association |
|---|---|---|---|---|---|---|---|
| | H.S. Grad | Some College | College Grad | Grad/Prof School | | | |
| | Min Perf | Avg Perf | Little Above avg | Much Above avg | Top | | |
| 1. Educational Expectations | | | | | | | |
| Blacks | 24.1 | 10.3 | 48.3 | 17.2 | | 29 | CHI = 4.3   p = .34 |
| Whites | 25.5 | 17.0 | 44.7 | 12.8 | | 47 | V = .24   G = .03 |
| 2. Occupational Eminence Expectations | | | | | | | |
| Blacks | 6.5 | 16.5 | 6.5 | 25.8 | 45.2 | 31 | CHI = 8.8   p = .07 |
| Whites | 12.8 | 14.9 | 19.1 | 36.2 | 17.0 | 47 | V = .34   G = .19 |

288

| | Low | Medium | High | | | |
|---|---|---|---|---|---|---|
| 3. Self-Esteem | | | | | | |
| Blacks | 6.5 | 80.6 | 12.9 | 31 | CHI = 1.4 | p = .5 |
| Whites | 2.1 | 78.7 | 19.1 | 47 | V = .13 | G = .28 |
| 4. Mastery Orientation | | | | | | |
| Blacks | 9.7 | 51.9 | 37.0 | 31 | CHI = 9.5 | p = .01* |
| Whites | 0.0 | 80.9 | 19.1 | 47 | V = .35 | G = −.23 |
| 5. Achievement Values | | | | | | |
| Blacks | 10.0 | 30.0 | 60.0 | 31 | CHI = 7.5 | p = .11 |
| Whites | 12.7 | 53.2 | 34.0 | 47 | V = .31 | G = −.41 |
| 6. Occupational Aspirations | | | | | | |
| Blacks | 11.1 | 51.9 | 37.0 | 31 | CHI = 7.2 | p = .03* |
| Whites | 11.9 | 21.4 | 66.7 | 47 | V = .32 | G = .41 |
| 7. Academic Self-Concept | | | | | | |
| Blacks | 0.0 | 58.1 | 41.9 | | CHI = 1.2 | p = .56 |
| Whites | 2.1 | 48.9 | 48.9 | | V = .12 | G = .11 |

CHI = Chisquare Statistic; G = Gamma Statistic; V = Cramer's V Statistic
* = Relationship significant at .05 level or beyond.

occupational expectations, generally expecting to move into higher compensation-status-demand occupations than did their black counterparts. In this sense, the occupational expectations reported by black and white sons tended to mirror occupational disparities by race in the contemporary labor force. Black sons sensed themselves to be in greater control of their lives. This race difference obviously contradicts self-evident black–white differences throughout the society in the possession of resources linked to effective personal control over one's life and environment. Of the two racial groups, black sons valued achievement most highly and stated higher educational attainment expectations. On the other hand, black sons' self-esteem and academic self-concept levels were slightly lower.

## DISCUSSION

This study looked at socialization processes and outcomes in a biracial sample of families. Adolescent males in middle-income, two-parent families were the major focus of this research. Using a cross-cultural perspective, we sought to examine family characteristics, interpersonal dynamics, and socialization outcomes. A comprehensive model to guide the systematic assessment of key sources of causation in black child socialization and development is also proposed.

Although the primary purpose of this study was to further our understanding of black male adolescent socialization outcomes, its findings have clear implications of a more general nature. For example, the socialization complex model could be profitably applied in assessments of the socialization experiences and outcomes of different race/sex/age youngsters. This study's rejection of ethnocentric, normative perspectives in favor of perspectives more sensitive to the diverse cultural, situational, and value realities of this society is another widely generalizable result. Finally, this study demonstrates the general importance of disaggregation in social research.

Our ability to understand social processes is enhanced by breaking these down into their constituent parts and looking at how these parts are interrelated. We see clearly that fathers play important complementary, as well as contradictory, roles vis-a-vis mothers, thus data on both parents are required. Observed differences in parent child-rearing goals, practices and relationships across race, sex and race-sex identities offer further evidence of the need for disaggregated research designs. To the extent that future studies incorporate regional, class, age, and other variations, and disaggregate these variables for analyses, our understanding of child socialization and development will be greatly benefitted.

Having discussed the general implications of this research, we now ask, "What lessons does it teach us about black male adolescent socialization outcomes?" From a survey of specific findings, several significant patterns seem to emerge. In many respects, these patterns are culture-specific. For instance, the orientations of our respondent families to kin and community differ by race. Black families are characterized by child-rearing goal emphases, child care/rearing advice-seeking behaviors, parent control of social relationship patterns, and son other-approval sources that would seem to suggest greater engagement (relative to white families) with kinship and community groups.

Evidence also strongly suggests that relative to white mothers, black mothers occupy more central positions in their families. One notes, therefore, the profound influence of the black grandmother on the mother's child-rearing practices, and thus the next generation's socialization. The black mother frequently shares leisure time with the son and the son strongly identifies with her. Contrary to popular opinion, these black mothers' centrality to their families is not purchased at the fathers' expense. Instead, these black fathers are in the home, active in childcare and socialization, and sharing warm, close personal relationships with their sons. In an important sex-specific set of differences, mothers emerge—in both races—as support specialists in the rearing of sons, while fathers tend more to specialize as sanctioners of behavior (with punishments and rewards).

Our findings stimulate a wide variety of hypotheses. For instance, would the cultural differences observed here be sharper in a sample of low-income or Southern families? Or, to what extent do black family members recognize and actively reinforce the mother's centrality in family organization and functions? Are there clearly articulated norms in black families that emphasize offspring relations with people beyond the nuclear family? Would the above pattern of same-sex parent sanctions and different-sex parent support hold with a sample of adolescent females? These and numerous other hypotheses are suggested by this research. In this sense, it fulfills the heuristic intent of our exploratory effort.

In the past, researchers have placed negative evaluations on many of the findings which we interpret in a positive light. Thus, child-rearing goals such as obedience, consideration, loyalty, etc., were viewed as blind conformity rather than as the process of putting self second to the family. Here, the mother's central role in the family was not taken as a negation of the father's role, rather, it was seen as complementing the father's role. The child's close, approving relationships with people outside the nuclear family was not taken as evidence of his alienation from parents, but rather as his acceptance of a family ethic which emphasizes integration of individuals (and nuclear families) into larger kinship and community systems.

The point is, the story any data tell is very much influenced by researcher assumptions, values, and biases. I contend that black family socialization practices and outcomes are best viewed—and understood—against the backdrop provided by the black experiential context. Within this context, researchers have a more solid basis for deciding what constitutes positive or dysfunctional aspects of black child socialization and development.

It should be noted in conclusion that both the black and white male adolescents in this sample are healthy, highly motivated, well-adjusted youngsters. Their parents adopted different strategies and practices to reach comparable goals. Again, issues of different experiential contexts for the two races loom in importance. The values, resources, circumstances, and relations with the larger society differ for these black and white families. Hence different approaches to child socialization are required. The research agenda for the future must systematically specify features of person, environment and culture which distinguish black family socialization dynamics and their consequences.

## ACKNOWLEDGMENTS

An earlier version of this paper was presented during the 1981 Society for Research on Child Development meetings, Boston, April 2–5, 1981. The author acknowledges helpful comments from Study Group members, Arthur Mathis and Joseph Stevens. Data collection was funded by the Community and Family Study Center, University of Chicago. The author was supported by funds from the Rockefeller Foundation Postdoctoral Research Fellowship Program while writing this paper.

# Summary

Aimee Dorr
*University of California—Los Angeles*

The papers in this section, and the volume itself, fill a need that has existed since whites first brought blacks to this country, requiring them to both live among whites and be different from them. The need is to understand black life on its own terms, to know what variations exist in black life in this country, and to understand how these variations are related to socially significant outcomes.

In this regard, several themes emerge from the three papers in this section. One is the size of the family unit that effectively participates in the rearing of children. Another is the incursion of social institutions into adult caregivers' lives and therefore into children's lives. A third is the perspective taken on the black family vis-a-vis white culture. Brief summaries of the papers in this section will highlight these themes.

In the paper, "Race, Income, and Family Dynamics: A Study of Adolescent Male Socialization Processes and Outcomes," Allen describes three perspectives which have been brought to bear on the black family. Until the 1970s, the black family was seen as 'cultural deviant.' In the 1970s, a cultural equivalent perspective emerged in which the characteristics common to black and white families were sought. Those characteristics of black families which differentiated them from white families were often implicitly devalued. A more recent and less common perspective, the black family as a culture variant, is the one chosen by Allen. Black families in the United States are viewed as different from white families—unless shown to be otherwise. Black family forms and white family forms, as well as those of any other culturally identifiable group, are all taken as legitimate and functional.

The researcher's task then becomes one of describing family functioning and those variations that are important for child-rearing outcomes. Allen undertakes

293

such a descriptive and analytic task in his study of the relationships among parent and family background characteristics; parent child-rearing goals; parent child-rearing practices; parent–son interpersonal relationships; and child socialization outcomes in intact, middle-income, black and white families with adolescent sons. His findings point to the importance of a broad perspective and disaggregated data. Mothers play important roles in childrearing, but so do fathers. The extended family network is important, especially in the black family. Expert opinions can influence child-rearing practices, especially in the white family. These and other findings give us rich views of black and white family life. We have an opportunity to build a comparative understanding of how each type of family operates in the United States to produce healthy, well-functioning adolescent males.

LaPoint, Pickett, and Fairley tackle, in their paper, a group of families influenced by social institutions. "Enforced Family Separation: The Psychological Impact of Maternal Imprisonment on Black Children" explores childrearing from the perspectives of the incarcerated mother, the child, and the child's caregiver during the mother's incarceration. Moreover, childrearing prior to incarceration is also explored, thereby recognizing the historical framework within which mother, child, and caregiver experience the period of incarceration. Those mothers who functioned better prior to incarceration generally functioned better during incarceration.

For several children, incarceration of the mother did not lead to marked changes in child-rearing locale, participants, and experiences—although one ought not believe that this fact diminishes the significance of experiencing one's mother's incarceration. The LaPoint, Pickett, and Fairley paper is rich with description. It clearly shows the importance of an historical perspective, of the extended family network—particularly the maternal grandmother—and of the penal system as it impacts on the ways in which family members function. The significant experiences of some black families as they rear their children in the United States come alive in this paper, without normative judgments, evaluative statements, or comparisons to any other familial group.

Brookins' paper, "Black Children's Sex-Role Ideologies and Occupational Choices in Families of Employed Mothers," takes yet another approach to understanding black family life in a society where white perspectives have dominated. Like LaPoint, Pickett, and Fairley, Brookins studied only black families whereas Allen studied both black and white families. Unlike LaPoint, Pickett, and Fairley, Brookins repeatedly compares her findings with those obtained from white families, and occasionally from Hispanic families. The perspective is definitely that of the black family as a potential cultural variant. Variation itself is not viewed pejoratively.

Taking an admirably broad perspective, Brookins explores the confluence of maternal and paternal employment histories since the birth of the target child, maternal and paternal sex-role ideologies, maternal and paternal occupational satisfaction, social class of the family, sex of the child, and child intelligence, in determining a child's sex-role ideology and occupational plans. The focus is on the role of a broad contextual variable, maternal employment, but other variables and family members are not forgotten. The results again indicate the importance of approaches that go beyond the mother–child dyad. Fathers' occupations, attitudes, ideologies, and practices clearly mattered, as did mothers', for both boys' and girls' sex-role ideologies and occupational plans.

In their totality, these papers illustrate the variety of people who may effectively participate in childrearing. Without ever denying the possibility of a child's strong, or even primary, tie with the mother, they move beyond it. Fathers are shown to influence young elementary school aged children's sex-role ideologies and occupational plans. They even influence adolescent sons' beliefs, values, attitudes, and behaviors. But the family unit is not just the nuclear one. Extended family members, particularly the mother's mother, serve as important advice givers, norm setters, and even primary caregivers. They have direct and indirect influences on children's development. This recognition, that persons other than the mother are important for childrearing and socialization, is becoming increasingly evident in studies of families. When the work reported in the three papers in this section was started, it was surely among those in the vanguard in this respect.

The work is also exemplary in another respect: the inclusion of several types of variables and sources of measurement. In general, the studies do not employ simple paradigms for describing family life or exploring factors causally related to child outcomes. Parental work histories and earlier patterns of childcare are considered. The impacts of social institutions such as prisons, and the judicial system, are acknowledged. Social class is recognized as potentially influential.

The perspectives of mother, father, child, and alternate caregiver are all taken into account. Several are often used as sources for the same kind of data. Caregiver attitudes and practices pertaining to oneself and/or one's partner are assessed, as are those pertaining to the child. Several aspects of the child are addressed. Self-report, other report, and behavioral measures are obtained. The papers are rich in the multiplicity of views and variables considered. Naturally this leads to more complex findings that are harder to summarize in a few sentences and more likely to contain apparent contradictions. But surely findings derived from such a systematic view bring us closer to understanding family functioning than other findings can.

Of course, the sine qua non of the papers in this section is that they focus not just on family functioning, but on the functioning of black families in the United States. The papers by Allen, LaPoint, Pickett, Fairley, and Brookins help to provide direction for future research on the black family.

# THEORIES, POLICY IMPLICATIONS AND RECOMMENDATIONS

# Introduction

In Part III, the editors attempt to articulate the various themes regarding the growth and development of black children that have emerged throughout the volume. Five organizing principles considered important to the study of black child development are identified and discussed as well as four organizing perspectives regarded as necessary for empirical assessment of black children.

In light of these organizing principles and perspectives, the volume raises more questions than it answers. Thus, in a general fashion, a research agenda is set forth with 15 broad categories. While seemingly time dependent, the agenda will span a considerable period given the present pace of research and funding activity.

As black social scientists, we are concerned that there be a more conscientious articulation between research and social policy. The section on Action Implications and Agenda is an attempt to focus on recommendations that address policy issues that impact the lives of black—if not all—children in profound ways.

Finally, this volume culminates many years of hard work. A few words are provided as a reflection on that time period and its significance.

# 17

## Synthesis: Black Children Keep on Growing

Walter Recharde Allen
*University of Michigan*

Margaret B. Spencer
*Emory University*

Geraldine K. Brookins
*Jackson State University*

This volume presents new perspectives on the status of black child development in the United States. Our purpose, simply put, has been to redefine how black children and their families are treated in the literature. To accomplish this goal, we set the following objectives:

1. to study black children's development comprehensively, looking at social, emotional, and cognitive dimensions;
2. to explore the consequences of differing material circumstances, family characteristics, cultural patterns, and institutional settings for black child developmental outcomes;
3. to study the lives of black children with uncommon thoroughness and sensitivity.

The volume is an outgrowth of 3 years of work and planning. Twelve original empirical studies form the volume's core. These studies are divided into three major areas of concern; social competence, identity, and family. Critical summaries follow each topical area section. Four introductory papers outline theoretical, historical, life course, and ecological issues which should be considered in the study of black children. Together the introductory papers, empirical research papers, and topical area summaries offer alternatives to mainstream interpretations. Readers encountered alternative theoretical perspectives, research questions, empirical methods and interpretations intended to recast the study of black child development.

Important themes from the contributions to this volume can now be discussed. What were key or recurring points? What political, theoretical and parenting implications can be drawn from this volume? An agenda for the future, detailing useful research strategies and actions concludes this section. The agenda addresses the question, "What can researchers, helping professionals, and parents do to improve the lives of black children in this society?"

## Emergent Themes

Volume contributors have outlined a framework for the systematic, sensitive study of black child development. Each author wrestled with the difficult task of interpreting the black experience in this country. What are some salient, reliable empirical indicators? How are these related to one another? And most importantly, how do they shape the psyches and behaviors of growing black youngsters? In his paper, Ogbu reminds us that childrearing is a culturally organized formula, spanning the gap between life circumstances and necessary survival skills. Each of our authors has tried, in her or his own way, to unravel this formula; to decipher its code for black Americans. Each asks how the developmental paths of black children are related, through socialization practices, interpersonal relations and their families, to the circumstances of their existence.

The major themes from this volume can be summarized under two headings: Organizing Principles and Organizing Perspectives. Organizing principles are equivalent to founding assumptions: They encompass the basic premises about black children, black families and black life found in the different papers. Organizing perspectives refer to the models underlying and guiding the different authors' approaches to the study of black child development. That is, what variables and interrelationships do they consider important for study?

## Organizing Principles

Five organizing principles emerge as important considerations in the study of black child development. Contributors to this volume emphasize the need for orientations which are *multi-faceted, dynamic, revisionist, pluralistic* and *social-action* conscious.

The emphasis on a multi-faceted orientation is present in two forms, first as the call for multidisciplinary approaches and second as advocacy for ecological approaches. LaPointe, Pickett and Fairley urge researchers and human service professionals to increase their cooperation and coordination. In this way they will better understand and address the implications of maternal incarceration for affected children, mothers, and families. The paper by Holliday explores black child academic achievement in relation to the institutional settings provided by schools. She demonstrates that black children's school experiences are best understood as sets of attributes, attitudes and behaviors embedded in, and influenced by, distinct environments.

The necessity for a dynamic orientation is emphasized in various authors' references to time frames (societal, family, and individual). Cross' analysis of research findings from studies of black identity published between 1939 and 1977 reveal interesting patterns of change. He concludes that blacks have consistently had high senses of personal worth. However, now, unlike before, more blacks are characterized by black orientations (i.e., express positive identification with black group norms and values). Alejandro-Wright, Semaj, and Spencer trace developmental changes in black children's cognitions, self-perceptions and race consciousness as they grow older. While black preschoolers possess a basic awareness of race, it is not until late childhood that their concepts of race classification come to resemble those of adults in the society (Alejandro-Wright). Semaj and Spencer show that in the absence of socializing agents who actively counter society's negative evaluation of black children, the developmental trend for black children will likely be away from a collective, pro-black orientation to a no-preference or dual-consciousness stance as they age. At different stages of development, we see evidence of differing levels of correspondence between how positively black children evaluate self and group identity.

Multiple references to interactional exchanges between parents and children, and between black families and the larger society, are other examples of this dynamic emphasis. For example, Brookins interprets black mothers' labor force participation as necessary to the maintenance of family economic welfare. Mothers, their spouses and their children, in black families tend to view employment outside the home as a normal component of the maternal/wife roles. Children of employed mothers in her study exhibited more egalitarian sex-role ideologies, higher occupational aspirations, and better understanding of the society's occupational structure. Hare and Castenell stress the need for considering variations in black boys' self-esteem levels across settings (i.e., at home, at school, in the peer group). Where the black boys in their sample attributed less weight to school (and more to home) in the calculation of overall self-esteem, they were able to maintain high general self-esteem despite low grades and test scores in school. High achievement in the peer culture was often associated with poor school performance. Dill and Thomas' call for a comprehensive psychology, incorporating social and environmental bases of behavior, emphasizes this concern with interrelationships between groups of variables.

A revisionist orientation is apparent, to greater or lesser extent, in each of the contributions to this volume. Each author calls for changes in how developing black children are treated in the literature. They raise fundamental questions about theory, method, and research findings as these pertain to black children. McLoyd advances a new perspective on black children's play: Play is shown to be much more than undirected, frivolous activity. Systematic study of pretend play enables a deeper understanding of central values of Afro-American culture; how these values derive from life circumstances as well as how they are reflected in children's play. Abatso identifies high "coping" ability as an important determinant of college success. Young black adults with "coping personalities" adopted attitudes and behaviors more likely to produce positive academic results. Coping ability might represent a reliable, alternative criterion for college admissions decisions involving black students. In the spirit of this revisionist thrust, Franklin and Elder propose alternatives to the tradition of denigrative scholarship about black children and families, rooted in "assimilationist," pathogenic assumptions.

A pluralistic orientation is another feature common to the different papers. Authors emphasize comparative frames of reference for the analysis of black child development. It is critical that such comparisons be free of ethnocentric, elitist, and chauvinistic biases; biases which would have us accept white, middle-class, Protestant males as the standard against which all others are to be gauged. Moore compares differences in test performance between black children reared by white vs. black adoptive parents. She shows the content of children's socialization to vary according to race and social class of parents: Definitions of what constitutes a socially competent child (and adult) also vary by race and class. Allen studies healthy, well-adjusted, highly motivated black and white, male adolescents who arrived at the same point from different routes. He links parental socialization practices to their experiential context; approaches to child socialization are shown to vary by parent values, resources, and relations with the larger society. Spencer examines regional and age differences among black children in self-attitudes and notions of race, concluding that level of cognitive development and parent socialization practices are critical determinants. Dorr summarizes the need for pluralistic perspectives when she notes ". . . the need to understand black life on its own terms."

Social action orientations are present, in either explicit or implicit form, throughout the volume. Authors go beyond their findings to consider their implications for the lives of black children. In some instances, corrective actions are internally focussed, thus Ogbu asks us to examine the possibility that certain black community norms may actually support underachievement among black males in school. In other instances, corrective actions are externally focussed. Slaughter and McWorter, for example, criticize the research tradition which has stressed cultural assimilation as the ultimate solution for black people's problems in U.S. society. This tradition has fueled misdirected, ineffective social programs. Bronfenbrenner rejects "culture of poverty" explanations of black children's development. Instead, he recommends that scholars and nonscholars alike concentrate on reversing the worsening economic and social plights which deny blacks the basic resources necessary for dignified, human existence.

## Organizing Perspective(s)

Findings from this volume help to outline a framework for the systematic study of black child development. The emerging framework focuses on empirical assessment of black children's life circumstances; their perceptions or definitions of these circumstances; their adaptations or responses to these circumstances; and how their personalities develop.

Examinations of the objective conditions of black children's lives, their life circumstances, focus on contextual factors. In this connection, the authors explore the environments in which black life is enacted. More often than not the schools, family, and community settings of black children are shown to be potentially debilitating. Their "ecologies of deprivation" are characterized by poverty, poor health care, high crime rates, inferior educational opportunities, and limited life chances.

While concurring with conventional assessments about black children's life circumstances as less than satisfactory, this volume proposes an alternative, less deterministic view of consequences arising from this assessment. The various authors recognize the ability of human beings to rise above their circumstances, to "take what they have and use it to make what they need."

Subjective interpretations of life circumstances, their perception and definition, are one way that people mediate the effects of environment. Culture is the most general manifestation of this fact. Authors in this volume are, therefore, rightfully concerned with articulating the features of black American culture that enable families to produce healthy, motivated, self-respecting children despite the obvious obstacles. Their concern is with black culture generally, as well as with various subcultures in the black population. Thus, many papers emphasize the diversity internal to black communities and families. They point up the need for understanding the sources of differing traditions among blacks. Why are there always, in the same communities, families known for the positive achievements of their young, and others known for the negative reputations of theirs? Among the differentiating factors cited by authors in this volume are coping ability, race pride, high achievement motivation, and family traditions.

Adaptations and responses, or life styles, are another way for people to mediate the effects of life circumstances. We find from papers in this volume that families of low status sometimes prepare their children for upward mobility through anticipatory socialization. That is, they socialize their children into the norms and behaviors of middle-class people—despite lacking the appropriate material resources. In other cases, the extended family compensates for missing parents. Racial oppression and economic deprivation permeate the lives of most black Americans, yet findings in this volume reveal the possibility of responses which buffer and equip children to overcome.

Black children's developmental outcomes are also a major concern in this volume. Authors examine aspects of the children's social, affective, and cognitive traits across the developmental span from early childhood to young adulthood. Historical and contemporary factors combine to make academic achievement a particularly common outcome for study. It is also interesting to note the preponderant evidence of "bi-cultural patterns" among black children; their ability to shift between behaviors appropriate to black vs. white culture. Equally noteworthy is the resilience of these youngsters. Despite tremendous disadvantages, their average members emerge from childhood as competent adults.

The central concern of each contributor, and of this volume at large, is with understanding the whys and wherefores of black child development. How are the interactions between objective conditions, subjective interpretations, and life styles manipulated by parents, families, and other adults to produce functional human beings? What are the culturally organized child socialization formulae which connect black children's life circumstances and their development of necessary survival skills? This volume is an important first step in addressing these questions.

## Research Implications and Agenda

This volume raises many more questions than it answers. We felt it necessary, therefore, to outline an agenda of research questions concerning black child development to be addressed by future studies. For the sake of clarity, this research agenda is stated in general terms rather than as specific research hypotheses.

1. *Afro-American cultural orientations.* Social scientists have been slow to recognize and explore the reality of a distinctive Afro-American or black culture in this society. More detailed study of black culture is required particularly as it relates to the values and goals emphasized in the socialization of children. Ethnographic studies of black culture (such as John Gwaltney's *Drylongso*) might well provide the basis for formulation of research hypotheses to be examined using empirical research methods.

2. *Class status among black Americans.* The assignment of class status among black Americans has always been an elusive problem for social scientists. As a separate, less advantaged community, the criteria for status assignment in black communities differs from those in white communities. These differences are as much cultural as economic. Future research must examine the class structure of black communities, address the growth of the black middle class, and

establish the consequences of class status for black children's developmental experiences and outcomes.

3. *Interactions between class and culture in black life.* The failure to adequately separate class status from cultural identity among blacks has left as its legacy a tendency by researchers to gloss over the overlap between the two. We are unable to separate the effects of class from the effects of race. Closer attention needs to be paid to separating these factors and to pinpointing instances when the two are synonymous.

4. *Role of peers in black child socialization.* There is evidence of strong peer influences among black children. Yet, there are too few careful studies of such experiences in the lives of black youngsters. We need to understand the structure of peer relationships. How do these complement or thwart parents? How are black children socialized into, and by, peer groups? What functions do peer groups perform for children in school, community, and family settings?

5. *Implications of changing family structure.* The face of black family structure continues to change in our society. The gradual move away from two-parent families continues, as traditional, extended family living patterns shift. We must examine the implications of these changes for black children. What are the advantages and disadvantages of life in female-headed homes? How, and to what extent, are single-parent households involved with larger family systems?

6. *Black children and school.* School experiences continue to be difficult for many black youngsters. Their achievement levels are too low and dropout rates too high: There is need to account for these facts. What are the institutional and individual factors that act to produce academic underachievement among black children?

7. *Black children and the world of work.* Unemployment levels among black youth (and adults) are at all time highs. Two general research questions result. First, what factors contribute to high unemployment among black youth? Second, what are the life consequences of entering adulthood without ever having held a job? And, just how well do black youngsters understand the occupational structure of this society? How conversant are they with the range of occupational possibilities?

8. *Self-evaluation among black children.* Perception and evaluation of self influence how one behaves. More information is required about black children's attitudes toward themselves, their racial identification, and self-esteem. What are the sources and consequences of positive self-evaluations?

9. *Black families interface with other societal institutions.* Black parents and families do not operate in vacuo. Too little is known about how institutions like schools, churches, courts, and the media affect black children's development. We also need to know more about the strategies employed by parents and families to mediate these external influences. To what extent do black families rely on black churches or public schools for assistance with childrearing?

10. *Bio-Psycho-Social factors in black child development.* Interactions between physiological, psychological, and social factors in the lives of black children have received far too little systematic attention. We need to more carefully explore how these factors (operating individually and jointly) influence black children's development. What are the long range developmental consequences of childhood nutritional deficiencies?

11. *Ecological determinants of black child development.* Black child development is best evaluated in relation to the institutional, environmental, and interpersonal factors surrounding the individual. The combined and separate influences of these factors on black children's personalities needs to be clarified. Of special interest are the multiple ecologies that black children routinely move between; some predominantly white, and others predominantly black.

12. *Time as a conditioning factor in black child development.* Child socialization in black communities has changed fundamentally since Allison Davis and Robert Havighurst's pioneering study of black child development in 1945. Black children are now socialized for life in a desegregated society; the expectation is that they will routinely interact with whites as equals. Beyond this, our knowledge of how black child socialization has changed over time becomes hazy. For example, have there been dramatic shifts in the child-rearing goals and/or practices of black parents since the Civil Rights Movement? A clear understanding of how individuals change over time is also lacking. We are hard pressed to explain stability and change in the personalities of black children over a span of years (e.g., from ages three to 13). More research is necessary to gauge the import of changes over time (in the society and individuals) for black child development.

13. *Sex differences and black child development.* Sex is a vital differentiating factor in many sectors of life. Nevertheless, the research record remains murky, confusion abounds over the significance—if any—of gender of caregiver or child's gender for developmental outcomes. The record is particularly confusing in relation to black children. Researchers need to clarify how sex impacts and directs black child development in this society.

14. *Cross-cultural continuities in child development.* Efforts to identify continuities in child development across cultural or national boundaries are ham-

pered by research which limits comparisons to blacks versus whites. Such restricted, narrow comparisons also limit the degree to which within-group differences are understood. It is important, therefore, for researchers to undertake international comparisons of black child development. Are certain continuities apparent in the way blacks in France, Jamaica, New York City, and Kenya socialize their children? Do blacks in the U.S. rear their children much like minorities in other parts of the world (e.g., Oriental Jews in Israel, Muslims in India, Koreans in Japan, Laplanders in Sweden)?

15. *Appropriate theories, measures, and methods.* More research is needed that seriously questions the applicability of conventional theories, measures, and methods to the study of black child development. Researchers will need to evaluate conventional approaches to determine the appropriateness of their underlying values and assumptions to the realities of black Americans. Of special concern are culturally biased models that view nonwhites, the poor, and females as somehow deficient merely because they are different from the researcher (who is usually white, Protestant, middle-class and male).

## Action Implications and Agenda

Black children and their families currently face social and economic crises of such magnitude that their very survival is threatened. Spiraling inflation, soaring unemployment, and changing societal priorities greatly diminish the opportunities and quality of life for black children. We feel a special obligation to translate the practical implications of this volume into recommended actions aimed at alleviating the crises currently experienced by too many black (and minority and poor) children in this society. We do so not as disinterested, dispassionate, detached scholars, but rather as black professionals concerned with the futures of our children and our communities.

Social and behavioral research findings exert profound influence on public policy, which shapes the lives of an inordinate number of black children. Too often this simple connection is overlooked. It would be naive to believe that the day-to-day decisions of politicians, government officials, and human service professionals are completely determined by the most recently released research findings. It is equally naive to think that research findings have no consequences for how these people operate. Research findings taught in the classroom, reported in scholarly journals, distilled in the popular media, and discussed over cocktails, shape their ideas of both the appropriate and the possible. In making decisions, they draw upon these ideas in both conscious and unconscious ways.

Past research on black children and black families distorts their realities and defines them as pathological. As a result, social programs informed by this pejorative research tradition have been less than effective. Public policies intended to help black children have instead proven harmful. The research reported here provides a counterpoint. We encourage healthy skepticism about previous research findings from studies of black children and black families. We also encourage professionals to take carefully considered, and fully informed, action on behalf of black children.

Ironically, the actions this agenda calls for echo a similar call made by Allison Davis and John Dollard in 1940. Over the ensuing four decades much has changed in the lives of black people . . . Unfortunately, much has also remained the same. There are more black millionaires, physicians, professors, private contractors, and attorneys now than ever before. There also continue to be unacceptably high numbers of black children denied adequate health care, equal educational opportunity, and minimal living standards. The following recommendations suggest action which will insure that black (and minority) children who are currently disadvantaged receive their full benefits from this society. These recommendations are not intended to be all inclusive. Instead, they present our view of key arenas in children's lives for corrective action.

### Poverty

Black children and their families continue to be disproportionately represented in the ranks of this country's poor. Compared to whites, blacks earn less, have fewer capital resources, and are caught in systems of economic deprivation, experienced from generation to generation. Poverty conditions and life chances and experiences of black children in a variety of ways. In this society, the basic necessities of life—and any frills—are for sale. Those with limited or nonexistent purchasing power are therefore placed at a great disadvantage.

Action is required to improve the economic circumstances of black children and their families. We recommend:

  institution of an adequate guaranteed minimum family income. Where necessary, the incomes of working poor families should be supplemented.
  institution of a program of full employment involving the public and private sectors. Worker training/retraining activities would need to be a major component of such programs.
  equalization of worker salaries and earnings potential. Inequities in the wages paid to sole earner females and black males keep their families mired in poverty.

### Health Care

Black children and their families are deprived of adequate health care in this, the world's most medically advanced society. Disproportionate numbers of black children die in infancy, suffer poor nutrition, are not immunized, and die from accidents. Poor access to health care ends many young black lives prematurely and diminishes the quality of existence for others. Action is required to correct this situation. We recommend:

alternative financing of medical and health care services to insure their availability on the basis of need, rather than on the basis of ability to pay.

expansion of health care outlets, inducements for the location of health care
facilities in inner-city areas and increased recruitment/training of minority
physicians and health-care professionals to insure wider availability of
health care to black children.

establishment of comprehensive, preventive health programs emphasizing
early and periodic screening.

## Education

Educational attainment has steadily risen among black Americans. There is
reason to believe, however, that qualitative gains in their education have been
less pronounced. Black children lag behind whites on most objective measures of
achievement, their suspension rates are higher, and college entrance rates lower.
The educational experiences of black children are impaired through their enrollment at schools with larger numbers of underachieving students, more frequent
violence, fewer experienced teachers, and substandard facilities.

Action is necessary to improve the school experience for black children. We
recommend:

alternate financing approaches to eliminate current discrepancies in school
district resources dependent on the economic standing of the local communities in question.

development and implementation of individualized instructional programs
which employ "value added" approaches (i.e., emphasize student's improvement from variable starting points).

institute school personnel accountability systems that establish target achievement goals and assess school personnel performance in terms of these.

## Media

The electronic media in the form of television and radio exert an influence on
black children second only to parents. Children spend substantial amounts of
time absorbing the content of the most recent television programs and the most
popular songs. Yet parents exert little influence over the content of these messages. There is ample evidence that media messages are often detrimental to
black children's healthy development. The negative effects include advocacy of
violence, sexual indiscriminations, and conspicuous consumerism.

Necessary steps must be taken to maximize the positive effects of media and
to minimize any negative effects. We recommend:

regulation by parents of their children's media exposure patterns, restricting
them to television programs, radio stations, and movies that portray
positive messages.

monitor media broadcasts so as to encourage appropriate positive programming and to discourage inappropriate, negative programming.

### Child Care

If the model of a full-time homemaker, wife, ever had applicability in black communities, that time has long since passed. The majority of black mothers who can find jobs are employed outside the home. At the same time, the character of extended family involvements has changed so as to lessen the viability of these as child-care alternatives. The result has been an increased need for child-care services by black families. Limited availability of child-care options, high costs where these are available, and large numbers of black children in foster care make the provision of child care services to black families necessary. We recommend:

> expansion of low cost/community-based child-care programs to serve the needs of working parents. These services will need to be targeted toward children of different ages, from infancy to early adolescence.
> institution of training programs and referral resources available to child care providers.
> review and revamping of guidelines regulating black child placements in foster homes or group-care facilities.

## Responsibilities of the Black Community

Black communities have responsibilities extending to and beyond each of the problem areas above. They must pool and organize resources to insure that even where the government and larger society fail to fulfill their commitments, the needs of black children are being met. Self-help activities based in churches, social clubs, private homes, and available public meeting places must become the rule rather than the exception. This is a call for the recreation of community-based tutorial programs, social welfare cooperatives, and mutual support organizations of the sort commonly found in black communities at an earlier point in our history. It is a terrible irony that black Americans possess economic resources, educational achievements, and technical skills which would place us among the top 15 countries in the world were we an independent nation. Yet we mobilize the merest fraction of these vast resources in cooperative activities aimed at self-benefit. We continue to depend far too much on others for the fulfillment of our needs and for the protection of our young.

## Reflections

We purposely avoid referring to this, the final section of our comments, as a conclusion. Such reference would be highly inappropriate. Rather than ending, the task of creating a new scholarship about black child development is just beginning. It seems much longer than four years ago that this volume had its start. Over those years there were many hardships; and many lessons were learned.

Spurred by the pressing and obvious need for redefinition of the field, contributors to this volume undertook to fill the void. Little did we know the resistance which so straightforward a project (or so it seemed at the time) would generate. We have constantly encountered the question, "Why such a book?" People genuinely, if incorrectly, believed that black child development had been adequately addressed in the mainstream scholarship on child development. They saw no need for specific statements about black children. By the same token, beliefs that the cognitive realm was the most crucial—if not the only—focus for study of children's growth and development were widespread. We trust this volume provides a satisfactory challenge to such views. It is necessary to study how black children develop. It is necessary to study their social and emotional development.

We would be remiss if we did not comment on the vigor with which some resisted this project. Resistance was widespread. There were attempts to block funding, to ridicule the ideas advanced by this project, and to hamper efforts to publish these findings. As much as anything, this resistance was caused by the inertia common to established institutions. The institution of child development scholarship resisted this attempt to change its face. It mattered little that this impetus toward change came on the slippered feet of young black scholars, trained in top 10 universities; trained by mainstream mentors whose reputations were beyond reproach. The field, purely and simply, was uncomfortable with the notion that the thinking on black child development needed to be revised. There was discomfort with the thought that black children should be studied as a culturally distinct group. There was uncertainty over the wisdom of allowing a group of black scholars bent on self-definition, sufficient latitude to challenge accepted assumptions and models. The tension was of the sort described by Kuhn (1970) in *The Structure of Scientific Revolutions:* Advocates for established paradigms and world-views about black children resisted this volume's attempt to present alternatives.

We hasten to add that without the help of key people (some visionaries, others hard-nosed scientists) determined to subject the accepted to rigorous examination, this volume might not have come to be. For every attempt to sidetrack this project, there were equally determined efforts to insure its completion. Assistance and resistance to this project came from expected, as well as unexpected, quarters.

Our purpose in beginning this project was to stimulate dialogue and encourage reconsideration of perspectives on black children's development. Weary of studies that assumed blacks to be deficient, that ignored the reality of black culture, and that studied complex events in simplistic ways, we sought to propose alternatives. Our intention was to propose alternative perspectives, methods and interpretations in a nonreactive way—thus the emphasis on empirical studies. To engage in polemics would have been counterproductive. It is not sufficient to respond to charges that black child socialization and development is all patholog- ical by saying that is is all healthy. Both positions are unrealisitc. Human exis- tence is a composite of positives and negatives. The task of the scientist, there- fore, is to ascertain the structure of a given reality at a given place and time.

Our task has been to explore the lives of black children, to determine those features conducive to, or anithetical to, their processes of becoming. In this regard, our statement has applicability beyond black children and their develop- ment. In a broader sense, we attempt to understand the emergence of human personality. We hope that, out of this volume will come a better understanding of what all children require in order to develop into healthy, happy, productive human beings. We also hope that this volume will help to strengthen our soci- ety's commitment to providing these essential ingredients in the lives of all children, without regard to their race, income, sex, religion, or national origin.

# Afterword

Chester M. Pierce

What can be concluded following the reading of this book? Most will agree that the volume is well organized, carefully crafted, and scientifically credible. The editors and contributors have presented a body of qualitative and quantitative data which are useful, feasible, and practical. Throughout the volume are reassessments which suggest new directions for research and social policy. "Afterwards," this volume should rank as a landmark in studying and understanding racial factors in human development.

Each reader's experience will persuade considerations of what needs to be done in response to this book. Perhaps some will agree that, although this book is an excellent foundation for considering psychosocial aspects of development, an important future area will be to correlate more biological factors with the sort of theory and data presented. Other students may see the volume as leading us toward more robust ways of learning about cooperation. This possibility could well exert world-wide influence over the course of many years, since a task of humankind is to establish planetary citizenship. Still another, of many useful pathways this book guides us toward, is the more precise cataloging of what constitutes fundamental or universal human-specific behavior as opposed to behavior which has evolved from particular cultural, ethnic or indigenous features. "Afterwards," this volume should illuminate exciting pathways, especially for travelers journeying toward a firmer grasp of how to help more black people to live longer and to live better.

All who were augmented by the life of Dr. Jean V. Carew are grateful for this powerful remembrance of her never-ending effort to bring rigorous scientific studies by blacks (especially young scholars) to the field of child development. It is appropriate that colleagues and former students, black and white, from diverse disciplines have put together this volume to match both the love and generosity of spirit she had as a person with the vigor and objectivity she had as a researcher. "Afterwards," this volume should fuel our existential awareness of from whence we came. Many people will continue to be enriched by Jean's life despite her premature death.

# Bibliography

Aberle, D. F. (1962). Culture and socialization. In F. L. K. Hsu (Ed.), *Psychological Anthropology*. Evanston: Dorsey Press.

Aberle, D. F. (1968). The influence of linguistics on early culture and personality theory: In Robert A. Manners & David Kaplan (Eds.), *Theory in anthropology* (pp. 303–317). Chicago: University of Chicago Press.

Aberle, D. F. & Naegele, K. D. (1952). Middle-class fathers' occupational role and attitudes toward children. *American Journal of Orthopsychiatry, 22*, 366–378.

Abraham, R. (1976). Joking: the training of the man of words in talking broad. In Thomas Kochman (Ed.), *Rappin' and stylin' out: Communication in urban black America* (pp. 215–240). Chicago: University of Chicago Press.

Abrahams, R. D. (1962). Playing the Dozens. *Journal of American Folklore, 75,* 209–220.

Achenbach, T. M. & Edelrock, C. S. (1981). Behavioral problems and competencies reported by parents of normal and disturbed children aged four through sixteen. *Monographs of the Society for Research in Child Development, 46* (1, Serial No. 188).

Adorno, T., Frenkel-Brunswik, E., Levinson, D., and Sanford R. (1950). *The authoritarian personality*. New York: W. W. Norton.

Alejandro-Wright, M. (1975). The Black child's development of the concept of race. Unpublished manuscript, Harvard University.

Alejandro-Wright, M. (1979). The child's development of the concept of race: A socio-cognitive development study. Paper presented to the Society for Research in Child Development.

Alejandro-Wright, M. (1980). The child's development of the concept of race (Doctoral dissertation, Harvard University, 1980). *Dissertation Abstracts International,* in press.

Aldous, J. (1977). Family interaction patterns. *Annual Review of Sociology, 3,* 105–135.

Alkalimat, A. (1973). (Gerald A. McWorter). The ideology of black social science: In J. Ladner (Ed.), *The death of white sociology* (pp. 173–189). New York: Vintage.

Allen, W. (1975). *The antecedents of adolescent mobility aspirations*. Unpublished doctoral dissertation, University of Chicago.

Allen, W. (1978). Black family research in the United States: A review, assessment and extension. *Journal of Comparative Family Studies, 9,* 167–189.

317

Allen, W. (1978a). The search for applicable theories of black family life. *Journal of Marriage and the Family, 40,* 117–129.

Allen, W. (1978b). Race, family setting and adolescent achievement orientation. *Journal of Negro Education, 49,* 230–243.

Allen, W. (1979). Family roles, occupational statuses, and achievement among Black women in the United States. *SIGNS: Journal of Women in Culture and Society, 4*(4), 670–686.

Allport, G. (1958). *The nature of prejudice.* Garden City, NY: Doubleday Anchor Books.

Almquist, E. M., & Angrist, S. S. (1971). Role model influences on college women's career aspirations. *Merril-Palmer Quarterly, 17,* 263–279.

American Council on Education, Office of Research (1970). National norms of entering college freshmen. *5*(6).

American Council on Education, Office of Research (1973). The American freshman: National norms for Fall, 1973. Prepared by the staff of the Cooperative Institutional Research Program.

American Psychological Association (1982). *Ethical principles in the conduct of research with human participation.* Washington, D.C.: Author.

Anastasi, A. (1982). *Psychological testing.* New York: Macmillan.

Anderson, C. A. (1968). Education and society: In *International Encyclopedia of the Social Sciences,* Vol. 4 (pp. 517–525). New York: MacMillan Company and Free Press.

Anderson, J. D. (1978). Black cultural equality in American education: In W. Feinberg (Ed.), *Equality and social policy.* Urbana: University of Illinois Press (pp. 42–65).

Anderson, S., & Messick, S. (1974). Social competency in young children. *Developmental Psychology, 10,* 282–293.

Antonovsky, A. (1980). *Health, stress, and coping.* San Francisco: Jossey-Bass.

Arendt, H. (1951). *Origins of totalitarianism.* Cleveland: The World Publishing Company.

Armah, A. K. (1980). *The African world view: Counterstatements, pseudostatements, statements.* Unpublished manuscript.

Asante, M. K. (1980). *Afrocentricity: The theory of social change.* Buffalo, NY: Amulefi.

Asbough, J., Lavin, C. & Zacarria, L. (1973). Persistence and the disadvanteged college student. *Journal of Education Research, 65*(2), 64–67.

Aschenbrenner, J. (1978). Continuities and variations in black family structure: In Shimkins et al., (Eds.), *The Extended Family in Black Societies* (pp. 181–200). The Hague: Mouton.

Ascher, S. R., and Allen, V. L. (1969). Racial preference and social comparison processes. *Journal of Social Issues, 25,* 157–166.

Astin, A. W. (1971). *Predicting academic performance in college.* New York: The Free Press.

Astin, A. W. (1972). *College drop-outs: A national profile.* American Council on Education, Office of Research Reports, Vol. 7, No. 1.

Atkinson, J. W. (1964). *An introduction to motivation.* Princeton: D. Van Nostrand Co., Inc.

Atkinson, J. W., & Feather, N. T. (1966). *Theory of achievement motivation.* New York: Wiley & Sons.

Atkinson, J. W., Lens, W., & Malley, P. (1976). Motivation and ability: Interactive psychological determinants of intellective performance, educational achievement and each other. In W. Sewell, R. House, & D. Featherman, *Schooling and achievement in American Society.* New York: Academic Press.

Bachman, C., & Secord, P. (1963). Resistance to change in self-concept as a function of consensus among significant others. *Sociometry, 26,* 102–111.

Bachman, J. G. (1970). The impact of family background and intelligence on tenth grade boys, *Youth in transition,* Vol. 11. Ann Arbor: Institute for Social Research.

Baldwin, J. (1981). On the effect of racism, from a t.v. special on Harlem, Channel 13, New York, February 2.

Baldwin, J. A. (1979). Theory and research concerning the notion of Black self-hatred: A review and reinterpretation. *Journal of Black Psychology, 5*(2), 51–78.

Baltes, P. B. (1968). Longitudinal and cross-sectional sequences in the study of age and generation effects. *Human Development, 11,* 145–171.

Baltes, P. B., & Willis, S. C. (1979). Life-span developmental psychology, cognitive functioning and social policy: In M. R. Riley (Ed.), *Aging from birth to death* (pp. 15–25). Washington, D.C.: Westview Press.

Bandt, P., Meara, N., & Schmidt, L. (1974). A time to learn, a *Guide to academic and personal effectiveness.* New York: Holt, Rinehart & Winston.

Banducci, R. (1967). The effects of mothers' employment on the aspirations and expectations of the child. *Personnel and Guidance Journal, 46,* 263–267.

Bandura, A. (1978). The self system in reciprocal determinism. *American Psychologist, 33,* 344–358.

Banks, W. (1976). White preference in Blacks: A paradigm in search of a phenomenon. *Psychological Bulletin, 83*(6), 1179–1186.

Banks, W. C., & Rompf, W. J. (1973). Evaluative bias and preference behavior in black and white children. *Child Development, 44,* 776–783.

Banks, W. C., McQuater, G., & Hubbard, J. (1979). Toward a reconceptualization of the social-cognitive bases of achievement orientation in blacks: In A. W. Boykins, A. J. Franklin, and J. F. Yates (Eds.), *Research directions of black psychologists* (pp. 294–311). New York: Russell Sage.

Baratz, S., & Baratz, J. (1970). Early childhood intervention: The social science base of institutional racism. *Harvard Educational Review, 40*(1), 29–50.

Bardwick, J. M., & Douvan, E. (1972). Ambivalence: The socialization of women: In J. M. Bardwick (Ed.), *Readings on the psychology of women* (pp. 52–58). New York: Harper & Row.

Barker, R. G. & Wright, H. F. (1949). Psychological ecology and the problem of psychosocial development. *Child Development, 20,* 131–143.

Barnes, E. J. (1971). *The black community as the source of positive self-concepts for black children: A theoretical perspective.* Working paper commissioned by the Social Science Research Council. Prepared for the Self-concept Work Groups of the Learning and Educational Process Subcommittee on Compensatory Education. Pittsburgh: University of Pittsburgh.

Baron, H. (1971). The demand for black labor: historical notes on the political economy of racism. *Radical America 5*(2).

Barry, E. (1982). Legal services available to incarcerated parents and their children: An assessment of needs and services: In V. LaPoint and C. R. Mann (Eds.), *Incarcerated parents and their children.* Washington, D.C.: U.S. Government Printing Office.

Barry, H. III, Child, I. L. and Bacon, M. I. (1959). Relations of Childtraining to Subsistence Economy. *American Anthropologists, 61,* 51–63.

Bartz, K., & LeVine, E. (1978). Childrearing by black parents: A description and comparison to Anglo and Chicano parents. *Journal of Marriage and the Family, 40,* 709–720.

Battle, E. S. & Rotter, J. B. (1963). Children's feelings of personal control as related to social class and ethnic group. *Journal of Personality, 31,* 482–490.

Baumrind, D. (1970). Socialization and instrumental competence in young children. *Young Children, 26* 104–119.

Baumrind, D. (1971). Current patterns of parental authority. *Developmental Psychology Monograph, 41* (pt. 2), 1–103.

Baumrind, D. (1972). An exploratory study of socialization effects on black children. *Child Development, 43,* 261–267.

Baumrind, D. (1974). The development of instrumental competence through socialization. *Minnesota symposium on child psychology, 7.* Minneapolis, MN: University of Minnesota Press.

Baumrind, D. (1976). Subcultural variations in values defining social competence. Paper presented at Society for Research in Child Development, Western Regional Conference.

Baumrind, D. (1977). Subcultural variations in values defining social competence: An outsider's perspective on the black subculture. *Journal of Social Issues. 33*

Baumrind, D. & Black, A. E. (1967). Socialization patterns associated with dimensions of competence in preschool boys and girls. *Child Development, 38,* 291–327.

Baunarch, P. (1982). The families of inmate-mothers: Perceptions of the separation from their children: In V. LaPoint and C. R. Mann (Eds.), *Incarcerated parents and their children.* Washington, D.C.: U.S. Government Printing Office.

Beckham, R. (1976). *My life as a psychologist with Dr. Albert Sidney Beckham.* Paper presented at the annual meetings of the National Association of Black Psychologists, Chicago, August.

Beckum, L. (1973). *The Effects of Counseling and Reinforcement on Behaviors Important to the Improvement of Academic Self-Concept.* Stanford University technical Report No. 38, Stanford.

Bem, D. J. (1967). Self-perception: An alternative interpretation of cognitive dissonance phenomena. *Psychological Review, 74,* 183–200.

Benedict, R. (1949). *Race: Science and Politics.* New York: Viking Press.

Bennet, S. K., & Elder, G. H., Jr. (1979). Women's work in the family economy: A study of depression hardship in women's lives. *Journal of Family History, 3,* 153–176.

Bennett, J. W. (1969). *Northern plainsmen: adaptive strategy and agricultural life.* Arlington Heights, Ill.: AHM Publication.

Bennett, P. D.,& Lundgren, D. C. (1976). Racial self-concept of young children. *Journal of Interpersonal Relations, 5*(1), 3–14.

Bennett, W. S., & Gist, N. P. (1964). Class and family influences on student aspirations. *Social Forces, 43,* 147–173.

Bereiter, C., & Engelman, S. (1966). *Teaching disadvantaged children in the preschool.* Englewood Cliffs, N.J.: Prentice-Hall.

Berger, P. L. & Luckmann, T. (1966). *The social construction of reality.* New York: Doubleday-Anchor Books.

Berlyne, D. E. (1950). Novel and curiosity as determinants of exploratory behavior. *British Journal of Psychology, 3,* 68–80.

Bernstein, A., and Cowan, P. (1975). Children's concepts of how people get babies. *Child Development, 46,* 77–91.

Berry, J. W. (1971). Ecological and Cultural Factors in Spatial Perceptual Development. *Canadian Journal of Behavioral Science Review, 3*(4), 324–337.

Bialer, I. (1961). Conceptualization of success and failure in mentally retarded and normal children. *Journal of Personality, 29,* 303–320.

Billingsley, A. (1968). *Black families in white America.* Englewood Cliffs, N.J.: Prentice Hall.

Billingsley, A., & Giovannoni, J. (1972). *Children of the storm: black children and American welfare.* New York: Harcourt, Brace and Jovanovich.

Blackwell, J. E. (1975). *The Black community: diversity and unity.* New York: Dodd, Mead and Company.

Blair, T. L. (1977). *Retreat to the ghetto: the end of a dream?* New York: Hill and Wang.

Blassingame, J. (1972). *The slave community.* New York: Oxford.

Blau, P., & Duncan, O. (1967). *American Occupational Structure.* New York: Wiley.

Blood, R., & Wolfe, D. M. (1960). *Husbands and wives: The dynamics of married living.* Glenco, Ill.: Free Press.

Bloom, B. S. (1956). *Taxonomy of educational objectives.* New York: David McKay.

Bloom, B. S. (1976). *Human characteristics and school learning.* New York: McGraw-Hill Book Co.

Bloom, B. S., Davis, A., & Hess, R. (1965). *Compensatory education for cultural deprivation.* New York: Holt, Rinehart & Winston, Inc.

Blyth, D., Simmons, R., & Bush, D. (1978). The transition into early adolescence: A longitudinal comparison of youth in two educational contexts. *Sociology of Education, 51,* 149–162.

Bogue, D. (Ed.) (1974). *The basic writings of Ernest W. Burgess.* Chicago, IL: Community and Family Study Center.

Bonfanti, M. A., Felder, S. S., Loesch, M. L., & Vincent, N. S. (1974). *Enactment and perceptions of maternal role of incarcerated mother.* Unpublished master's thesis. Louisiana State University, New Orleans, LA.

Borth, A. (1970). Coping and defending in black classrooms: A study of non-intellectual correlates of achievement. Unpublished doctoral dissertation, University of Chicago.

Bowerman, C. E. (1964). Prediction studies: In H. T. Christensen (Ed.), *The handbook of marriage and family* (pp. 215–246). Chicago: Rand McNally.

Boykin, A. W. (1978). Psychological/behavioral verve in academic/task performance: a pre-theoretical consideration. *Journal of Negro Education, 47,* 343–354.

Boykin, A. W. (1979a). Black psychology and the research process: keeping the baby but throwing out the bath water: In A. W. Boykin, A. J. Franklin, & J. F. Yates (Eds.), *Research directions of black psychologists* (85–103). New York: Russell Sage Foundation.

Boykin, A. W. (1979b). Psychological/behavioral verve: Some theoretical explorations and empirical manifestations: In A. W. Boykin, A. J. Franklin, & J. F. Yates (Eds.), *Research directions of black psychologists* (pp. 351–367). New York: Russell Sage.

Boykin, A. W. (1980 November). *Reading achievement and the social cultural frame of reference of Afro-American children.* A paper presented at NIE Roundtable Discussion on Issues in Urban Reading, Washington, D.C.

Boykin, A. W., Anderson, F., & Yates, J. F. (1979). *Research directions of black psychologists.* New York: Russell Sage Foundation.

Braddock, J. H. (1980). Race, sports, and social mobility: a critical review. *Sociological Symposium, 30,* 28–38.

Brand, E., Ruiz, R., & Padilla, A. (1974). Ethnic identification and preference: a review. *Psychological Bulletin, 81*(11), 860–890.

Breer, P., & Locke, D. (1966). *Task experience as a source of attitudes.* Homewood, Illinois: Dorsey Press.

Bremner, R. (Ed.) (1974). *Children and youth in America: A documentary history.* (Vols. 2, 3). Cambridge: Harvard University.

Bridgeman, B., & Shipman, V. C. (1975). Disadvantageous Children and Their First School Experience. Project Head Start, Office for Child Development, U.S. Department of Health, Education and Welfare.

Brim, O. & Kagan, J. (Eds.) (1980). *Constancy and change in human behavior.* Cambridge, Mass.: Harvard University.

Brisbane, R. H. (1974). *Black activism: racial revolution in the United States, 1954–1970.* Valley Forge, PA: Judson Press.

Bronfenbrenner, U. (1965). Socialization and social class through time and space: In H. Proshansky (Ed.), *Basic Studies in Social Psychology* (pp. 349–365). New York: Holt, Rinehart and Winston.

Bronfenbrenner, U. (1970). *Two worlds of childhood: U.S. and U.S.S.R..* New York: Simon and Schuster.

Bronfenbrenner, U. (1971a). Beyond the deficit model in child and family policy. *Teachers College Record, 81*(1), 95–104.

Bronfenbrenner, U. (1977). Toward an experimental ecology of human development. *American Psychologist, 32,* 513–531.

Bronfenbrenner, U. (1979a). Contexts of child rearing: problems and prospects. *American Psychologist, 34*(10), 844–850.

Bronfenbrenner, U. (1979b). *The ecology of human development: experiments by nature and design.* Cambridge, MA: Harvard University.

Brookins, G. K. (1977). Maternal employment: its impact on the sex roles and occupational choices of middle and working class black children. Unpublished doctoral dissertation, Harvard University.

Brookover, W., et al. (1965). *Self concept of ability and school achievement II*. Lansing: Michigan State University.

Brookover, W., Erickson, E., & Joiner, L. M. (1967). *Self-concept of ability and school achievement, III*. Final Report of Cooperative Research Project Number 2831. Michigan State University.

Brookover, W., LePere, J., Hammacher, T., & Erickson, E. (1965). *Self-concept of ability and school achievement, II*. East Lansing: Michigan State University.

Brookover, W. B., Paterson, A., & Thomas, S. (1962). *Self-concept of ability and school achievement*. Final report of Cooperative Research Project Number 845. Michigan State University.

Brophy, J. E. (1970). Mothers as teachers of their own preschool children: The influence of socioeconomic status and task structure on teaching specificity. *Child Development, 41*, 79–94.

Brophy, J. E. & Good, T. L. (1974). *Teacher-student relationships: causes and consequences*. New York: Holt, Rinehart & Winston.

Brown, H., Adams, R. G., & Kellam, S. G. (1981). A longitudinal study of teenage motherhood and symptoms of distress. The Woodlawn Community Project. *Research in Community and Mental Health 2*, 183–213.

Brown, M. (1974). Some determinants of persistence and initiation of achievement-related activities: in J. Atkinson & J. Raynor (Eds.), *Motivation and achievement*. Washington, D.C.: Winston & Sons. pp. 320–335.

Bruber, H., & Voneche, J. (1977). *The essential Piaget*. New York: Basic Books.

Bruner, J., Goodnow, J. & Austin, C. (1956). *A study of thinking*. New York: John Wiley.

Bruner, J. S., Jolly, A., & Sylva, K. (Eds.) (1976). *Play: its role in development and evolution*. New York: Basic Books.

Bryan, J. G. (1950). A method for the exact determination of the characteristics equation and latent vectors of a matrix with applications to the discriminant function for more than two groups. Unpublished doctoral dissertation, Harvard University.

Buckles, D., & LaFazia, M. (1973). Child care for mothers in prison: in B. Ross and C. Shireman (Eds.), *Social work practice and social justice* (pp. 44–50). New York: National Association of Social Workers.

Buhler, K. (1930). *The mental development of the child*. New York: Harcourt, Brace.

Bullock, P. (1973). *Aspirations vs. opportunity: "Careers" in the inner city*. Ann Arbor: The University of Michigan Press.

Burgess, E. W., & Bogue, D. (Eds.) (1964). *Contributions to urban sociology*. Chicago: University of Chicago.

Burgess, E. W., & Cottrell, L. S. (1939). *Predicting success or failure in a marriage*. New York: Prentice-Hall.

Burgess, E. W., Locke, H. J., & Thomas, M. M. (1971). *The family: From tradition to companionship* (4th ed.). New York: Von Nostrand.

Burns, S. M., & Brainerd, C. J. (1979). Effects of constructive and dramatic perspective taking in very young children. *Developmental Psychology, 15*, 512–521.

Buros, O. K. (Ed.) (1965). *The sixth mental measurements yearbook*. Highland Park, N.J.: Gryphon Press.

Bush, D., Simmons, R., Hutchinson, B., & Blyth, D. (1977–78). Adolescent perception of sex roles in 1968 and 1975. The *Public Opinion Quarterly, 41*, 459–474.

Bushnell, D., & Zagaris, I. (1972). *Strategies for change*. Washington, D.C.: American Association of Junior Colleges.

Busk, P., Ford., R., & Schulman, J. (1973). Effects of school's racial composition on the self-concept of black and white students. *The Journal of Educational Research, 67*, 57–63.

Butler, R. O. (1976). Black children's racial preference: A selected review of the literature. *Journal of Afro-American Issues, 4*(6), 168–171.

Butts, H. (1963). Skin color perception and self-esteem. *Journal of Negro Education, 32,* 122–128.
Calhoun, G., Kurfiss, J., & Warren, P. (1976). A comparison of self concept and self-esteem of black and white boys. *Clearing House, 50,* 131–133.
Caplan, F., & Caplan, T. (1973). *The power of play.* Garden City, N.Y.: Anchor Books.
Capital Punishment 1978 (1979). (National Prisoner Statistics Bulletin SD-NPS-CP-7) Washington, D.C.: U.S. Government Printing Office.
Carnegie Commission on Higher Education (1970a). *A chance to learn: An action agenda for equal opportunity in higher education.* New York: McGraw-Hill Book Co.
Carnegie Commission on Higher Education (1970b). *The open-door college: Policies for community colleges.* New York: McGraw-Hill Book Co.
Castenell, L. A. (1981). *Achievement motivation: An area-specific analysis.* Doctoral dissertation. Graduate College-University of Illionois, Urbana, Ill.
Cayton, H., & Drake, St.C. (1945). *Black metropolis: A study of Negro life in a Northern city.* New York: Harcourt Brace.
Chaillé, C. (1978). The child's conceptions of play, pretending, and toys: Sequences and structural parallel. *Human Development, 21,* 201–210.
Chapman, J. R. (1980). *Economic realities and the female offender.* Massachusetts: D.C. Heath.
Cherlin, A. J. (1981). *Marriage, divorce, remarriage: Marital formation and dissolution in the postwar United States.* Cambridge, Mass.: Harvard University Press.
Chimezie, A. (1976). The dozens: An African heritage theory. *Journal of Black Studies, 6,* 401–420.
Chin, R., & Benne, K. (1969). General strategies for effecting changes in human systems: In W. G. Bennis, K. D. Benne & R. Chin (Eds.), *Planning of change* (pp. 32–59). New York: Holt, Rinehart & Winston.
Cicourel, A. V., & Kitsuse, J. I. (1963). *The educational decision makers.* Indianapolis: Bobbs-Merrill.
Clark, A., Hocevar, D., & Dembo, M. (1980). The role of cognitive development in children's explanations and preferences for skin color. *Developmental Psychology, 16*(4), 332–339.
Clark, B. R. (1960). *The open-door college: A case study.* New York: McGraw-Hill Book Co.
Clark, E. T. (1967). Influence of sex and social class on occupational preference and perception. *Personnel and Guidance Journal, 45,* 440–444.
Clark, K. B. & Clark, M. K. (1939). The development of consciousness of self and the emergence of racial identity in Negro preschool children. *Journal of Social Psychology, 10,* 591–599.
Clark, K. B., & Clark, M. K. (1940). Skin color as a factor in racial identification of Negro preschool children. *Journal of Social Psychology, 11,* 159–169.
Clark, K. B. & Clark, M. K. (1947). Racial identification and preference in Negro children: In T. Newcomb and E. Hartley (Eds.), *Readings in Social Psychology* (pp. 602–611). New York: Henry Holt.
Clark, K. B., & Clark, M. K. (1972). Racial identification and preference in Negro children: In G. E. Swanson, T. M. Newcomb, & E. L. Hartley (Eds.), *Readings in Social Psychology* (Revised Edition) (pp. 551–560). New York: Holt.
Cocking, R. R., & Siegel, I. E. (1979). The concept of decalage as it applies to representational thinking: In H. Smith & M. B. Franklin (Eds.), *Symbolic functioning in childhood.* Hillsdale, N.J.: Lawrence Erlbaum Associates.
Coe, R. D., Duncan, G. J., & Hill, M. S. (1982). *Dynamic aspects of poverty and welfare use in the United States.* Prepared for Conference on Problems of Poverty, Clark University.
Coelho, G., Hamburg, D., & Adams, J. (1974). *Coping and adaptation.* New York: Basic Books.
Cohen, R. (1969). Conceptual sytles, culture conflict, and noverbal tests of intelligence. *American Anthropologist, 71,* 828–856.
Cohen, Y. A. (1971). The shaping of men's minds: Adaptation to the imperatives of culture. In M.

L. Wax, S. Diamond & F. O. Gearing (Eds.) *Anthropological Perspectives on Education.* (pp. 19–50) N.Y.: Basic Books.

Cole, M., & Bruner, J. (1971). Cultural differences and inferences about psychological processes. *American Psychologist, 26,* 867–876.

Cole, M. V., John-Steiner, V., Scribner, S. & Souberman, E. (Eds.). (1978). *Mind in Society.* Cambridge: Harvard University Press.

Cole, S. (1981). The influence of self-selection on the distribution of rewards. Center for the Social Sciences. Preprint, Columbia University.

Coleman, J. S., Campbell, E., et al. (1966). *Equality of educational opportunity.* Washington, D.C.: U.S. Department of Health, Education & Welfare.

Coles, R. (1965). It's the same but it's different. *Daedalus, 94,* 1107–1132.

Comer, J. (1974). The black American child in school. In E. J. Anthony and C. Koupernik (Eds.), *The child in his family* (vol. 3). New York: John Wiley and Sons.

Connolly, D. J. & Bruner, J. S. (1974). Introduction: Competence: its nature and nurture: In K. J. Connolly & J. S. Bruner (Eds.), *The Growth of Competence* (pp. 3–7). London: Academic Press.

Conyers, J., & Epps, E. (1974). A profile of black sociologists: In J. Blackwell & M. Janowitz (Eds.), *Black Sociologists: Historical and contemporary perspectives* (pp. 231–252). Chicago: University of Chicago.

Cooke, G. (1974). Socialization of the black male: Research implications. In Lawrence E. Gary, (Ed.) *Social Research and the Black Community: Selected Issues and Priorities* (pp. 76–87). Washington, D.C.: Howard University.

Cooley, C. (1912). *Human nature and the social order.* New York: Scribner's.

Cooley, W. W., & Lahanes, P. R. (1966). *Multivariate procedures for the behavioral sciences.* New York: Wiley & Sons.

Coopersmith, S. (1967). *The antecedents of self-esteem.* San Francisco: Freeman.

Coopersmith, S. (1975). *Coopersmith self-esteem inventory.* Lafayette, CA: Self-Esteem Institute.

Cox, O. C. (1948). *Caste, class, and race.* New York: Doubleday.

Crain, R., & Weisman, C. (1972). *Discrimination, Personality, and Achievement.* New York: Seminar.

Crites, L. (1976). *The female offender.* Massachusetts: D. C. Heath.

Cross, P. (1968). *The junior college student: Research description.* Princeton, New Jersey: Educational Testing Service.

Cross, W. E., Jr. (1978a). The Thomas and Cross models on psychological Nigrescence: A literature review. *Journal of Black Psychology, 4*(1), 13–31.

Cross, W. E., Jr. (1978b). The Mediax project: The socioemotional domain. Position Paper Prepared for Mediax Associates of Westport, Ct.

Cross, W. E., Jr. (1978c). Black families and Black identity: A literature review. *Western Journal of Black Studies, 2*(2), 111–124.

Cross, W. E., Jr. (1979). *Black families and Black identity: Rediscovering the distinction between personal identity and reference group orientation.* Paper Presented at the International Seminar on "The Child and the Family"; Gustavus Adolphus College, St. Peter, Minnesota.

Cross, W. E. (1979). *Black families and Black identity development: Rediscovering the distinction between self-esteem and reference group orientation.* Unpublished manuscript.

Cross, W. E. (1980). *Black identity: Rediscovering the distinction between personal identity and reference group orientation.* Paper presented at the meeting of the Society for Research on Child Development Study Group on the Social and Affective Development of the Minority Group Child.

Cross, W. E. (1980, November). *Exploring ecological determinants of black and white identity and development in children: Social networks and everyday activities of three year olds.* Paper presented at the SCRD Study Group Meeting held in Atlanta, Ga.

Cross, W. E., & Bronfenbrenner, U., & Cochran, M. (1977). *Black families and the socialization of*

*Black children: An ecological approach* (Research proposal received and funded by ACYF 1977–1980).

Cummings, S. (1977). Family socialization and fatalism among black adolescents. *Journal of Negro Education, 46,* 62–75.

Daehlin, D., & Hynes, J. (1974). Program developments: a mothers' discussion group in a women's prison. *Child Welfare, 54*(7), 464–470.

Dansky, J. L., & Silverman, I. W. (1976). Effects of play on associative fluency in preschool children: In J. Bruner, A. Jolly, & K. Sylva (Eds.), *Play: Its role in development and evolution* (pp. 650–654). New York: Basic Books.

Dave, R. H. (1963). *The identification and measurement of environmental variables that are related to educational achievement.* Unpublished Doctoral Dissertation, University of Chicago.

Davis, A. (1948). *Social-class influence on learning.* Cambridge: Harvard University Press.

Davis, A. (1971). Cognitive style: Methodological and cognitive considerations. *Child Development, 42,* 1447–1459.

Davis, A., & Dollard, J. (1964). *Children of bondage.* New York: Harper and Row. (Originally published, 1940).

Davis, A., & Havighurst, R. (1946). Social class and color differences in childrearing. *American Sociological Review, 2,* 698–710.

Davis, A., Gardner, B., & Gardner, M. (1937). *Deep South: A social anthropological study of caste and class.* Chicago: University of Chicago Press.

Dawes, R., & Corrigan, B. (1974). Linear models in decision making. *Psychological Bulletin, 81,* 95–106.

deCharms, R. (1968). *Personal causation.* New York: Academic Press.

deCharms, R., & Dave, P. (1965). Hope of success, fear of failure, subjective probability, and risk-taking behavior. *Journal of Personality and Social psychology, 1,* 558–568.

Deutsch, C. P. (1973). Social class and child development. In B. M. Caldwell & H. N. Ricciuti (Eds.), *Review of child development research* (Vol. 3) (pp. 233–282). Chicago: University of Chicago Press.

Deutsch, M., Fishman, J., Kogan, L., North, R., & Whiteman, M. (1964). Guidelines for testing minority children. *Journal of Social Issues, 20,* 129–145.

Devries, R. (1969). Constancy of generic identity in the years three to six. Monographs of the *Society for Research in Child Development, 34* (3, Serial No. 127).

Dewey, J. (1967). The reflex-arc concept. In J. Ratner (Ed.) *Philosophy, psychology and social practice.* Toms River, New Jersey: Capricorn Books.

Dewey, J. & Bentley, A. (1973). The knowing and the known: In R. Handy & E.C. Harwood (Eds.), *Useful proceudres of inquiry* (pp. 89–190). Great Barrington, MA: Behavioral Research Council. (originally published, 1949).

DeVos, G. (1973). *Socialization for achievement: Essays on the cultural psychology of the Japanese.* Berkeley: University of California Press.

De Vos, G. (1975). Ethnic Pluralism: Conflict and accommodation. In G. De Vos and L. Romanucci-Ross (Eds.), *Ethnic identity: Cultural continuities and change.* Palo Alto: Manfield.

Diner, S. (1975). Department and discipline: The department of sociology at the University of Chicago, 1892–1920. *Minerva, 13*(4), 514–553.

Dixon, D., & Saltz, E. (1977). The role of imagery on concept acquisition in lower SES children. *Child Development, 48,* 288–291.

Dixon, V., & Foster, B. (1971). *Beyond black or white.* Boston: Little, Brown.

DiCesare, A. C., Sedlacek, W. C., & Brooks, Jr., G. C. (1972). Nonintellectual correlates of black student attrition. *Journal of College Student Personnel, 13,* 319–324.

Doll, E. A. (1947). *Vineland social maturity scale: Manual of directions.* Minneapolis, MN: Educational Test Bureau.

Dollard J. (1939). The dozens: Dialect of insult. *American Image, 1,* 3–25.

Douglas, P. (1981). The war on black children. *Black Enterprise, 10*(4), 22–27.

Douvall, E. B. (1955). Conceptions of mother roles by five and six year old children of working and non-working mothers. *Dissertation Abstracts, 15,* 1609.

Douvan, E. (1958). Social status and success striving: In J. W. Atkinson (Ed.), *Motives in fantasy, action and society* (pp. 509–517). Princeton, New Jersey: Van Nostrand.

Drake, St. C. (1974). In the mirror of black scholarship: W. Allison Davis and Deep South. *Harvard Educational Review.* Monograph No. *2,* 42–54.

Drake, St. C. (1975). *Black intellectuals and black liberation.* Paper presented to the Conference on Pull the Covers Off of Imperialism. Fisk University, Nashville, Tennessee, January, 1975. A report of this conference was published in the *Black Scholar, 6*(5), 54–56.

Drake, St. C., & Cayton, H. (1945). *Black metropolis.* New York: Harcourt, Brace and World.

Dreger, R. M. (1968). Comparative psychological studies of Negroes and whites in the United States: 1959–1965. *Psychological Bulletin Monograph Supplement, 70*(2), 1–58.

Dreger, R. M. (1973). Temperment: In K. Miller and R. Dreger (Eds.), *Comparative studies of blacks and whites in the United States.* New York: Seminar.

Dreger, R. M., & Miller, K. S. (1968). Comparative psychological studies of Negroes and whites in the United States—1959–1965. *Psychological Bulletin Monograph, 70,* 3.

Drew, E., & Teehan, J. (1963). Parental attitudes and academic achievement: In W. W. Charters, & N. L. Gage (Eds.), *Readings in Social Psychology of Education.* Boston: Allyn and Bacon, Inc.

DuBois, W. E. B. (1961). *The souls of black folk.* Greenwich, Conn.: Fawcett, (Originally published 1903).

DuBois, W. E. B. (1967). *The Philadelphia Negro.* New York: Schocken, (Originally published, 1899).

DuBois, W. E. B. (1968). The talented tenth. Reprinted in *ibid.,* pp. 385–403; quotes from *The autobiography of W. E. B. Dubois.* New York: International Publishers, p. 236.

DuBois, W. E. B. (1971). The conservation of races. Reprinted in J. Lester (Ed.), *The seventh son: The thought and writings of W. E. B. DuBois* (Vol. 1) (pp. 176–183). New York: Vintage Books. (Originally published in 1897).

Dubose, D. (1977). Women in prison—a neglected issue. In P. Eck & C. English (Eds.), *Incarceration—benefits and drawbacks.* Texas: University of Texas (Arlington).

Dulan, C. G. (1978). Ethnic identification and stereotyping by black children in desegregated elementary schools. *Dissertation Abstracts International, 38,* (10-A), 6352–A.

Duncan, O. D. (1961). A socioeconomic index for all occupations. In A. J. Riess (Ed), *Occupations and social status.* New York: Free Press.

Dunham, R. G. (1963). Achievement motivation as predictive of academic performance: A multivariate analysis. *Journal of Education Research, 67,* (No. 2), 70–72.

Dunn, L. & Dobzhansky, T. (1952). *Heredity, race and society.* New York: New American Library of World Literature, Inc.

Durkheim, E. (1964). *The Division of labor in society.* New York: Free Press.

Durrett, M. E. and Davy, A. (1970). Racial awareness in young Mexican-American, Negro and Anglo children. *Young Children, 26*(1), 16–24.

Duvall, E. (1947). Conceptions of parenthood. *American Journal of Sociology, 52,* 193–203.

Eckberg, D. L. (1979). *Intelligence and race.* New York: Praeger.

Edelman, M. W. (1980). *A portrait of inequality—black and white children in America.* Washington, D.C.: The Children's Defense Fund.

Edwards, D. (1974). Blacks versus whites: When is race a relevant variable? *Journal of Personality and Social Psychology, 29,* 39–49.

Edwards, R. C., Reich, M. and Gordon, D. M. (Eds.) (1975). *Labor Market Segmentation.* Lexington, Massachusetts: D. C. Heath.

Edwards, G. F. (Ed.) (1968). *E. Franklin Frazier on race relations: Selected writings.* Chicago: University of Chicago.

Eifermann, R. R. (1971). Social play in childhood: In R. E. Herron & B. Sutton-Smith (Eds.), *Child's play* (pp. 270–297). New York: Wiley.

Elder, G. H., Jr. (1974). *Children of the Great Depression*. Chicago: University of Chicago Press.

Elder, G. H., Jr. (1984). Family and Kinship: Historical and life course perspectives: In R. Parke (Ed.), *The family*. Chicago: University of Chicago Press.

Elder, G. H. Jr. & Rockwell, R. C. (1979). The life course and human development. *International Journal of Behavioral Development 2*, pp. 1–21.

Elder, J. L., & Pederson, D. R. (1978). Preschool children's use of objects in symbolic play. *Child Development, 49*, 500–504.

Elkind, D. (1963). The child's conception of his religious denomination, III: The Protestant child. *Journal of Genetic Psychology, 103*, 291–303.

Elkins, S. (1959). *Slavery: A problem in American institutional and intellectual life*. Chicago: University of Chicago.

El'Konin, D. (1966). Symbolics and its functions in the play of children. *Soviet Education, 8*, 35–41.

Ellis, H. D. & Newman, S. N. (1971). Gowster, ivy-leaguer, hustler, conservative, mackman, and continental: A functional analysis of six ghetto roles: In Eleanor Bruke Leacock, (Ed.), *The Culture of poverty: A critique* (299–314). New York: Simon and Schuster.

Ellis, M. J. (1973). *Why people play*. Englewood Cliffs: Prentice-Hall.

Ellwood, D. T., & Wise, D. A. (1982). Youth employment in the 1970s: The changing circumstances of young adults: In R. R. Nelson & S. Skidmore (Eds.), *The high cost of living* (pp. 59–108). Washington, D.C.: National Academy of Sciences.

Emmerich, W., Goldman, K. S., Kirsch, B. & Sharabany, R. (1977). Evidence for a transitional phase in the development of gender constancy. *Child Development, 48*, 930–936.

Epps, E. G. (1967). Impact of school desegregation on self-evaluation and achievement orientation. *Law and Contemporary Problems*, Summer 1978, *42*(3), 57–76.

Epps, E. G. (1966). Motivation and Performance of Negro Students. Unpublished paper. Institute for Social Research, University of Michigan, Ann Arbor, Michigan.

Epps, E. G. (1969a). *Family and achievement: A study of the relation of family background to achievement orientation and performance among urban Negro high school students*. Final Report of Project #5-1006. U.S. Department of Health, Education, and Welfare. Ann Arbor: Institute for Social Research, University of Michigan.

Epps, E. G. (1969b). Correlates of academic achievement among northern and southern urban negro students. *Journal of Social Issues, 25*(3), 55–70.

Epps, E. (1971). *Achievement orientation and racial attitudes among urban black high school students*. Unpublished manuscript: University of Chicago.

Epps, E. (1973). *Race relations: Current perspectives*. Massachusetts: Winthrop.

Epps, E. (1975). Impact of school desegregation on aspirations, self-concept and other aspects of personality. *Law and Contemporary Problems, 50*, 300–313.

Epstein, Y. M., Krupat, E., & Obudho, C. (1976). Clean is beautiful: Identification and preference as a function of race and cleanliness. *Journal of Social Issues, 32*(2), 109–110.

Erickson, E. (1942). Hitler's imagery and German youth. *Psychiatry, 5*, 475–493.

Erickson, E. (1950). *Childhood and society*. New York: Norton.

Erickson, E. (1967). Identity and the life cycle: Selected papers. *Psychological Issues*, 1959, Monograph 1.

Erickson, E. (1968). *Identity, youth, and crisis*. New York: Norton.

Eysenck, H. (1971). *The I.Q. argument*. LaSalle, Ill.: Library Press.

Fannon, F. (1967). *Black skin, white masks* (translated by C. Markman). New York: Grove Press.

Farley, Reynolds (1968). The urbanization of Negros in the United States. *Journal of Social History, 1*(3), 241–258.

Faris, R. (1967). *Chicago sociology: 1920–1932*. San Francisco: Chandler.

Feagin, J. R. (1970). Black women in the American work force: In C. Willie (Ed.), *The family life of black people* (pp. 23–35). Columbus, OH: Charles E. Merrill.

Fein, G. G. (1975). A transformational analysis of pretending. *Developmental Psychology, 11,* 291–296.

Fein, G. G. (in press). Pretend Play in Childhood: An integrative review. *Child Development.*

Feitelson, D., & Ross, G. (1973). The neglected factor—play. *Human Development, 16,* 202–223.

Female Offenders Resource Center (American Bar Association) (1976). *Female offenders: Problems and programs.* Washington, D.C.: Author.

Ferman, L. A., Kornbluh, J. L., & Miller, J. A., (Eds.) (1968). *Negros and jobs: A book of readings.* Ann Arbor: The University of Michigan Press.

Festinger, L. (1954). A theory of social comparison processes. *Human Relations, 7,* 117–140.

Feyerabend, P. (1970). Problems and empiricism, Part II: In R. Colodny (Ed.), *Nature and Function of Scientific Theories* (pp. 275–353). Pittsburgh: University of Pittsburgh Press.

Fichter, J. H. (1967). Graduates of predominantly Negro colleges class of 1964. Washington, D.C.: U.S. Department of Health, Education and Welfare.

Fink, R. (1976). The role of imaginative play in cognitive development. *Psychological Reports, 39,* 895–906.

Fishbein, H. D. (1976). *Evolution, development, and children's learning.* Pacific Palisades, CA: Goodyear.

Fisher, R. A. (1936). The use of multiple measurements in taxonomic problems. *Annals of Eugenics, 8,* 276–386.

Fiske, D. (1963). Problems in measuring personality: In J. Wepman and R. Heine (Eds.), *Theories of personality* (pp. 249–263). Chicago: Aldine.

Flavell, J. H. (1972). An analysis of cognitive-developmental sequences. *Genetic Psychology Monograph, 86,* 279–350.

Folb, E. A. (1980). *Runnin' down some lines: The language and culture of black teenagers.* Cambridge: Harvard University Press.

Forehand, G. A., Rogosta, M., & Rock, D. A. (1976). *Conditions and processes of effective school desegregation.* Princeton, N.J.: Educational Testing Service.

Foster, H. L. (1974). *Ribbin', jivin', and playin' the dozens: The unrecognized dilemma of inner city schools.* Cambridge, Mass.: Ballinger.

Fouther-Austin, A. (1978). Education, personality development and mental hygiene. *Dissertation Abstracts International, 38*(8-A), 4650–A.

Fowler, J. W. (1981). Stages in faith: The structural-developmental approach. In Thomas Hennessey, *A Symposium on moral development education.* San Francisco: Harper and Row.

Franklin, J. H. (Ed.) (1968). *Color and race.* New York: Houghton-Mifflin.

Franklin, V. P. (1980a). Black social scientists and the mental testing movement: In R. Jones (Ed.), *Black psychology* (sec. ed.) (pp. 215–226). New York: Harper and Row.

Franklin, V. P. (1980b). Continuity and discontinuity in black and immigrant minority education: A historical perspective. In *Educating an urban people: The New York City experience.* New York: Teachers College Press.

Frazier, E. F. (1932). *The Negro family in Chicago.* Chicago: University of Chicago.

Frazier, E. F. (1957a). *The Negro in the United States* (Rev. Ed.) [orig. published in 1949] (674–678) New York: Macmillan.

Frazier, E. F. (1957b). *Black bourgeoisie.* Illinois: Free Press.

Frazier, E. F. (1964). *The Negro family in the United States* (Rev. Ed.). New York: Macmillan. (Originally published, 1939. Republished in 1966 by the University of Chicago Press).

Frazier, E. F. (1968a). Negro Harlem: An ecological study: In G. F. Edwards (Ed.), *E. Franklin Frazier on race relations: Selected writings* (pp. 142–160). Chicago: University of Chicago.

Frazier, E. F. (1968b). Desegregation as an object of sociological study: In G. F. Edwards (Ed.) *E. Franklin Frazier on race relations.* Chicago: University of Chicago.

French, L. (1976). The incarcerated black female: The case of social double jeopardy. *Journal of Social and Behavioral Sciences, 22,* 334–342.

Freud, A. (1946). *The ego and mechanisms of defense.* New York: International University Press.

Freud, S. (1949). *An outline of psychoanalysis.* New York: International University Press.

Freyberg, J. (1973). Increasing the imaginative play of urban disadvantaged kindergarten children through systematic training: In J. L. Singer (Ed.), *The child's world of make-believe* (pp. 129–154). New York: Academic Press.

Furstenberg, F. F., Jr. (1976). *Unplanned parenthood: The social consequences of teenage childbearing.* New York: Free Press.

Furstenberg, F. F., Jr., & Crawford, A. G. (1978). Family support: Helping teenage mothers to cope. *Family Planning Perspectives, 10,* 322–333.

Furth, H. (1978). Young children's understanding of society: In H. McGurk (Ed.), *Issues in childhood social development* (pp. 228–256). London: Methuen.

Galler, E. H. (1951). Influence of social class on children's choices of occupation. *Elementary School Journal, 51,* 439–445.

Garbarino, J. (1982). Children and families in the social environment. New York: Aldine Press.

Garvey, C. (1974). Some properties of social play. *Merrill Palmer Quarterly, 20,* 163–180.

Garvey, C. (1977). *Play.* Cambridge: Harvard University Press.

Gary, L. (1974). *Social research and the black community.* Washington, D.C.: Institute for Urban Affairs and Research, Howard University.

Gary, L. (1978). Mental health: The problem and the product: In L. Gary (Ed.), *Mental health—a challenge to the black community* (pp. 26–47). Pennsylvania: Dorrance.

Gecas, V. (1979). The influences of social class on socialization. In W. Burr, R. Hill, F. I. Nye & I. Reiss (Eds.), *Contemporary theories about the family, Vol. I: Research-based theories* (pp. 365–404). New York: The Free Press.

Geschwender, J. (1978). *Racial stratification in America.* Dubuque, Iowa: William C. Brown.

Gesten, E. L. (1976). Health resources inventory: The development of a measure of the personal and social competene of primary-grade children. *Journal of Consulting and Clinical Psychology, 44,* 775–786.

Gibson, M. A. (1976). Approaches to multicultural education in the United States: Some concepts and assumptions. *Anthropology and Education Quarterly, 7,* 7–18.

Ginsburg, H. & Opper, S. (1969). *Piaget's theory of intellectual development: An introduction.* NY: Prentice-Hall.

Ginzberg, E., Ginzburg, S. W., Azelrod, S., & Herma, J. L. (1951). *Occupational choice: An approach to a general theory.* New York: Columbia University Press.

Ginzberg, R. (Ed.) (1962). *One hundred years of lynchings.* New York: Lancer.

Gitter, A. G., Black, H., & Mostofsky, D. (1972). Race and sex in the perception of emotion. *Journal of Social Issues, 28,* 63–78.

Gitter, G., Mostofsky, I., & Satow, Y. (1972). The effect of skin color and physiognomy on racial misidentification. *The Journal of Social Psychology, 88,* 139–143.

Glaser, E., & Ross, H. (1970). *A study of successful persons from seriously disadvantaged backgrounds.* Washington, D.C.: Office of Manpower Programs, Department of Labor.

Glazer, N. (1971). Blacks and ethnic groups: The difference, and the political difference it makes. In N. Huggins, M. Kilson, & D. Fox (Eds.), *Key issues in the Afro-American experience.* (Vol. II) New York: Harcourt Brace.

Glazer, N., & Moynihan, D. (1963). *Beyond the melting pot.* Cambridge, Mass.: M.I.T. Press.

Glick, R., & Neto, V. (1977). *The national study of women's correctional programs.* U.S. Department of Justice Publication No. 027-000-00528, Washington, D.C.: U.S. Government Printing Office.

Goldberg, M. L. (1971). Socio-psychological issues in the education of the disadvantaged. In A.

Harry Passow, (Ed.) *Urban Education in the 1970s* (pp. 61–93). New York: Teacher's College Press.

Golden, M., Birns, B., Bridger, W., & Moss, A. (1971). Social class differentiation among black preschool children. *Child Development, 42,* 37–45.

Goldschmidt, W. (1971). Introduction: The theory of cultural adaptation: In Robert B. Edgerton, *The Individual in Cultural Adaptation: A Study of Four East African Peoples* (pp. 1–22). Berkeley: University of California Press.

Goldstein, C., Koopman, E. and Goldstein, H. (1979). Racial attitudes in young children as a function of interracial-contact in the public schools. *American Journal of Orthopsychiatry, 49*(1), 89–99.

Goldstein, J., Freud, A., & Solnit, A. (1979a). *Before the best interests of the child.* New York: The Free Press.

Golomb, C. (1979). Pretense play: A cognitive perspective. In N. Smith & M. Franklin (Eds.), *Symbolic functioning in childhood* (pp. 101–116). New York: Wiley.

Gonzalez, N. S. (1961). Family organization in five types of migratory wage labor. *American Anthropologists, 63*(6), 1264–1280.

Goodman, M. E. (1952). *Race awareness in young children.* NY: Crowell-Collier, 1964. Cambridge, Massachusetts: Addison-Wesley.

Goodspeed, T. (1972). *A history of the University of Chicago: The first quarter-century.* Chicago: University of Chicago. (Originally published, 1916.)

Gordon, C. (1969). *Looking Ahead: Self-Conceptions, Race, and Family Factors as Determinants of Adolescent Achievement Orientation.* Cambridge: Social Relations Department, Harvard University.

Gordon, C. (1972). *Looking ahead: Self-conceptions, race and family as determinants of adolescent orientation to achievement.* Washington, D.C.: American Sociological Association.

Gordon, V. V. (1976). Methodologies of black self-concept research. A critique. *Journal of Afro-American Issues, 4*(3 & 4), 373–381.

Gordon, V. V. (1977). *The self-concept of Black Americans.* Washington, D.C.: University Press of America.

Gouldner, R. (1972). *Child studies through fantasy: Cognitive-affective patterns in development.* New York: Quadrangle Books.

Grant, L. (1984). Black female's "place" in desegregated classrooms. *Sociology of Education, 57,* April 1984, 98–111.

Grant, L. (1982). *Development of Different Schooling Experiences for Children of Varying Race-Sex Statuses. Doctoral dissertation.* University of Michigan, Ann Arbor, Michigan.

Gray, S. W., Ramsey, B., & Klaus, R. A. (1981). *From 3 to 20: The early training project.* Baltimore: University Park Press.

Gray-Little, B. (1982). Marital quality and power processes among black couples. *Journal of Marriage and the Family. 44,* 633–646.

Greeley, A. (1974). *Ethnicity in the United States.* New York: Wiley.

Greeley, A., & Rossi, P. (1966). *The education of Catholic Americans.* Chicago: Aldine Press.

Green, B. (1956). A method of scalogram analysis using summary statistics. *Psychometrica, 21,* 79–88.

Green, H. (1981). Black women in the criminal justice system. *The Urban League Review, 6,* 55–61.

Greene, D., & Winter, D. (1971). Motives, involvements and leadership among black college students. *Journal of Personality, 39*(3), 319–332.

Greene, H. (1946). *Holders of doctorates among American Negroes: An education and social study of Negroes who have earned doctoral degrees in course, 1876–1943.* Boston: Meador.

Greenwald, H. & Oppenheim, D. (1968). Reported magnitude of self-identification among Negro children—artifact? *Journal of Personality and Social Psychology, 8,* 49–52.

Gregor, A. J. & McPherson, D. A. (1966). Racial attitudes among white and negro children in a deep south standard metropolitan area. *Journal of Social Psychology, 68,* 95–106.

Grier, W. H., & Cobbs, P. M. (1968). *Black rage,* New York: Basic Books.

Grier, W. H., & Cobbs, P. M. (1971). *The Jesus bag.* New York: Bantam.

Griffin, Q., & Korchin, S. (1980). Personality competence in black male adolescents. *Journal of Youth and Adolescence, 9*(3), 211–225.

Griffiths, R. (1935). *A study of imagination in early childhood.* London: Kegan Paul.

Grodon, J. (1965). *The poor of Harlem: Social functioning in the underclass.* Washington, D.C.: Report to the Welfare Administration.

Guillory, B. (1974). *The black family: A case for change and survival in white America.* Doctoral dissertation, Tulane University, New Orleans, LA.

Gurin, P. (1969). Internal-external control in the motivational dynamics of negro youth. *Journal of Social Issues. 25,* pp. 29–53.

Gurin, P., & Epps, E. G. (1975). *Black consciousness, identity and achievement.* New York: Wiley.

Gurin, P., & Gurin, G. (1969). *Internal-external control in the motivational dynamics of negro youth.* Ann Arbor, Michigan: Survey Research Center, University of Michigan.

Gurin, P., & Katz, D. (1966). *Motivation and aspiration in the Negro college.* Ann Arbor, Michigan: University of Michigan.

Guthrie, R. (1976). *Even the rat was white.* New York: Harper and Row.

Gutman, H. (1976). *The black family in slavery and freedom, 1850–1925.* New York: Pantheon.

Haan, N. (1963). Proposed model of ego functioning: Coping and defense mechanisms in relationship to I.Q. change. *Psychological Monographs: General and Applied, 77*(8), 1–23.

Hagestad, G. O. (1981). Problems and promises in the social psychology of intergenerational relations. In R. Fogel, E. Hatfield, S. Kiesler, & J. March (Eds.), *Stability and Change in the Family* (pp. 11–46). New York: Academic Press.

Hale, J. (1980). The socialization of black children. *Dimensions, 9,* 43–48.

Haley, K. (1977). Mothers behind bars: A look at the parental rights of incarcerated women. *New England Journal on Prison Law, 4*(1), 141–155.

Hall, E. (1971). *Motivation and achievement in Negro and white students.* Unpublished doctoral dissertation, Department of Psychology, University of Chicago.

Halpern, F. (1973). *Survival: Black/white.* New York: Pergammon Press.

Hamburg, D. A., & Adams, J. E. (1967). A perspective on coping: Seeking and utilizing information in major transitions. *Archives of General Psychiatry, 17,* 277–284.

Hannerz, U. (1969). *Soulside: Inquiries into ghetto culture and community.* New York: Columbia University Press.

Hare, B. R. (1975). The Relationship of Social Background to the Dimensions of Self-Concept. Doctoral dissertation. University of Chicago, *Dissertation Abstracts International, 36,* 4350A.

Hare, B. R. (1977a). Racial and socioeconomic variation in preadolescent area-specific and general self-esteem. *International Journal of Intercultural Relations, 1*(3), 31–51.

Hare, B. R. (1977b). Black and white self-esteem in social science: An overview. *Journal of Negro Education, 46*(2), 141–156.

Hare, B. R. (1979a). Black girls: A comparative analysis of self-perception and achievement by race, sex, and socioeconomic background. *Report No. 271, The Johns Hopkins University Center for the Social Organization of Schools.*

Hare, B. R. (1979b). School desegregation variations in self-perception and achievement: An analysis of three national samples by race, SES, sex and region. Unpublished paper presented at the *American Education Research Association Annual Meeting.* San Francisco, CA.

Hare, B. R. (1980a). *Looking underneath the central tendency: Sex differences within race and race differences within sex.* Prepared for Summer Institute on Life Span Human Development, Center for Advanced Study, Stanford University. Stanford, Calif.

Hare, B. R. (1980b). Self-perception and academic achievement variations in a desegregated setting. *American Journal of Psychiatry, 137*, 683–689.

Hare, N. (1976). What black intellectuals misunderstand about the black family. *Black World, 25*(5), 4–15.

Hareven, T. K. (1981). *Family time and industrial time*. New York: Cambridge University Press.

Harlow, H. F., & Harlow, M. K. (1966). Learning to love. *American Scientist, 54*, 244–272.

Harootunian, B., & Morse, R. (1968). *Characteristics of Negro and white high school students prior to desegregation*. Washington, D.C.: U.S. Gov't. Printing Office.

Harris, M. (1979). Research strategies and the structure of science: In *Culture materialism: The struggle for a science of culture* (pp. 5–28). NY: Random House.

Harrison, B. (1972). *Education, Training, and the Urban Ghetto*. Baltimore, Md.: The Johns Hopkins University Press.

Hartley, R. (1960). Children's concepts of male and female roles. Merril-Palmer Quarterly, 6, 83–91.

Hartley, R. (1961a). What aspects of child behavior should be studied in relation to maternal employment: In A. E. Siegal (Ed.), *Research: Issues related to effects of maternal employment on children* (pp. 41–50). University Park, Pa.: Pennsylvania State University.

Hartley, R. (1961b). Current patterns in sex roles: Children's perspectives. *Journal of the National Association of Women, Deans and Counselors, 25*, 3–13.

Hartmann, H. (1958). *Ego psychology and the problem of adaptation* (translated by D. Rapaport). New York: International University Press.

Harvey, W. B. (1977). *The Black male: Attempted victim of cultural assassination*. Unpublished paper presented at the Fourth Annual National Conference on the Black Family, Louisville, Kentucky.

Havighurst, R. (1969). Social class factors in coping style and competence. Committee on Human Development, University of Chicago, unpublished paper.

Haynes, T., & Johnson, L. (1980). *Changing perspectives on black families in empirical research: Selected journals, 1965–1979*. (Unpublished manuscript), Washington, D.C.: The Urban Institute.

Hays, W. L. (1972). *Statistics for the Social Sciences* (2nd Ed.). New York: Holt, Rinehart and Winston, Inc.

Heider, F. (1958). *The psychology of interpersonal relations*. New York: Wiley.

Heiss, J. (1975). *The case of the black family: A sociological inquiry*. New York: Columbia University Press.

Henriques, Z. (1977). Intervention programs for incarcerated mothers and their children. Paper presented to the meeting of the American Correctional Association, Milwaukee, Wisconsin.

Herrnstein, R. (1971, September). I.Q. *Atlantic Monthly, 118*, pp. 44–64.

Herron, R. E., & Sutton-Smith, B. (Eds.) (1971). *Child's play*. New York: Wiley.

Herskovits, M. J. (1936). The significance of West Africa for Negro research. *The Journal of Negro History, 21*, pp. 15–30.

Herskovits, M. J. (1941). *The Myth of the Negro Past*. Boston: Beacon Press.

Hess, R. (1970). Social class and ethnic influences on socialization. In P. Mussen (Ed.), *Carmichael's manual on child psychology* (Vol. 2) (pp. 457–458). New York: Wiley.

Hess, R., & Bear, R. (Eds.) (1968). *Early education: Current theory, research and practice*. Chicago: Aldine.

Hess, R., & Shipman, V. (1965). Early experience and the socialization of cognitive modes in children. *Child Development, 34*, 869–886.

Hess, R., & Shipman, V. (1970). Cognitive elements in maternal behavior: In J. Hill (Ed.), *Minnesota Symposia on Child Psychology* (Vol. 1). Minneapolis: University of Minnesota, 1967, 58. 1970, 457–558.

Hickerson, R. (1980). *Survival strategies and role models in the ghetto.* Unpublished manuscript, Department of Anthropology, University of California, Berkeley.

Hill, K., & Sarason, S. (1966). The relation of test anxiety and defensiveness to test and school performance over the elementary-school years: A future longitudinal study. *Monograph of the Society for Research in Child Development, 31* (2, Serial No. 104).

Hill, R. (1964). Methodological issues in family development research. *Family Processes, 3,* 186–206.

Hill, R. (1972). *The strengths of black families.* New York: Emerson-Hall.

Hinds, L. (1980). The impact of incarceration on low-income families. Washington, D.C.: National Community Action Agency Executive Directors Association.

Hofferth, S. L. (1984). Children's trajectories to adulthood. In G. H. Elder, Jr. (Ed.), *Life course dynamics: From 1963 to the 1980s.* Ithaca: Cornell University Press.

Hoffman, L. W., & Nye, F. I. (Eds.). (1974). *Working mothers.* San Francisco, CA: Jossey-Bass.

Hoffman, L. W. (1974). Effects of maternal employment on the child—a review of the research, *Developmental Psychology, 10,* 204–228.

Hoffman, S. (1977). *What happens when a mother goes to prison?: An overview of relevant legal and psychological considerations.* Snowmass, Colorado: Annual Meeting of the American Psychology-Law Society. (ERIC Document Reproduction Service No. ED154322).

Hogan, D. P. (1981). *Transitions and social change.* New York: Academic Press.

Holleb, D. (1972). *Colleges and the urban poor.* Lexington, Mass.: Lexington Books, D. C. Heath.

Holliday, B. G. (1978). *The ecological mapping of behavioral competencies of latency age black children in the life spheres of home, neighborhood and school.* Unpublished doctoral dissertation, University of Texas, Austin.

Holliday, B. G. (1981). The imperatives of development and ecology: Lessons learned from black children: In J. McAdoo, H. McAdoo, & W. E. Cross, Jr. (Eds.), *Fifth conference on empirical research in black psychology* (pp. 50–64). Washington, D.C.: National Institute of Mental Health.

Hollingshead, A. B. (1957). *Two factor index of social position.* New Haven, Connecticutt.

Hollingshead, A. B., & Redlich, F. (1958). *Social class and mental illness: A community study.* New York: Wiley.

Holt, G. S. (1972). Stylin' outta the black pulpit: In Thomas Kochman, (Ed.), *Rappin' and stylin' out: Communication in urban black America* (pp. 189–204). Urbana: University of Illinois.

Horner, M. S. (1968). *Sex differences in achievement motivation and performance in competitive and noncompetitive situations.* Unpublished doctoral dissertation, University of Michigan.

Horner, M. S. (1972). Toward an understanding of achievement related conflicts in women. *Journal of Social Issues, 28*(2), 157–168.

Horowitz, R. E. (1939). Racial aspects of self-identification in nursery school children. *Journal of Psychology, 7,* 91–99.

Horton, J. (1970). Time and cool people. In L. Rainwater, (Ed.), *Soul.* (pp. 31–50). Chicago: Aldine Press.

Hraba, J. & Grant, G. (1970). Black is beautiful. A reexamination of racial preference and identity. *Journal of Personality and Social Psychology, 16*(3), 398–402.

Hudson, J. (1972). The Hustling Ethic. In Thomas Kochman, (Ed.), *Rappin' and stylin' out: Communication in urban black America* (pp. 410–424). Chicago: University of Ill. Press.

Huizinga, J. (1950). *Homo Ludens: A study of the play element in culture.* Boston: Beacon Press.

Hunt, D. E., & Hardt, R. H. (1969). The effects of upward bound programs on the attitudes, motivation, and academic achievement of Negro students. *Journal of Social Issues, 225,* 122–124.

Hunt, J., McV. (1969). *The challenge of incompetence and poverty: Papers on the role of early education.* Urbana: University of Ill.

Hunt, J., McV. & Hunt, L. (1977). Racial inequality and self-image . . . identity maintenance as identity diffusion. *Sociology and Social Research, 61*(4), 539–559.

Hunter, A. (1980). Why Chicago? The rise of the Chicago school of urban social science. *American Behavioral Scientist, 24*(2), 215–227.

Hunter, D. (1980, August). My Turn: Ducks Vs. Hard Rocks. *Newsweek*, p. 14–15.

Hyman, H. (1953). The value systems of different classes. In S. Lipset (Ed.), *Class status and power*. Illinois: Free Press.

Hyman, H., & Reed, J. S. (1969). Black matriarchy reconsidered: Evidence from secondary analysis of sample surveys. *Public Opinion Quarterly, 33*, 346–354.

Hyman, J. J., & Singer, E. (1968). *Readings in reference group theory and research*. New York: McGraw-Hill.

Inhelder, B. & Piaget, J. (1964). *The early growth of logic in the child classification and seriation*. NY: Harper & Row.

Inkeles, A. (1968). Society, social structure, and child socialization. In John A. Clausen, (Ed.), *Socialization and Society* (pp. 73–129). Boston: Little, Brown.

Isaacs, H. R. (1968). Group identity and political change: The role of color and physical characteristics: In J. H. Franklin (Ed.), *Color and race* (pp. 75–97). Boston: Houghton Mifflin.

Isaacs, S. (1930). *Intellectual growth in young children*. New York: Harcourt Brace.

Janowitz, M. (1972). Professionalization of sociology. *American Journal of Sociology, 78*, 105–135.

Janowitz, M. (1978). *The last half-century: Societal change and politics in America*. Chicago: University of Chicago.

Jencks, C., *et al.* (1972). *Inequality: A reassessment of the effect of family and schooling in America*. New York: Harper Colophon.

Jensen, A. R. (1969). How much can be boost IQ and scholastic achievement? *Harvard Educational Review, 39*, 1–123.

Johnson, C. (1967). *Growing up in the black belt*. New York: Schocken. (Originally published, 1941.)

Johnson, C. (1934). *Shadow of the plantation*. Chicago: University of Chicago Press.

Johnson, C., & Weatherford, W. (1934). *Race relations: Adjustment of whites and negroes in the United States*. Boston: D. C. Heath.

Johnson, J. E. (1976). Relations of divergent thinking and intelligence test scores with social and nonsocial make-believe play of preschool children. *Child Development, 47*, 1200–1203.

Jones, J. M. (1972). *Prejudice and Racism*. Reading, Mass.: Addison-Wesley.

Kagan, J. (1958). The concept of identification. *Psychological Review, 65*, 296–305.

Kallingal, A. (1971). The prediction of grades for black and white students at Michigan State University. *Journal of Educational Measurement, 8*(4), 263–265.

Kamin, L. (1974). *The science and politics of I.Q.* Potomac, Maryland: Erlbaum Associates.

Kaplan, D. & Manners, R. M. (1970). *Culture theory*. Englewood Cliffs, N.J.: Prentice-Hall.

Karabel, J. (1967–68). Community college and social stratification. *Harvard Educational Review, 66*, 6–13.

Kardiner, A., & Oversey, L. (1951). *The mark of oppression*. New York: Norton.

Karnes, M., Teska, J., Hodgins, A., & Badger, E. (1970). Educational intervention at home by mothers of disadvantaged infants. *Child Development, 41*, 925–935.

Katz, I. (1967). The socialization of academic motivation in minority group children: In D. Levine (Ed.), *Nebraska Symposium on Motivation* (pp. 133–196). Lincoln, Neb.: University of Nebraska Press.

Katz, I. (1968). Academic motivation and equal educational opportunity. *Harvard Educational Review*, XXXVIII.

Katz, I. (1969). A critique of personality approaches to negro children, with research suggestions. *Journal of Social Issues, 25*, (3), 13–27.

Katz, I., & Benjamin, L. (1960). Effects of white authoritarianism on biracial work groups. *Journal of Abnormal and Social Psychology, 61,* 448–456.

Katz, I., & Cohen, M. (1962). The effects of training Negroes upon cooperative problem solving in biracial teams. *Journal of Abnormal and Social Psychology, 64,* 319–325.

Katz, I., & Deutsch, M. (Eds.) (1968). *Social class, race and psychological Development.* New York: Holt, Rinehart and Winston.

Katz, I., Epps, E. G., & Axelson, L. J. (1964). Effect upon Negro digit-symbol performance of anticipated comparison with whites and with other Negroes. *Journal of Abnormal and Social Psychology, 69,* 77–83.

Katz, I., Henchy, T., & Allen, H. (1968). Effects of race of tester, approval-disapproval and need on learning in negro boys. *Journal of Personality and Social Psychology, 8,* 38–42.

Katz, P. A. (1976). The acquisition of racial attitudes in children. In P. A. Katz (Ed.), *Towards the elimination of racism.* NY: Pergamon Press.

Keil, C. (1966). *Urban blues.* Chicago: University of Chicago Press.

Kellam, S. G., Ensminger, M. E., & Turner, R. J. (1977). Family structure and the mental health of children. *Archives of General Psychiatry, 34,* 1012–1022.

Kellam, S. G., Adams, R. G., Brown, C. H., & Ensminger, M. E. (1982). The long-term evolution of the family structure of teenage and older mothers. *Journal of Marriage and the Family, 44,* 343–359.

Kelley, H. H. (1967). Attribution theory in social psychology. In D. Levine (Ed.), *Nebraska Symposium on Motivation.* Omaha: University of Nebraska Press, 192–238.

Kerber, S. & Bommarito, B. (1965). Preschool education for the developing cortex: In Kerber and Bommarito, (Eds.), *The schools and the urban crisis* (pp. 345–349). New York: Holt, Rinehart and Winston.

King, J. (1976). African survivals in the black American family—key factors in stability. *Journal of Afro-American Issues, 4*(2), 153–167.

Kirchner, E. P., & Vondracek, S. I. (1973). *What do you want to be when you grow up? Vocational choice in children aged three to six.* Paper presented at the biennial meeting of the Society for Research in Child Development, Philadelphia.

Kirk, R. E. (1968). *Experimental design: Procedures for the behavioral sciences.* Belmont, CA: Brooks/Cole.

Kish, L. (1965). *Survey sampling.* New York: Wiley.

Klein, D. (1976). The etiology of female crime: A review of the literature. *Issues in Criminology, 8,* 5–31.

Kleinke, C. and Nicholson, T. (1979). Black and white children's awareness of defacto race and sex differences. *Developmental Psychology, 15*(1), 84–86.

Knoell, D. M. (1965). Factors effecting performance of transfer students from two- to four-year colleges: With implications for coordination and articulation. *Junior College Journal, 35,* 5–9.

Knowles, L. L. & Prewitt, K. (Eds.) (1969). *Institutional racism in America,* Englewood Cliffs, NJ: Prentice-Hall.

Kochman, T. (1972). *Rappin' and stylin' out.* Chicago: University of Illinois Press.

Kogan, N. (1976). *Cognitive styles in infancy and early childhood.* Hillsdale, N.J.: Wiley.

Kohlberg, L. (1963). Stage and sequence: The cognitive-developmental approach to socialization: In D. Goslin (Ed.), *Handbook of Socialization: Theory and Research* (pp. 347–480). New York: Rand McNally and Col.

Kohlberg, L. (1966). A cognitive-developmental analysis of children's sex-role concepts and attitudes: In E. Maccoby (Ed.), *The development of sex differences* (pp. 82–113). Stanford, Calif. Stanford University Press.

Kohlberg, L. (1969). Stage and sequence: The cognitive-developmental approach to socialization. In Goslin (Ed.), *Handbook of Socialization Theory and Research.* (pp. 347–480) Chicago: Rand McNally.

Kohlberg, L. & Ullian, D. (1974). Stages in the development of psychosexual concepts and attitudes: In R. Friedman, R. Richart and R. Vande Wiele (Eds.), *Sex Differences in Behavior.* New York: Wiley.

Kohlberg, L., & Zigler, E. (1967). The impact of cognitive maturity on the development of sex role attitudes in the years four to eight. *Genetic Psychology Monographs, 75,* 89–165.

Kohn, M. (1969a). *Class and conformity: A study in values.* Homewood, Ill.: Dorsey Press.

Kohn, M. L. (1969b). Social class and parent-child relationships: An interpretation: In Rose Laub Coser, (Ed.), *Life Cycle and Achievement in America* (pp. 21–48). New York: Harper and Row.

Kuhn, M., & McPartland, T. (1965). An empirical investigation of self attitudes. *American Sociological Review, 19,* 68–75.

Kuhn, T. S. (1970). *The Structure of Scientific Revolutions,* 2nd edition. Chicago: University of Chicago Press.

Kunkel, P., & Kennard, S. S. (1971). *Spout spring: A black community.* New York: Holt, Rinehart and Winston.

Kuvlesky, W. P., & Bealer, R. C. (1966). A clarification of the concept of occupational choice. *Rural Sociology, 31,* 268–276.

Labov, W. (1972). *Language in the inner city: Studies in the black english vernacular.* Philadelphia: The University of Pennsylvania Press.

Labov, W. (1972). Academic ignorance and black intelligence. *Atlantic Monthly, 229*(6), 59–67.

Ladner, J. (1971). *Tomorrow's tomorrow: The black woman.* New York: Doubleday.

Ladner, J. (Ed.) (1973). *The death of white sociology.* New York: Vintage Books.

Ladner, J. A. (1978). Growing up black. In Juanita H. Williams, (Ed.), *Psychology of Women: Selected Writings* (pp. 212–224). New York: W. W. Norton & Co.

Lakatos, I. (1970). Falsification and the methodology of scientific research programes. In I. Lakatos and A. Musgrave (Eds.), *Criticism and the Growth of Knowledge.* Cambridge: Cambridge University Press.

Lambert, N., Windmiller, M. & Cole, L. (1974). *AAMD adaptive behavior scale, public school version, 1974 version.* Washington, D.C.: American Association on Mental Deficiency.

Landis, J. R., & Scarpitti, F. R. (1965). Perceptions regarding value orientation and legitimate opportunity. *Social Forces, 44,* 83–91.

Landreth, C., & Johnson, B. (1953). Young children's responses to a picture inset test designed to reveal reactions to persons of different skin color. *Child Development, 24,* 63–80.

Lavin, D. E. (1965). *The prediction of academic performance.* New York: Russell Sage Foundation.

Lazar, I., & Darlington, R. (1979). *Lasting effects after preschool,* DHEW publications, No. (OHDS) 79-30179.

Lazarus, R., Averill, J., & Opton, E. (1974). The psychology of coping: Issues of research and assessment. *Coping and adaptation.* (pp. 249–315.) New York: Basic Books.

LaPoint, V. (1977). Mothers inside, children outside: Some issues surrounding imprisoned mothers and their children. *Proceedings of the 107th Annual Congress of Corrections of the American Correctional Association.* Maryland: American Correctional Association, 274–284.

LaPoint, V. (1980). *The impact of incarceration on families: Research and policy issues.* Paper presented to the Research Forum on Family Issues, National Advisory Committee of the White House Conference on Families, Washington, D.C.

LaPoint, V., & Mann, C. R. (1982). *Incarcerated parents and their children.* Washington, D.C.: U.S. Government Printing Office.

Leacock, E. B. (1969). *Teaching and learning in city schools.* New York: Basic Books.

Lecky, P. (1945). *Self-consistency: A theory of personality.* New York: Island Press.

Lerner, G. (Ed.) (1973). *Black women in white America.* New York: Vintage Books.

Lesser, G., Fifer, G., & Clark, D. (1965). Mental abilities of children from different social class and cultural groups. *Monographs of the Society for Research in Child Development, 30,* (serial no. 102).

Lessing, E. E. (1969). Racial differences in indices of ego functioning relevant to academic achievement. *Journal of Genetic Psychology, 115,* 153–167.

Lester, J. (1971). *The seventh son: the thoughts and writings of W. E. B. DuBois. Vol. 1,* N.Y.: Vintage Books.

Levine, L. (1977). *Black culture and Black consciousness: Afro-American folk thought from slavery to freedom.* New York: Oxford University Press.

LeVine, R. A. (1977). Child Rearing as Cultural Adaptation. In P. Herbert Leiderman, S. T. Tulkin and A. Rosenfeld, (Eds.), *Culture and Infancy: Variations In The Human Experience,* (pp. 15–27). New York: Academic Press.

Levinson, D. J. (1980). Toward a conception of the adult life course: In N. J. Smelser & E. H. Erikson (Eds.), *Themes of work and love in adulthood* (pp. 265–290). Cambridge, Mass.: Harvard University Press.

Lewin, K. (1948). *Resolving social conflicts.* New York: Harper & Row.

Lewin, K. (1951). *Field theory in social science.* New York: Harper & Row.

Lewin, K. (1954). Behavior and development as a function of the total situation: In L. Charmichael (Ed.), *Manual of child psychology* (2nd ed.). New York: Wiley.

Lewis, D. (1975). The black family: Socialization and sex roles. *Phylon, 36,* 221–237.

Lewis, H. (1936). *Social differentiation in the Negro community* Master's thesis, Department of Sociology, University of Chicago.

Lewis, H. (1955). *Blackways of Kent.* Chapel Hill: University of North Carolina.

Lewis, M., & Brooks-Gunn, J. (1979). *Social cognition and the acquisition of self.* New York: Plenum Press.

Lewis, O. (1966). The culture of poverty. *Scientific American, 215,* pp. 19–25.

LeVine, R. A. (1967). *Dreams and deeds: Achievement motivations in Nigeria.* Chicago: University of Chicago Press.

Lieberman, J. N. (1965). Playfulness and divergent thinking: An investigation of their relationship at the kindergarten level. *Journal of Genetic Psychology, 107,* 219–224.

Lightfoot, S. L. (1978). *Worlds Apart: Relationships Between Families and Schools.* New York: Basic Books.

Linn, R. L., & Werts, C. E. (1971). Considerations for studies of test bias. *Journal of Educational Measurement, 8,* 1–4.

Lippman, W. (1914). *Drift and mastery.* New York: Mitchell Kennerly.

Loevinger, J., & Wessler, R. (1970). *Measuring ego development, Vol. 1.* San Francisco: Jossey-Bass.

Logan, R. (1969). *The betrayal of the Negro, from Rutherford B. Hayes to Woodrow Wilson.* London: Collier-Macmillan.

Looft, W. R. (1971). Sex differences in the expression of vocational aspirations by elementary school children. *Developmental Psychology, 5,* 336.

Lovell, J. (1972). *Black song: The forge and the flame.* New York: Macmillan.

Lovinger, S. L. (1974). Sociodramatic play and language development in preschool disadvantaged children. *Psychology in the Schools, 11,* 312–320.

Lundberg, D., Sheekley, A., & Voekler, T. (1975). *An exploration of the feelings and attitudes of women separated from their children due to incarceration.* Unpublished master's thesis, Portland State University.

Lyman, S. (1972). *The black American in sociological thought: A failure of perspective.* New York: Capricorn.

Lynd, R. S., & Lynd, H. M. (1929). *Middletown: A study in contemporary American culture.* New York: Harcourt, Brace.

Maccoby, E., & Gibbs, P. K. (1954). Methods in childrearing in two social classes. In W. Martin & C. B. Stendler (Eds.), *Readings in child psychology* (pp. 390–396). New York: Harcourt, Brace.

Maccoby, E., & Jacklin, C. (1974). *The psychology of sex differences*. Stanford, Calif.: Stanford University Press.

Maehr, M., & Lysy, A. (1978). Motivating students of diverse sociocultural backgrounds to achieve. *International Journal of Intercultural Relations, 2*(1), 38–70.

Maehr, M. L. (1971). Atkinson's theory of achievement motivation: First step toward a theory of academic motivation. *Review of Educational Research, 41*(2), 143–161.

Mahan, J. (1976). Black and white children's racial identification and preference. *Journal of Black Psychology, 3*(1), 47–58.

Mann, C. R. (1980). Personal communication.

Marcus, D. & Overton, W. (1974). The development of cognitive gender constancy and sex role preferences. *Child Development, 49,* 434–444.

Marcuse, H. (1964). *One-dimensional man*. Boston: Beacon Press.

Marcuse, H. (1960). *Reason and Revolution*. Boston: Beacon Press.

Martin, B. (1975). Parent-child relations: In F. D. Horowitz (Ed.), *Review of child development research* (Volume 4) (pp. 463–540). Chicago: University of Chicago Press.

Martin, E., & Martin, J. (1978). *The black extended family*. Chicago: University of Chicago.

Martin, T. (1976). *Race first*. Westport, CT: Greenwood Press.

Matthews, F. (1977). *Quest for an American sociology*. Montreal: McGill-Queen's University Press.

Matthews, W. (1977). Modes of transformation in the initiation of fantasy play. *Developmental Psychology, 13,* 212–216.

Mayer, P. (1970). *Socialization: The approach from social anthropology*. London: Tavistock.

McAdoo, H. (1973). An assessment of racial attitudes and self-concepts in urban Black children. Office of Child Development, No. OCD-CD-282.

McAdoo, H. P. (1977, December). The development of self-concept and race attitudes in black children: A longitudinal study. *The Third Conference on Empirical Research in Black Psychology,* Cross, W. E., (Ed.) NIE(DHEW), 47–64.

McAdoo, H. P. (1978). Factors related to upwardly mobile Black families. *Journal of Marriage and the Family, 40,* 61–69.

McAdoo, H. P. (1979). Father-child interaction patterns and self-esteem in Black preschool children. *Young Children, 34,* 46–53.

McAdoo, H. P. (1980). Black mothers and the extended family support network. In La Frances Rodgers-Rose (Ed.), *The Black Woman*. Beverly Hills, CA: Sage.

McCall, C. (1980). Pleasanton Children's Center program—second year report and evaluation, 1979–1980. California: National Council on Crime and Delinquency.

McCarthy, B. R. (1980). Inmate mothers: The problems of separation and reintegration. *Journal of Offender Counseling, Services and Rehabilitation, 4*(3), 199–212.

McCarthy, J., & Yancey, W. (1971). Uncle Tom and Mr. Charlie: Meta physical pathos in the study of racism and personal disorganization. *American Journal of Sociology, 71*(4), 648–672.

McClelland, D. (1961). *The achieving society*. Princeton, NJ: Van Nostrand.

McClelland, D. C., & Atkinson, J. (1953). *The achievement motive*. New York: Appleton-Century.

McCord, W., Howard, J., Friedberg, B. & Harwood, E. (1969). *Life styles in the black ghetto*. New York: W. W. Norton.

McCubbin, H. I., Joy, C. B., Cauble A. E., Comeau, J. K., Patterson, J. M., & Needle, R. H. (1980). Family stress and coping: A decade review. *Journal of Marriage and the Family, 42,* 855–871.

McDill, E., Meyers, E., & Rigby, L. (1966). *Sources of educational climate in high schools*. Baltimore: Johns Hopkins University.

McGhee, P. E., Ethudge, O. L. & Benz, N. A. (1981). Effects of level of toy structure on preschool children's pretend play. Unpublished manuscript. Lubbock, Tex.: Texas Technological University.

McGowan, B., & Blumenthal, K. (1978). *Why punish the children?—A study of children of women prisoners.* New Jersey: National Council on Crime and Delinquency.

McGuire, W., & Padawer-Singer, A. (1976). Trait salience in the spontaneous self-concept. *Journal of Personality and Social Psychology, 33,* 745–754.

McLoyd, V. C. (1979). Verbal interaction in social play: Mixed-age, preschool dyads. *Journal of Black Studies, 9,* 469–488.

McLoyd, V. C. (1980). Verbally expressed modes of transformation in the fantasy play of black preschool children. *Child Development, 51,* 1133–1139.

McLoyd, V. C. (1981). *Social class differences in sociodramatic play: A critical review.* Unpublished manuscript. Ann Arbor: University of Michigan.

McQueen, R., & Browning, C. (1960). Intelligence and educational achievement of a matched sample of white and Negro students. *School and Society, 88,* 327–329.

McWorter, G. (1967). *The political sociology of the Negro: A selective review of the literature.* New York: Anti-Defamation League of B'nai B'rith.

Mead, G. H. (1934). *Mind, self and society: From the standpoint of a behaviorist.* Chicago: University of Chicago Press.

Mead, M. (1939). *From the South Seas: Studies of adolescence and sex in primitive societies.* New York: William Morrow.

Means, R. (1980). Fighting words on the future of the earth. *Mother Jones, 5*(10), 12–38.

Mechanic, D. (1962). *Students under stress.* New York: Free Press.

Mednick, M. T., & Puryear, G. R. (1975). Motivational and personality factors related to career goals of black college women. *Journal of Social and Behavioral Sciences, 21*(1), 1–30.

Mehrabian, A. (1968). Male and female scales of the tendency to achieve. *Educational and Psychological measurement, 28,* 493–502.

Mehrabian, A. (1969). Measures of achieving tendency. *Educational and Psychology Measurement, 29,* 445–451.

Mercer, J. R. & Lewis, J. F. (1980). *System of multicultural pluralistic assessment (SOMPA)—Adaptive behavior inventory for children.* New York: The Psychological Corporation.

Merton, R. K. (1968). *Social theory and social structure.* New York: Free Press.

Middleton, R., & Putney, S. (1960). Dominance in decisions in the family: Race and class differences. *American Journal of Sociology, 65,* 605–609.

Miller, D., & Swanson, G. (1958). *The changing American parent.* New York: Wiley.

Miller, D. M., & O'Connor, P. (1969). Achiever personality and academic success among disadvantaged college students. *Journal of Social Issues, 25,* 103–116.

Miller, L. (Ed.) (1974). *The testing of black students—A symposium.* Englewood Cliffs, New Jersey: Prentice-Hall, Inc.

Miller, S. M. (1975). The effects of maternal employment of sex role perception, interest, and self-esteem in kindergarten girls. Mimeo.

Milner, C. A. (1970). *Black pimps and their prostitutes: Social organization and value system of a ghetto occupational subculture.* Unpublished dissertation, Department of Anthropology, University of California, Berkeley.

Minuchin, P., Biber, R., Shapiro, E., & Zimiles, H. (1969). *The Psychological impact of school experience.* New York: Basic Books, Inc.

Mischel, W. (1966). A social learning view of sex differences in behavior. In E. Maccoby, (Ed.), *The development of sex differences* (pp. 56–81). Palo Alto: Stanford University Press.

Mischel, W. (1970). Sex typing the socialization in P. H. Mussen (Ed.), *Charmichael's manual of child psychology,* (pp. 3–72) Vol. 2, New York: Wiley.

Mitchell-Kernan, C. (1972). Signifying, loud-talking, and marking. In Thomas Kochman, (Ed.), *Rappin' and stylin' out: Communication in urban black America* (pp. 315–335). Chicago: University of Illinois Press.

Mobley, B. D. (1973). *Self-concept and the conceptualization of ethnic identity: The black experience.* Unpublished doctoral dissertation, Purdue University. (University Microfilm #74-5017.)

Moen, P., Kain, E., & Elder, G. H., Jr. (1983). Economic conditions and family life: Contemporary and historical perspectives: In R. Nelson (Ed.), *American families and the economy* (pp. 213–254). Washington: National Academy Press.

Montague, A. (1972). *Statement on Race* (3rd Ed.). New York: Oxford University Press.

Moore, E. (1980). *The effects of cultural style on black children's intelligence test achievement.* Unpublished Doctoral Dissertation, University of Chicago.

Moore, N. V., Evertson, C. M., & Brophy, J. E. (1974). Solitary play: Some functional reconsiderations. *Developmental Psychology, 10,* 830–834.

Moos, R. H. (1979). *Evaluating educational environments: Procedures, measures, findings and policy implications.* San Francisco, CA: Jossey-Bass.

Morland, J. K. (1958). Racial recognition by nursery school children in Lynchburg, Va. *Social Forces, 37,* 132–137.

Morland, K. (1966). A comparison of race awareness in northern and southern children. *American Journal of Orthopsychiatry, 36,* 23–31.

Moynihan, D. (1965). *The Negro family: The case for national action.* U.S. Department of Labor: Office of Planning and Research.

Murphy, L. (1962). *The widening world of childhood.* New York: Basic Books.

Murphy, L. B. (1972): Infants' play and cognitive development. In M. W. Piers (Ed.), *Play and cognitive development* (pp. 119–126). New York: Norton.

Myers, H. F., Rana, P. G., & Harris, M. (1979). *Black child development in America 1972–77.* Connecticutt: Greenwood Press.

Myrdal, G. (1944). *An American dilemma: The negro problem and modern democracy. (pp. 928–930), New York: Harper and Row.*

*National assessment of education progress. (1976). Education for citizenship* (Citizenship/Social Studies Report No. 07-CS-01). Washington, D.C.: U.S. Government Printing Office.

National Coalition for Jail Reform. (1984). *Women in Jails.* Washington, D.C.: Author.

National Minority Advisory Council on Criminal Justice (1982). The inequality of justice: A report on crime and the administration of justice for the minority community. Washington, D.C.: Department of Justice.

National Urban Coalition. (1976). *Final summary report and recommendations of the national minority conference on human experimentation.* Washington, D.C.: Author.

Nelson, R. R. & Skidmore, S. (1982). American families and the economy: *The high cost of living.*

Newman, D. K., Amidei, B. K., Carter, D. D., Kruvant, W. J. & Russell, J. S. (1978). *Protest, politics, and prosperity: black Americans and white institutions, 1940–1975.* New York: Pantheon Books.

Netting, R. (1968). *Hill farmers of Nigeria: Cultural ecology of the Jos Plateau.* Seattle: University of Washington Press.

Newmann, E. A. (1971). *The elements of play.* New York: MSS Information Co.

*New York Times,* 14 August 1982, p. 18.

Nichols, P., & Anderson, V. (1973). Intellectual performance, race, and socioeconomic status. *Social Biology, 20,* 367–374.

Nie, N. H. et al. (1975). *Statistical package for the social sciences.* Second Edition. New York: McGraw-Hill Book Co.

Nobles, W. (1976). *A formulative and empirical study of black families.* Final report to Department of Health, Education and Welfare, Office of Child Development.

Nobles, W. W. & Traver, S. (1976). Black parental involvement in education: The African connection. *In Child welfare and child development: Alton M. Childs Series* (pp. 23–36). Atlanta, Ga.: Atlanta University School of Social Work.

Nobles, W. W. (1978a). African consciousness and liberation struggles: Implications for the development and construction of scientific paradigms. In R. L. Williams (Ed.), *Selected Papers. Beyond Survival: The Practical Role of Black Psychology in Enhancing Black Life.* The St. Louis Association of Black Psychologists.

Nobles, W. W. (1973). Psychological research and the black self-concept: A critical review. *Journal of Social Issues, 29*(1), 11–31.

Nobles, W. W. (1978). Toward an empirical and theoretical framework for defining Black families. *Journal of Marriage and the Family, 40*, 679–688.

Nunnally, J. (1967). *Psychometric theory.* New York: McGraw-Hill Book Co.

Nuttall, R. L. (1964). Some correlates of high need for achievement among urban northern Negroes. *Journal of Abnormal and Social Psychology, 68*, 593–600.

Ogbu, J. U. (1974). Cultural discontinuities and schooling. *Anthropology and Education Quarterly, 13*, pp. 290–307.

Ogbu, J. U. (1974). *The next generation: An ethnography of education in an urban neighborhood.* New York: Academic Press.

Ogbu, J. U. (1978). *Minority education and caste: The American system in cross-cultural perspective.* New York: Academic Press.

Ogbu, J. U. (1979). Social stratification and Socialization of Competence. *Anthropology and Education Quarterly, 10*, 3–20.

Ogbu, J. U. (1980). *An Ecological Approach to Minority Education.* Unp. Ms.

Ogbu, J. U. (1981a). Education, clientage, and social mobility: caste and social change in the United States and Nigeria. In G. D. Berreman, (Ed.), *Social inequality: comparative and developmental approaches* (pp. 277–306). New York: Academic Press.

Ogbu, J. U. (1981b). Origins of human competence: A cultural-ecological perspective. *Child Development, 52*, 413–429.

Ogbu, J. U. (in press). *Cultural Discontinuities and Schooling.*

Ogletree, E. (1969). Skin color preference of the Negro child. *Journal of Social Psychology, 79*(1), 143–144.

Oppenheimer, V. K. (1981). The changing nature of life-cycle squeezes: Implications for the socioeconomic position of the elderly. In R. W. Fugel et al. (Eds.), *Aging: Stability and change in the family* (pp. 47–81). New York: Academic Press.

Overton, W. F., & Jackson, J. P. (1973). The representation of imagined objects in action sequences: A developmental study. *Child Development, 44*, 309–314.

Owens, C. (1977). *Mental health and black offenders.* Massachusetts: D. C. Health & Co.

Owens, C., & Bell, J. (1977). *Blacks and criminal justice.* Mass.: D. C. Health.

Pallone, N. G., Hurley, R. B., & Rickard, F. S. (1973). Further data on key influences of occupational aspirations among minority youth. *Journal of Counseling Psychology, 20*, 484–486.

Pallone, N. G., Rickard, F. S., & Hurley, R. B. (1970). Key influences of occupational preference among black youths. *Journal of Counseling Psychology, 17*, 498–50.

Park, R. (1952). *Human communities: The city and human ecology.* Glencoe: Free Press.

Parsons, T. (1959). The school class as social system: Some of its functions in American society. *Harvard Educational Review, 29*, 297–318.

Parten, M. (1932). Social participation among preschool children. *Journal of Abnormal and Social Psychology, 27*, 243–269.

Passow, H. A. (Ed.) (1963). *Education in depressed areas.* New York: Teachers College, Columbia University.

Paton, S., Walberg, H., & Yeh, E. (1973). Ethnicity, environmental control, and academic self-concept in Chicago. *American Educational Research Journal, 10*, 85–99.

Peck, R. (1968). Developing internationally acceptable concepts and measures of effective coping behavior. University of Texas at Austin: Presented at the annual meeting of the American Psychological Association, Washington, D. C.

Peller, L. (1952). Models of children's play. *Mental Hygiene, 36*, 66–83.

Peoples College (1975). *Introduction to Afro-American Studies* (Vols. 1, 2). Chicago: Author.

Perkins, E. (1975). *Home is a dirty street.* Chicago: Third World Press.

Perlman, H. (1982). Incarcerated parents and their children—the uniform law commissioner's model sentencing and corrections act: In V. LaPoint & C. R. Mann (Eds.), *Incarcerated parents and their children.* Washington, D.C.: U.S. Government Printing Office. In preparation.

Peters, E. F. (1971). Factors which contribute to youths' vocational choice. *Journal of Applied Psychology, 25,* 428–430.

Peters, M. (1978). Notes from the guest editor. *Journal of Marriage and the Family, 40,* 655–658.

Pettigrew, T. F. (1964). *A profile of the Negro American.* Princeton, N.J.: Van Nostrand.

Pfeifer, C. M. & Sedlacek, W. (1971). The validity of academic predictors for black and white students at a predominantly white university. *Journal of Educational Measurement, 8*(4), 253–261.

Phillips, R. (1945). Doll play as a function of the realism of the materials and the length of the experimental session. *Child Development, 16,* 123–143.

Piaget, J. (1950). *The psychology of intelligence.* New York: Harcourt, Brace.

Piaget, J. (1952). *The origins of intelligence in children* (translated by M. Cook). New York: International University Press.

Piaget, J. (1960). *The Child's Conception of the World.* Totowa, New Jersey: Little Field, Adams and Co.

Piaget, J. (1962). *Play, dreams, and imitation in childhood.* New York: Norton.

Piaget, J. (1972). *Judgement and Reasoning in the Child.* Totowa, New Jersey: Little Field, Adams and Co.

Piaget, J., & Inhelder, B. (1964). *The Early Growth of Logic in the Child: Classification and Seriation.* London: Routledge and Kegan Paul, Ltd.

Piaget, J. (1967). *Six psychological studies.* New York: Vintage Press.

Piaget, J., & Inhelder, B. (1969). *The psychology of the child.* N.Y.: Basic Books.

Piers, M. W. (Ed.) (1972). *Play and development.* New York: Norton.

Plas, J. M. (1981). The psychologist in the school community: A liasion role. *School Psychology Review, 10,* 72–81.

Pleck, E. (1970). A mother's wages: Income earning among married Italian and black women, 1896–1911: In M. Gordon (Ed.), *The American family socio-historical perspective* (pp. 490–510). New York: St. Martin Press.

Pollard, D. S. (1982). *Perspectives of Black parents regarding the socialization of their children.* Seventh Conference on Empirical Research in Black Psychology, Hampton, Virginia.

Porter, J. (1971). *Black child, white child: The development of racial attitudes.* Cambridge: Harvard University Press.

Porter, J., & Washington, R. (1979). Black identity and self-esteem: A review of studies of black self-concept, 1968–1978. *Annual Review of Sociology, 5,* 53–74.

Poussaint, A., & Arkinson, C. (1973). Black Youth and Motivation: In Edgar G. Epps, (Ed.), *Race Relations: Current Perspectives* (pp. 167–177). Cambridge, Mass.: Winthrop Publishing Co.

Poussaint, A. F., & Atkinson, C. (1970). Black youth and motivation. *The Black Scholar, 1*(5), 43–51.

Powell, C. J. (1973). Self-concept in white and black children: In W. C. Kramer & B. Brown (Eds.), *Racism and mental health.* Pittsburgh: University of Pittsburgh Press.

Powell, G. (1974). *Black Monday's children.* New York: Appleton Century Croft.

Powell, G., & Fuller, M. (1970). *School desegregation and self-concept.* Paper presented at meeting of the American Orthopsychiatric Association, San Francisco.

*Prisoners in state and federal institutions on December 31, 1978* (1980). National Prisoner Statistics Report No. SD-NPS-PSF-6/NCJ-64671. Washington, D.C.: U.S. Government Printing Office.

Proshansky, H. (1966). The development of intergroup attitudes. In L. Hoffman & M. Hoffman

(Eds.), *Review of Child Development Research* (Vol. 2) (pp. 311–371). New York: Russell Sage Foundation.

Proshansky, H., & Newton, P. (1973). Color: The nature and meaning of Negro self-identity: In P. Watson (Ed.), *Psychology and Race*. (pp. 176–212) Harmondsworth, Middlesex, England: Penguin Books, Inc.

Proshansky, H., & Newton, P. (1968). The nature and meaning of Negro-identification: In Deutsch et al. (Eds.), *Social class, race and development*. New York: Irvington. 178–218.

Prude, J. (1976). The family in context. *Labor History, 17*, 422–435.

Pulaski, J. (1970). Play as a function of toy structure and fantasy predisposition. *Child Development, 41*, 531–537.

Quilitch, H. R., & Risley, T. R. (1973). The effects of play materials on social play. *Journal of Applied Behavior Analysis, 6*, 573–578.

Rafter, N. H. & Natalizia, E. M. (1981). Marxist feminism: implications for criminal justice. *Crime and delinquency, 27*, pp. 81–98.

Rainwater, L. (1970). *Behind ghetto walls: Black families in a federal slum*. Chicago: Aldine.

Rainwater, L. (1966). Crucible of identity: The Negro lower-class family. *Daedlus, 95*(1), 172–216.

Rainwater, L. & Yancy, W. (1967). *The Moynihan report and the politics of controversy*. Cambridge: MIT Press.

Ralston, McC. D. (1974). *Master plan for the city colleges of Chicago*. Sunnyvale, California: Westinghouse Learning Corp.

Ramirez, III, M., & Price-Williams, D. (1976). Achievement motivation in children of three ethnic groups in the United States. *Journal of Cross-Cultural Psychology, 7*, 49–60.

Ramirez, M. & Castenada, A. (1974). *Cultural democracy, bicognitive development and education*. New York: Academic Press.

Rao, C. R. (1948). The utilization of multiple measurements in problems of biological classification. *Journal of the Royal Statistical Society, Series B, 10*, 159–193.

Raynor, J. (1974). Future orientation in the study of achievement motivation. In J. Atkinson & J. Raynor (Eds.), *Motivation and achievement*. Washington, D.C.: V. H. Winston.

Rehberg, R., Schaefer, W., & Sinclair, J. (1970). Toward a temporal sequence of adolescent achievement variables. *American Sociological Review, 35*, 34–47.

Reid, I. (1940). *In a minor key: Negro youth in story and fact*. New York: Harper and Row.

Reid, I. (1972). *Together black women*. New York: The Third Press.

Reid, I., & Cohen, L. (1973). Achievement orientation, intellectual achievement, responsibility and choice between degree of certificate courses in colleges of education. *British Journal of Educational Psychology, 43*, 63–66.

Richardson, S. A. & Green, A. (1971). When is black beautiful? Colored and white children's reaction to skin color. *British Journal of Education, 41*, 62–69.

Riegel, K. F. (1976). The dialectics of human development. *American Psychologist, 31*, 689–699.

Riessman, F. (1962). *The culturally deprived child*. New York: Harper & Row.

Riley, M. W. (1973). Aging and cohort succession: Interpretations and misinterpretations. *Public Opinion Quarterly, 37*, 35–49.

Riley, M. W. (1979). Introduction: Life-course perspectives. In M. W. Riley (Ed.), *Aging from birth to death* (pp. 3–14). Washington, D.C.: Westview Press.

Rist, R. C. (1973). *The urban school: A factor for failure*. Cambridge, MA: MIT Press.

Robovits, P., & Maehr, M. L. (1973). Pygmalian Black and white. *Journal of Personality and Social Psychology, 25*(2), 210–218.

Rodgers-Rose, L. (Ed.) (1980). *The black woman*. Beverly Hills, California: Sage Publications, Inc.

Rodman, H. (1963–4). The lower-class value stretch. *Social Forces, 42*, 205–215.

Roe, A. (1956). *The psychology of occupations*. New York: John Wiley & Sons.

Roebeck, M. C. (1978). *Infants and children: Their development and learning*. New York: McGraw-Hill.

Rollins, B., & Thomas, D. (1979). Parental support, power and control techniques in the socialization of children: In W. Burr, R. Hill, F. I. Nye and I. Reiss (Eds.), *Contemporary theories about the family, Vol. 1: Research-based theories* (pp. 317–364). New York: The Free Press.

Rose, P. (1968). *The subject is race*. New York: Oxford.

Rosen, B. C. (1956). Race, ethnicity, and the achievement syndrome. *American Sociological Review, 24*, 47–60.

Rosen, B. C., Crockett, H. J., & Nunn, C. E. (1969). *Achievement in American society*. Cambridge, Mass.: Schenkman Publishers, Inc.

Rosen, C. E. (1974). The effects of sociodramatic play on problem-solving behavior among culturally disadvantaged preschool children. *Child Development, 45*, 920–927.

Rosenberg, M. (1965). *Society and the adolescent self-image*. Princeton, New Jersey: Princeton University Press.

Rosenberg, M. (1968). *The logic of survey analysis*. New York: Basic Books.

Rosenberg, M. (1973). What significant others. *The American Behavioral Scientist, 16*, 829–860.

Rosenberg, M. (1975). The dissonant context and the adolescent self-concept: In S. Dragastin & S. H. Ecder (Eds.), *Adolescence in the life cycle: Psychological changes and social context* (pp. 97–116). Washington, D.C.: Hemisphere Publications.

Rosenberg, M. (1977). Contextual dissonance effects: Nature and causes. *Psychiatry, 40*(3), 205–217.

Rosenberg, M. (1979a). *Conceiving the self*. New York: Basic Books.

Rosenberg, M. (1979b). Disposition concepts in behavioral science. In R. K. Merton, J. S. Coleman, & P. H. Rossi (Eds.), *Qualitative and quantitative social research: Essays in honor of Paul F. Lazarsfeld* (pp. 245–260). New York: Free Press.

Rosenberg, M., & Pearlin, L. (1978). Social class and self-esteem among children and adults. *American Journal of Sociology, 84*(1), 53–77.

Rosenberg, M., & Simmons, R. (1971). *Black and white self esteem: The urban school child*. Washington, D.C.: American Sociological Association.

Rosenkrantz, L., Joshua, V. (1982). Children of incarcerated parents: A hidden population. *Children Today, 11*, 2–6.

Rosenthal, R. A. (1971). *Pathways to identity: Aspects of the experience of black youth*. Cambridge, Massachusetts: Final Report. Harvard University, 1971, ERIC, ED 053.

Ross, A. M. & Hill, H. (Eds.) (1967). *Employment, race, and poverty: A critical study of the disadvantaged: status of Negro workers from 1865–1965*. New York: Harcourt, Brace and World.

Rotter, J. E. (1966). Generalized expectancies for internal versus external control of reinforcement. *Psychological Monographs: General and Applied, 80*(1), 609.

Rubin, K. H. (Ed.) (1980). Children's play. *New Directions for Child Development, 9*.

Rubovitz, P., & Maehr, M. C. (1973). Pygmalion black and white. *Journal of Personality and Social Psychology, 25*, pp. 210–218.

Rudwick, B. (1971). *The black sociologists: The first half century*. Belmont: Wadsworth.

Ruhland, D., & Feld, S. (1977). The development of achievement motivation in black and white children. *Child Development, 48*, 1362–1368.

Rummel, R. J. (1970). *Applied factor analysis*. New York: Northwestern University Press.

Saltz, E., & Johnson, J. (1974). Training for thematic-fantasy play in culturally disadvantaged children: Preliminary results. *Journal of Educational Psychology, 66*, 623–630.

Saltz, E., Dixon, D., & Johnson, J. (1977). Training disadvantaged preschoolers on various fantasy activities: Effects on cognitive functioning and impulse control. *Child Development, 48*, 367–380.

Sametz, L. (1980). Children of incarcerated women. *Social Work, 25*(4), 298–303.

Sampel, D. D., & Seymour, W. R. (1971). Academic success of black students: A dilemma. *Journal of College Student Personnel, 12,* 243–247.

Sanders, K. M., & Harper, L. V. (1976). Free play fantasy behavior in preschool children: Relations among gender, age, season, and location. *Child Development, 47,* 1182–1185.

Sarason, S., Hill, K. T., & Zimbardo, P. G. (1964). A longitudinal study of the relation of text anxiety to performance on intelligence and achievement tests. *Monograph of the Society for Research on Child Development, 29*(7, Serial No. 98).

Sarason, S. B., Davidson, K. S., Lighthall, F. F., White, R. R., & Ruebush, B. K. (1960). *Anxiety in elementary school children.* New York: Wiley and Sons.

Sarbin, T. R. (1970). The culture of poverty, social identity, and cognitive outcomes. In V. Allen (Ed.), *Psychological Factors in Poverty* (pp. 29–46). Chicago: Markham.

Scanzoni, J. H. (1971). *The black family in modern society.* Boston: Allyn & Bacon.

Schaie, K. W. (1970). A reinterpretation of age-related changes in cognitive structure and functioning. In L. R. Goulet & P. H. Baltes (Eds.), *Life span developmental psychology: Research and theory* (pp. 486–507). New York: Academic Press.

Schlosberg, H. (1947). The concept of play. *Psychological Review, 54,* 229–231.

Scholtz, B., & Ellis, M. (1975). Repeated exposure to objects and peers in a play setting. *Journal of Experimental Child Psychology, 19,* 448–455.

Schroeder, J., & Cohen, B. C. (Eds.) (1971). *The wonderful world of toys, games, and dolls: 1860–1930.* Northfield, Ill.: Digest.

Schulz, D. A. (1969). *Coming up Black: Patterns of Ghetto Socialization.* Englewood Cliffs, N.J.: Prentice-Hall, Inc.

Schulz, D. A. (1968). Variations in the father role in complete families of the Negro lower class. *Social Science Quarterly, 49,* 651–659.

Schwartzman, H. (1976). The anthropological study of children's play. *Annual Review of Anthropology, 5,* 289–328.

Schwartzman, H. B. (1978). *Transformations: The anthropology of children's play.* New York: Plenum.

Sciara, F. J. (1971). Perception of Negro boys regarding color and occupational status. *Child Study Journal, 1,* 203–211.

Scott, J. W. (1976). *The black revolts: Racial stratification in the U.S.A.* Cambridge, Mass.: Schenkman Pub. Co.

Sears, R. (1975). Your ancients revisited: A history of child development. In E. Mavis Hetherington (Ed.), *Review of child development research* (pp. 1–74). Chicago: University of Chicago.

Sears, R., Maccoby, E., & Levin, H. (1957). *Patterns of child rearing.* Illinois: Ron Peterson.

Sedlacke, W. E., & Brooks, Jr., B. C. (1972). Predictors of academic success for university students in special programs. Research Report #4-72. Cultural Study Center, University of Maryland.

Seegmiller, B. (1980). Sex-role differentiation in preschoolers: Effects of maternal employment. *The Journal of Psychology, 104,* 185–189.

Seitz, V., Abelson, W., Levine, E. & Zigler, E. (1975). Effects of place of testing on Peabody Picture Vocabulary Test scores of disadvantaged head start and non-head start children. *Child Development, 46,* 481–486.

Selman, R. (1971). Taking another's perspective: Role-taking development in early childhood. *Child Development, 42,* 1172–1734.

Semaj, L. T. (1979a). Reconceptualizing the development of racial preference in children: The role of cognition. In W. E. Cross, & A. Harrison (Eds.), *The fourth conference on empirical research in black psychology* (pp. 180–198). Published by the Africana Studies Center and NIE(DHEW).

Semaj, L. T. (1979b). Racial identification and preference in children: A cognitive developmental approach. (Doctoral dissertation, Rutgers—The State University of New Jersey, 1978.) *Dissertation Abstracts International,* May *39*(11), 5661–5662 (b) Order # 7910436.

Semaj, L. T. (1979c). *Ethno-racial identity and black children: A social cognitive approach.* (Research proposal funded by Human Ecology College Grants, Cornell University and Foundation for Child Development, 1979–81).

Semaj, L. T. (1980). *Models for a psychology of black liberation.* Unpublished manuscript, Cornell University.

Semaj, L. T. (1981). *Afrikanity, cognition, and extended self-identity.* Paper presented at the SRCD Study Group Meeting held in Atlanta, Ga.

Senn, M. (1975). Insights on the child development movement in the United States. *Monographs of the Society for Research in Child Development, 40* (3–4, Serial No. 161).

Sewell, W. H., Haller, A. O. & Portes, A. (1957). The educational and early occupational attainment process. *American Sociological Review, 22,* 67–73.

Shantz, C. (1975). *The development of social cognition.* Chicago: The University of Chicago Press.

Shavelson, R., Hubner, J., Hubner, R., & Stanton, G. (1976). Self-concept validation of construct interpretation. *Review of Educational Research, 16*(3), 407–441.

Sherif, M., & Sherif, C. (1964). *Reference groups: Exploration into conformity and deviation of adolescents.* Chicago: Henry Regnery Company.

Shils, E. (1970). Tradition, ecology and institution in the history of sociology. *Daedalus, 99*(4), 760–825.

Shimkin, D. B., Shimkin, E. M., & Frate, D. A. (Eds.) (1978). *The extended family in Black societies.* The Hague: Mouton.

Shoemaker, A. (1980). Construct validity of area-specific self-esteem: The Hare self-esteem scale. *Educational and Psychological Measurement. 40,* 495–501.

Shuey, A. M. (1966). *The testing of negro intelligence.* New York: Social Science Press.

Sidle, A., Moos, R., Adams, J., & Cady, P. (1969). Development of a coping scale: A preliminary study. *Archives of General Psychiatry, 20,* 226–232.

Siegel, C. L. F. (1973). Sex differences in the occupational choices of second graders. *Journal of Vocational Behavior, 3,* 15–19.

Sigel, I. E. & McBane, B. (1967). Cognitive competence and level of symbolization among 5-year-old children: In J. Hellmuth (Ed.), *The disadvantaged child. Vol. 1.* (pp. 434–453). New York: Brunner/Mazel.

Sigel, I. E., Anderson, L. M., & Shapiro, H. (1966). Categorization behavior of lower-and middle-class Negro preschool children: Differences in dealing with representation of familiar objects. *Journal of Negro Education, 3,* 218–229.

Sigel, I. E., & Cocking, R. R. (1977). Cognition and communication: A dialectic paradigm for development. In M. Lewis & L. A. Rosenblum (Eds.), *Interaction, conversation, and the development of language.* New York: Wiley.

Silber, E., Hamburg, O. A., & Coehlho, G. V., et al. (1962). Adaptive behavior in competent adolescents: Coping with the anticipation of college. *Archives of General Psychiatry, 5,* 354–365.

Silverstein, B. & Krate, R. (1975). *Children of the dark ghetto: A developmental psychology,* New York: Praeger.

Simmons, R. (1978). Black and high self-esteem. A puzzle. *Social Psychology, 41*(1), 54–57.

Simmons, R., Brown, L., Bush, D. M., & Blythe, D. A. (1978). Self-esteem and achievement of black and white adolescents. *Social Problems, 26*(1), 86–96.

Simmons, R., & Rosenberg, F. (1975). Sex, sex roles and self-image. *Journal of Youth and Adolescence, 4*(3), 229–258.

Simmons, R., Rosenberg, M., & Rosenberg, F. (1973). Disturbance in the self-image at adolescence. *American Sociological Review, 38,* 553–568.

Singer, J. (Ed.) (1973). *The child's world of make-believe: Experimental studies of imaginative play.* New York: Academic Press.

Singer, J. L. (1966). *Daydreaming.* New York: Random House.

Sitkei, E., & Meyers, C. (1969). Comparative structure of intellect in middle and lower class four year olds of two ethnic groups. *Developmental Psychology, 1,* 592–604.

Slade, P. J. (1977). An examination of ethnic-esteem and personal self-esteem among urban black senior high school and college students. *Dissertation Abstracts International*, (4-B), *38*, 1961-B.

Slaughter, D. T. (1973). Psychological scientism and the black scholar. *School Review*, *81*(3), 461–476.

Slaughter, D. T. (1977). Relation of early parent–teacher socialization influences to achievement orientation and self-esteem in middle childhood among low-income black children. In J. Glidewell (Ed.), *The social context of learning and development* (pp. 101–131). New York: Gardner Press.

Slaughter, D. T. (1982). What is the future of head start? *Young Children, 37*, 3–9.

Smilansky, S. (1968). *The effects of sociodramatic play on disadvantaged preschool children*. New York: Wiley.

Smith, C. P. (1969). The origin and expression of achievement related motives in children. In C. P. Smith (Ed.), *Achievement-related motives in children* (pp. 102–150). New York: Russell Sage.

Smith, C. U., & Killian, L. (1974). Black sociologists and social protest. In J. E. Blackwell & M. Janowitz (Eds.), *Black sociologists: Historical and contemporary perspectives* (pp. 197–202). Chicago: University of Chicago Press.

Smith, M., & Brache, C. (1962–3). When school and home focus on achievement. *Educational Leadership, 20*, 314–318.

Smith, M. B. (1968). Competence and socialization. *Socialization and society*. Boston: Little, Brown.

Smith, S. (1978). Research in the mental health of black people: In L. Gary (Ed.), *Mental health—a challenge to the black community* (pp. 314–359). Pennsylvania: Dorrance & Company.

Smith, W. D., Burlew, A. K., & Mosley, M. H. (1978). *Minority issues in mental health*. Massachusetts: Addison-Wesley.

Smitherman, G. (1977). *Talkin' and testifyin': The language of Black America*. Boston: Houghton-Mifflin.

Sorce, J. (1977, March). The role of physiognomy in the development of racial awareness. Paper presented at the biennial meetings of the Society for Research in Child Development, New Orleans, LA.

Spear, A. (1967). *Black Chicago: The making of a Negro ghetto, 1890–1920*. Chicago: University of Chicago.

Spencer, M. B. (1977). The social-cognitive and personality development of the Black preschool child. An exploratory study of developmental process. *Dissertation Abstracts International, 38*(2–B), 970–B.

Spencer, M. B. (1980). Race dissonance research on Black children: Stable life course phenomenon or fluid indicator of intraindividual plasticity and unique cohort effect. Paper prepared for the 5th Empirical Research Meeting on Black Psychology, Washington, D.C.

Spencer, M. B. (1982a). Personal and group identity of black children: An alternative synthesis. *Genetic Psychology Monographs, 106*, 59–84.

Spencer, M. B. (1982b). Preschool children's social cognition and cultural cognition: A cognitive developmental interpretation of race dissonance findings. *Journal of Psychology, 112*, 275–286.

Spencer, M. B. (1983). Children's cultural values and parental child rearing strategies. *Developmental Review, 3*. pp. 351–370.

Spencer, M. B. (1984). *Post-crisis follow-up research: Personal-social adjustment of minority group children*. Final report (Part II) of Project Number 5-R01-PHS-MH-31106 funded by the National Institute of Mental Health, (in progress).

Spencer, M. B. (in press). Black children's race awareness, racial attitudes and self-concept: A reinterpretation. *Journal of Child Psychology and Psychiatry*.

Spencer, M. B., & Horowitz, F. D. (1973). Effects of systematic social and token reinforcement on the modification of racial and color concept attitudes in black and white preschool children. *Developmental Psychologist, 9*(2), 246–254.

Sroufe, A. (1970). A methodological and philosophical critique of intervention oriented research. *Developmental Psychology, 2*(1), 140–145.

St. John, N. (1975). *School desegregation outcomes for children.* New York: Wiley.

St. John, N. (1971). Thirty-six teachers: Their characteristics and outcomes for black and white pupils. *American Educational Research Journal, 8,* 635–648.

Stack, C. B. (1974). *All our kin: Strategies for survival in a black urban community.* New York: Harper and Row.

Stanton, A. (1980). *When mothers go to jail.* Mass.: D. C. Health.

Staples, R. (1974). The black family in evolutionary perspective. *Black Scholar, 5,* 2–9.

Staples, R. (1978). Masculinity and race: The dual dilemma of Black men. *Journal of Social Issues, 34,* 169–183.

Staples, R., & Mirande, A. (1980). Racial and cultural variations among American families: A decennial review of the literature on minority families. *Journal of Marriage and the Family, 42,* 887–904.

Steinke, B. K., & Kaczkowski, H. R. (1961). Parents' influence on the occupational choice of 9th grade girls. *Vocational Guidance Quarterly, 9,* 101–103.

Stephan, W. (1978). School desegregation: An evaluation of predictions made in Brown vs. Board of Education. *Psychological Bulletin, 85*(2), 217–238.

Stephan, W., & Rosenfield, D. (1978). Effects of desegregation on race relations and self-esteem. *Journal of Educational Psychology, 70*(5), 670–679.

Stern, W. (1924). *Psychology of early childhood.* New York: Holt.

Stewart, L. H. (1959). Mother–son identification and vocational interest. *Genetic Psychological Monographs, 60,* 31–43.

Stodolsky, S. S., & Lesser, G. (1967). Learning patterns in the disadvantaged. *Harvard Educational Review, 37,* 546–593.

Stodolsky, S. S., & Lesser, G. (1971). Learning patterns in the disadvantaged. Challenging the myths. *Harvard Educational Review, 3,* 22–69.

Stokols, D. (1977). Origins and directions of environmental-behavioral research. In D. Stokols (Eds.), *Perspectives on environment and behavior: Theory, research and application.* New York: Plenum Press.

Storm, P. A. (1971). An investigation of self-concept, race image and race preference in racial minority and majority children. *Dissertation Abstracts International, 31,* 6246-6247-B.

Storr, R. (1966). *Harper's university: The beginnings.* Chicago: University of Chicago.

Stott, D. H. & Sykes, E. G. (1967). *Bristol social adjustment guides.* San Diego: Educational and Industrial Testing Service.

Strickland, A. (1966). *History of the Chicago Urban League.* Urbana: University of Illinois.

Strickland, W. (1979). The road since Brown: The Americanization of the race. *Black Scholar, 11,* 2–8.

Strodtbeck, F. L. (1958). Family interaction, values and achievement. In D. C. McClelland, et al. (Eds.), *Talent and society.* Princeton, New Jersey: VanNostrand.

Strumpfer, D. F. W. (1973). Failure to find space relationships between family constellation and achievement motivation. *Journal of Psychology, 85,* 29–36.

Super, D. E. (1953). A theory of vocational development. *The American Psychologist, 8,* 185–190.

Sutton-Smith, B. (1971). The role of play in cognitive development. In R. E. Herron & B. Sutton-Smith (Eds.), *Child's play* (pp. 252–260). New York: Wiley.

Sutton-Smith, B. (1972a). Play as a transformational set. *Journal of Health, Physical Education, and Recreation, 43,* 32–33.

Sutton-Smith, B. (1972b). *The folkgames of children.* Austin: University of Texas Press.

Sylva, K., Bruner, J., & Genova, P. (1976). The role of play in the problem-solving of children 3–5 years old. In J. Bruner, A. Jolly, & K. Sylva (Eds.), *Play: Its role in development and evolution* (pp. 244–257). New York: Basic Books.

Tangri, S. S. (1972). Determinants of occupational role innovation among college women. *Journal of Social Issues, 28,* 117–199.

Tatsuoka, M. (1970). Discriminant analysis. Selected topics in advanced statistics. Champaign, Illinois: Institute for Personality and Ability Testing, No. 6.

Taylor, R. (1976). Psychosocial development among Black children and youth: A re-examination. *American Journal of Ortho-Psychiatry, 46*(1), 4–19.

Teeland, L. A. (1971). *The relevance of the concept of reference groups to the sociology of knowledge.* Report #12, Department of Sociology, University of Grothenburg.

Temp, G. (1971). Validity of the SAT for blacks and whites in thirteen integrated institutions. *Journal of Education Measurement, 8*(4), 245–251.

Thomas, A., & Sillen, S. (1972). *Racism and psychiatry.* Secaucus, N.J.: Citadel Press.

Thomas, D. L., Franks, D., & Calonico, J. (1970). Role-taking and power in social psychology. *American Sociological Review, 37,* 605–614.

Thomas, G. (1980). Race and sex group equity in higher education: Institutional and major field enrollment statuses. *American Educational Research Journal, 17*(2), 171–181.

Thomas, W. I. (1904). Race psychology: Standpoint and questionnaire. *American Journal of Sociology, 17,* 745.

Thomas, W. I., & Znaniecki, F. (1918–20). *The Polish peasant in Europe and America* (Vols. 1–5). Chicago: University of Chicago.

Thomas, W. L. (1967). *The Thomas self-concept values test manual.* Chicago: E. Clement Stone.

Thorndike, R. L. (1971). Educational measurement for the seventies. In R. L. Thorndike (Ed.), *Educational Measurement,* 2nd Edition (pp. 750–764). Washington, D.C.: American Council on Education.

Tinto, V. (1973). College proximity and rates of college attendance. *American Educational Research Journal,* 277–293.

Tizard, B., & Harvey, D. (Eds.) (1977). *Biology of play.* Philadelphia: Lippincott.

Tomlinson, T. M. (1980, May). *Student ability, student background and student achievement: Another look at life in effective schools.* A paper presented at conference on effective school, sponsored by the Office of Minority Education, ETS, New York.

Torgerson, W. S. (1965). *Theory and Methods of Scaling.* New York: John Wiley & Son, Inc.

Traurig, H., Marjorum, G., & Musk, H. (1982). Issues related to incarcerated women and their children in the context of a total institution. In V. LaPoint & C. R. Mann (Eds.), *Incarcerated parents and their children.* Washington, D.C.: U.S. Government Printing Office. In preparation.

Trent, R. D. (1957). The relation between expressed self-acceptance and expressed attitudes toward Negroes and whites among Negro children. *Journal of Genetic Psychology, 91,* 25–31.

Trotman, F. (1977). Race, I.Q., and the middle class. *Journal of Educational Psychology, 69,* 266–273.

Tukey, J. W. (1949). Dyadic ANOVA, an analysis of variance for vectors. *Human Biology, 21,* 65–110.

Tulkin, S. (1972). An analysis of the concept of cultural deprivation. *Developmental Psychology, 6*(2), 326–339.

Turner, R. (1964). *The social context of ambition.* San Francisco: Chandler.

Turner, R. (Ed.) (1967). *Robert E. Park: On social control and collective behavior.* Chicago: University of Chicago.

U.S. Bureau of the Census. (1982). *Current population reports.* Series P-60, #1934. Money income and poverty status of families and persons in the United States: 1981. Washington, D.C.: U.S. Government Printing Office.

U.S. Children's Bureau. (1967). *The story of the White House conferences on children and youth: 1909–1960.* Washington, D.C.: U.S. Government Printing Office.

U.S. Department of Justice. (1979a). *Profile of state prison inmates* (SD-NPS-SR-4). Washington, D.C.

U.S. Department of Justice. (1979b). *The profile report: The inmate information.* Washington, D.C.

U.S. Department of Justice. (1980). Criminal justice research solicitation: Center for the study of race, crime and social policy. Washington, D.C.: National Institute of Justice.

U.S. Department of Justice. (1983). *Prisoners in state and federal institutions on December 31, 1981.* (National Prisoner Statistics Bulletin, No. NCJ-86485). Washington, D.C.: Bureau of Justice Statistics, J.S. Department of Justice.

Urry, J. (1973). *Reference groups and the theory of revolution.* London: Routledge and Kegan Paul.

Valentine, C. A. (1971). Deficit, difference and bicultural models of Afro-American behavior. *Harvard Educational Review, 41*(2), 137–57.

Van den Berghe, P. (1980). Review of *Minority Education and caste* by John U. Ogbu (N. Y.: Academic Press, 1978). *Comparative Education Review, 24,* 126–130.

Vandenberg, B. (1978). Play and development from an ethological perspective. *American Psychologist, 33,* 724–738.

Vandenberg, B. (1981). Environmental and cognitive factors in social play. *Journal of Experimental Child Psychology, 31,* 169–175.

Vaughan, P. B. (1977). A developmental study of race esteem and self-esteem of Black boys and girls in third and seventh grade. *Dissertation Abstracts International, 38*(6–A), 3735–A.

Vernon, P. E. (1969). *Intelligence and cultural environment.* London: Methuen & Co.

Veroff, J. (1969). Social comparison and the development of achievement motivation. In C. P. Smith (Ed.), *Achievement-related motives in children* (pp. 46–101). New York: Russell Sage.

Veroff, S. (1965). Theoretical backgrounds for studying origins of human motives. *Merrill-Palmer Quarterly of Behavior Development, 11,* 3–18.

Vygotsky, L. (1962). *Thought and language.* Cambridge, Mass.: The MIT Press.

Vygotsky, L. S. (1978). The role of play in development: In M. Cole, V. John-Steiner, S. Scribner, & E. Souberman (Eds.), *Mind in Society.* Cambridge: Harvard University Press.

Wallace, W. Some elements of sociological theory in studies of Black Americans. In J. Blackwell & M. J. Janowitz (Eds.), *Black sociologists* (pp. 299–311). Chicago: University of Chicago.

Waller, W. (1938). *The family: A dynamic interpretation.* New York: The Dryden Press.

Walters, J., & Stinnett, N. (1971). Parent–child relationships: A decade review of research. *Journal of Marriage and the Family, 33,* 70–111.

Walters, J., & Walters, L. (1980). Parent–child relationships: A review, 1970–1979. *Journal of Marriage and the Family, 42,* 807–822.

Ward, S. J., & Braun, J. (1972). Self-esteem and racial preference in Black children. *American Journal of Orthopsychiatry, 42*(4), 644–647.

Warner, W. L. (1949). *Social class in America.* Chicago: Science Research Associates.

Warner, W. L., Meeker, M., & Eells, K. (1949). *Social class in America.* Chicago: Science Research Associates.

Warner, W. L., Havighurst, R., & Loeb, M. (1944). *Who shall be educated?* New York: Harper.

Warner, W. L. (1941)., Junker, B., & Adams, W. *Color and human nature.* Washington, D.C.: American Council on Education.

Washington, J. (Ed.) (1979). *The declining significance of race: a dialogue among black and white social scientists.* Philadelphia: AfroAmerican Studies Program, University of Pennsylvania.

Watts, R. B. (1982). Incarcerated parents and their children—a view from the judiciary. In V. LaPoint & C. R. Mann (Eds.), *Incarcerated parents and their children.* Washington, D.C.: U.S. Government Printing Office. In preparation.

Webber, T. (1978). *Deep like the rivers: Education in the slave quarter community, 1831–1865.* New York: W. W. Norton and Co.

Wehrly, B. L. (1973). Children's occupational knowledge. *Vocational Guidance Quarterly, 22,* 124–129.

Weiner, B., & Potepan, P. A. (1970). Personality characteristics and affective reactions toward exams of superior and failing college students. *Journal of Educational Psychology, 61,* 144–151.

Werner, E., Simonian, K., & Smith, R. (1968). Ethnic and socioeconomic status differences in abilities and achievement among preschool and school age children in Hawaii. *Journal of Social psychology, 75,* 43–59.

Werner, H. (1958). *Comparative Psychology of Mental Development*. New York: International Universities Press, Inc..

West, C. K., Fish, J. A., & Stevens, R. J. (1980). General self-concept, self-concept of academic ability and school achievement: Implications for "causes" of self-concept. *The Australian Journal of Education, 24*(2), 194–213.

Weston, P. J., & Mednick, M. T. (1970). Race, social class and the motive to avoid success in women. *Journal of Cross Cultural Psychology, 1*(3), 283–291.

White, B. (1978). *Experience and environment*. Vol. 2. Englewood Cliffs, N.J.: Prentice-Hall.

White, B., Kaplan, B. T. & Attanuchi, H. (1979). *The origins of human competence: The final report of the Harvard Preschool Project*. Lexington, Mass.: D. C. Heath.

White, J. (1972). Toward a black psychology. In R. Jones (Eds.), *Black psychology* (pp. 43–50). New York: Harper & Row.

White, K. M. (1971). Conceptual style and conceptual ability in kindergarten through the eighth grade. *Child Development, 42*, 1652–1656.

White, L., & Smith, T. (Eds.), (1929). *Chicago: An experiment in social science research*. Chicago: University of Chicago.

White, R. (1959). Motivation reconsidered: The concept of competence. *Psychological Review, 66*, 297–333.

White, R. (1960). Competence and psychosexual states of development. *Nebraska Symposium on Motivation, 8*, 97–141.

White, R. (1974). Strategies of adaptation: An attempt at systematic description. In G. Coelho, D. Hamburg & J. Adams (Eds.). *Coping and adaptation* (pp. 47–68). New York: Basic Books.

White, S. H. (1973). Federal programs for young children: Review and recommendations. Volume 1 goals and standards of public programs for children. Washington, D.C.: U.S. Government Printing Office.

Whiteman, M., & Deutsch, M. (1968). Social disadvantage as related to intellective and language development: In M. Deutsch, I. Katz, and A. Jensen (Eds.), *Social class, race, and psychological development* (pp. 86–114). New York: Holt, Rhinehart, and Winston.

Whiteman, M. (Ed.) (1980). *Reactions to Ann Arbor: Vernacular black english and education*. Arlington, Va.: Center for Applied Linguistics.

Wilensky, H. L. (1981). Family life cycle, work and the quality of life: Reflections on the roots of happiness, despair, and indifference in modern society: In B. Gardell & G. M. Johannson (Eds.), *Working life* (pp. 235–265). New York: Wiley.

Wilkenson, D. Y. (1974). Racial socialization through children's toys: A sociohistorical examination. *Journal of Black Studies, 5*, 96–109.

Williams-Burns, W. (1977). An investigation into the self-esteem level and skin color perceptions of self-portraits of advantaged Afro-American children in New Orleans, La. *Dissertation Abstracts International, 38*(2–A), 686–A.

Williams, A. P. (1972). Dynamics of a black audience. In Thomas Kochman, (Ed.), *Rappin' and stylin' out: Communications in black urban America* (pp. 101–106). Urbana: University of Illinois Press.

Williams, I. J. (1975). *An investigation of the developmental states of Black consciousness*. Unpublished doctoral dissertation. University of Cincinnati.

Williams, J. E. & Morland, K. J. (1976). *Race, color, and the young child*. Chapel Hill: University of North Carolina Press.

Williams, R., & Byars, H. (1968). Negro self-esteem in transitional society. *Personnel and Guidance Journal, 47*, 120–125.

Williams, R. L. (1980). The death of white research in the black community: In R. L. Jones (Ed.), *Black psychology* (pp. 403–417). New York: Harper & Row.

Willie, C. V. (1976). *A new look at black families*. New York: General Hall.

Willie, C. V. (Ed.) (1979). *Caste and class controversy*. New York: General Hall, Inc.

Wilson, W. J. (1978). *The declining significance of race: Blacks and changing American institutions*. Chicago: University of Chicago Press.

Winer, B. J. (1971). *Statistical principles in experimental design*. (2nd ed.) New York: McGraw-Hill.

Winterbottom, M. (1958). The relation of need for achievement to learning experience in independence and mastery. In J. W. Atkinson (Ed.), *Motives in fantasy, action, and society* (pp. 453–478). Princeton: Van Nostrand.

Wirth, L. (Ed.) (1940). *Eleven twenty-six: A decade of social science research*. Chicago: University of Chicago Press.

Wolf, S. (1980). Commentary: High time for synthesis. *Forum on Medicine, 3*(8), 502–503.

Wolk, S., & Ducette, J. (1971). Locus of control and achievement motivation: Theoretical overlap and methodological divergence. *Psychological Reports, 29,* 755–758.

Woodring, P. (1975). The development of teacher education. In K. Ryan (Ed.), *Teacher Education. The seventy-fourth yearbook of the National Society for the Study of Education* (Part 2) (pp. 1–25). Chicago: University of Chicago.

Woodson, R. L. (1977). *Black perspectives on crime and the criminal justice system*. Boston, MA.: G. K. Hall & Co.

Woodson, C. G. (1969). *The miseducation of the Negro*. Washington, D.C.: The Associated Publishers. Originally published 1933.

Wright, E. O. (1973). *The politics of punishment*. New York: Harper & Row.

Wright, R. N. (1953). *The outsider*. New York: Harper.

Wylie, R. (1961). *The self concept*. Nebraska: University of Nebraska Press.

Wylie, R. C. (1979). *The self-concept* (Vol. 2). Theory and research on selected topics. Lincoln: University of Nebraska.

Yancey, W., Ericksen, E., & Juliani, R. (1976). Emerging ethnicity: A review and reformulation. *American Sociological Review, 41,* 391–403

Yates, F., Collins, W., & Boykin, A. W. (1974). Some approaches to black academic motivation in predominantly white universities. *Journal of Social and Behavioral Sciences, 20*(3), 19–36.

Young, V. (1970). Family and childhood in a southern Georgia community. *American anthropologist, 72,* 269–288.

Young, V. H. (1974). A black American socialization pattern. *American Ethnologist, 1,* 415–431.

Zaccaria, L., & Creaser, J. (1971). Factors related to persistence in an urban commuter university. *Journal of College Student Personnel, 12,* 286–291.

Zigler, E., Ableson, W., & Seitz, V. (1973). Motivational factors in the performance of economically disadvantaged children on the Peabody Picture Vocabulary Test. *Child Development, 44,* 294–303.

Zigler, E. & Butterfield, E. (1968). Motivational aspects of changes in IQ performance of culturally deprived nursery school children. *Child Development, 39,* 1–14.

Zigler, E., & Child, I. L. (1969). Socialization. In C. Lindzey and E. Aronson (Eds.), *Handbook of social psychology,* 2nd Edition, Vol. III (pp. 458–489). Reading, Massachusetts: Addison-Wesley.

Zigler, E., & Valentine, J. (Eds.) (1979). *Project Head Start: A legacy of the war on poverty*. New York: Free Press.

# Author Index

# Subject Index